TRAUMA FOR BEGINNERS

TRAUMA FOR BEGINNERS

MEDITATIONS AND COMMENTARIES

—

William M. Redpath

BARBERRY PRESS
Lexington, Massachusetts
2019

Please note that *Trauma for Beginners* is documentary and reflects the personal experience and ideational explorations of the author. The book is not to be interpreted as an independent guide for self-healing. If you intend to follow any of the strategies of the book, do so only under the supervision of a medical doctor or other health professional.

Copyright © 2019 William M. Redpath.

All Rights Reserved. No part of this book may be reproduced or transmitted in any form or by any means, electronic or mechanical, including photocopying, recording or by any information storage and retrieval system, without permission from the publisher. Reviewers may quote brief excerpts.

Published by Barberrry Press
Lexington, Massachusetts

Trauma Energetics, Held-Energy Systems^{SM}, a process for educating individuals about how trauma is stored in the mind-body, is patent pending.

Trauma Energetics, Held-Energy Systems^{SM}, is a registered trade/service mark.

Grateful acknowledgment is made for the use of the following copyrighted material:

Excerpts from WAITING FOR GODOT copyright © 1954 by Grove Press, Inc.; Copyright © renewed 1982 by Samuel Beckett. Used by permission of Grove/Atlantic, Inc. Any third party use of this material, outside of this publication, is prohibited.

Joseph Conrad. The Secret Sharer and Other Stories, Dover Publications, Thrift Edition, New York 1993. ISBN -13: 978-0-486-27546-8; ISBN-10: 0-486-27546-9.

"a man who had fallen among thieves". Copyright 1926, 1954, © 1991 by the Trustees for the E. E. Cummings Trust. Copyright © 1985 by George James Firmage, from COMPLETE POEMS: 1904-1962 by E. E. Cummings, edited by George J. Firmage. Used by permission of Liveright Publishing Corporation.

Excerpt from The Seven Storey Mountain by Thomas Merton. Copyright 1948 by Houghton Mifflin Harcourt Publishing Company; copyright renewed 1976 by the Trustees of The Merton Legacy Trust Reprinted by permission of Houghton Mifflin Harcourt Publishing Company. All rights reserved.

Plato. The Republic, Benjamin Jowett, translator. Dover Thrift Edition, Dover Publications, New York, 2000. ISBN 0-486-41121-4.

Positive Health, for permission to use the author's article: Trauma Energetics: Working With the Breath. This article was published in Positive Health PH Online Issue 80. September 2002 (www.positivehealth.com/energy-medicine/trauma-energetics-working-with-the-breath).

"The Insusceptibles". Copyright © 2016 by the Adrienne Rich Literary Trust. Copyright © 1955 by Adrienne Rich., from COLLECTED POEMS: 1950-2012 by Adrienne Rich. Used by permission of W.W. Norton & Company, Inc, 1993. ISBN 0-39-3034-186.

Sophocles, Robert Fagles, translator. The Three Theban Plays. Penguin Classics, 1984. ISBN 978-0140444254.

Printed in the United States of America

First Edition, Version 1.0

ISBN 978-0-9647730-1-1

Cover Art by Carson Wiser

Book Design by Kory Kirby

For my teachers —
family, friends, students, and colleagues

CONTENTS

ACKNOWLEDGMENTS	ix
AUTHOR'S NOTE	xi
ENLIGHTENMENT AND HISTORY	1
BEING	7
LIBERTY, HISTORY, AND BEING	27
DISCOVERING THE BREATH	43
THE BREATH OF LIFE	59
NOTES ON ALCHEMY	67
ADVANCED SESSION	73
ENERGETICS AND THE GESTALT	97
MORE POEMS AND THE GESTALT	131
THEOLOGICAL CONCEPTS AND ENERGY	173
LITERATURE, ENERGY, AND DEVELOPMENT	229
GESTALT IN LITERATURE	243
GESTALT IN LITERATURE: GODOT	265
SEXUALITY, ENERGY, AND SPIRITUALITY	281
MARRIAGE AS GESTALT	307
FURTHER APPLICATIONS: NOAH	317
SUCCESSFUL LIFE – ADDENDUM TO NOAH SPEECH	333
EDUCATIONAL EXTRAPOLATION	337
INDEX	346

ACKNOWLEDGMENTS

I should like to thank the following friends and associates who have participated directly and indirectly in the development of this collection of meditations and commentaries. In discussions and in some cases, sessions, in relationships professional and in friendship, they have generously supported my elaborations which appear here, though they have their own ideas; insofar as we can claim anything, the following idea sequences are mine as I hold them, and I take responsibility for them.

I thank my wife Judith Jordan, Bruce Poulter, David Carr, Haskell Cohen, Frances Mervin, Kevin Stolz, Marcela Ot'alora Gomez, Suzanne Weinberg, Jeanne Garrison, Suzanne Loughlin, John Walsh, Margaret Reed Weiss, Roger Paine. Also, my students at the Arlington School, and of course my clients, dedicated and brilliant.

As my father used to quote, we are supported in our endeavors by a cloud (or did he mean crowd?) of witnesses. Either way, there are many others in my social encounters and friendship who have given me challenge and support, including Randall Paulsen and Sally Bowie, my brother Robert and my sister-in-law Cecily, Sam Fisk and Linda Coe, and my sister Jeannie Becton and my brother-in-law, Henry Becton, Charles Dietrick, Joseph Pleck, Christopher Sullivan, and Tyler Carpenter.

I continue to be indebted to my initial work with Peter Levine. Like others exposed to his insights, I have examined tragedy, held-energy systems and shock now for decades. We are definitely not the first to approach the importance of understanding trauma to humanity, and many of the theory and insights renewed by Peter illuminate and run parallel with each of our understandings. My basic premise is that from the first of civilization consciousness, trauma has been a central concern. It should be the central concern; it involves where we begin.

AUTHOR'S NOTE

Culled from years of experience in variegated realms, including tragic theory, psychology, and intellectual history, I am sharing very simple insights, including about preverbal experience.

The following texts are meditations and commentaries – conversational in intention. They are composed with many sentences denser than readers may be used to. If you find the compressions too much, please be patient with me and with yourself. There may be rewards ahead.

Some depths can be garnered from complexity, including ideational and syntactical. They ultimately and regularly may reduce to essence, beyond words.

If you get used to the rhythm and sequence of the ideas, it is my hope that these may take you, reader, to a different level of understanding, commensurate with the preverbal experiences being described.

With good wishes.

There is only one sentence, only one word, only one breath.

CHAPTER ONE:

ENLIGHTENMENT AND HISTORY

Preamble

It has been over twenty-three years since I published my first book, *Trauma Energetics A Study of Held-Energy Systems* [ISBN 0-9647730-0-7], a compressed, well-meant commentary on discoveries I made about held-energy systems, linked to certain classical humanistic texts; and now I have more to add. I trust that those initial insights will be deemed refined and expanded upon here. I have included more traditional literary texts exegesized in ways to help figure out how the brain links its humanistic thought capacities with more meditational skills. Perhaps I can reduce the levels of complexity which includes huge realms of preverbal experience.

I have also chosen to minimize framing some of the insight sequences with references and footnotes. For my readers, most of these areas are already known and encrusted. My goal is to allow whatever idea decisiveness to occur between us, who have certain levels of reading and cognitive expertise. I am hoping that the commentaries will help return us to our centers, which I find are not readily found in the volumetric and shuttle of traditional scholarship.

What I discovered in the early 1990's was a way into brain process which follows certain easily-applied rubrics resulting often in "miraculous" transformations – miraculous only in the sense if you didn't know what you were doing, and not doing. What has emerged over the subsequent years of working with individuals with these approaches is simple and not new; people in the past knew about what I have re-discovered, but the knowledge appears to have been lost, or not sustained – characteristically difficult to hold.

I have come to think our human life objective can be to live fully, moving toward the spiritual and cognitive destination of enlightenment by witnessing resolution of old dissociative patterns which clutter our thought and behavior; so that we can exist in inward and outward freedom as we confront reality. This anthem is sung by someone who has worked as an educator and therapist throughout his adult life, been privilegedly educated but also has been fortunate enough to garner inner time and the accoutrements of that, including a strong and increasingly differentiated contemplative practice.

So the goals are achievable, if you can forge three meals a day, a room of one's own, some sort of spacious security. And sometimes, often, they are achievable without those supports (as well as obscured by such supports). And having time may be in itself a challenge to delineating the territories I am about to describe. We spend most of our days and nights in ritual and habit; the experience of inner freedom may begin as an acquired taste; I find it becomes a reason to live.

How do we accomplish or embody this option to resolve, to have it at the ready as part of our self-organization, a card in our hand of cards? The Buddha educates us about ending the cycle of rebirth and of suffering. The question prior to this objective is to know, "Is there suffering? And how do we experience this?"

We can acknowledge the perhaps already clear to us presence of sustained uncomfortable conflicts, quirks, and inner squiggles which come in the way of a balanced, reality-based, righteous action and mind-set. We sense we are at the sides of things or at the bad, toxic center of things. No matter at what age, one way we sense that we are not on clear center is that we wonder whether we already are wasting time, culturally and socially, but more significantly personally – our time, our life. This evaluation comes from within as well as from our exchanges with the world without.

And I respond, "At some levels, we waste the gift of life; and it is often difficult to do something about that." Curiously, we are what we are, so how, as God's (Whatever's) creatures, can we be wasting our time – our life is all God's anyway? Does God waste Its creation? From our current positions of fragmentation in our neurochemistry (and I use neurochemistry to signify our consciousness that fundamentally at every moment, whatever we think we are arises from within a neurochemical sea), we "waste" something, probably energy, certainly our capacity to discern; but figuring out what or how that waste is or what it means may require more specific, less casual focus and evaluation, particularly if we want to redress our imbalances. Among other parts of our experience, our excesses, and our self-evaluations, and our fatigue, reveal our suffering and strategically, the awareness in the structure of linear time itself that things could, or should be different.

What if we discover through trial and error that these, our stumble-inciting challenges, are simply incompletions which proffer completion, and with our spiritual skills, the vision of their integration which the lack of is so troubling to us, propels our consciousness into a sense of waste, or frustration, or dissatisfaction, or suffering. We have left things undone, and badly done some, many others. What experiences do not yield to second guessing?

In short, how does the range of dysfunctional, immature, even pernicious patternings, including addictions and abuse – which we probably internally sense and know – manifest? What are its shapes, its forms? Why can't we just wash them off our body, like dirt? Can we attack the old – shall we call them in a spectrum sort of way dissociative – patterns directly or if not, how do we approach them? Do the restorations, the redemptions, if you will, require Twelve Steps, or fourteen Stations of a Cross? Do our realizations of suffering help us to make things better?

"Getting and spending, we lay waste our powers"— *Wordsworth*

Wordsworth withstanding, we throw away our time by habitually performing maintenance activities in a meaningless way, by delay, by non-conscient experience, by refusal or inability to learn and to grow. For lack of centered focus, we waste existence and time itself in war, starvation, a-relationality, misguided intention, and ignorance. In current popular terms, we are not mindful; and this malaptitude compromises our already incomplete sense of time and of history.

When our actions proceed from a, for lack of a better word, spiritual pivot point, righteous action springs out of core centeredness: there is no sense of waste or of loss. Yet even for some who have developed companies, discovered new research insights, written books, won prizes, raised families, and waged peace, we may come to an awareness that our times have been unresolved (because) our actions have not been centered. They have been mere activities.

If we somehow bring our personal patterns into integrity, into the dissolving power of resolution, then what has been incomplete may be of no consequence; finally, nothing is lost, and something is gained. We will see that even the fragmentations we have experienced feed into a deeper wholeness:

something we have known and longed for. In some way, we have garnered patterns in order to solve their problematicity; and we may be surprised at what these lessons are. Because at some levels, we ourselves may be the last person in the room to perceive the waste.

Time becomes important

Irresolution involves a sense of conflicted or suspended time and of problematic historical sequence, both for the individual and for society. Suddenly, time becomes important, not for just measuring events, but for tracing sequences of behavior – proffer and response, cause and effect, meaning and non-meaning – as well as the sense of their thwartings.

With the relatively recently evolved strategy of linear time as our means for structuring sequence, we may appropriate a focus which magnifies or minimizes the ways we evaluate our complex experience of what is happening in what we laughingly might call the moment. And history, as an organized sense of memory about what has occurred, becomes central to our current apperception of current identity. As a sensed phenomenon, history and its handmaiden, memory, should take us into the present tense, which, like a pastry tube, may have differing widths or points of focus.

I find that acknowledged history, written and verbal, as a personal and cultural phenomenon is always referring to the phenomenon of the present, where we may discover we can conscientiously discriminate about the nature of origin, wherein we will discover that beginning and source are more difficult to evaluate and to connect with and embody than we think. For most of us, the present tense is envisioned as singular, which implies a gestalt awareness of boundary.

Scholarly historians view one "present tense" after another and somehow connect them; or, more likely, maybe that conjoining is the central illusion of their magic show. In each selected time frame, there may be no single moment, and thus narrative or causal connection may conceal brain-sensed chaos. We could post this insight on the realizations-to-realize bucket-list for foot-soldiers prior to the battle of Verdun, or some TET Offensive.

Sometimes written history can be organized around various points in the so-called past, when things "occur", such as World War I begins in August, 1914 (or when does it *begin*?). But as with personal memory, the historical weave can be, in current colloquial terms, spun; and our desire to see the present thoroughly presented in all its layered complexity and simplicity remains. The stories we tell appear to reveal not just that things happen, but how things come about, and these narratives are presents, strung – high above the airy unknown. They often appear to overrun the sense of being at the center of the present for each of us – being which is preverbal, silent, still, and contains void.

In his book *How to Change Your Mind* [Michael Pollan. *How to Change Your Mind, What the New Science of Psychedelics Teaches Us About Consciousness, Dying, Addiction, Depression, and Transcendence.* Penguin Press, 2018. ISBN 978-1594204227], Michael Pollan discusses his understanding of a *default mode network*, a brain function wherein most of what we experience in our so-called consciousness is prefigured, prewired, by the past (including genetics), and that we use only some current "reality" details from what we are currently experiencing to trigger a preset set of relational understandings. Our common-place adjustment to the recognition of this network might read, "I do not have to reinvent the world; I already know it because I bring a whole set of memories and synaptical learnings to the new situation, whose features trigger the old."

The cognitive issue about what is real may be acknowledged when, as infants, we understand that our mother is basically the same person, no matter what dress she is wearing (though, importantly, her mood or disposition may vary). Under the influence of hallucinogens (as well as other meditational, spiritual, and therapeutic practices), these pre-characterized sequences pull back or are suppressed, and we are confronted with the power to reformulate the basic assumptions of our library of experience, individual and cultural, which are the primary determinants of the rails upon which our engine runs.

Critical, then, to healing process, we may be able to reconfigure traumatically held memories and synaptic tracks which then are triggered in their altered (more realistic?) Forms. Though we have been bitten by a dog as a child, the new site says, "Not every dog will bite; though some may." I think in some curious way, this "new" theorem or understanding could be clarifying Blake's experience of the paradox of Innocence and Experience.

Our default mode network is prefiguring from past experience, while some portion of our system is facing our reality as new. Too much of either state/capacity screws up our ability to generate and experience real action. Our creativity involves reworking the relationship between Experience and Innocence, which, Pollen might argue, is conducted within the default mode network and its interface to contemporary sense data. That this interface could be acknowledged and reworked is part of the enlightenment lineage, this time with a neurochemical twist. Speaking psychodynamically, spiritually, and cognitively may help us to recalibrate how nearsighted or farsighted we are.

On the road to being able to approximate – dance with – (Ultimate) reality, one mark of inner freedom might be the capacity to renegotiate to this relationship within ourselves between the gifts of the past – genetics, civilization, upbringing (nurture), and significantly trauma held-energy systems (our own and those around us) – and a voidy present. And it might take some inner time to integrate these phenomena at revised levels; we might run into a sense of waste and miscue, both as to how we think and feel and how we act. For one, we might realize that real action is not activity. These discriminations might lead us to a revision of our understanding of freedom and of how easily or difficult it may be to embody and sustain developmental and spiritual liberty.

Trauma significantly prefigures

So, the following insight cluster contained in this book could rarefy to a realization that a most important task for us involves history: how it is shaped, garnered, limited and expanded, and how trauma – the way it is evoked and maintained in our human systems and consciousness and its related dissociative patterns – significantly prefigures and distorts our sense of time, action, and perception of reality, external and internal. What we may discover is that we have only a fragile understanding of how we store (our) history within ourselves, and that to attend to this frontier of awareness may bring fears but also accomplishments currently considered beyond the expected boundaries of our sense of normal and possible.

As we learn to expand our sense of inner freedom and to reduce the rigidities with which our held-energy systems – shock sites – command and push to the front of our consciousness for resolution, we shall confront the present more directly, including the void at the center of the present – a factor of fear and ego-obliteration as well as of freedom.

From this perspective, our current personal and social crises explicate numinous brainscapes where each of us can witness important, soul-based transformations. This vision is not unprecedented – "history" is chock-full of such awareness; but each turn of the earth brings us to a greater realization of the pervasive presence of traumatic process in all that we humans do. The traumata are stored in the default mode network agency and are referred to with consequential force, particularly as we in some important ways, cannot see them. Thus, we are our traumata until we are not.

CHAPTER TWO:

BEING

What is essential about us

Perhaps paradoxically, we try to find out what is essential about us when we are freed of transient vicissitudes of personality and physical encumbrances; we search for that which is freed by time sequence altogether, not dependent upon age or gender or tribal affiliation: what we look like and what, or how we experience ourselves as just being.

Obviously, there have been tons of investigations about what we are, including notably in recent Western intellectual thought early examinations of the American Indian as the "natural" man, or Descartes attempting to reach some essential, irreducible level of consciousness awareness, or Rousseau's meditations on education. Or current studies of surviving aboriginal natives in Australia. Or from endless psychological research. And in Eastern thought, well, a lot more.

In this meditation lineage, or shall we fashionably call it conversation, what differentiating intelligence frequently comes to is some single point in presumed linear time when we are doing nothing but breathing and metabolizing. In this moment we are not archers nor the recipient of their arrows, nor the arrows, nor the bows. (In some definitions of present moment, we are all of these simultaneously). From this site of potential, everything we aim to "do" is a form of becoming, involving a sense of causal sequence, including decay. The state, or maybe better, condition prior to this we identify as being.

We could call this moment present tense and mean some sort of abstract aspect of linear sequence separate from human process. But the present can be experienced at varying levels of embodied intensity, and the singularity of such awareness could be an awareness of being, from within and viewed from outside of ourselves. In obverse Buddhist terms, for humans, the present can involve recognition of and the setting aside of our attachments, to things, ideas, and emotions as we come to know who – what we are. Setting aside our attachment – which in some sense embodies illusion – our merit badges of identity, being is the only thing we are.

Our vocabulary and syntax can escort us to our experience beyond syntax. We use the verb/noun/gerund/participle, etc., *being* to declare the problem of identity. It includes or frames, or locates a focus in time which throughout is basically singular, a point; in this, our concern with being significantly includes and expresses gestalt awareness. We may be talking about a brain function or capacity as well as experience. And our meditation on *being*, or is-ness, or similar linguistic strategies includes focusing on where(-from) and how the word itself comes about.

Being

The focal study of this lineage or strategy, or problem, or concern – or word – has been called Being, its philosophical lineage ontology, and it is difficult to describe its features, because of its essential, preverbal though not immaterial nature. The history of philosophical and psychological examination of Being is extensive; in fact because of its essential characterization factor, we might argue it has been our main consistent human concern – along with the (related) nature of God. We might say all therapies and theologies address our experience of Being.

And Being seems to have the qualities of a black box phenomenon, where we cannot easily look directly at this, our core (and then tell ourselves and our neighbors what we have seen and what we know). Using cross-hair focus, we can fire an electron into Being, but as with an accelerator, we know about the center only from its aftermath. Because Being is not just a concept, but a (the) state, and an experience, discussions about it, in time, can quickly overlap and confuse.

Yet Being is the harbor out of which all movement occurs, all personality expresses, all senses of present tenses derive. And Being encompasses at least two time sequences, so-called linear external clock within calendar time, and inward metabolic, energetic time, which has its own realms and priorities – forms in spaciality which we experience as having their own sequences, even though they also "occur" within linear time.

Because of its complexity, it may be wise to assemble impressions about this experience/insight we call Being. By a process of elimination, Being is what is left after thought and characterization; again, Being is not our attachment(s). Being is like sitting quietly with nothing on our mind, only deeper – including something or some process. The state of Being usually can be experienced only partially because it is an energetic High which quickly incites some Second Shoe of trauma process: metabolically, we can't sustain it easily, though it is always somewhere in (and ultimately at the center of) the room.

A word about the energetic High. I shall characterize it with a capital letter because it becomes for me an entity, not something which I can easily identify, either by neurochemistry or emotion. But the pattern which it describes has been noted before, at least as early as Aristotle. It is the state which may be used in prediction, and certainly can be seen in the patterns' wake, looking back upon an energetic sequence.

What we wonder at is how a golfer or tennis pro can sustain concentration and effectiveness as the superiority of his actions lead him to a winning score. Some inner sequence gets activated by the perfection of his moves, their clarity, at which a second phase or I call it the Second Shoe, occurs, and the clarity is lost.

As a phrase, the Second Shoe refers, as I have heard it, to the experience of a dweller in an old-style tenement, where the floor-plan of each apartment is the same as the ones above and below it. In our bedroom, we are under our neighbor's bedroom, and at night as we hear him take off and drop his first shoe on the floor, we wait to hear him drop his second. If he is cruel, or in trouble, we will not hear the second shoe, and we will be up all night worrying about the incompletion of his regular activities as he gets ready for bed.

I think this High is where in the neurochemistry the residual held-energy systems relating to previous traumata are triggered or activated. We are suddenly or not so suddenly confounded by an additional text which demands reading. Lottery won, debts come due.

In this sense, the High predicts the Second Shoe, the appearance of the trauma pattern with which we are then left. It may be a potential guideline, to say what causes the trauma pattern to emerge: it is the High. This sequence was noted by Aristotle when he describes the "fall" of the tragic hero as following a prideful " moment". He thought that the hero had to be capable of encompassing an exalted site or chemistry, in order for the sequence to be demonstrated. Lesser characters, or lesser characteristics within a person would not engage this energetic movement and were not exalted, or they were identified as comic individuals. From whatever site, the High had to be brain-experienced as exalted, to trigger the Second Shoe.

Inspired by Luther's Reformation, in the 19th century dramatists were concerned with giving the same potentiality of exaltation to more ordinary people like Ibsen's Solness, the Master Builder, and in the 20th Century, Miller's Salesman Willy Loman. More often these tragic formulations were left to people in the media, politicians and stars, who would not be able to sustain their glamour, and would "fall", as their held-energy systems took over to reveal, in supermarket trash newspapers, their corruption and abject ignorance.

In fact, the democratization of the appearance of the trauma patterns is a major popularization of what everyone experiences, only we have not recognized it as such. It would be nice if I could locate the neurochemistry with greater accuracy than by the name of the High, but so far I cannot. Some will say that the term is too vague to be useful, yet I think what is original to this focal sequence is to break the ordinary (sentimental) elaborations on why the falls occur.

It is too easy to say we fall like Eve because of something bad we have done, rather than recording psycho-dynamically the actual sequence (neurochemical) which occurs between the High and the aberrant – but eventually predictable and trustworthy – appearance of the held-energy system. Over time, this discrimination will be the commonplace way of understanding such phenomena. And will help individuals and their surround with focusing appropriately on what is happening.

The lineages

There are lineages both Western and Eastern, including senses of the present tense, and is-ness – usually meditations on the nature of Being which seek to establish some generative starting point; they characterize what is essentially elemental to us as human creatures. And they are thus linked, preverbally in music and art, but frequently in words, which takes the thoughtful person right back to the preverbal origins of language itself. These meditations include key verbs, such as *be*, and *is*, and they quickly roil out of control; we cannot maintain efficacious focus.

The experience of Being may show up in transforming moments when we sense some(thing) radical – location – within us at what we would have to call a neurochemical level. Here, it may have something to do with what has been called primitive brain. What shows up is some deep level of integration-motion both initially dislocating (perhaps disturbing) and enlightening; achieving awareness or joining its basic nature has the hallmarks of movement and hope, and sufficiency. Being seems beyond the criticism of moral understanding or personality; Plato indicates it as connected to or described by what he calls The Good (well beyond the dualistic "attachments" of and to good and bad).

So, as perceiver of time, our remembered history – and thus of our sense of self – is confounded by at least two problems in ordinary time, which itself turns out to be not so ordinary after all. The first is Being, its definition, its experience. Practically, we can be alone in a room, yet we are internally busy with list-making, or dreams, or memories. Being means all those concerns peal away, and there is survival without anxiety.

In the state of "pure Being", we may experience ourselves to just be. To Be can mean dropping not only inner dialogues but even the inward sense of loneliness, and beyond that, of being – alone. Because of the reductionistic, funneling element in our experience of Being, Being is imperative. When Hamlet says, "To be, or not to be, that is the question," Shakespeare appears to be taking us into this essentializing problem/sequence. Here Shakespeare may be referring to Being as intimately connected with the mystery of time, which is what Being intimately involves.

There seem to be some cognitively-stated discoveries about Being, usually projections of personality or the constructs of conscious experience, which say that in the narrowed and reducing focal point of Being, there are certain insights which may apply, though even these too may drift or slough away. And though Being may be thought to be in linear time, in sensing it, essentially linear time fades away. This means that we can talk about Being contextually, what it leads to in our becoming ways – our potentiality – but that is not the same as the experience of centeredness.

Void

Like the universe it inhabits, Being apparently includes void, which is nothingness, appearing in partnership with our somethingness. That God's universe has what we perceive as emptiness at its center is something we embody, with varying degrees of our incarnative blend of spirit and matter. With the existentialists, and now the astro-physicists, we posit that Being includes void; in this sense, void is not outside of Being.

All plural or dualistic constructions about Being at some point in our understanding of the so-called present tense, enter or become singular or are characterized as a unity. Even that embodied insight is only a partial expressive circumambulation of Being.

One interesting note: when describing Being, we can encounter the importance of focus, as in differentiated sequencing. For some observers, Being expresses itself within a single moment, or some similar "atomic" formulation. By its syntactical placement as a single word, it is singular and reductive. Though we might meditate on some complex grid, we usually don't talk, or think of "Beings" when we are describing the inner experience of a so-called individual.

In this sense, Being can be simultaneous with reality, and reality's definition. Applying Buddhist strategies, Being is without illusion; it reflects discrimination and the capacity to differentiate moments into single moments – into a single, unified moment or moment with unity: beginning, middle, and end. Here, meditationally, we could focus on angels and pinheads.

Being inspires our concern with focus. Can we move single-mindedly, tolerate such departure from the illusion of plurality and discover a one-God reality and sustain it? I will comment on this later.

Being is intimately connected to Soul, the lifetime organizing principle of what we are: as unitary, unified, creatures. I think Soul refers to the initiating memory of unity which (at least) occurs when we are one cell, not two: diploid, not haploid; or perhaps even better, the process whereby haploid momentously transforms into diploid. And we refer to that remembered organizing unity every time a cell divides, and yet we also are one.

Concomitantly, the cognitive discovery of *unit (particle)*, and of one, includes a mythic component which allows us to conceive of ourselves as one, irreducibly one. This pointillist proficiency is profound; every time we apply it, to individuals, to nations, to worlds, to atoms, to the psychological gestalt, some control is rendered, some efficacy with truth is gained. Truth embodies this singular unity, as if our brain must touch base with this "unity factor" each time it connects with diversity and plurality; otherwise we don't know. And if we don't know, we cannot understand.

In direct ways, the experience of Being and singularity is linked to sensate body experiences very early on, and progress toward this discriminating power is related to brain maturation.

For beginners

Soul and Being are linked word-concepts describing us humans as energetic creatures, and, for starters, each singular. With every start, Being is stated and somehow paradoxically so. The paradox of "beginning" is incorporated in our approach to Being, the word, the concept, and the dedicated experience.

Somewhat appropriately, the site of Being is often meditationally characterized by Stillpoint, wherein in the energetic of our neurochemistries, as T.S. Eliot notes, there is no movement, no need for movement, no restriction from movement. A corollary of this meditational and neurochemical site discovering, which can be found in our earliest experiences, *in utero* and after, is that when the debris of civilization urgently seeking resolution but not finding it, gets too much, like Noah, and like the infant, we find the Ark of Stillpoint, upon which we can float above our flooding sensations until we re-group and reconnect with the "exterior". Being at least has to include this approaching sense of pause, though that approach is not Being.

Locke's *tabula rasa* may (or may not) somewhat obliquely refer to this sense of Being at the beginning; he locates it in early infancy, but I think Being is prior to that; and he sees it as something which is subsequently influenced by education and experience, whereas Being is always Being, apparently not educatable nor transformable.

We can propose that at the center of all creation is Stillpoint and at the center of Being is Stillpoint, spare, simple, silent, and luxuriant. To discover our free relationship potential with an open and empty reality comes to us when we experience our energetic inner light – what mystics may call Source. Experienced energetically from within, our de-traumatized core amounts to light, and people have called this experience/realization enlightenment, with the derived perception/insight that we are God's creatures, all of us, and that we share the fate of our participation as creatures with fellow creatures of this energetic destiny.

The following excerpt from Thomas Merton's *The Seven-Storied Mountain* [Harcourt Brace. ISBN 0-15-601086-0. p311-2] describes his encounter with Source light. Note how Catholic Merton contextualizes his experience, but its perameters take him to qualities which characterize Being.

> But what a thing it was, this awareness: it was so intangible, and yet it struck me like a thunderclap. It was a light that was so bright that it had no relation to any visible light and so profound and so intimate that it seemed like a neutralization of every lesser experience.

And yet the thing that struck me most of all was that this light was in a certain sense "ordinary" – it was a light (and this most of all was what took my breath away) that was offered to all, to everybody, and there was nothing fancy or strange about it. It was the light of faith deepened and reduced to an extreme and sudden obviousness.

It was as if I had been suddenly illuminated by being blinded by the manifestation of God's presence.

The reason why this light was blinding and neutralizing was that there was and could be simply nothing in it of sense or imagination. When I call it a light that is a metaphor which I am using, long after the fact. But at the moment, another overwhelming thing about this awareness was that it disarmed all images, all metaphors, and cut through the whole skein of species and phantasms with which we naturally do our thinking.

It ignored all sense experience in order to strike directly at the heart of truth, as if a sudden and immediate contact had been established between my intellect and the Truth Who was now physically really and substantially before me on the altar. But this contact was not something speculative and abstract: it was concrete and experimental and belonged to the order of knowledge, yes, but more still to the order of love.

Another thing about it was that this light was something far above and beyond the level of any desire or any appetite I had ever yet been aware of. It was purified of all emotion and cleansed of everything that savored of sensible yearnings. It was love as clean and direct as vision: and it flew straight to the possession of the Truth it loved.

And the first articulate thought that came to my mind was:

"Heaven is right here in front of me: Heaven, Heaven!"

It lasted only a moment: but it left a breathless joy and a clean peace and happiness that stayed for hours and it was something I have never forgotten.

If we see our history as the gradual collective sequencing toward this enlightenment-embodying goal (and process), without which we are not less than nothing but rather to the side of nothing (which I sometimes sense as worse) – then our story collection of historical focus pares our efforts toward the expression about this clean center; and all our activities are propelled toward this site. Eastern and Western thinkers refer to this site as pure, its evolving sequence purification. From this site of Being, all righteous actions form out of "otherwise" activities and the movement out-toward this site reduces our preoccupations with our usual messy variora. History, remembered past, with its narratives, resolves, dissolves into Being. As encountered in its many, complex levels, history is a shot across humanity's cluttered bow.

Shall we be surprised that Being as a state of understanding as well as of awareness, is always immanent, yet it is harder to know than almost anything? Being is at least preverbal, both in the developmental sense of rooted before we have words – before the language centers are readily available and synaptically experienced – and, relatedly, Being is what is cognitively prior to language, even if we have the words. It is thus hard (to put a word on it) to find translatable, expressible descriptions, if express is what we want to do.

And those of us who are educated to prize cognitive and verbal skills as aids to knowledge and control of our lives, may get distracted by the verbal centers of our brain at the expense of sensing deeper reality. Being takes us past these verbal and cognitive centers of the brain. (And here I think we may have garnered a perspective upon reality which can be expressed cognitively somehow through paradox.)

Being divided

We also know from myth and the exploration of the psyche particularly in the intensification of concern about Being in the 19th Century and after (though proceeded by millennia of commentaries), that though "whole" and "unitary", Being can be approached as if it is divided. And from division, in some people's view, Being must be returned to singularity. These are difficult, sometimes arcane slopes. We also know from Hebrew and Greek traditions among others, that it can be relational, as in having a Covenant with exterior (and interior) Ultimaticity, and as Orestes develops with Athena. Yet these potentials are not Being itself.

We also know that because Being is prior to words, it may be best not to try to name it; preverbal experience takes us closer to the center, where silence, inner and outer, reigns. We also know that if we use words, we can find out the power of our cognitive and word brain centers which must yield to silence, which itself transcends narrative. In some sense, the meditations about the nature of God – a proposed "Ultimate Reality" whatever – duplicate and overlap the more humanistic and humanistically differentiating experience of Being.

In the neurochemical state of Being, there is tranquility and, in true proportion and justice, no anxiety; this space is what we fidgety creatures have as our core, not Being as a mere vacation spa for busy-bodies. Here we can experience transcendence, beyond ordinary time and narrative, though

Being as known by humans is also within time, linear and constant within the – every and ever – present.

Because it is so central to even our active life and thought, there is a lot of cultural talk and historical conversation about the state of Being, its vectors and what it leads to. For the purposes of this discussion, Being is meditationally located at the Stillpoint center, with void. It is what we give children in "Time Outs", only more systemically profound, and without the usual "Outs", and the usual "Time".

We can be quiet on the outside, we can be quiet on the inside, but there is an inward structural phenomenon where we are alone even with our (non-)self which may take years of experience to "allow". To experience Being (which is also what we are no matter what we are aware of) means dropping even this sense of loneliness, and beyond this, of alone, which implies relationship.

In prayerful meditation we can be alone with our God, yet Being means a step within and beyond that; it is developmentally, cognitively prior to God, God being at least that which exists beyond our common sense of self. Thus Being refines; the verb nature of Being helps to set our concerns, our thoughts aside. It is at the beginning; in a significant, natural way, it is origin. And like God, it includes Omega, the ending or the pause. Regressively, Being refers to our intelligence when we first are, the pre-divided first cell. And it becomes time as memory and synaptic connections create our sense of continuity which we propose and call (Self).

Again, as perceivers of time, our remembered history is confounded by at least two problems in ordinary time. The first is Being, its definition, its experience, its usefulness. It is hard to define and to experience, like water to the fish, and one of the first ways we enter the room of Being may be through the door of our sense of waste, and concurrent alternative possibility; here may be where suffering begins, or begins to be visible. Ultimately, the decision to focus on Being may be itself the (evolutional?) signal of a turning away from the despair included in dissociative process.

My philosopher friend David comments that those who, as currently practicing, focus on Being as a state of consciousness to be pursued at any and all costs often lose connection with the world; moment by moment, we live a seriously compromised existence, filled with constant error. What needs reframing then is that those of us who are attached to narrative may have to struggle to re-achieve the importance of Stillpoint, even amidst the most crucial and anxiety-driven narratives. If we don't know what Stillpoint senses like, we may not know anything – we live unrighteous lives. The acknowledgment of Stillpoint can be a hallmark of integrity; and it is a neurochemistry.

A second problem in time

A second problem in how we understand our experience of ordinary time is that our shock systems make it hard to perceive or maintain what has been called Being, the center of who we are, without encumbrances of anxiety or bias. What stands in the way of our embodying the ascending intensification of the clarity at the center of Being is our immobilized shock memory (which also in held, densified, de-oxygenated form contains Stillpoint and its Source radiance). We have two still "positions", Stillpoint, and held-energy nexuses of shock.

Because of the apparently (impulsive? anxiety-determined?) urgencies to complete early traumatic shock-memorialized patterning, we cannot browse leisurely into preverbal states – both interior and inward – and see that Being is what our core is and is at the center of whatever contract or covenant we have with Ultimate Reality. In the minefield of traumatic memory, we are East of Eden, expelled from the clarity and refinement of the integrative state we might initially call Edenic Being by our own survival mechanism, the perpetuate experience of shock and its persistent form of shock memory, or held-energy systems. And at this black site, Being is longed for, but not visible.

Eden, the day shock enters

An initial word here about Eden, about which I have found there is a lot to consider. One reason we have Adam and Eve and the Garden is as an attempt to mythically master early preverbal prenatal, natal, and infantile states of awareness; in this sense, Adam and Eve are truly our first parents, the first statement of, or our attempt to define what analysts might call the early iconographic parental introjects. Implied in the poetry of Genesis is the insight that there are first parents, beginnings, to the subsequent process of our lives. We now know from current focus on fairy tales and creation myths that there are different stages of understanding of how we come about, as well as how we comprehend the world which includes parents. Viewed from this point, the myths of Genesis can be mined for developmental understanding, complete, partial, factual, and accurate to our developing brain as infant and as growing child. They also encompass meditational points of consciousness, beginning at least at conception, if not "karmically" before.

Thus, as far as infantile awareness goes, what is Eden about? Eden is not quite Being, because Eden contains God and activity and Adam and Eve, and narrative, within and against the suspended sense of linear time (or limitless time) which is Being. From the point of Being as I am now considering it, Eden is a mythic approximation of an early meditational point, even of earliest developmental sites, but not origin itself. God places Adam in the Garden, a stage later or after Being.

Eden characterizes an incarnative sense of Being integrating with the world or, if you will, the Other; but I think Eden is meditationally secondary to Being, though Eden indicates that Being can dwell harmoniously in the matter-of-fact world, in (naked) narrative. In terms of the Expulsion, Eden is prior to traumatic experience, whether that is experienced or deduced.

As a state of unified consciousness, Being is without shock, even though the potential to evoke shock enables the entire neurochemical system to eventually discover Being's centrality, sometimes many years from the initiating situation. What understanding emerges is that shock is manifold, and it is hard to see any of us even getting born, not to mention created, without, as sustaining midwife, shock somehow being evoked to preserve the often tenuous option of survival.

In a curious, even possibly paradoxical way, shock can appear posited against Being, its presence immediately surrounding and sometimes penetrating Being. The narrative of Satan has been characterized as God's closest angel, who opposes God; this "fallen" and beguiling characterization may express the sudden, rescuing and alternative quality of shock as it intrudes upon our ordinary consciousness, just as the shock-inciting triggering occasion – the car accident – itself does.

Our accommodation to the awareness of shock (presuming we have it) is after its implementation, not prior to it. The paradox of Innocence and Experience may shed some light upon this sequence; it is not so much a question of which comes first but how does the presence of shock influence and sustain our sense of both polarities. So shock's entry into our consciousness may involve an awareness of primitive process – primitive brain and its spine – hence the image of the tree and the serpent.

Being is at the soul level, organizing and sustaining presence in and in relationship to the outside world. The historicity of remembered trauma is the residual interaction of our capacity to experience shock and thereby to sustain our entire system through suspended animation triggered by sensate crisis. As he falls toward breaking his crown, Jack goes into shock, or hold.

Our trauma "memories" are always present and apparently their complex neurochemistries are at the ready for resolution or completion. They are pushing to the front of the line, into the present moment, in which the restoration of our clean, clear sense of Being can be recovered. We want the clarity and freedom of a shock-reduced, shock-decompressed existence; even a world in which shock does not have to rescue us as it does. Our Experienced sense of self seeks the Innocence where shock need not apply.

In various portions of our system, we return to Eden as the incarnative Garden wherein we cultivate our focus upon Being. In other – many – portions, we are already there, surviving, thriving, and Being-balanced, right down to, through, and past our mitochondria.

Thus, the second issue in human time involves trauma memory as it emerges and colors our perception of the present. The experience of trauma process, particularly as it is stored in memory, by memory function, creates an uneasy sense of waste and lack of centeredness, yet the fact of the existence of shock has enabled us to survive through substantial crises and imperfections in ourselves and in the surrounding world we inhabit. Shock, at the center of traumatic memory, obscures and confounds as well as retains our present sense of Being. Its presence can be characterized as held-energy (see *Trauma Energetics: A Study of Held-Energy Systems*).

Its accompanying determinate sense of inevitable, mind-boggling (unjust?) fate places the shock mechanism at the heart of tragedy; whose stories catalogue the ways in which perpetuant held-energy systems force dramatis personae (dramatic "people" – the people or people-fragments characterized in dramas) to move toward resolution. And because of the nature of the shock-initiating crises, tragedies reveal the memory re-engagement process as cataclysmic.

Is it any wonder that these characters, or portions of personality, are seen to be the somehow institutors of their own hapless demise? Greek tragedy and Aristotelian tragic theory are among the first sustained Western attempts to identify and to grid the extenuating place which held-energy systems take in our lives. And in the long run, they may provide a way through the conundrums which as shock-storing, memorializing, curating creatures we are, until we are not.

Trigger

As a neurochemical and energetic phenomenon, our somehow recollected trauma sequence is set off in a current moment by abundance of some sort, some energetic or material "High" (the Greeks sometimes identified it as *hubris*, or pride – an energetic overweaning), after which there is what I have called the Second Shoe of re-emergent traumatic experience(s).

In a curious way, a similar sequence of immediacy applies to the energetics of trauma patterning as it surfaces into current present moments. Some inner or exterior state conveys we have won a spiritual, energetic, and/or material lottery and now, sure as shootin' – the triggering word applies – the old debts of immobilization, stored as trauma memories, many of which we have taken on quite early as cultural, ethnic, racial, and sexual parts, come forward for resolution.

These Second Shoe patterns arrive with a radical swiftness and subtle power which can lay us flat if we don't know how to read them. And they are filled with, or amount to toxicity. Our brain rushes to complete some compressed holding pattern created in the suspension of its neurochemistry when it moved into immobilizing shock, often years ago; and we are confronted with our responses to current situations which somehow don't quite apply; and we promulgate messes which "seek" centered experience, but therein we often never get it.

Brain's perception of the inciting present is that the now situation is similar enough for the remembered shock system to finally and successfully unfold, to dissolve in an appropriate, relational way; the brain seeks to restore itself to the Being beginning: a pristine, even meditationally pre-Edenic mode, vibrationally pure, antique, fresh, limitless, without anxiety, and open.

Again, I use the term pre-Edenic here to acknowledge that Eden contains Being, attempts Being, connects harmoniously with Being, but is already "corrupted" or possibly confounded by its (cognitive) narrative. We live in "imperfect" consciousness because while Being may be experienced perfectly in narrative (in Eden), narrative experience includes shock-potentiality. Because of the problems of scale, infantile and grandiose, myelanated and growing, contextual and isolate, we take on the whole of civilization when we take on these, our trauma sites.

Being is like having a credit card which turns out to have lots of add-on features, some of which we are still learning, long after we sign up for one. Yet Being is achieved meditationally and cognitively by focusing on singularity, our individual unity; this means discarding as we can the usual suspects, our – illusory – attachments. Here, Being is unified consciousness.

Barnacled by time

To this thwarted, unfolding movement, brain expects the outer world to respond in an appropriate and healing way, something which was only radically, partially experienced in the shock-inducing original moment. Additionally, our initial memories are barnacled by time and synaptic usage, so getting to the original bottom of things, where ultimate change could and needs to occur, is difficult. People in therapy know they frequently go over and over a certain situation until it is satisfactorily resolved, if they are lucky enough to get that.

Shock enables the entire human system to maintain itself in a survival mode, and it has succeeded; only it has one further step to go, the completion of the momentum which has been memorized, memorialized as held-energy: we can return to the state of unencumbered, unattached Being from which sacred and decent existence can be experienced. Some call this Centering, with Being being the center point. (It is interesting that one would use the term *point* to bring time and space to singularity). This resolution gives us the mind-state of enlightenment, at various levels of clarity. And to achieve this transformation of held-energy, brain apparently needs some kind of "holding."

As a kind of healing/holding, getting a true reading of an historical sequence, which could be seen as the movement toward enlightenment, and its impingements, turns out to be problematic. Not only are the human actors in the (some) present – presumably what is being described by historical records – biased: dissociated. They are prejudiced in very circumscribing ways; for this task, prejudice itself is very limiting.

While we all may share the Edenic goal of embodying, incarnating Being, our roads to that goal appear to vary, and we may not be aware of its variations which seem so different, both within ourselves and in social recognition of others. And in a room with others, there are apparently other (competing?) irresolutions, all seeking completions.

To admit their similarities, or the similitude of their resolution goals, might be like disowning our specifically stored past, both ours as individuals and ours as inheritors of traumatic patternings in our culture. The vectors of the original shock impingements upon energetic flows within our neurochemistries seem to demand that these held-energy systems be followed down in some specific brain sequence, duplicating in some kind of jimmy-rigged reverse order the way the original shock system was discovered and utilized. Like Theseus, having "transformed" the Minotaur at its center, now chasing back his string, turns corner by turned corner, to the outside of the Labyrinth. Or watching a reversed family video of a diver arising feet first out of the water and returning backwards to standing on the front edge of the diving board.

Yet my clients and I have discovered that the resolutions of these so-called historical memories can often take place at lightning speed, with complex subtlety and dazzling re-organization which can only be glimpsed. Currently, slowing down the process takes skill, patience, and luck.

So the recording of the past must somehow acknowledge the shock mechanism and its semi-permanent place as held-energy systems in our perceptions and distortions of the present. This is a major hurdle when it comes to memory taking us ultimately to Being. Again, here is the second problem with time and our only partial understanding of the problem stated by our approximation of the past, presumably addressed in the issues surrounding history, memory, and awareness. Centered, we are unified and unitary.

Successful life

Given the above-outlined situation, we may need to characterize an increasingly successful life, not a perfect one; though over time an increasingly successful life may look like an assembly of perfectly sung notes, with trauma-determined variations. Success, of course, appears in many realms, including financial, political, personal, metabolic, and spiritual; success implies integrity, including a viable rendering of reality, and a sense of wholeness about something, including a whole life. But I find it is the spiritual, or better, energetically clear success which can be our ultimate benchmark and its handmaiden, our psychological manifestations; for these foci are fulcrum sites where inner energetic stability may be found and recognized and maintained; for they can engage at the soul level, where our deepest organization as an integrated individual occurs. They have to do with Being and with garnering toward Being.

Young adults swim in the high-water turbulence of hormone and energetic process, but they are not necessarily at the peak of their embodied experience. In fact, they are often perhaps just beginning to see what the problem is which the apparently confounded adults around them are working on.

After two decades of brain self-scanning (approximately 6,307,200,000 times, not including nine months – an additional, say, 23,920,000 times), our personal arrogance may begin to diminish, and we are increasingly humbled by life's persisting questions and their refusal to resolve. We quickly encounter random disasters, addictions, self-destructive patternings and the like, and we are brought down by these distractions.

With these preoccupative experiences in high definition, shock-filled trauma pattern resolution appears to be the name of the human game, and in the great myths – of Arthur, Hercules, Quixote, Odysseus, Moses, Oedipus, Jesus, and Buddha, of the Zens and of the Sufis, to name a few – theirs is the lineage about pattern resolution which we teach or are taught, and, in a manner of speaking, pattern resolution is the only lineage, mythic or "in fact", which matters.

And there is functionally only one sequence, simple and difficult, to learn, in order to have a clear day. Or a clear moment. When we hit some inner turbulence, the question we can ask ourselves is, "What needs to happen here; what seeks completion?" From this resultant completion "clarity", or enlightenment, we shall be able directly to witness reality: on a clear day.

Hints of clarity are always present, and clear emotions and states of awareness are the ones we prize, woven into the fabric of more difficult states because they seem to happen within a self which is capable of tolerating them. Identifiable emotions such as love, hate, jealousy – usual suspects – are often used as signposts toward the refinement of clarity, but in themselves, they are not at the center.

Psychologists may refer to the dissociative, shock-infested states we are in and comment, "But you are not in touch with your feelings," as if that will do the trick. As proffered, this strategy/insight rarely does – which leads me to think there is often a bait and switch aspect to the therapeutic offer to help me get in touch with my feelings. My feelings, complex and simple, have not led me to greater clarity, though greater clarity has included greater capacity to understand and frame – position – feeling states.

When I am clear, the feelings fold and open, advance and retreat as they will, and I observe them dynamically and participate in them as fully as I can, or better, do. Somehow, the traditional approaches of "getting in touch" don't match the subtlety of the process, which may include witnessing, not touching.

An acquaintance informs me that he gradually allows his orgasms to overwhelm him in order to see, to understand, and to experience; he does not merely luge through the chute in order to bring the pleasurable irritability to ecstatic conclusion. As a result, he garners a differentiated view, perhaps a quite raw and subtle view of vivid, complex, energetic natural process. And he reports being able to watch the orgasmic aftermath with equal intensity as the preceding enthralling storm, noticing how the system restores itself from Being to Being. At their best, all experiences, including sensations and feelings, may lead us back to Being.

How clear can I be here?

As we develop, these feeling states become important as they serve the deeper question: how clear can I be here? What truth can I see, and at what levels will that truth satisfy me? What do I have to do to guarantee my fair share of these experiences, to experience the full range and impact of these moments? How much habit and discipline will help me? What material needs are necessary to meet and sustain these moments and strings of moments, connecting with the higher forms of consciousness toward which I am driven? Upon first or second glance at these highs, it turns out they can scare me, sometimes profoundly, and I will avoid my presumed desire for clarity at some sites, for days, months, and sometimes years.

Yet my longing is for a level of development so that when I die, St. Peter, or its mythic equivalent, can ask me, "What did you see/do in your life?", and I can reply, "I have seen, witnessed, and embodied reality, the truth. I have sustained Being." All important myths are about strategies toward achieving this end. So I find it clear from the great religious transitions and traditions what success can mean: it can mean connecting with ultimate truth; and embodying the God-head within that truth, the essence of wisdom. "I have held the card of Being in my hand in order that it be played."

God-head

The concept of God-head suggests a state of conscient being wherein we are able to witness Ultimate Reality, including the activating belief system in a creator which we engender as children when we realize we have been "created" (and continue to be creating). Such witnessing might include the neurochemistries of faith as archival residue of early ideation about reality, but not necessarily; then we approach the witnessing process as an issue of faith, rather than with more complex, simplifying understanding.

God-head involves intelligence, but if we do not acknowledge the ways faith acts upon our consciousness whether we like it or not, faith will become the elephant in the room and skew our perceptions. To view reality, we need our intelligence to be rarified by integrating earliest forms of belief, if only to set them aside, or folded into a deeper context.

Success and perfection of consciousness mean enlightenment. If we are in this state of awareness, we perform and experience acts of compassion, toward ourselves and toward others, explicating such awareness from a spacious sense of possibility.

CHAPTER THREE:

LIBERTY, HISTORY, AND BEING

Liberty and Being

Liberty is both a word-idea and an experience. Yet from the language centers of the brain, our essential liberty can be intuited, expressed, but can it be known? For all the shouting surrounding the term, liberty is a quality and attribute of Being and is informed by preverbal states perhaps separate (or separatable) from the language centers of the brain.

Liberty can be understood as taking the same space as Being, a state we can initially approximate and view, perhaps best, from paradox, hardly our standard concept of liberty. Liberty is a neuro-chemical state or experience beyond paradox and beyond ideas. Liberty includes the freedom to be as well as to do. Liberty is both within and without. Liberty involves freedom from held-traumatic process, and liberty implies the achievement of Stillpoint, our inner energetic, meditational state where, as has been described, there is no movement, no need for movement, and no restriction from movement.

In their freeform sequences, Olympic skaters convey the paradox of discipline and pure energetic elevation. We look for both expressions in the performance, but we seek to witness the topping of the practiced order with some pure god-driven drive, which is ecstatic and without formality: we want to witness and vicariously experience "mere" embodiment.

No matter how subtly or happily introduced, ideas are regularly an intrusion upon this clarity, often in some second phase of the idea's existence within our consciousness. The first carries the aura of liberation, and all our enthusiasms attach to the synaptical sequence and soon become institutionalized. This is a neurophysiological energetic process, and it can be observed and described.

Ideas or idea-clusters themselves can give us a glimpse of this experience of liberty, and we can be moved by their sequence in narratives of story and song. That we can abstract themes from narrative levels of awareness gives us some sense of rolling reality which enables us to grasp or position ourselves above details, unattached, itself a liberal cognition.

We are self-destructive in at least two senses: self-destruction as a way toward ego-less enlightenment; and self-destruction in that we do not understand the real interaction between impacted, projective systems we call humans: real interactions with catastrophic results. The experience of liberty and freedom, often relatedly interchangeable word-ideas, is essential toward bringing focus to the reality to which these ideas refer. With focus as our tool, like Being, liberty can be seen to be singular, a site of unity; and in some ways, a site of integrity.

Being and invisibility

Though they seem to bring a kind of concrete clarity, ideas contain invisibility, and the longer we differentiate our experience, the more we discover the essential part invisibility plays in our idea systems. In a debate, when we are asked to argue a premise, in fact we have to learn both sides of the debate proposition, not just one. In order to be fully in command of our position, if we dare call it that, we need to see both sides and to argue empathically from both sides. This capacity may explicate an invisible middle ground.

William Blake withstanding, Innocence and Experience express a paradox, just as chicken/egg firstness is a paradox. We can't have one without the other, its apparent "opposite". In subtle ways, ideas are about paradoxes, and in their polarizing function, dangerous illusions about the approximation of reality can occur.

Usually, in debate, when we achieve this "bipolarity", we fall away from taking sides, and we see the true complexity of the proposition under discussion and rediscover an invisible – even – mystery. Like confounded Job, we cover our mouth, or we fall back and try to bring other individuals to the same ideational place we occupy, as in the case of abortion arguments. But the complexity of this paradox experience means that at times we seek the apparent firmness of polarity; we think ideas are about one thing. Because their apparent singularity reminds us of truth.

If we have to do it with ideas, where is the best vantage point from which to witness the God-head? Or embody it. Certainly it includes specifically witnessing the outside world; and it also includes viewing/experiencing inner awareness states of Being. Ideas are about something, but what if they include void? Or what cannot be seen? At what point, or by what bridge, can they dissolve into Being? Is Being the only truth which satisfies?

Ideas seem to have a more permanent identity than journalistic reportage, and they give us some flexibility of approach, hence their importance as sites from which to view the Canyon. Because we can center ourselves a bit with ideas, they become important; but do we know what they are? Their influence can be profound, to the extent that certain idea sequences can be seen as leading toward a world view which appears mortally threatened, and we find we are prepared to die – for our ideationally expressed aggregate of idea sequences.

But the idea systems are often interchangeable, and in a very real sense the deaths of our systems, including our own deaths, are meaningless on some absolute scale: we and all our longings die; by definition, God is what sustains – and remains. The interface of one system with other systems is predicated on the following such-as questions. What do we do about: that unruly child, our attitudes toward authority, our experience of sexuality? Our approach to ultimate truth – through paradox? Do we use books? Do we use individuals? How to train these individuals who interpret the books? How much dissent can we tolerate and is that wise? Where do we set our limits? How do we hold ideas – can ideas be possessed, and by whom?

Ideas and idea systems provide some motivation for implementation, for action, yet they also provide a venue toward enlightenment, which dwells in the state of Being. When we ask these questions about ideas, we are holding them within a state of Being which transcends any ideational system we have. Here enlightenment cannot be bought, or possessed – perhaps only experienced.

Enlightenment and history

As I have noted before, the movement toward enlightenment, not always a linear progress, and beyond objectification, has a number of crucial areas of focus including the study of history. Apparently a simple linear record of time and experience, history includes complex, layered attributes of focus. For individuals, it begins in the internalization of habit and discipline related to our growing identity; it is known through our experience of repetition and memory.

Garnered through repeated time sequences which give us a taste of the (once present) past, history is confirmed in our interactions with our parents and family, and later with friends and society. In academic and religion lineages, we are instructed in the so–called past, where facts emerge and are organized in time sequences, with beginnings, middles, and ends.

History acknowledges the remarkable brain-fact of memory. As infants, memory becomes the foundation of personality, agency, and relationship. Yet from our own experience and that of others, we slowly learn that memory can be altered, reportage spun, the reality of time expanded or contracted; people, including ourselves, lie or get confused, or, currently, mis-speak. Nailing an event somehow includes surfing idea systems which float in and out of recorded dates. Placement and sequence follow rules and customs not always obvious, rational, or consistent.

Memory research

For some time now, experimenters are researching memory, to the point where someone on the radio recently notes (not surprisingly) that our memories are flawed and basically synaptically encrusted. The original memory as laid-down neurochemistry gets reduplicated, stacked, if you will, until the "first occasion" is not what we recall, but millions of scanned moments surrounding this initial, prompting sequence.

We are lucky to be able to identify what "happens" in a present moment with any hope of ultimate veracity: if we assume that the first synaptic pass on an event contains some process/access called truth. A memory is like an aquarium into which we peer, replacing water and plants, fish, over time, until while some structure remains, the entire experience has been transformed by prejudice, bias, proclivity, pain, and pleasure.

To that add substantial personal chemistries of dissociation, shock-inspired, shock-immersed distortions of what we think happened, and of what we are – the whole kit and caboodle; our capacity to discern reality insofar as what may be crucially tied to what we identify as the passage of time, history's presumed bailiwick, is, to say the least, challenged. We are not talking merely about idealism or kicking stones, here; we are talking about how we aggrandize what has occurred with how we shelve these occurrences, including what kind of meaning systems we fashion, what patterns we reveal, which we avoid. In his examination of the effect of hallucinogens upon consciousness, Pollan identifies this function within the default mode network.

There are moments when it is not clear whether as God's creatures, we are meant to envision the so-called past. Within the current struggles with fundamentalist thought and evolution, there are critical juxtapositions which highlight this question; for some, the idea of evolution itself involves a new and mordant leap into a shapeless future.

In order to make the history playing-field fair and even worthwhile engaging with, we must first examine what happens when we remove the simplest equivocations which qualify our statements, our ideas. We are left seeking viewing positions without bias, without anxiety – we must "recollect in tranquility", from without and from within. This is one area where the idea and reality of progress might begin to mean something: who are we to presume accuracy? How do we get clear? If clarity involves the deepest parts of the brain stem, how can these be viewed, not to mention functionally accessed? How unanxious can we be about events which traumatize – which evoke the trauma mechanism?

How many histories examine how the enacters regard time sequence and their personal distortions as part of the list of happenings? From what trauma-framed doors do each of the participants enter the peace conference room, and what patterns are seeking resolution therein?

Discovering

While it is not the professional historians' done thing to discover how important history or the past as we organize it can be to our sense of Being, I have recently been working with clients who are trying to access early childhood occasions, usually garnered and framed within abusive, or sudden shocking interactions. They are stuck in patterns of action and response which seriously compromise their well-being as adults.

The traumatic mechanisms, designed to enable overwhelmed systems to sustain themselves in crisis, no longer quite apply, and the individuals are caught in the held-energy systems of dissociation. Their time is wasted, and they are suffering, and this condition can effect people's vulnerability, both emotional and physiological, in the most mortal ways.

If the memories are not vividly stored, they have to be gleaned from energetic states, recorded in dreams, reveries, current patternings, and the like. Sometimes this journey into the past is like heading into a fog with an abyss at its center. Even though the client and I are eager to bring movement and "life" back to these formidable impaction sites, often there is a resistance (Freud's term) to awareness which is palpable and can be reentered as if the brain is experiencing its life-threatening stimulus again, without oxygen. No brain in its right mind will "enter" these sites, even though they are borne within its entire system and scanned at least ten times a second; characteristically, energetically, such focused reentry may be like a death.

Here the study of history is direct, immanent, and its bramble of detail significant. The held-energy site of trauma "memory" awaits a Prince Charming to awaken it with a restorative kiss. The truth is that our so-called history as held, not to mention acknowledged, by the individual is a highly compromised, sometime thing.

There are occasions when we rely on our trauma impactions and patterns, which occur like floaters in the eye, to orient against even higher levels of awareness, because the freedom we experience there may have an unfocused, initially disorienting feel to it. We want it so bad we can taste it, yet given actual clarity and freedom, including freedom from linear time and sequence, we can be profoundly afraid and can tolerate only little bits of liberty.

The purpose of studying, developing history

As a result, here, I find the purpose of studying, developing history is to witness trauma patternings and to watch them dissolve into preverbal states of Being. Here, we might begin to establish constructs about the nature of some (revised) kinds of success.

These resultant semi-Edenic states of consciousness are useful and beneficial to social and personal order. In them lies the vision, if not the experience of a true connectedness, to ultimate reality and back again to some understanding of incarnate existence. Paradoxically, and noted – not for the first time – when "we enter the present", traditional markers of time dissolve, and it would appear we become "a-historical". Valhalla burns, the state disappears.

History's lessons

Into these voidy or void-inclusive places whole civilizations can be poured, rendered, essentialized, learned from, and dissolved. We talk as if history teaches us lessons, but these lessons rarely are delineated in digestible forms; and they don't generally lead us back to Being.

The lessons of war, for example. With some hopefulness, World War I was envisioned to be the war to end all wars, and it could be still if we find out how to learn from it – how to see its patterns: all subsequent conflicts, World War II and the like, can be seen as extensions of whatever was declared then.

For this sustained objective, most significantly, a new global awareness is now embedded in the initial concept of a world war which is fulfilling itself in the environment, globally perceived, including the world-wide web and the cloud – destined to change our parochial understandings of where we are and what our rights and responsibilities are. Any world war is global in its implications: by characterizing the fragmentations of personality, connection and systems leading up to World War I, Barbara Tuchman's *The Guns of August* for one illustrates our morbid encapsulations which seem haplessly universal to humanity – to the point of lethal farce.

Currently our understanding indicates we have not learned much from our reviews of this particular (Western) past, so our new wars remain cognitized under its shadow, if only as an anchoring point for discussions trying to identify where we are. And as mere repetitions, these military varietals are probably insufficiently instructive as a result.

For perhaps the first time in modern (again Western) awareness, with World War I we acknowledge that war must be concluded as a way to do whatever war seems to do. This voiced – thought – idea does not make glamorous or even necessary the activities of armed conflict. We seek the war to end all wars, but – and – we misunderstand what that ending would look like. Because of its trauma-based premises, war ends war, until it does not.

Thus our current wars appear to be despair-filled exigencies, rendered by leaders with dissociative consciousness, caught up in sequences of proposal and response. The awareness which would end these conflicts, death-ridden and retraumatizing as they are, horrendous and distracting for all those caught up in their maelstroms, is barely tolerated. We spend our days putting out brush fires, justifying why we are where we are. And, traumatically sealed, where we are not.

Intelligent about the past

Given our experience with the distortions trauma confounds our private sense of present, how can we teach ourselves to be intelligent about the past, our own and that of our community, including its global nature? How is the past bred into us? How can we deepen and expand our understanding of the so-called, crucial past?

With clients and students thusly interested, I have examined how what we call the past is stored in the memory functions of the brain, particularly how such memories, bound by shock, are immobilized. Insofar as these memories or memory convictions, contained in (largely preverbal) held-energy systems, are fixed, or encrusted, the systems of cognitive consciousness can do little to alter the trajectories of the future, including retraumatizing through repetition of destructive, deoxygenated (energetic) patterns which express themselves in radical narrative.

This aspect of the study of history is often acknowledged by traditional historians, who argue for history's place in the pantheon of academic gods, as leading us to an understanding of what we think has already happened in order not to repeat our ignorant, ignoring mistakes.

Though channeled from God, we cannot substantially learn about our history of behavior, even from Ten Commandments. Witnessed from an enlightened state, commandments are processed as merely commandments. Commandment here suggests a forceful, attention-getting intervention; it bespeaks a weakness in the face of perhaps otherwise-chaotic inner experience. Yet when fully sourced, commandments could be experienced as polite and gentle advisories, reminders of the path toward Being, which arise out of our own righteousness. But how much do we deeply understand about the past or how to deal with its issues from the place, even such as commandment? For the enlightened or righteous person, there is no need for Commandments; coming from their center, they would not perform these "errors". They would not be interested.

History becomes the opportunity to witness

History as study and as phenomenon becomes the opportunity to witness trauma patterns which are forcing themselves into consciousness through ideation and activities, often idiosyncratic and destructive and chronic. But in the realms of narrative sequencing lie tons of trauma, distorting how those sequences are shelved and implemented. It becomes hard to establish facts, the safety net against the free-fall of personal, personality chaos.

To that, we obviate the possible personal and social value in identifying the endlessness of patterning which threatens our ability to transform. It may be more important that at some levels, the conflicts and battlefields of gender, race, religion, neurochemistry, and prenatal development need to be witnessed and observed empathically. This could be the voice of the culture and each of its teacher priests, to say, in the face of internal turmoil and tumult: "The world can be perceived as a whole and can be viewed as such by a single individual and communicated in a sharing of this so-called civilization." Which may amount to a very thin, threaded grid, poised over void.

If such is the holistic platform I propose to speak from and to encourage my students to be able to manifest, no idea can be excluded, no aspect of experience can be obviated. Sex, drugs, violence, war, peace, god, God, heroines, are all linking positions from which to view the battlefields of civilization, and we excise one at our pedagogical peril. We retraumatize by default, particularly in the face of individual traumata which encompass these areas. And we seem to be expected to know what our true history looks like, and to know why we have got it mostly wrong. Do our studies of ideas and activity sequences escort us back to Being?

The studies of each of these dominant processes can be approached through literature and language, which also is abused, and needs to be held accurately as a tool toward a broad, universal form of learning, particularly to learning's edge, the edge of Being. This means that all approaches, which are multiplex, must be made reference to, as a gestalt, if the integration is to be demonstrated by the teacher and encouraged by the student, who wishes to share with its teacher a similar set of individuating skills.

In its most current forms, the rhetoric for exploring texts, such as bibles, appears at a dead end, wherein scholars and teachers dwell in and at minutiae to no effect. The obsessional explication of the enticements to the spirit can be deadeners, particularly for an audience of late adolescents who are amid resolution of their traumata and a sense of inner possibility, hope – energetic movement – where before there has been none. If we do not address this issue, I think our teaching has little depth and is a reduplication of the abuse which earlier was hurled upon us elders in the name of education, by teachers similarly abused.

Sometimes teachers of literature are so enthralled by the language centers of the brain that words have a magical power, capable of generating feelings and commitment; so the educators work their way down to the poem's sounds and word order, and which includes at their best, preverbal levels of understanding, at their worst, obsessive distraction from reality. The elevation of experience through words dominates our educational forms. Yet often the verbal territories become rarified in a way which appears arcane and without essential, neurochemistry-liberating meaning.

Projection and projections

One related pivot point toward this goal: the phenomenon of projection may be directly related to traumatic process, and I think it should be taught about in our schools. Projection generally means taking something inner and placing it outward, usually on some Other – person, group, or deity. We project when there is some inner process which is difficult or unacceptable within; this mechanism is included in scapegoating, where some selected (chosen?) one carries sins of the world out beyond some boundary and away. Projection is usually connected to apparently unassailable traumatic holding, and in our inner economy, it promises a way through an otherwise deadly nexus of shock and stalemate. But it is a defense.

In the time of the Vietnam War, which was concurrent with the 100th anniversary of the American Civil War, America projected upon the conflict in Vietnam its own dilemmas, its lack of resolution in 1961 of the issues raised by the crisis in 1861. Lead by a southern president, we sought to intervene on behalf of the liberty for South Vietnam against a totalitarian North. Only when America became ready to readdress issues of civil rights with its democratic resources at many levels was it possible to withdraw from the foreign scapegoat. And the retreat from the projection site of Vietnam literally occurred at the clusters of the anniversaries surrounding the founding of the United States. Clinicians note the importance of anniversaries to the process of their clients. This insight is carried out in the axis lining up of the walls of Maya Lin's Vietnam Memorial in Washington, DC.

If we were to agree that there would be no acting out of the projections and projective processes which arise from traumatic holding, what would we allow in the explication of freedom? The High of Being/freedom would lead us directly back to our next, unresolved trauma – I think Being as an experience or potentiating reality most always does – which we then project onto the world and expect the world to somehow mirror/fulfill – in order to garner healing. Marriage, society, family, government allow us to confront this simple sequence, and we frequently feel destroyed when we discover our own imprisonment within these forms. Often, the new messenger brings the opportunity to see the ways in which we have been imprisoned all these years; and somehow we kill him/her/it. Otherwise, and better, we can sometimes go back to our (own) drawing board.

What we project upon the outside world often takes the form of some kind of cruel domination or another. But in our intercourse with the world, what if we were to say, "I will not do that. We shall not fulfill your expectations for a partner with which your pattern can be projectively mirrored, though critically, not completed?" Can we forget the outside's mirroring function as guarantee for inside development? Whatever the exterior crisis which interferes with its own traumatic impact, can we not let it keep us away from our task?

If someone bombs us, can we respond by seeking to restrain them without calling them our enemy? Can we refuse to wage war, to name someone our enemy, particularly when they are projectively seeking an enemy to exteriorize the domestic, inner problem they face? One "lesson" from World War I could be we shall not declare anyone our enemy; that is to promote a self-destructive action, including destroying the Other. We shall negotiate, use force to stop behaviors, but we shall not declare enemies, bad guys, etc.

All identities are projective, until they are not

Each cell must plump and like a delicate sponge, take in and release with a miraculous discrimination. Each cell carries Eden within its Being intelligence. All other interactions as described are projective, until they are not. All identities are projective, until they are not. At societal levels, must not each tribal, collective identity return to God, *i.e.,* the unknown, not the known God?

The compression of trauma commands our attention, and we die of it; though often we cannot identify the point of related impact: which butterfly sets off the maelstrom? But what we experience as random inner appearances are in reality extensions of a sequence of vulnerability initiated by the outside, patternings we have taken on. In this sense we are not to blame, though because of our held-energy systems, we are vulnerable, and, curiously responsible.

Enlightenment carries us past words, into insights whose activity leads us to silence. The only real movement, our motive for all activities, can be seen as the resolution of traumatic patterning, and the reestablishment of Stillpoint at the center of our wholeness. The activities which are plural in nature then become action, which is unitary and holistic. It is the simultaneity of this encompassing which establishes us as clear, a sense which we tune up for and which brain reports back to itself as clear.

While we have a global awareness, with global history, and global intellectual history, the Western Judeo-Christian lineage consolidates a continuing focus upon trauma and its role in our understanding of time and Being and shock. The Book of Genesis and the revisionist Gospels can be seen as all of a whole, beginning with the Edenic portrait, with its dissociative aftermath – the Expulsion – culminating in the hopefully clarifying and developmentally individual-specific myth of the spiritual hero, a gestalt singularity of a collective consciousness, whose demise mythically fulfills the drive toward resolution and toward Being.

While their interpretations yield separate and separating insights, the basic energetic and developmental truth of these stories is grounded upon the energetic phenomenon being described. Our progress, if we are looking for one, is the measure of the specific developmental site of traumatic holding and its curiously literal (*i.e.*, energetic and neurochemical) narrative.

Until we had secular developmental psychology, and intellectual history, which both are increasingly site-specific, at the individual and with individuation, their burden of awareness was carried by theology and its "authority". At their best, people went to church or synagogue or temple to absorb collective wisdom and get life strategies.

So no matter what war is promulgated, what peace garnered, what liberty moment fastened down or experienced, the collective and individual movement toward the appropriation of Being can be seen as the universal subtext. And could it be a disservice to say we want everybody to be good Christians and good Jews and now good Muslims? Is that not a dead end? Perhaps better to proffer we want everybody to access their sense of Being. The theological framing of developmental insight may be understandable, but so far it has been too easily misunderstood and disastrously, if humanly held. And full of achieving Being, all too suddenly, we now run into a variation upon the Peter Principle [*Dr. Laurence J. Peter and Raymond Hill. The Peter Principle. William Morrow and Company, 1969, current Harper Collins paperback. ISBN 978-0-06-209206-9*].

The Peter Principle

As a deft secular rephrasing of the trauma mechanism, we rise to the level of our incompetence. I carry the Peter Principle insight a bit further. We choose our professions intuitively because they provide an arena narratively close to some personal traumatic pattern; and we labor in the vineyards until the Second Shoe arrives, in the form of some crisis when it is clear we know "nothing" about what we are doing: promoted and full of success, we then proceed to demonstrate crisis and scandal and curious behavior.

In business theory, we incorrectly apply the skills from one level of successful proficiency to some other next level and thus appear incapable, but this move is easily explainable. We have to learn to shift gears. But a deeper pattern occurs with so-called success which does not quite apply to going from one level of success to another. At the core of success is a trauma pattern which seeks resolution, and it comes due or is visible after some "successful" achievement. Shakespeare notes the patterning when Hamlet tells Horatio:

> Ay, marry, is't:
> But to my mind, though I am native here
> And to the manner born, it is a custom
> More honour'd in the breach than the observance.
> This heavy-headed revel east and west
> Makes us traduced and tax'd of other nations:
> They clepe us drunkards, and with swinish phrase
> Soil our addition; and indeed it takes
> From our achievements, though perform'd at height,
> The pith and marrow of our attribute.
> So, oft it chances in particular men,
> That for some vicious mole of nature in them,
> As, in their birth – wherein they are not guilty,
> Since nature cannot choose his origin–
> By the o'ergrowth of some complexion,
> Oft breaking down the pales and forts of reason,
> Or by some habit that too much o'er-leavens
> The form of plausive manners, that these men,
> Carrying, I say, the stamp of one defect,
> Being nature's livery, or fortune's star,–

> Their virtues else – be they as pure as grace,
> As infinite as man may undergo–
> Shall in the general censure take corruption
> From that particular fault: the dram of eale
> Doth all the noble substance of a doubt
> To his own scandal.
>
> *Hamlet I:iv:13-38*

Here Shakespeare identifies how a single (trauma) pattern, "a vicious mole", seeking resolution amid the garden of an otherwise noble and balanced personality, brings itself forth calamitously; the defense will out, framing and obscuring what precedes it. It is interesting that Shakespeare understands how the trauma pattern is the result of some occasion which may not be within the carrier's control, and that it is developmental, related even to birth, or patterns absorbed by the individual from its parents or its environment.

Within my understanding, the Peter Principle may deeply express something about shock, at the nominal, nominating center of our motivation. Thus we run into classic professional paradoxes: the minister without faith, the doctor who cannot heal herself, the teacher who cannot learn, the house builder who does not understand space, the architect who does not understand the practicalities of living in the space, the judge who is a closet criminal, the criminal who is a closet judge, the avid homosexual who carries a thick vein of heterosexuality in its mines.

The appearance of the incompetence pattern can be quite apparently destructive, and as in the case of dictators and bullies of all sorts, comes inopportunely due involving entire groups of people. We entrust our government to self-selecting people who essentially do not know how to govern or be governed. At their best, they are learners, and, woe to everyone around them, when their Second Shoe appears for delivery after some success. And is it not crucial that their individual shock-infested understandings do not get projected upon the reality which involves millions of people?

Enlightenment remains the endpoint of these myths, the resolution from shock-induced incompetence, or said better, dissociation. This focus comes after some High – getting elected, being appointed, being anointed, answering an infantile riddle, becoming a star. Then our dissociative sequencing rushes forward, and we are back in diapers, depression, and addiction.

What's next

Entire lives and civilizations can be asked this question: "What is seeking resolution here?" And is there any resolution achieved? Our understanding of time and patterning return to our middling, muddling apprehension of Being, with its crucial add-on of pattern-resolution: "What happens next?" There is very little historical perspective on this next state, though in the Odyssey, the hero moves inland until he can endure or face some paradox or point of origin-al unknowing, some site of shock, whereat Odysseus' shouldered oar is not recognized as such. With Being, we may be able to return to beginner's mind.

The Christian myth indicates a resolving transcendent and luminous neurochemistry which ascends and realigns in a left-right brain. For the Oedipus at Colonus, there is a similar ascension as the trauma form dissolves amid thunder and lightning, restoring the myth's carrier, Theseus, to humane leadership, from which he governs Athens with enlightenment.

How much of this "opportunity" do we ordinary citizens get in our lifetimes is a question, but the stories imply that we are all Oedipus – or better, all Theseus – all Christ (not necessarily coterminus with Jesus, who carries and narrates the Christ energetic). We just don't quite know how. Knowing how to read their sequence means we also are the sequence; developmentally; we already have been crucified and somehow are preparing to come out an other end. At some level, it's a synaptical, perhaps SSRI thing.

Over recent centuries, the confounding mix of exchanges between Catholics, Jews and Protestants, (and now) Muslims, Buddhists and Hindus, frequently mortal, testifies to how these insights, which are basically shared, can be adversarially held. We get the idea that there is some basic threshold of cultural maturities forever waiting to be crossed.

In the Eastern meditational lineages, these pathways are well documented and experienced, though not necessarily well-heard. History then can focus on the dynamic movement of activities into action, which can then be assembled or delineated as patterns, sequences, and finally states of clarified Being. The way the hero holds the resolution sequence is as important, more important than the shock sequence itself.

The Hegelian unfolding of history includes brain movement toward trauma resolution; it is present in all our interactions and appears to sponsor them, at the activity level. But because these resolutions are usually partial (if they occur at all), we do not quite know what follows full resolution because our focus on this lineage of catastrophe and shock has been obscured by defenses and virtually never achieved, or publically "recorded". Again, we position on the cusp of enlightenment.

If this is so, then the vicissitude of narratives of history and myth are merely the grid upon, during which, we weave our carpet. And while there are story variants, essentially there is one sequence, the dissolution of shock into Being, black into radiance. What follows that, we hardly know. As creatures apparently mated – fated – to history, we are out of ordinary time.

With all this concern about trauma and its centrality in formulating strategies to approach its dissolution, I recall how somewhat early on, I turned for explication to an old agency, our subtle, classless realm – our sixth sense – the breath.

CHAPTER FOUR:

DISCOVERING THE BREATH

Here follows a summary of further explorations in technique, most particularly relating to the breath, also augmented here from an article by me. [Positive Health. PH Online Issue 80. September, 2002. (www.positivehealth.com/article/ energy-medicine/trauma-energetics-working-with-the-breath)]

Working with the breath

When I first began working with the breath, as it is sometimes called, I would follow the directions of my teachers, and they would help me breathe in the universe and breathe it out. I could hold this objective for moments at a time, but soon I became bored or exhausted, and my attention would wander. Additional data in my "scan" intruded upon the stated objective and quickly overwhelmed my process. When I asked fellow breathers how they were doing, they shrugged their shoulders and reported they were equally confounded.

I had been meditating, sort of, for years, including summers spent since childhood in a Quaker community whose Friends Meeting services featured silence. I had taken on Transcendental Meditation in the 1960's, and my instructors seemed hapless in their inability to help me deal with the inner process which a mantra evoked in me. At each meditational crisis, I was advised to return to my sitting and hang out with what came up and then to let it go. I was not consulted about whether I wanted to let it go or not, not to mention whether or not I could let it go – and at what level.

My inner "system" was too problematically active for this strategy, and, forced to desert it when I felt there was important information thus being ignored, I became discouraged, as I found many other novice and experienced meditators were. If we considered ourselves as self-scanning organisms, we had trouble discriminating what was important in the scan and what was not, and how to focus on or transmute these differences.

I drifted in and out of meditation practice, but I never found teachers who would or could take me on on my own terms, *i.e.*, the terms I was facing within myself. They kept telling me to go to some inner place other than where I was; or once occasionally centered in the present, I was advised to perform some practice flourish which took me away from the center as I experienced it, as if I were in a shared realm of insight with my teachers when I was not. They advised me to "Let go" rather than "Watch your brain let go." Intuitively, I felt they were very right and somehow, very wrong, and the distinction I drew around this issue of intentionality and witnessing became central to what I subsequently discovered.

One important exception to my frustrating experience with meditation came with Vimala Thakar, a woman who had studied under an old favorite of mine, Krishnamurti; and she remains, the clearest teacher I have ever encountered. Thakar articulates a vision of stillness and silence at the center of Creation and of Being which is consistent and deep. Though implementing this vision again returned me to my own (fragmented) recognizance, I drew strength from her simplicity about what centering involved: a return to what I came to call Stillpoint.

Discovering the black

In the early 1990's, with the help of insights developed over 30 years of focus upon what I later consolidated as my life-time study of trauma, I developed (now called) Trauma Energetics, Held Energy-Systems^{SM} (TE), a non-intentional modality for evoking the self-healing powers of the brain, specifically in those parts of the neurochemistry which are traumatically held [*Positive Health Online: Trauma Energetics, Issue 60, 2001*]. Therein I discovered that with the deepest trauma sites which have not been resolved with the help of other techniques, my clients could get movement and the resolution of the trauma site and its shocky neurochemistries if we merely focused upon some aspect of the internal scan energetically represented by color and shape as described by the client.

In this approach I ask the client to draw or to describe the energetic portrait of the brain or other areas of the mind-body without ideas, emotions, sometimes even without sensations. What emerges is a full weather-map/brainscape, filled with shapes and energetic statements of some aspects of the entire human system. Some people with greater experience than I thought we were working at the so-called energetic subtle body levels of experience, though other specialists who experienced TE reported we were not.

I discovered that the critical color stating where the brain itself is in "recorded" or memorized shock is black, because, as in physics, black is where there is no movement. Also, when the dense, hardened forms of the black dissolve, color or movement returns, and with it, the reduction and elimination of the dissociative narrative symptoms which plague consciousness. In this sense, the artistic insight that black contains all colors is curiously confirmed.

Black has a number of qualities which can be internally sensed and witnessed as held energy. And if the client focuses on the black as held energy, without physical or emotional narrative, the held-energy system begins to move, transmute, and resolve, resulting in often dramatic reduction of symptom, pain, personality problems, addictions, and the like.

In 1994, I published *Trauma Energetics, A Study of Held Energy-Systems* [ISBN 0-9647730-0-7], consolidating the initial insights, and I waited about a year before I could persuade someone I trained to supervise a session for myself. I naively discovered the modality's power and potential for clarity. When I worked with a client, I somehow knew what the black was and empathically could sense and see it, and I could identify an appropriate next place to focus in the conjoint meditational endeavor we were engaging in. When focusing on the black on my own, for myself, I had difficulty, particularly if I applied the technique independent of a supervising practitioner.

Trauma takes our breath away

Then, a few years ago, I realized that trauma takes our breath away. And that the sites of held energy which I and my clients scan, are predominantly experienced as shallow-breathed and oxygen-depleted, sometimes to the point of suffocation. Attempting to resolve my own traumata independent of a practitioner, I realized that if I could not easily scan for the black in my own process, at least I could scan my own breath and seek out the sites of shock recorded in its shallowest sequences. All I had to do was witness them, this in an area whose mortal implications would normally incite anxiety.

I began to observe my own breath, again without intention, watching how it assembled itself, how unruly, fragmented, and disorganized it could be, how there were times when I was lucky to have a unified sequence, much less a complete one. This focus upon the disorganized orchestra of my breathing process changed everything.

Whereas before, I could not be dragged to ordinary meditational breath work, now I could not stop watching. My whole day became a waking meditation, focused on what was happening with the breath as it fashioned itself in my awareness. A friend noted, "You have spent much of your life studying the Greek classics. How wonderful for you now for the first time to be visiting Athens."

"I don't care where I am, as long as I can breathe," I replied, and my friend's eyebrows rose.

In my pursuit of the black, as my student Michael pointed out, unwittingly I had reinvented the ancient alchemical wheel; I later discovered that early alchemists focused on the black, which long ago was labeled the *negrido*. In my process, I saw that the black and lack of oxygen are two hallmarks of the memorialized site of trauma which must be addressed energetically if the deepest traumata are to be resolved. Here is the hometown of shock itself: the streets of black, shock, and deoxygenation coincide. And that by witnessing the breath, I could discover the sites as well as with the visualized black; and, better yet, that the client and I could move effectively back and forth between these two modes, apparently accessing the causal levels of why people have difficulty letting go of stressful patterns. I realized that if the energetic and with it neurochemical change did not also occur in the breath – and with it some deep metabolic sequencing – the change probably would not be sustained.

The black of held energy

The black of held energy is potent and inwardly experienced as risky to approach; no brain in its right mind will go to a place, even in its own system, where there is compromised oxygenation. I could roughly see how the compromising of the breath in the system could result in drastic curtailments of functioning, hence disease and immunity weaknesses could be sponsored at such sites. The Russian research on the relationship between cancer and oxygenation slid into understanding, as did other, similar strategy studies, including about inflammation. If residual trauma compromises our sense of time, time distortions are carried in the bound cells of the lungs.

And that if the immune system were to be reoxygenated at some "institutional", causal level, all kinds of old and new balances could be achieved. But why did the presence of deep breathing not necessarily lead to resolution of the trauma? All we needed to do was to take some systematic breaths, directly pouring fresh oxygen into the deoxygenated gaps, and everything should be all right; right?

My alchemical understanding of the black characterized that the energy was at the interface between so-called spirit and so-called matter. In incarnation strategy, the densification into sub-molecular, tissue, and organ systems could be directly observed at the energetic level, and it could be observed in the breath as well, which had particularity as well as wave-like aspects.

I found that clients perform all sorts of quasi-superstitious maneuvers with their breath and with their intention in order to deal with these deoxygenated places. To get the changes where the changes need to occur, there was no point in utilizing voluntary breath; the regular, autonomic, involuntary breath offered an avenue into the trauma sites which were declaring themselves ten times a second for resolution through and within each breath.

Thus I did not teach new ways of breathing, as in taking the client to a kind of alternative amusement park; rather, I escorted clients to the breaths they had, including trauma sites, each time witnessing involuntary breath as our baseline observation point. What they showed me were systems as fragmented and precarious as my own.

Graphic representations of the breath

I came to ask the client for an initial graphic representation of the breath, which, when one comes to think of it, is not easy to do. How do we draw – or better, sketch – our breath? Or characterize it? Furthermore, if we use words, we can only very roughly approximate this very complex preverbal experience. After a while, I refined the scan into in and out breaths, focusing on the important transitions between the in and out and out and in breath phases. I later discovered these formulations were not unprecedented in various scientific and non-scientific lineages.

These strategies evolved as the client and I searched for ways to acknowledge and not interfere with the breath. We could set our focus on the transition between the so-called somatic and autonomic systems, the voluntary and involuntary breaths, trying to keep to the (deeper) involuntary breaths.

As we do with the black, our approach is to witness selectively. I find this to be essential to the full resolution of the held neurochemistry we seek to observe. Breathing into the pain, sending light into the black, all involve some intention, which is fine when these gambits work, as I personally have experienced. But the clients who come to me have been frustrated by these approaches because their patterns don't change, or they revert.

Picking up the mail bag

On the American plains, trains race through small towns and a special hooked-arm device at their sides allows the high-speed mail cars to pick up the bag filled with local mail (suspended on a hook-like post) without slowing down. I use this image-idea to take what the brain offers as it scans its self-sustaining breath process. I ask clients to observe these retrieved forms of the breath as observable forms, and to focus directly at those sections which brain describes as dysfunctional or not smooth enough. "What does brain say needs to happen here?" I ask, using *brain* as a generic term to mean the entire intelligence system, including its energetic and neurochemical basis. And the client reports something like, "It needs more balance, or more smoothing out." We then take brain to the problematic site in the breath and reexamine it, or we take the mailbag image of its dysfunctional sequencing, as it were, and begin to work with those graphics.

In this latter phase, the black soon appears, and we are off and running again (or better, holding still). After some sequential transforming witnessing, we return to the breath to see what changes have occurred. The results are often dramatic and often bring about healing crises or similar neurochemical shifts resulting in greater clarity and a sense of profound evening and sequential oxygenation. By focusing at these energetic levels, the client can sense immediate changes at physiological levels: muscles relax, or developmentally rotate, odd completion tingling occurs, the mind-body settles in deeply and "newly".

Clients wonder whether this is a natural process, or that we are getting results as a result of rebirthing or yoga-type breathing protocols, which clearly involve intentionality to bring the brain to these usually early developmental sectors. I caution against hyperventilation and keep the client observing where the breath is, rather than where it could be.

Even with experienced meditators, I find that staying with the complex and traumatically impacted breath we have inspires a – High – vibratory state which in turn immediately brings forward for resolution the deoxygenated patterns surrounding and within traumatic shock. And that the shock often appears to register prior to active lungs, *i.e.*, in prenatal experience.

It is this two-phase sequence which initially devastated my early attempts to do breath meditation. It perhaps led my teachers to proffer, "Observe the breath" but not to tell me to describe the results or where to focus specifically within those observed results. Nor would they say what I might expect, nor that the experience could be shared point by point with them. I was left alone to piece together whatever I could, devil take the hindmost. In those moments when I sensed no single breath but rather fragments barely held together by string or chewing gum, I thought the directive to "Observe the breath" either ignorant, sadistic, or some Zen paradox initiation – threshold to enlightenment, this latter objective continuing to be magnificently elusive.

Re-centering

Trauma Energetics, Held-Energy Systems^{SM} work offers a unified strategy of trauma, namely that trauma is anything which knocks us off our center, and that in order for rebalancing change to last, that *off-center* position must reset itself without intention. A concomitant idea is that, by direct (and in most cases exceptional) focus, brain can begin to confront the otherwise layered confounding aspects of what seems to be a simple activity, laid against or within a simple past and present.

The resultant concern with the workings of memory and event storage, in short, of history itself, comes to the forefront, and more about that later. What does happen is that it is possible to watch the resolution internally at an energetic level, thereby being able to identify significant change, or the lack of it. With my clients, the imagery that evolves is like segments of solid geometry and cartoon animation.

Viewed from within the experience, so to speak, the breath has structure, as well as location, though that is not so easy to define. I have trained clients to witness the edge of the breath to discover the surface of the lining of the lungs, where lungs and air interface. Here, it is possible to sense areas of lung surface as in traumatic process.

Gloria

Gloria, a deeply anxious client, and one familiar with TE strategies, precipitously developed an apparently narcoleptic-type process wherein she would suddenly collapse into unconsciousness, then, moments later, return to upright and regular conversation, then, moments later, slump over. Her life was thus totally disrupted, and she had to crawl into my office wearing a head-protecting helmet. We conducted the session on a floor mattress.

When I asked whether she could hear me during the 30-second slump phases, she said she could. Having trained her to watch the edge of the breath, I asked her to sense the ratio of oxygen intake and CO_2 outflow, which I suspected was out of balance, making necessary a drop into a rebalancing dormant mode, into which she "collapsed". I talked her through two of these moments, and on the second one she awakened with a startled look. "There is oxygen coming in, but the CO_2 exhaust gets backed up," she reported. "Nothing is going out. How can I change that?" she asked.

"I don't know," I replied. "But maybe your system can work on it. I don't think intention will help, but perhaps you can focus specifically on the energetics of the sites we observed." The next day she returned, striding helmetless into the office; she reported that after some focusing, the pattern had rebalanced, which to this day, some years later, her reports indicate the entire pattern dissolution has been sustained.

The strategy here is that the lining of the lungs at the air/alveoli interface encompasses a huge number of agencies and vectors. The in-coming oxygen is, as it were, zipcoded specifically for delivery into specific inner sites in the body, depending upon declared need and overall systems analysis by so-called brain. If the respiratory system is in shock at the intake level, entire inland regions are compromised, with resultant inflammation, including immunity and endocrine systems. If these early lung-surface, alveolar sentinels are compromised by shock, then they do not function well, and with them, inland systems lacking clear oxygen supply, which is not just rendered as numbers of oxygen molecules, but as vectors of information.

The event boundary

To that restoration goal, the most deliberate of the strategies I have devised so far involves locating some severe site of deoxygenation, some impossible, complexly dead-end place in the energetic which cannot climb itself out of stolidity into classic Source radiance. After a few seconds of observations, no change occurs. I invite the client to allow brain to provide an "event boundary" around this phenomenon, including all its problematicity, then invite witnessing an involuntary or voluntary breath and allow breathing to abut the boundary, but not intend into the depleted situation itself. In the old Reichian days, with some considerable, but not predictable success, we used to "breathe into the pain", or in other similar ways save the besieged Alamo by directly bringing in new supplies. John Wayne to the rescue. But that is not what my clients and I now do.

As by way of circumscribing the suffocation site, I initially suggested, "Set a line around the suffocation site."

"Is the line three-dimensional, or does it totally surround the trauma memory, or only at ground level?" the client asked.

"Make it a fence?" I proffered. But fences could have openings, and clients would ask me, "What kind of fence – with spaces?" It was obvious I was not clear enough for this ultimately delicate procedure; that there is a spatial problem of rendering sides or limits to the experience, something which in the original traumatic process apparently had not occurred, at least not in some recognizable way. The whole suffocating memory phenomenon is forever and eternal, and not embodied.

And by thus externally setting the required and desired limiting boundary around the situation, we were avoiding the more fundamental learning sequence contained in the chaotic boundarylessness. As with Heisenberg, our way to observing the phenomenon was changing, even predetermining the phenomenon, and brain would pay us back by not learning/establishing a new pathway. At every point, as much as we can, we need to follow brain's process, on its terms, if we are going to get the clearest, deepest, and most sustained resolution.

Set any kind of boundary

Amid a variety of differing client structures, increasingly I found myself saying, "Around the impacted area, set any kind of boundary which seems right." The complexity of the surrounding ego-creative imagined boundary systems developed by the client for the delineation and containment of the problem site is often Byzantine, though clients may feel quite at home, even dependent upon these boundaries for orientation.

And I came to see that the problems of compression and two-dimensionality vs. three-dimensionality needed some different approach, not that these earlier formats were completely ineffective. We needed a term which could do honor to the clients' creditable difficulties with the strategy. That included setting the problem in a brain-manageable way, for after a time both client and I knew that the most secure energetics are expressed as pure radiance, even rather than light within some kind of particulate structure; then the proposed suffocant structure disappears. And very often, the client can watch brain bring about the dissolution into radiance.

At best, the radiance is an oscillating transcendent brilliance of blurry wave-particle. And that brain often resists this radiance, long-desiring of it as brain might appear to be. The extended impact of traumatic process includes a disturbance of brain's capacity to know the limit(s) of the damage site, limits which could be reworked, but on brain's terms, rather than on the exterior authority of the creative "I", or the supervisory police function of setting the yellow tape around the scene of the accident, or of the teacher who observes classroom chaos and by way of setting limits, barks, "Stop this right away!" We can say we need limits, but at the trauma site, such intervention may be experienced as an imposition on the now partially functional chaos, somehow external, irrelevant, and itself compoundingly distorting: apparently the chaos must be viewed untrammeled in order to be resolved.

This strategy, functional in all of these above-mentioned ways, must still move with respect into the fundamental mind-set of discovery rather than grid-like imposition. Teachers, psychologists, as well as theologians, perhaps need to share even more than they currently do with their clients/parishioners – that the end point of this kind of knowledge confronts and engages in mystery, and that all of our structures and symbol-intrigues must bring us to such a hopefully playful center.

Recently on the radio I heard the term "event boundary" in reference to some business jargon appropriation of astrophysics black-hole studies, and I thought, "That term includes time and spatiality in an usefully encompassing yet site-specific way." Furthermore, I thought it best to take the creation of the boundary as ego-less as possible, so the directive has become, "Allow brain to provide an event boundary around the site." This strategy has turned out very productive, because the boundary which emerges is of "original" interest, and in its structure can tell us even more about the way brain processes the site in its complexity and in the portrait it gives of cellular processing of the trauma experience.

In the same way, every unified black particle can express by its density or hollowness the extent of the first occasion of shock and the way each individual cellular intelligence has been distorted or apparently altered. As I have noted before, frequently the trauma site is brain-characterized as two-dimensional because it is describing traumatic compression; and often, it is also somehow infinite and boundary-less. Thus restoring the neurochemistry involves watching the two-dimensional form fluff out into three dimensions, and the initiating event emerges with an Aristotelean beginning, middle, and end, with natural limits to its efficacy in determining the current present. I know that this phenomenon comments on and effects the way memory function stores our "history".

Going crazy

Back to the strategy. There are two time-neurochemistries at work here. The first (A), states the early unresolved deoxygenated trauma site, going back to significant early, spindle traumatized stages in development. It is *event-boundaried*, which allows for primal, non-judged evaluation and delineation of where the boundary can (even may) – not should – occur. The second (B), takes place in the neurochemical present, where there is no umbilicus wrapped around one's neck, nor a mother and infant who are drugged by natal anaesthetics. The client focuses on the graphic sense of the impossible, immobile (A), and simultaneously brings ordinary (sometimes in-voluntary) current breath up next to but not into the pattern site. I usually name the current breath after the town in which the session is taking place: "Take Boulder, May 2, 2010 breath...."

Using these graphics, we juxtapose the two neurochemistries (if that is what we are doing), and the client remains focused on the graphic boundary, sometimes characterized as a midline between A and B, witnessing only.

Usually, black appears on this line. The cursor of attention "straddles" the two phenomena, suffocation and plenty, and brain goes (a little) crazy as it tries to justify, in the carpenter sense, the juxtaposition. It is a hard-to-follow series of crazy moments as the brain recalculates the two modes in an English muddle-through sort of way, with tectonic shifts and realignments quickly occurring. Thus allowing the cat to toss in the air, the oxygen will land brain on its feet automatically, institutionally, at a systemic causal level, so that no (exhausting) will is needed to solve the problem. All the client has to "do" is witness the random animation of the transition, which in fact, if understood as such, is an enthralling vista.

The result is that the client reports the unpredicted resolution, partial or complete, of the initial (A) pattern in a new and manifest way, as if the system is oxygenating from a completely different vector, by new lungs. We have a recharacterizing improvement within the Alamo site of suffocation, without the oxygen cavalry entering the besieged fortress. Oxygen has been re-sourced from within the site of deprivation, not from without. Brain reorganizes on its own terms, within its own rubrics and channels, subtly and wholesomely.

Juxtaposition

This juxtaposition technique is processed without conscious intention, though it is deliberate in that client and I train brain to observe a chaotic, "crazy" processing, but in a specific, witnessing way. As the client understands the function of this process, it becomes part of their toolbox gambits and capacities, not something to be feared or associated with the fear of loss of oxygen, which can be comprehended as the core issue underpinning all anxiety, no matter what its narrative forms. Over time, this way of siting on the midline *between* rather than *in* the breaths becomes an acquired taste, not just an experience of terror.

I opine this juxtaposition evokes the only real form of craziness there is, and one which is desirable and creative, leading as it does, to greater centeredness, radiance, and connection at all points in the system to what mystics call Source. Other forms of craziness ("word salads", psychotic ideation, some forms of dementia, some flagrant dissociative processes) are statements of toxicity and have within them difficult, but not impossible blacks, sometimes connected to phenomena which the brain characterizes as foreign to itself (inorganic human-formulated anaesthetics, drugs, alcohol, nicotinic acid, etc.).

This idea of juxtaposition has been present in the Western classical literature of healing since the Hebrews and the Greeks, including in particularly distinctive forms in the Edenic myth, Plato's "Allegory of the Cave", the medieval theatre of juxtapostion, the poetry of John Donne and John Keats, Freud's analytic, and contemporary therapies including Quantum Therapy, and possibly some aspects of EMDR (Eye Movement Desensitization and Reprocessing). In the Eastern modalities of Zen koans and Sufi paradox, and their variants in the parables of Jesus, the paths to juxtaposition are beautifully organized and well-trod.

What differentiates these historical approaches from the ones I have devised is that these latter strategies are (the specific client's) brain's own energetic graphics and with them we can witness the importance of focusing on those forms, at certain points, graphically, as opposed to narratively, emotionally, and cognitively.

We can use publically-held myths and literary images as referent points – we always have, but it seems to me perhaps at times revolutionary to insist that we begin and sustain attention with the specific imagery/reportage each (client's) brain provides. Culturally, this approach aligns itself with the analytic/therapeutic focus upon individuals who are specifically resolving each and every trauma; and it involves a lot of time-consuming work. While other more generalized approaches to social reform, including law and economics, may be very important, the scale of healing viewed from this perspective is intimate and individually huge. It involves potentially every single person on the planet and the transformation of each and every held-energy system.

Our personal systems change or they don't

Which is not to say everyone seeks such focus or potential for transformation. And while interpretation strategies may comfort, aid and abet through generalized awareness, either our personal systems change or they don't. And most of the clients I have seen experience what they call the shallowness of regular therapeutic modalities wherein for years they have faithfully turned up for their sessions, with no real change of their held-energy systems.

Artists, shamans, and other radical experiencers have long appreciated the importance of so-called madness, and some have lost their way, even disastrously. But the tradition, as stated for example in Shakespeare's *King Lear*, shows that our center can be found amid the inner storm, and that one can creatively witness the power of brain to bring about its own healing, separate from, for lack of a better term, ego. The Buddhist tradition offers visions of tranquility in which ego–less states are cultivated. But one must confront these places in the chemistry compromised by deoxygenation, again a task no brain in its right mind will take on readily without support or guidance.

In this sense, suicidal ideation can appear linked as a symptom of lack of oxygen and may be transformed through breathwork, a connection also alluded to by Gertrude, queen and mother of the suffering, death-pondering, "to be or not to be" Hamlet.

> *Queen:* Be thou assured, if words be made of breath,
> And breath of life, I have no life to breathe
> What thou hast said to me.
>
> *Hamlet, III, iv, 199-201.*

The breath is an occasion where the incarnation of spirit can be observed, its densification into matter witnessed, and the loci of toxicity and traumatic shock can be directly, causally addressed. The power of such focus to bring healing resolution and transformation is profound and has been known for millennia, with varying degrees of specificity and success. To me, the importance of adding this realm of focus to the client's toolbox is manifest, and it can be folded into the soufflé of standard as well as alternative therapies.

When other breath strategies have failed to bring resolution, often for the client, the observed breath is voluntary, intentional, and is intentionally witnessed. The client has not been supported in going to the least oxygenated sites, where the immobility of the black is expressed, and in remaining witness to the energetic processes in those places within the traumatically-bound neurochemistries.

When these unsafe deoxygenations are juxtaposed with current (safe) breath, a confoundment occurs, and brain relocates its center without wilful, emotional or cognitive intervention into the specific trauma site in fascinating, unpredictable ways. As mentioned earlier, this resolution brings with it often a new sense of oxygen direction, as if our breath is coming from some new area of the lungs. And the levels of stress and anxiety are significantly reduced as the trauma pattern resolves, and with it, problematic narrative symptomology.

More about juxtaposition

In summary, when I tried saying, "Place an event boundary around the immobilized phenomenon," what turned up was that brain would set up its own formulation of the boundary, which would tell us more about the phenomenon and how sealed or porous it needed to be. It gave us a playing arena to understand what brain was doing with the experience, unruly or dead end as it might be, or seem to be. Then the second stage could be addressed, namely the juxtaposition of the place of suffocation with the "exterior" where there is no significant limit to oxygen. The scanner does not try to take the oxygen into the place of need, which is what most people do. The deepest levels of accommodation and transformation, the inner memory system apparently needs to change on its own, without intervention or direct input. In these cases, this appears to be the (only) way substantial change can occur.

"Get in touch with your anger"

I recall therapists ordering, "You must get in touch with your anger," and then I would express it intentionally in psychodramatic ways, with or without batakas (harmless foam bats used to strike surrogate abusers). There would be momentary release, which was interesting, and there was an afterglow, which was pleasing, but delicious "Chinese" meal that it was, the anger returned soon after.

Expressive discharge of the anger was apparently not enough. There was something institutional, even structural, about the undischarged anger, which of course there was. Unless the held-energy system fluffed out, the anger was always there as part of brain's attempt to expand and complete the traumatically compressed energy; that was simple and all it was. So the narrative site of where the anger should be directed was not the prefigurative question. No more simplistic targeted rage at men or women or mothers and fathers (or children).

Addendum:

The most recent Nobel prize in medicine has been given to reseachers who examine the relationship between full oxygenation and dissociative, deoxygenative sites, particularly how cells sense for oxygen availability. Currently they are looking for a means to effect, detoxify the human status quo which, they propose, leads to major and minor disease coordinates, often relating to so-called inflammation. How will we get brain itself to make the adjustment. One current understanding is that the transformation, which I think begins with traumatic shock experience and residual held-energy systems, must be allowed to happen, rather than counting on external interventions, but the allowing must be guided and focused by consciousness.

CHAPTER FIVE:

THE BREATH OF LIFE

Breath advisories

The breath is subtle and the breath is infinite. It may be productive to assume that insofar as our breath process holds trauma memory, all trauma forms will also conclude, resolving into the breath. They seem to be meant to dissolve and vaporize into atmosphere. In the past, the site of disappearance-into was often located as the ether. In quiescent normalcy, the trauma forms are returned into the sea of air. As in Plato, the Forms themselves as forms are perhaps the last phase prior to dissolution or transmogrification into Radiance, the so-called Good (see *Republic, p123*), pure Being.

When we ask, "What needs to happen here?", the ultimate answer is that the form must differentiate, fractionate, dissolve, much like Star Wars' Deathstar; it transmutes internally into vapor, as it were, into the etheric beyond (both within and without). And the breath is where we can ultimately witness this sequence. We want to view the process in some way we have not been able to heretofore. This witnessing is existential: it pertains to Being, to consciousness viewing itself without prejudice, with empathy and compassion, because this neurochemistry is ultimately the only way to the truth; this framing is a meditational position from which true, serious action may occur.

Scientific methodology attempts to accommodate to the fundamentally dissociative agency wherewith, hapfully, we seek to find things out, and it is partially, even institutionally successful; yet its results are scanned, absorbed by mind-sets infested with dissociation. We should not be surprised by the misuse of the information it garners, predictably away from serious action. All other actions can be characterized diminutively as activities – dissociative, and driven by the movement toward resolution, with a concomitant promise that the stuck place of shock will have something to do with activities, either in concluding or in impeding the action, corrupting it.

Harriett is able to watch a trauma site resolve, and as she does so, she sees its connection to the breath, so that there is very little she has to say. There are long moments of silent dissolve. I ask her if the breathing is new, and she responds, "It is fresh."

We do not usually characterize our own breath as fresh, or new, structurally and physically, dwelling as it does at some finite cove amid the sea of air through which we move. The atmosphere (except on the New Jersey Turnpike and similarly challenging sanctuaries) is relatively the same. And when we are in moments of breathing, the air is relatively the same. But our lungs are not. They are like bats' ears, sonaurally extending, pulling back, aiming, receiving, discharging. They are a primary organ of perception, communicating primally the relationships between inside and outside.

Our condition is explicated at this commerce dock, where exports are cast out and imports are negotiated and tagged for delivery inland, perhaps site specific. If the energetically-held traumata do not arrive at this last platform for resolution (which they always do in some fashion), the pattern continues, even to and "causing" death. Othello suffocates Desdemona.

Bringing structural change to the breath is perhaps the ultimate revolt against the tyrannies of embedded shock and its narratives. Changing the economies of metabolism with the breath means allowing the breath(s) to find its own levels, expansive, unencumbered, and clear. States of traumatic compression decompress, and with them, totalitarian and authoritarian modes expressed in personality, even in political and social narratives.

The breath of life is Adam

Adam is the first person in the world, after God, which we, as child consciousness, are. Our first patterns include significantly who we are. At some level, later to be differentiated, first we are light and breath. We are the *atman*, the breath, invisible; and Adam, the first person, is psychodynamically the mother. Later Adam is who we are. And a second person emerges from the body of the first, and Eve is that person; and we are Eve: the Mother, and recollecting its origins, the Child.

The (mythic, Freudian, Christian) third person, the Father, may be mythically born out of the Mother, who is the only birth-giving creature in the infant's panoply of agency, until it is clear he is not. These strategies overlap and are concurrent until they are sorted out by the child, who is at the center of all these myth-movements. Each new Edenic "character" is an attempt to delineate the constant relationship of Self to Other, Self always taking on the form of the relevant, immediate, fathomable Other. Our Child identity includes very much what surrounds and holds us.

Observing the breath, doing exercises, all may be beside the resolution point. Where the relationship between the energy and the will (or the doing function) is punitive, or forcing – even with good intentions – the developmental process will not be fulfilled. We know when a problem has been solved. Short of that we dwell in decadence – traumatic structure and its substructures.

The Line contains void

Dancers and athletes, architects, spiritual intuitives, singers and body workers refer to the Line. The Line contains void. We move and are moved by its discordance. Space includes void. All energetic interfaces include void at their center, and often the traumatic holding prevents us from seeing it. The black contains light, white Source, from which we are alienated by enveloping, encrusting shock memory.

We must first get used to void, see its usefulness, its spaciousness within us, within our atoms, at their center. As we comprehend their atomic center, also void, we will see its extension within ourselves, within the so-called extended self, and into the world "beyond".

Void is within the breath, and it not only separates, but it gives us a sense of God – whatever that is; we project upon God the power of the breath (He "breathed into his nostrils the breath of life; and man became a living being." *Genesis 1:7*), and the written, poetic Genesis encompasses only a bit of this developmental differentiation.

Between the juxtapositions of color, red and orange, adjacent primaries like red and yellow, pastels like pink (red and white) or purple (red and blue), there is frequently black. For this meditational work, the pastels – like turquoise – are not to be trusted as "pure" vibration states; they contain and express held traumatic history. The otherwise energetic wash, which would be a smooth transition, is rendered as black, a hard black line. Entering that line – and into its dissolution – brings a transformation, a rebalancing which can be immediately sensed.

Prior to this directness, there is an invisibility factor, wherein the black obscures the light within. We avoid the black within because it is the recollection of shock, wherein we were life-threatened; and because it demands resolution, we scan for it at least ten times per second. Our failure to resolve this continuing irritating nexus is expressed in the complexity of being invisible, wordplay intended. Being is sensed, not thought; to thought, Being is in the realm of invisibility. In addition, at the center, Being includes void.

First Particle/First particle

If we ask brain to magnify an held-energy system, we can approach some of them at a medium level of enlargement and get transformation. For most situations, we can increase the magnification, usually upon that sector which is black – or its variants, grey, metal, etc. – until we are at the particle level – the millions or trillions of particles which make up the form, or the conglomerate of memory which the form combines into. Then we can see how brain characterizes the pluralized form of the larger system. Whether this is the truth about the particle or not, does not matter to transformation. What or how the brain describes it does.

We can then place brain focus between the first particles and the adjacent particles, or the first particle of the system and the first particle of the next or adjacent system or color bank, whatever. Usually the boundary issues arise quickly and are stated "electromagnetically".

Vice-like headache

A student has a vice-like headache. I ask her to tell me what the colors are or shapes amid the frontal lobe where she is pointing the headache is. "Is there color?" I ask. She responds, "I know, I have done this before. You'll ask me to characterize my anger toward my mother and give it a color. It doesn't work."

I reply, "No, what I am suggesting is something different." She finally shrugs and says, "All right. It is sort of red."

I respond, "Go to the edge of the red and tell me what is the next phenomenon." She says, "It's white."

I: Go to the interface between the red and the white, and tell me what the boundary looks like.

She: It's fuzzy.

I: Stay in the fuzziness. Go into the midline of the fuzziness.

She bursts out laughing, she cannot stop.

I: Why are you laughing?

She: The headache is gone.

She continues to laugh hard and long.

She: I am on the edge of tears.

I: Let them come, they include enzymes which need to be shed.

She continues to laugh and cry for a few moments. Then, wiping her eyes, she gets back to work.

Increasingly we go to the interface between adjacent colors, assuming they are dividing into vivid colors because of some held energy; otherwise they would be golden or radiant white. Like green and yellow. They are complementary colors, and both contain yellow. Usually if we show brain the division it is manifesting, something will change.

A matter of timing

Let us suppose the First Moment is always clear. It is our Second Moment, which contains the Second Shoe, which has triangulation, conflict, dissociation in it, of it.

Theologically, the First Moment is always clear – starkly bright, non-toxic, generous, having center, Being center. Concomitant with all apparent randomness, here is unifying essence. And it is somehow independent of us, its often-dazzled observers. Apperceiving the volumetric of First Moment takes time: we are often easily overwhelmed. Emily Dickenson refers to this inner light as prepossessing, needing slow acclimation.

The Second Shoe is dissociative, and the High(-er) the initial vibrational moment – perhaps nanoseconds away – the greater urgency is of the timing of the Second Shoe which presents the trauma pattern seeking resolution. Thus, Ultimate Reality has a clear, even (pre-)Edenic proportionality to it;

it is ever present, no matter how confounded or toxic we creatures of the Second Shoe are.

We come to think that our trauma patterns are who we are, and of course, in a matter of speaking, they are who we are – until we are not. Then we are clear.

We can descend from Being into participation in Ultimate Reality as Adam and Eve, before the Fall. Or, with greater complexity, as Adam, before Eve. Only the Mother is on our screen. Perhaps we are only partially aware of ourselves *in vacuo*, without the First Person. That comes later, against and within the maternal support we gain, *in utero* and out. How will we stand on our own two feet? With help, and then, by ourself. As individuals, all our history can be characterized along this individuating grid.

Where will our sexuality lead us, onto what journeys, what discoveries? We say we are this, we feel driven by that, and sometimes it becomes difficult to say which story we are leading or are led by. But the clear truth is we are in Being, incarnating into Eden, forever and ever, no matter what we proclaim our sexuality to be.

Apprehending Ultimate Reality

The closer we come to apprehending the nature of Ultimate Reality, the more we realize that we cannot, should not name it. Naming it will destroy our acumen, our focus, which at two levels, historical and at the Being level, must be preverbal.

The reason for naming Ultimate Reality is historical: in order to exhaust what cognitively we already are doing, namely naming; we thus get the patterns out on the table so we can see our distortion-filled awareness. Here, the names are the background noise which confounds our viewing, and I sense that through all the verbiage and conceptualizations most theological texts ultimately return us to a profound silence.

Ultimate Reality also cannot be cognitively undertaken – it is too complex, or too simple. We quickly run our brain to its limits, and through ultimate vocabulary, seek to apprehend its over-the-top quality. We long to be with the animals, who apparently only indirectly seek what we call awareness, which may be in fact somewhat different from our "real" engagement with the truth.

Can we perceive the (any) Initial Moment – sustain or slow it down?

Through art, sports, and slow motion photography, we can, but it is the determinative emotional context with which we see the First or Initial Moment which disturbs our perspective and distorts our vision, we, the carriers of this vision.

If the First Moment is immutable and ever present, can we change the Second, or the way we pick up and hold the Second? Can we effect transition and transformation between the First and the Second Moments? Once we are in the Second Moment, we appear to have choice, and no choice; the toxicity overwhelms and destroys (us), or somehow reminds us we have merely responded upon impulse, upon lightning flashes of response dreadfully leading us into the shallow and the predictable.

All the evening news is repetition of the same few outline stories: someone accidentally shoots his son, someone stands up to tyranny, a war carries everything with it down the tube, a child is rescued. And the weather. Our news repeats, our response patterns duplicate, and we are remaindered bereft: there is nothing new; no sense of having learned anything – such information-filled news has nothing to teach. Which would be to teach about the fateful relationship between the First Moment and the Second.

Can we expand the First Moment? Yes and no. The First Moment contains what individuals have called Eternity. It is also atomic site-specific. As we expand and contract, we can see its faceted essence, its multiplicity as well as its unity. But it is dependent upon the viewer to say what aspects are being viewed. The problem with Ultimate Reality is that for us humans it is viewer dependent, until it is not. I think that is why God becomes an attractive term to mean that Ultimate which lies beyond our usual consciousness and existence.

The resolution of this issue comes when there is a surprise, and some element comes at us out of left field. Then we are reduced to silence, which is the safe and perhaps the only locus within which to view Ultimate Reality. Then the universe is characterized, could be characterized by our own two-phased dynamic, inbreath and outbreath.

Job's complaint

Job's complaint could be one of overstimulation, as well as the monotony of catastrophe's occasions. Everything we say about Ultimate Reality is projection, until it is not. But Job ultimately covers his mouth, all the better to see You with. Perhaps he is holding out until silence escorts him into non-attached Being, free of the dualistic narrative of God and Satan arguing over him.

If we are in post-Fall consciousness, all experience carries burden. Like for Cain, work becomes travail, childbirth agony, death punishment, science the harbinger of hope. We are East of that neurochemistry (Abel's) of balance between inside and out, between core "self" and empathic perception of what lies beyond and within us. And our absence is exhausting.

To take responsibility for our plight, we must admit that we do not know where we are: our sense of our own history is seriously compromised by trauma and memory. Most of what we recall, if it matters at all, is partial and laced with if not prevarication, with its sibling, defense. Thus the evolution of history is a highly selective discipline of if not overt misrepresentation, of diversion. Myths interface with facts, selected and spun with the unspoken prejudices of victors, victims, forgotten inconsequentials and consequentials, raked with the harrow of certainty so-called remembered. We have just started to face the deeper problem of recording the history of Being, which paradoxically approximates the fathomless. When we ask what Adam and Eve do in the Garden, we marvel at incarnation, of Being transitioning into Becoming. And Becoming dissolving back to Being.

If we can barely account for our self, how can we sustain a consistent vision of our communities? How will our searching for the life-raft of identity be sated within the purveyance of Ultimate Reality? Or should we just forget the whole thing and dance and kiss and kill and eat our daily bread, taking our chances and hoping for good luck? Life so conducted can slalom around the nasty and brutish flags, and through focus, can lengthen, in terms of temporal longitude, and maybe lengthen existence within some personal inward scale.

If Eden is the place of incarnate Being, wherefrom centered, righteous activity can evolve into action, also Edenic, what helps keep us from that sequence is our natural, God-made phenomenon of traumatic process, and memory distorted by our residual enshocked system. But the reason to take traumatic holding out might seem to be to restore Edenic consciousness; but behind that is the reaccessing of Being. So far, we live in a Great Compromise.

CHAPTER SIX

NOTES ON ALCHEMY

The alchemical tradition

Alchemists have been most commonly remembered for attempting to transform lead into gold. Secondarily, though maybe not to many of them, alchemists sought personal transformation. These goals required powers of observation, spiritual discipline, and certain assumptions about the nature of human reality. From within these ancient, often arcane alchemical traditions, we can locate main threads leading directly to our contemporary understanding of life.

Alchemists perused a correspondence between our human inner world and the outer world; yet much of alchemy faltered under an assumption – curiously held – that the same spiritual and physical rules applied to both personal realms and the world which is not human. As quasi-magician/healers, alchemists thought they should be able to do the same outwardly as inwardly. If they could achieve some semblance of vibrational "gold" internally, by identical means they could achieve the same or similar transformations in the real, external world, and thus become rich. This has never happened.

But in this process, something else did. Among others, Aristotle noted that all things can be subdivided, that matter is particulate, atomic. All things in the material world can be cognitively subdivided and viewed at various levels of subdivision. Our linguistic experience reflects this insight, so that apple or apples can be divided into a single apple, that apple divided into regions within the apple (skin, core, seed, pulp), those regions divided into particulate forms which somehow glue themselves together (molecules, atoms, electrons, etc.). This insight leads to our current understanding of chemistry – including amazing plastic – as well as atomic and subatomic physics and the atom bomb.

A further level of alchemical understanding was that the human body is also particulate and can be subdivided as a chemistry and affected by those subdivisions and by the interaction with the material world, including in its subdivisible forms. This insight leads to our understanding of neuro-chemistry, with its sentinels including the antidepressants as well as antipsychotic medications, all still-evolving specificity.

The final level of alchemical understanding, and related to the previous one, was that as human chemistries, from within our systems, we can effect transformations of our experience at its chemical levels. This insight has brought us to contemplate that movement or point which predates, prefigures, and determines even the smallest particulate form and its organization. This point has been identified within fields of subtle energy which surround and suffuse our organic systems.

Historically we have been able to locate ourselves at the infusion or incarnation of so-called spirit into matter, and thus into spiritual formulations about reality, both inner and outer. From this platform, we can move toward metaphysics, prayer, and experiences designed to bring us to enlightenment, which is also a neurochemical state. It is this incarnative level which I wish to discuss.

Related as they may have been to Gnostic insight, alchemists were in spiritual, even Christian terms, probing for irregularities of feeling and attitude which had been accounted as sin. They were ascribing divine functionaries in the transformational process, both looking at it and seeking to account for the changes which did occur, including spiritual and personality transformations. For this they had a number of concepts which helped them orient themselves.

By focusing along this range of particularity and causality, alchemists developed a number of concepts of how to evoke changes. Changes were of particular interest to those who wanted to account for why things seem to go wrong – in Buddhist, human terms, why there was suffering.

1. Most significant was the understanding of projection: that we are not sure of the exact relationship between outside and inside, and that often we set outside what we know from within and vice versa.

2. The *negrido*, or black: an appreciation of the importance of the phenomenon of energetic black at some what we might now call neurochemical level.

3. The vision of what happened when the black revises: the order of transformation which can be observed from within or by arcane methods, deduced from without. The primary movement of invisible spirit is reflected in the move between the black, wherein there is no movement and the energy is held, into the color gold, whose radiance represents what we might now call fine-tuned, even transcendent personality balance. This is the gold of Christ energy, Buddha consciousness, and Moses viewing the Burning Bush, among others.

4. As Jung notes, because of their density when inwardly viewed, these held-energy systems were called the philosopher's stone, which resembled the Christ, whose pattern of held-energy and resurrection were similar – even identical – though it was dangerous to say so. The medieval political and religious climate demanded mythification and mystification of the process, and alchemists apparently agreed that the techniques were not to be divulged for fear of misuse. And when there is real transformation, the held-energy systems appear not to allow for manipulation, for our brain revolts against the tyranny of will and intention and will not allow the deepest levels of suffering to unlock by using traditional modes of power (over) or subterfuge.

Alchemists diverted

So often, the alchemists were diverted from this vision at a series of levels, getting distracted from the direct apprehension of human chemistry. The attempt to transform human chemistry from within, allowing for what we now call the self-healing capacities of the brain to declare themselves has remained elusive perhaps because of the issue of intention. Because pain and or suffering can predominate our awareness, it is hard to argue for bringing no intention to these sites. "For God's sakes," our system cries, "take this toothache away! Don't give me process, I want results!"

The alchemists did discover the negrido, the presence at a subtle energetic "vibration" of black, immobilized energy, and they knew its importance as harbinger of transformation. But approaching vibrational states chemically had some dead ends; the alchemists often got caught in the subsequent redness, and whiteness which appeared to the inward gazer. They were looking intuitively at what occurs internally, not waiting for the gold, which they also wanted, and beyond that, the white, and beyond that, the clear.

This intuition was that a human could induce a transformation of inner chemistry to a golden radiance which our soul longs for, thereby sensing connection to the deepest and farthest reaches of Being and Source. The transformation of lead (whose grey color contains black) into gold, spoke as a paradigm for our spiritual longing for enlightenment, through recognition of chemistry and projections. Understandably, this vision led to the physical excesses and greed of kings who were duped by people transforming in the outer world, they said, lead into gold. We now know that more exceptional reworkings of earth's substances are possible than that one, which in some sense now seems a ridiculous task.

At base, the alchemical tradition can be seen as spiritual, for it took the subdivisions of experience and gratified these subdivisions by focusing upon them. From this lineage, we get scientific methods as a way to focus on the elusive phenomena of reality in the face of a consciousness which is clouded or traumatically held. As a discipline focusing on the incarnation of spirit into matter, alchemy is about trauma, first, then about the chemistry in and by which it is rendered.

Gnostic gospels

The Gnostic gospels and insight acknowledge the hermaphroditic nature of the soul: it has both masculine and feminine aspects. Its sexual identity is not primary, but the energetic connection rendered through the specific genital gender is, and that is polymorphous. Does our soul respond to all of its experience from a perspective of equality? This observation about ourselves is perceived through trauma-determined energetics, for our view of the norm – which proposes equality – while true, is not what appears to brain.

We are drawn into patterns which then become through habit what we are; we do not see them as what we are not. Whatever I am, I am not my patterns, only the carrier of those patterns. The soul is beyond patterning and is beyond its body, hence its energetic proposal of itself as energetic. What the writers of the Gnostic gospels and the alchemists appear to have in common is this apperception.

But alchemical preoccupation with the symbolic and with symbols was haphazard and superstitious. Rather than penetrate at each point of the symbolic configuration into the energetic level – toward apperception of Being – the occupants of this mysterious land fell into arcane and elaborate pre/pro-scriptions about what each symbol meant. Yet each symbol is an invitation to return to the non-verbal energetic, rather than to move into further linguistic elaboration of meaning.

The turning toward the black affords a real vector or axis wherein we can build a systems approach not to diagnosis but to transformation. We are moving not toward diagnosis but towards transformation. The lists in diagnosis may tell us some things, but not a lot. Wholeness must be pursued from the point where it does not move – not where there is fragmentation, but from where there is no movement.

The "metaphysical" gold was what they were looking for – an inner vibrational state which yields enlightenment and turns the viewer into a chemistry trauma free, hence capable of sensing the wealth of information flowing through him/herself, so that such spiritual enlightenment had the effect of making one rich, even saturated with information and condition, the very thing people sought for in the amassing of the metal gold.

Every one carries

In this sense, everyone carries the Christ energetic, an insight Jesus knew and taught. Yet within the Church, such insight could be spun and its dissemination lead to a break in social trust and could catastrophically threaten the Church's exclusionistic franchise on the mythic rendering of the truth about trauma embodied in the life and fate of Jesus; and which claimed that there was only one Christ, and the Church was its only salvation/insurance policy agent.

Rather than seeing the "only" insight as an access to the developmental site being described – infantile, organizational, historical, trauma-informed, trauma-experienced, and significant – the problem was rendered as one about heresy. And people who were escorting individuals into energetic consciousness where the "real" gold can be found, were replacing a societal authoritarianism with a revolutionary reliance upon the authority of inner experience and inner authority, something Jesus (and later, Luther, among many others) would have understood.

To propose that everyone carries the Christ energy within would be heresy enough for a social system which brought order (as well as retraumatization) to huge parts of the then Western civilization; such insight would be Church insider trading, something perhaps the Templars, among perhaps others, individually and in groups, knew something about. To demonstrate this sequence, as alchemist, you would have to choose your clients pretty carefully: who could and who could not tolerate such spiritual individuation; it was potentially ecstatic but also dangerous work. And as a side order of fries, the scientific world of direct observation of reality took a quantum leap of availability and efficacy in world consciousness and development.

CHAPTER SEVEN:

ADVANCED SESSION

Session preamble

In the past, arising out of Rolfing sessions where this energy work started, I would hold the prone Client's head (at the end of the table) throughout each session. Now I don't do that. We sit facing each other, or the Client lies down nearby on a couch or table, or we face each other across a desk, or in chairs, or by telephone, or by Internet. Some clients want the physical proximity, so they work with me in the same room. For others, the Internet is suitable – sometimes it is the only way possible for people living in China or Chile.

In some settings where touch is therapeutically problematic, at certain moments in the sessions I have shaken hands with the Client or given them high fives which I explain as grounding gestures to remind their "primitive brain" as Clients peruse these esoteric absorptive sites that there is someone else in the room.

I have noted that in some analytic and therapeutic modes, the Clients determine and have to think through what they want. In TE, the Practitioner facilitates as a guide toward guidelessness. He/she points out, suggests where to go, depending upon their experience, both directly empathic and from recall. Some trails are recognizable, and from trial and error, the Facilitator can predict certain sequences, so he/she can be specific: "Here, let me show you something interesting."

In guided meditations, a Facilitator takes you to certain image sites, whereas here, the images and neurochemical portraits and vistas are totally generated by the Client. The Facilitator's skill is in identifying where and how to look, again based upon its experience and intuition. Hence the Practitioner voice can be quite directive, though as rapport is developed between them, the meditative pair are collegial, facing the task of merely witnessing, with no "ego" or intention beyond that. The objective is to generate healing movement at, for lack of a better term, primitive brain levels; the stated premise is "Let me show you something about how trauma is stored in the brain/system." Thus, initially, the Practitioner may begin the session with "Where do you want to start?" After a number of sessions, this question becomes a significant framing strategy for the Client.

The following session is both typical and exceptional. Because of my current focus on TE as a meditational modality, I call the Client The Meditator, and myself The Practitioner. But both labels apply to both people in the session. I haven't found yet a better way to call us.

The Meditator here has experienced many prior sessions with me, and we have a working rapport that includes a sense of shorthand. Like a skilled mountain climber, he knows the ropes. So there is an economy of presentation and accuracy on his part which is exemplary and allows for depth and real change, which he in some measure gets in the presenting pattern. At the end of the session he reports a deeper tranquility in the site which had been turbulent.

Unlike the session recorded in my first book, this one includes the strategy of event boundary, which is primarily built upon focusing on the compromised oxygenation in the breath at the trauma site. Together, we move back and forth between the black and breath areas lacking oxygen, both essentially the same strategy.

Advanced Session

	TIME		DIALOGUE	COMMENTS
1	0:00	P	Ok, so let's start in and tell me where you want to start.	This is the usual initiating statement of the Practitioner. For individuals new to the process, I invite them to draw a top view of their brain and to draw a brain weathermap, including pressures, pains, swirls, colors, segmentations, something they are not used to looking at. I am not seeking information applied through an understanding of the anatomy of the brain or the function of the parts of the brain attendant to various gestures or aptitude. For Clients who have TE experience, they intuit where they want to start, knowing that what they "see" now is the best way to recall earlier positions they have bookmarked. We start with what the current vistas show.
2	0:10	C	Um, there's energy collecting in the center of my forehead (P: Mmhm) so I'm gonna start there.	This Client has had lots of TE experience, and his reportage indicates a sensitivity to energy patterns, which can be fixed or moving. Some of the challenge of this work is learning how to slow down brain process so it can be observed.
3	0:16	P	Alright	
4	0:17		[pause]	TE strategy supports longish pauses, negotiated with the Practitioner, allowing for inward observation by the Client. Sometimes the brainscape is so fast or opaque that the initial training both for the Client and the relationship with the Practitioner takes some time to develop trust and accuracy of reportage. The Practitioner often completes the Client's sentences to enhance the Client's priority upon focusing and observing, not getting the words describing the energetics fully accurately. Description is a challenging task anyway, from primitive brain to language centers to another person. And, like the recording secretary, if the Practitioner gets it sort of right, that usually is enough to lead both Practitioner and Client to the sites where correspondence of understanding between Self and Other may become more significant and require more differentiated observation.

5	0:30	C	It's like water. I was swimming today and it feels like that.	Client reports influence of earlier activity in his understanding of what he is looking at, some orienting combination of interior and exterior experience.
6	0:35	P	Alright. [pause] It's corr... it's as if it were coming upon your forehead, as in swimming or– (C: It's more...) just like, just the fluidity of it?	The Practitioner supports further, more detailed explication of the inner experience as well as to indicate to the Client how close he is to empathic accuracy of focus on both their parts.
7	0:48	C	It's more like the feeling of being in the water.	Client locates the boundary between interior and exterior, often an important discrimination in areas of perception where the inner energetic boundaries may appear to cross over or blur.
8	0:51	P	Ok.	Practitioner supports and acknowledges the Client's discrimination.
9	0:52	C	Sort of like a rocking back and forth...	Client adds to the description, for himself and for the Practitioner.
10	0:55	P	Ok.	Practitioner follows from the position of recording secretary as well as empathic perceiver of the reportage.
11	0:57	C	and that allows me to drop down.	Client reports an energetic interior with accuracy.
12	0:59		[pause]	Client is experiencing something having to do with location of focus as well as movement of focal position within the interior brainscape.
13	1:07	P	You're further back in the skull? [pause] Or down the throat? Or just down –	Practitioner wants to locate the experience in the head if possible. Some locations have a free-floating quality, particularly in dissociative "neuro-chemistries" including those of foreign substance.

14	1:12	C	Down in the...down in the throat.	Client approximates the location (interpretation) involving the sense of down. In early development of body image as well as body sequences, as in birth, "down" includes an evaluation of some complexity.
15	1:15	P	Ok.	
16	1:16	C	And down, just a...underwater, but I can still breathe a little. [yawns]	Client reports the inner experience with poised accuracy, including the cognitive framing that he can acknowledge that though "underwater" (possibly before lung breath), he can still breathe – and yawn).
17	1:24		[pause]	
18	1:33	C	Yeah, and I get to the bottom and...	Client is entering the inner experience, which may include a "regressive" reexperiencing of a prenatal state, some might call a memory, though it also may be traumatically framed. The held-energy framing is more the subject of our focus than the narrative content of the so-called memory.
19	1:37		[pause]	More Client processing.
20	1:48	C	and it becomes more intense, it becomes more like pulsating, the energy in my head.	The Client reports the effect of his focus upon his current inward experience. Brain is reworking something here, including the recognition that this past experience is structurally co-existing and determining portions of the current time and space which may be different. Its "necessity" may be not so necessary.
21	1:54	P	And how far down are you would you say?	Practitioner helps ground the focusing capacity, though he knows the capacity of focus has its own rules which both he and the Client need to follow, not influence or intend.
22	1:57	C	In my stomach.	The last commentary was about the head. Now we are in the stomach.

23	1:59	P	In the stomach. We've done this, we've taken this journey before in some ways, haven't we?	Practitioner reminds Client of earlier movement sequences they, as spelunkers, have experienced. He also clarifies the conjoint effort being made by saying, "We".
24	2:05	C	I think so.	Client approximates the recollection insight but does not nail it.
25	2:06	P	Yeah…[unintelligible]…but tonight it's… what it is.	Practitioner becomes colleague to this uncertainty, pulls back from a perspective which may not be useful here. Sometimes the Practitioner may say, "I don't think that comment may be useful here." The objective is to follow brain's sequence, which both Client and Practitioner are trying to do.
26	2:13	C	Yes.	Client settles in on this agreement. In a sense, both Practitioner and Client share collegial objective: direct observation of brain phenomena, in particular, the way trauma is stored.
27	2:16	P	What's it like at the stomach level?	Practitioner asks the next question as he intuitively garners it empathically sited as he is in bodyscape which Client has described.
28	2:21	C	Shallow. Hot. [pause] Compressed.	These are terms related to traumatic holding. They come up frequently, including the heat, as in inflammation and/or "healing crisis".
29	2:27	P	Mmhm.	Practitioner acknowledges Client's experienced use of the terms and his understanding that the Client can observe what they have seen before; that thereby they are closer to sensing the epicenter of the trauma system, which shall be "recorded" in the black.
30	2:29	C	Not too much oxygen. There's some, but not too much.	Oxygen (or better, the lack of oxygen) is crucial to the explication of the trauma site. "Trauma takes your breath away." And its siting is maintained, and eventually discharged with(in) the breath, whose structure and experience by us is transformed, restored, and augmented. There is truth in the meditation traditions which opine, "Everything is in the breath."
31	2:33	P	Mmhm.	Agreement about where we are.

32	2:34		[pause]	More Client inward observation of a situation with some stasis, or movement which is happening so newly or fast as defies instant translation.
33	2:43	C	The energy manifests into a form that... is bearing down on me.	Client descibes the energetic of a trauma site whose date and narrative are not clear (nor necessarily will they be).
34	2:49	P	Thank you. [pause] And the form, does that have a color, can the, does the brain characterize it in terms of color?	Practitioner is moved to thank the Client for his clarity and expertise and sharing. This move is not one encountered in most "therapeutic" exchanges. Practitioner indicates interest in the energetic explication at a vibrational level, hence color.
35	3:00	C	Yeah there's, there's um, gray, and dark purple.	The black in the grey may be at the core. The presence of dark purple also contains black, even though it is framed in a modified, even defensively protective way.
36	3:06		[pause]	More Client observation, accommodation to perhaps this new level of information.
37	3:11	P	And that's the cloud or the force or the -	Practitioner reenforces the portrait for himself and for the Client.
38	3:13	C	Yeah, it's like a cloud force that pushes me down	Client confirms what he (and they) are looking at.
39	3:17	P	Yeah. [pause] So the interface between that and what you would identify as the "me" is... is, has gray and purple and then what's the color, ah or the boundary, where there is a [space] for you?	Practitioner senses the narrative level of the energetic which promotes an "engineering" spatial question of relationship between self and other, which he voices.
40	3:34	C	It's clear.	Client is direct and supported in his response. "Clear" is the highest color vibration, approximating the state of Being at the center of all experience. Both Client and Practitioner have this understanding.

41	3:35	P	It's clear.	Practitioner is also direct and matches Client's enthusiasm.
42	3:37	C	Yeah.	Client re-acknowledges impact of shock-free energetic vibratory elevation.
43	3:38	P	Fantastic. [pause] Let's go right to that boundary then.	Practitioner responds enthusiastically, like a miner seeing ore in the pan. Where to go now? Either deal with the surround or experience the clear. Intuitively, the Practitioner proffers the latter.
44	3:43		[pause]	Client processes the scan, which includes difficulties as the integration process proceeds.
45	3:46	C	It's explosive, when I get down.	Client characterizes the energetic and the relationship of the (two) states which are being brought together, reported from the lower site.
46	3:49	P	Yeah, – yeah, yeah, that's, that's very interesting. [pause] Like it's, it's, it's gonna, it's just gonna blow up.	Practitioner picks up the situation and frames it. He senses the direction and frames it from a somewhat distanced position, indirectly reminding the Client that the pattern may blow up but not necessarily the whole Client. Explosive patterning usually indicates traumatic compression.
47	3:59	C	Yes.	Client agrees.
48	4:04	P	Let's take, let's see if we can, if you can tolerate this, let's take it down to a point, to particle level, and get to the first particle of the Clear, well Clear doesn't exactly have a particle but, Clear has something.	Practitioner works through a direction to take as an approach to the explosive nature of the situation. If Client can focus into the middle of the site, remaining at the observational level, no matter what else happens, primitive brain will orient in response to the focus point, not just the explosive environment which has been evoked.
49	4:16	C	Mmhm.	Client takes on the proposal as a strategy – here everything conscious is a strategy to see the truth at this level.

50	4:17	P	And then, on the other side of that boundary is the purple and the gray which would have white, blue, red, and black. [pause] And if you could take a, take your brain right to that interface and watch what happens. It may be too volatile.	Practitioner refines the strategy as he has picked it up. He reminds the Client that within the explosive drama, there is agency (though curiously not intention – no scenery is being moved) of focus. He does not need to be subsumed by the explosivity (which may only be some sort of defense). He aligns with Client and the observing objective. When observed, the way primitive brain holds the held-energy system changes. But, as Practitioner reminds Client, the focus may not be achieved due to energetic turbulence.
51	4:37	C	Mmhm.	Client is already into the process, which the Practitioner may or may not have gotten (approximately) right.
52	4:38	C	[long pause]	Client is immersed in observation.
53	5:109	C	It makes, um... [pause] Umm, there's a feeling when I don't want to do something but I know I have to, or maybe I did something that I feel like I shouldn't have, it's like a... it's like a feeling of emptiness in my chest, and the juxtaposition of these two states or particles makes me feel like that.	
54	5:36	P	Yeah, ok.	Practitioner supports complexity as well as Client's skill in this verbalization.
55	5:38	C	And it's like, it's almost the opposite of volatility, it's not that they're exploding at each other, it's that... oh... integration or um, or resolution that would cause that sort of feeling.	Client describes a process which is true (anticipated by lines 48-50), both sequentially and emotional. Practitioner senses something unusually clear and brilliantly resourceful and yet not unprecedented in this kind of focusing.

56	5:52		[pause]	More Client processing.
57	6:01	C	And it's again –	Client breaks silence with description of some observed repetition.
58	6:01	P	What...go ahead.	Practitioner starts to ask what is being repeated, intuits this is intrusive to Client's observation.
59	6:04	C	It's feeling like... um, if I can release the tension, that these particles will dissolve.	Client is describing the current vista of understanding and energetic sequence. Brain reports what needs to happen.
60	6:16	P	Yes.	Practitioner supports the Client's reportage.
61	6:17	C	It's nothng, it's nothing more than that.	Client reports the simplicity of the achieved perspective. What has been confounding (the trauma site and the presence of shock) is no longer daunting or "explosive", the latter description perhaps suggesting something about the original site of shock implantation.
62	6:19	P	Yeah, I don't think it is... I agree, I agree. I mean, I think that's a good reading. Let's put an event boundary... around, this interface, in some way, I know that's not, it doesn't have that complete, easy clarity about that.	Practitioner reports from his perspective, which includes internal information as well as empathic readings from what has been described and the way it has been described. He senses the difficulty of the problem being confronted, including the implied juxtapositions; and he proposes an event boundary, which is a strategy which surrounds the juxtaposition (the Client renders the boundary in any visual or non- visual way which suits him). The Client then straddles the boundary so that 1/2 of the screen scan is inside the boundary, 1/2 outside. The interior includes the chronically oxygen-depleted trauma site. The exterior side of the screen includes the real time of the current environment, where there is plenty of oxygen. The Client then brings the two sides together, two time zones (past and present) into juxtaposition. The usual experience is one of tectonic proportions. Brain confronts the fact it is maintaining two different systems, and focus can be maintained for often only milliseconds. The strategy of bringing oxygen into the depleted system is actively denied. The aftermath is a shift of some proportion in the way the held-energy system is held.

63	6:37		[pause]	Experienced, the Client is effecting the event boundary strategy.
64	6:55	C	[yawns]	Brain reworks the pattern of oxygen absorption.
65	6:56		[pause]	More reworking, usually fast and preverbal.
66	7:12	C	There is an energy on the um, black and purple side. There is... light, it's just accessing it. And trusting that it'll be there.	Client reports the aftermath of the event boundary strategy, including light (oxygen) where there had been none.
67	7:25	P	Yeah.	Practitioner follows what has been noted.
68	7:27	C	To let it dissolve, that it'll still be there after it dissolves.	Client describes a complex energetic sequence strategy here.
69	7:31	P	Yes. What needs to happen here to make that more secure? If we could control it anyway, you know, you could say, "Well, I would like this." But what needs to happen here?	Practitioner refines the approach of witness where Client might bring intention into the graphics of the site. He states the perspective of witnessing at a specific site in response to what brain has just described.
70	7:47	C	I need to let go of my fear of these things dissolving.	Client phrases the problem in a perhaps psychodynamic way, which may state a partial truth but is not useful in this modality. Such thoughts are ordinary but they tend to lead the Client into a box where nothing can be witnessed, hence changed.
71	7:53	P	Mmhm.	Practitioner murmurs support but is unspecific about what phase of the Client process he is observing.
72	7:57	C	And I think that means actually going into them themselves.	Client comes to the TE-characteristic strategy, of witnessing the black sites with discriminating specificity, rather than dealing with cause and effect. Whatever change occurs will occur in the context of brain's own processing of the site, something Practitioner and Client probably better not mess around with. The resultant calculations are too complex, too organic, to be cognitively rendered.

73	8:00	P	Yes, yeah. I think that's, I agree. [pause] Let's go for the hardest, let's go for the hardest part. Like one of the blacks, I would think. Not necessarily, but generally I would think... see if you can tell me how brain characterizes that.	Practitioner is moved to proffer going for the darkest part of the site, including the hardest part the Client can tolerate. There can be agreement as to what this hardest part witnessing includes, a question of judgment and perception. There is a thrill at being able to look at the preverbal precoursers of patterns which end up in character, emotion, personality, pain, suffering, and stalemate.
74	8:21	C	Dark, dangerous.	Client reports brain's framing of this stuck place.
75	8:24	P	Yeah?	Practitioner is a bystander here, with an "Oh my gosh" as it were hayseed response.
76	8:25	C	Um, makes me think of past experiences with depression.	Client connects this site with earlier experiences in his life, including previous TE sessions.
77	8:31	P	Yeah. Now we haven't see that for awhile.	Practitioner colludes with this recollection, framing it.
78	8:35	C	Not directly.	Client is reworking what he is now witnessing with the past, including an increased discriminative focus.
79	8:42	P	Let's ease into it. Let's not, let's just take our, we can put our feet up a little bit on this one. We don't have be aggressively... boy scout... um... Teddy Roosevelt.	Practitioner supports difficulty of the move, including proffering discretion, rather than exceptional enthusiasm of someone who is hitting some sort of paydirt. He includes an hopefully relevant, playful historical reference to the noted Rough Rider, perhaps addicted to fight/flight adrenaline. Such references by Practitioner and Client often occur in this work, providing temporary relief or sideline experience before reentering the intense playing field of observation.
80	8:58	C	Mmhm.	Client is busy but notes Practitioners comment.

81			[pause]	
82	8:59	P	Why don't you circle the form? And tell me if there are any entry points to it.	Practitioner senses the process is more complex than it initially seemed. He re-proffers the event boundary strategy.
83	9:03	C	[long pause, with occasional "hmms" from C]	Client is focusing and observing profoundly and in his own way and does not share his process with the Practitioner except to murmur.
84	9:10	C	Yeah, I can stand up in this place.	Client synthesizes and garners a statement which links to the earliest sense of an oppressive form coming down upon him (see lines 30-39). Something has been integrated and the energetic vista has changed.
85	9:42	P	Mmhm.	Practitioner affirms.
86	9:47	C	I can stand up. [pause] And that's significant.	Client reports shift and acknowledges its significance for his system, including the transforming of the shock in the traumatic held-energy system.
87	9:48	P	Yes, I think so. [pause] And is the standing up something you've [already] accomplished or something that you've just learned?	Practitioner senses/agrees. He asks the next question about how to frame the capacity to stand. This is important to establish an historical context, which has its own complexity. That includes whose pattern this is, is the site encapsulated from other sites wherein the Client can stand in very ordinary ways, etc.
88	9:54	C	Um, I'm, accomplished at it now, but not within this state.	Client reports accurately that this is a developmental accomplishment within a traumatically-bound state of consciousness. It is a completion.
89	10:05	P	Right, got it. [pause] So this is fairly early.	Practitioner acknowledges the Client's reportage and pauses, then phrases the next insight/question about what they have been working on.
90	10:12		[pause]	
	10:18			

91	10:31	C	Ok, I'm... it's actually, the... my chest, or my stomach, the, the bad feeling, it's actually opening it up, um...	Client is already experiencing the aftermath of the focusing process at a feeling, experiential level.
92	10:49	P	So you're feeling it, more of it?	Practitioner further specifies the Client's process.
93	10:53	C	Yes, and letting it absorb other feelings.	Client explicates what he is experiencing.
94	10:57	P	Yes, yeah, let's let that happen if you can tolerate it. I'm, I'm here. I'm happy to be with you. This is just exactly where I want to be. I don't want to be anyplace else.	Practitioner frames the process for both of them as witnesses, including a tolerance thermostat which implies they can call off the play, go to the sidelines, if necessary. He adds the ecomium of desirability in the face of the aloneness of the Client. In the earliest environments for the Client facilitators or therapists rarely state their satisfaction about being with the Client, who is transforming out of held suffering into movement.
95	11:08		[long pause]	Client is reworking the historically bound version of what is happening and to whom it is happening. These are moments of "grace," beyond the capacity of both client and practitioner to control.
96	11:36	C	Yeah, it's standing with your arms spread so you aren't protecting your stomach.	Client reports a free energetic narrative involving the body stance.
97	11:44	P	Mmhm.	Practitioner assents to the validity of this reportage.
98	11:45		[pause]	More shared silence as Client watches the energetic rework.
99	12:02	P	That's neat. [pause] It also seems early to me.	Practitioner carries the description further, including the insight about when this shock "situation" may have literally first occurred.
100	12:12	C	Mmhm.	Client acknowledges the strategy.

101	12:16	P	Would you say your stomach has been wounded? Or that there's a memory there of stomach wounding or pelvis wounding?	Practitioner positions the experience to some (ordinary) historical scan.
102	12:23	C	Yeah, actually, somehow.	Client supports strategy, carrying his subsequent reportage to a deeper, more inclusive sense of historical responsiveness, and responsibility.
103	13:27	P	Yeah.	Practitioner is at a level playing field with Client in terms of sense of time and traumatic process.
104	12:28		[pause]	
105	12:36	P	Prenatalists talk about that, you know, about... the separation, the actual umbilical separation as being very, being very problematic.	Practitioner offers a prenatal strategy to explain or narrate what Client has been and continues to be reworking.
106	12:51	C	Mm.	Client takes in historical strategy but has not left the inner experience which continues to flush out, to expand and integrate, something Client can actually witness at multiple experiential levels.
107	12:54	P	And of course circumcision isn't our favorite, um, favorite ah, pastime.	Practitioner offers another cognitive strategy. It turns out that narrative diagnosis or the depiction of what has happened is more complex than one would think. Brain may accept a narrative for a time only to realize it does not go deep enough to conclude the entire pattern. In some sense the trauma site stacks on earlier sites; and it does not matter what witnesses propose, as long as pattern movement and "shock memory" dissolution occurs. Here are proffered two (popular) strategies, but they are offered somewhat ironically, because from earlier experience with this meditational form, Client knows how the narrative or the desire for a firm narrative can betray or delay the real solution, which involves the held-energy of black in the system. In some sense the dissolution of the held-energy system is all that matters.

108	13:03	C	Mmhm.	Client places this strategy on some inner shelf.
109	13:05	P	Baseball is.	Practitioner declares, "we are in fluid, ironic states of consciousness here, which we can share."
110	13:06		[long pause]	Client thoughtful.
111	13:32	C	Yeah, it's like energy is opening everything, it's not just my chest anymore, it's everything.	The held-energy system is dissolving. The black of shock is no longer the primary information which brain is having to experience. The information is quickly expanding throughout the mind-body. The formerly compressed cells are now allowed to stretch to their normal, and exceptional profiles.
112	13:39	P	There we go. That's earlier, I think that's uh, you're seeing an earlier, more open space.	Practitioner confirms and suggests how to frame the experience in possible, flexible ways.
113	13:46		[pause]	Client is absorbed in his process. Other than silence, no other communication is needed.
114	14:03	C	My eyes are closed but if feels like the ceiling is very high, it goes on forever.	Client reports energetic extension which mystics might opine means the crown chakra has opened. The insight is that we are connected universally to everything, from our core outwards (and inwards).
115	14:10	P	Yes, ok that's fine.	Practitioner expresses confidence which Client is also expressing.
116	14:12	C	Like things are extending out and becoming infinite.	Client continues describing energetic completions which are ok.
117	14:16	P	Yeah. Is that a, is that an improvement?	Practitioner asks next framing question.

118	14:21	P	Yeah, right, right. It's new in this place?	Practitioner reframes the problem of integration.
119	14:25	C	Um, well if I can sustain it, somehow.	Client has had experience with the phases of absorption and integration and knows second and tertiary phases of the rocket may bring new challenges for sustaining the new information.
120	14:30	C	Yes.	Both Client and Practioner are conjoined in their understanding of how this all works.
121	14:31	P	Good.	The information being processed is not a reworking of an old pattern but brain experiences it as new. We have given brain a new toy to play with.
122	14:34	C	Yes, yes, yes.	Client confirms.
123	14:40	P	Yeah.	Practitioner confirms. We have results – movement.
124	14:41	C	[takes in breaths]	Pattern is reworking, integrating (recapitulating) at an oxygen breath level.
125	14:50	C	[exhales] I think I can practice staying open.	Client begins framing next step.
126	15:02	P	Yup. Shall we continue a little bit longer or is a good place… to stop?	Practitioner senses an additional step, but checks in with Client about fatigue.
127	15:12	C	Um, do you have a suggestion for what to do next? Usually I know but…	Client seems amenable to continuing and ackowledges his TE expertise.
128	15:19	P	I just follow the directions on the package. I think, my sense is that we could play a couple more minutes and just see what that sustaining looks like and what next…I think the next, you can anticipate that the next stage of whatever trauma you're looking, working on will come forward. But it's very important for you to know that you can sustain this, this chemistry. Because eventually the second, the Second Shoe on this is going to be a further chance for you to, more sustain the original high or original openness.	Perhaps unnecessarily, Practitioner acts as coach, reiterating goals.

129	15:56	C	Hm.	Client considers strategy.
130	15:57	P	And for you to play the piano with that openness might be really extraordinary.	Practitioner addresses Client's professional goals.
131	16:01	C	Mmhm.	Client assents.
132	16:02	P	As for my associations you'd want to sort of remember that and you could practice that. As well as, you know practicing whatever you're… I think a lot of what you practice includes not only the notes but also the energy of what's going through your body right?	Practitioner addresses larger, longer goals.
133	16:18	C	Yeah.	
134	16:21	P	So, and if you're playing from your heart, or from your gut, these realms are important.	Practitioner illustrates integration process and its realistic applications.
135	16:31	C	Mmhm.	
136	16:34	P	That's what I have to say about it.	(Practitioner overselling the car?)
137	16:35	C	Yeah.	Client responds, sort of.
138	16:36	P	But I know that I, I'm anticipating the Second Shoe on this, and I don't know that's, you know, you don't want to lose sight on the fact that you have this now. So you maybe need to hold onto it for awhile until you can, until the brain sort of, gets to understand that it's possible to be there and then comes up with something new.	Practitioner proffers a more integrative strategy.

139	16:59	C	Mmhm.	Client follows what is being said, somewhat. Interior process is still occurring.
140	17:00		[pause]	
141	17:06	P	Very interesting, quite....	
142	17:08	C	Yeah, I'm still open, I think –	
143	17:10	P	That's neat. [pause] If you were to live your, lift your arms while you're open, how would that feel?	Practitioner suggests an integrative strategy involving the body image or even spirit body with the (kinesthetic) body.
144	17:29	C	[exhales] Good, good.	Client lifts his arms.
145	17:32	P	Mmhm. [pause]	
146	17:37	C	Yeah.	
147	17:38		[pause]	
148	17:50	C	Yeah. I'm looking around the room it's like I can take in the energy of different objects in the room.	Client notes apperceptive shifts.
149	17:59	P	Yes, isn't that interesting?	"Interesting" here means commonplace "interesting" as well as TE application meaning "(primitive) brain is engaged".
150	17:50	C	Yeah, I've done a little of that before, but it hasn't felt this, it hasn't gone to my stomach before.	
151	18:08	P	Right, just imagine a baby trying to comprehend the world, the environment.	

152	18:13	C	Mm.	
153	18:14	P	With these ener-...with this going through it. Yeah. Your lungs are doing something cause you're yawning. Maybe partly because it's late but uh...	
154	18:30	C	Mmhm. [pause] I think I should stop and um... see what happens tomorrow.	Client senses end of session sequence.
155	18:45	P	Alright.	
156	18:46	C	Honestly, if I can um, if I can keep this openness.	
157	18:50	P	Yup, you'll see. Brain wants it open, it's easiest that way, so ah, it's a natural artistic insight which if you're fully, in full performance level of great openness, that's in fact where you want to be.	Summary framing of Client's experience.
158	19:07	C	Yeah.	
159	19:10	P	And you may struggle with learning the texts of whatever music you have or the, whatever you're doing, um, in order to get to that place but that's, that's, that's a real place in you, that openness.	

160	19:25	C	Yeah.	
161	19:26	P	And it will serve your art, but it will also serve your soul.	
162	19:34	C	Yeah.	
163	19:35		[pause]	
164	19:42	C	Ok.	
165	19:44	P	Ok. Alright, that's good work.	
166	19:49	C	Alright.	
167	19:50	P	Interesting, really interesting stuff.	Practitioner reflects general and real respect and appreciation for where they have been. As above, in TE 'interesting" also can mean "Have we got the primitive brain interested in the trauma pattern?"
168	19:52		Yeah.	

The aftermath

The aftermath: we want as much integration and broad neurochemical absorption of the new material as possible. This means that at the end of a session, we wisely may assume it is as if we have been in an accident and that includes the good feeling and clarity and sense that there is movement where before there was none. Thus post-session Meditators move carefully, even sleep, or rest or go into fetal curl or the like. Take a shower, drink water, meditate, watch the proceedings, be amazed at the observable speed and slowness of brain's integration of the new information, whatever. One regular client notes a two-day absorptive Re-calculation sequence following each session.

Often the effect will be both immediate and long term. It resembles the silver bullet we all hope for, when we finally "get it", yet having got it, we are sometimes thrown off our pace because of the new information. Our prayer is, "Send me the magic bullet and the patience, perspective, self-mothering, self-soothing, to absorb the skewed newness, the integrative process, with due diligence."

Often the second phase includes renewed traumata emerging. Suddenly and slowly. Often the new skewed system can be discomfiting, and yet viewed as process, it can be instructive. How we integrate can reveal processes which must be reviewed as well as rearranged on the shelf.

What happens in the aftermath

What happens in the aftermath of a session or sessions. Variations on the same insight.

1. You may experience a radical shift, wherein (perhaps suddenly) you have no longer addictive patterns or obsessional loops of thought or behavior, including smoking, drinking, and fighting. Some of such changes affecting your sense of inner space may take some getting used to.

    You may find yourself looking for, and looking forward to sustained space; experiencing void; experiencing Stillpoint. I think the setting of Stillpoint into the pond of our awareness and self-encouragement is a profound intervention; it subtly affects everything we do.

2. There may be a lifting off of internal pressure or weight, an increased lightness and manifest depth to your proceedings. Sense how the serotonin, if that is what it is, humors and coddles the perspective.

   You may find you can peruse the adjusting brainscape while over days and weeks it realigns. Never assume that some bad new site or sequence will last; never assume that the stuck place is anything more than a stuck place (and that's where you want to focus). It may take some time to recognized and experience the inner space in contra-juxtaposition to familiar sharp tensions or conflicts. Some senses of freedom can be initially disorienting. Blurred or fuzzy, you may have to wait for the newly efficient chemistry to establish itself. Some difficult moves will illustrate why you initially could not achieve resolution from them.

3. You may experience pockets of brain sequence which seem smoother, even invisible to heretofore obsessionalisms. You may feel invisibly supported, allowing for some new gesture of freedom by a revising (disappearing?) Self. If a set of conflicting vectors resolves, you will be left with a radiant space which contains the old history, but that history is no longer problematic, or of concern. Interestingly enough, such freedom may take some getting used to; some clients report it frightening. We ask for freedom and think we will rush to and embrace it easily. At these meditational levels, I find I am not so sure about how much freedom I want or can live with.

4. You may experience sequencing reversals, bits of neurochemistry which in some nameless way go to an edge and "complete' with the sense of rightness leading to a new (and hopeful) future. The serotonin kicks in.

5. You may have headaches and energetic sequences where you can sense brain turning internally and quieting, reworking connections. These can include pressure shifts, heating up, muscle movements, twitching, a limb spasming and turning internally and then quieting, sobbing or crying unaccountably, sharp pain. Usually, the rages soften as the cells puff and shrink into their fulfilling place and proportion. As inflammation subsides, a deeper calm manifests. Watching these

recalculating sequences, usually too fast to verbally characterize, can be experienced as a privilege. Their speed as well as their slowness can seem (seem?) miraculous.

6. You may see how dependent (addicted) you have been to the trauma fight/flight mechanism and its accompanying adrenalin, for your day-to-day orientation. Removing this rescue "dock" includes breathing changes which alter consciousness, cravings, suffocation patterning, and "new-lung" experiences. Playing with the trauma sites from the breath you have (including the acquired taste of seeking out the shallowest places you can tolerate) may increase your sense of direction, of mastery, of purpose.

7. Be prepared for early developmental process, including pre-natal rotations, to occur and complete, in subtle, sometimes powerful ways. Here, the game, if we conceive it as such, is resolution and integration.

8. One question emerges: "How deep do you want to go? How far into the complexity, the shallowness, the obtuseness of illusion do you want to go – to the loving, radiant center where Self dissolves? Maybe not right now, maybe now. Both Practitioner and Meditator participate in this evaluation.

9. People get interested in the developmental process, the sequencing and its trauma-induced obstructions. A respect develops for the inner energetic process and its priority as the place where observation can evoke the deeper changes desired, linked to but separate from narrative. Some of the first commentaries from initiates amount to "This is weird." Trauma leaves markers, and they can be attended to.

CHAPTER EIGHT:

ENERGETICS AND THE GESTALT

Early statements of the problem

The attention paid to what is called integrity has been civilizations long. One might argue integrity is the hallmark of civilized living, its definition and its promise. In our own so-called Western tradition, the preoccupation with setting things right from a catastrophically-divided situation may begin within the Judeo-Christian myth of the Garden of Eden, which describes a Perfection out of which mankind Falls, and from which Re-Gaining of Perfection is promised within an insight sequence surrounding a crucial expression of the relationship of the Individual to Its tribal and universal Identity. As stated and assimilated, the images from this trajectory evoke the restoration of a fundamental theological integration which has been somehow (and surprisingly regularly) lost.

If we can witness how parts are becoming whole, we may have a clue to seeing how and where we heal, including viewing the healing sequence specifically, contained and sometimes concealed by narrative. There is a twin-stroke engine here which describes the trauma mechanism or sequence as it functions in our daily life. The First Shoe is what I have called The High; the Second Shoe is a statement having something to do with shock memory, coming hard upon the First. This is a memory sequence, not the first experience of shock installation which takes place in the moments of an accident.

And gestalt understanding takes us below narrative closer to the preverbal energetic where actual resolution and transcendent healing between parts, at the boundary lines between parts, are. The energetic landscape provides focal points of witness where we can see how things come together, or don't; we get a sense of where to focus, upon not just Snow White, but upon the juxtaposition between her snow white skin and the raven black of her hair. I perceive that the concerns of the gestalt are the concerns of the trauma sites and their energetic layout in our human systems. With the boundary understanding which gestalt insight brings, we may be closer to returning – out of narrative – into pure Being.

Ultimately, gestalt understanding arrests time, in particular, dissociative time, and we can observe Being, which is whole-some, and unitary. Hopefully, our brain will hold the present in wholeness for a time. Which is not to say that other forms of held-time, including words and commas, and sentences and poems do not offer the chance to witness; but they are linked moments, linking to other links – not whole ones.

Centaurs...mermaids

From the Greek and earlier Mediterranean cultures, we Westerners recall centaurs, satyrs, minotaurs, and mermaids – half-person, half-animal forms from classical myth. Visually, there is a traditional transition line usually at the creature's torso, which illustrates we are segmented, divided – human and animal. Often the upper half is the humanoid face and breast, while the pelvis and legs or fins, are animal. In his minotaur etching series, Picasso engagingly reverses this tradition: the head on his naked male human body, in bed with a naked woman, is that of a bull, with humanoid expressiveness in its mouth, animal nose, and eyes.

What is significant about these forms, I think, is not only their shocking contemporaneousness, but that we can energetically approach a dividing line in our awareness between our animal and our human or ordinary and conscious identity. These ancient thus-divided forms seem to me a curiously culturally premature representation, holding a wisdom which has been carried and maintained through generations which understand and do not understand its essential insight. We keep turning a corner and rediscovering their importance.

In the mythic images, in sculpture and drawing, it is not clear whether the drawn line rigidly separates out the two aspects as if for the first time – I have discovered I am two – or is to be seen as an attempt to bring them as separate functions into integrity, into one – I am somehow divided, and I need to become one. Here might be three steps to civilized consciousness:

Step 1. We discover, often, cognitively, we are in some ways divided into two or more parts; and

Step 2. We find ways to bring the separations together. Brain often achieves this integration instantaneously once the "split" is witnessed.

Significantly, achieving (1) can automatically bring about (2), but not from some levels of approach or so-called self-awareness.

Step 3. The third stage is the realization and sustaining of integrity. From the divided images, we can envision that this point in the sequence, the line between upper and lower functions will dissolve and as in an animated film, the full human form will emerge, or full radiance will carry us beyond our ordinary, trauma-determined perceptions of human form within our body images of ourselves.

What causes the split in the first place may be some developmental sequence which becomes fixed within some primal traumatic process, partially named or expressed in the narrative myth which describes it. And in terms of structural priority, we can remember that prior to the narrative of Eden is Being itself.

The Labyrinth

In the Minoan myth of the Labyrinth, we gain access to such central truth after passing through corridors and turning corners. In one version, arriving at the core problem – the divided creature – Theseus slays the Minotaur, half-man half-bull. Historically, this may relate to the real King Theseus ending the direct sacrifice of youths as part of the Labyrinthian culture. But I sense the most successful encounter between Minotaur and hero involves a more loving, perhaps witnessing embrace: the process of slaying meets the formidability of the Minotaur – shall we call it event – with violence, as similarly violence (Leda) engenders the Fall of Troy. But it seems to me this slaying violence is hapless, head-banging, immature, and re-traumatizing stuff.

A slower, more equilibrated sequence of empathic understanding will dissolve the Minotaur permanently and transform and assimilate its energies, toward greater empowerment of the individual experiencing them. Otherwise, like some current politicians, Theseus is condemned to repeat the intentioned obliteration of the recurring pattern, only a partial resolution. At this level, violence in the name of resolution kills and maims, leaving the trauma pattern, or portions of it, to return. Furthermore, with this violent strategy, we never get back to Being, though that's the promise.

I see a parallel structure in the Riddle of the Sphinx, wherein the Mother is assembled, her parts or aspects stitched together or grouped – face and breast of a woman, body of a lion (her power), wings (for the witnessing infant, her ability to walk, and walk away and towards), a sharp tail (something to do with pain she can inflict or about endings), and her Riddle. I see the assembly of the Sphinx's parts similar to the Minotaur, the dividing line is both a separation and the possibility of linking cognitively separate parts together. But in these hovering assemblies of both the Sphinx and the Minotaur, there is at best only partially experienced unity.

In the case of the Sphinx, the Child is approached by the Mother who is going to eat the Child (as the Child eats "at" the Mother). The Riddle encompasses the insight that we children are early versions of the adult world, and by answering the Riddle, we join it as "equals" in the problem of existence, including our death. Disarmed, the Sphinx hurls itself into the sea, a similar unnegotiable violence to that of the slaughtered Minotaur. Both solutions have significant incompletions.

In the mythic narrative, the Sphinx is replaced by the Mother, whom we marry in personable relational form: Jocasta. The child-generation we have with her has a casual add-on feel to it, like the abrupt movement between the Virgin Births of Adam and Eve to the more realistic births of Cain and Abel and the rest of human reality. Ordinary parents have ordinary children, and we jump to this new level of understanding without missing a beat.

The new level is perhaps stitched together with the old, and there may be some violence in the initial juxtaposition. What needs to come together may involve a transition bridge of chaos, one which in our fear, anxiety, and deoxygenation, we do not think we can safely experience. Like Evel Knievel, we have the security of the jumping off and the landing, with the in-between chasm negotiated by a heart-stopping momentum – and we hold our breath.

The settlement (rapprochement?) between Theseus and the Minotaur could involve a mutual melt, or an incorporation, or an embrace of love. As Auden notes, Jack and his Giant may be better as lovers, not mortal enemies. As he returns to the entrance of the Labyrinth,

> *Ariadne:* You've changed.
> *Theseus:* I have.
> *Ariadne:* You look stronger, yet more vulnerable.
> *Theseus:* I can carry that now.
> *Ariadne:* It's a different kind of strength.
> *Theseus:* Yes.
> *Ariadne:* How did it go with the Minotaur?
> *Theseus:* I slayed him. At least that is what he said to me.
> *Ariadne:* Said?
> *Theseus:* He said, "You slay me."
> *Ariadne:* And then you slayed him?
> *Theseus:* No, I replied, "You slay me, too."

Without violence

Developmentally, we could slide or phase or evolve from one neurochemical site to another, without violence; this transition process, even movement can be part of what we mean by "understand". With the introduction of shock and its natural necessity, we are in an altered stage of awareness, of our neurochemistry, if you will – at and past Being; on behalf of this doubled, divided world and Self-view, we want to slide into Being decorously, even though our introduction to the presence of shock is usually abrupt, and under often catastrophic conditions.

The problem, which the Minoans among others subsequently have seen, is that anyone – ok, almost anyone – can achieve the developmental, meditational center of the problem of the Labyrinth, here, our "divided" or double-aspected self (brain). Once acclimated to the witnessed core, the issue for our heroic Theseus quickly transforms into "Now, how do I get out of here?" Or, to put it another way, "How do I integrate what I have learned at the core with the 'real' outside world?"

In a recapitulation of umbilicus and birth events, Ariadne has advised Theseus to position a string at his journey's start at the outside gate of the

Labyrinth (where they sell the All-Day and Family Rate tickets?), and, unlike hapless Hansel and Gretel, to maintain an effective unwinding working exit strategy as he heads right into, into the core (or so it seems).

In mythic form, this connecting strategy is what integrity involves; we can go to our core, but we need to integrate that inner understanding with our personal embodied surround as well as with the outside world in which bills have to be paid (and lovers abandoned?). In Plato's Allegory of the Cave, the Philosopher/King returns to his fellow prisoners to assist them as they move out of their trauma-determined awareness.

It is a little like God, who realizes that at some point the growing blastocyst will leave the uterus, so right from the start, certainly at implantation, a tissue process separates the placental event from the nurturant uterine wall and activates at birth to allow the placenta eventually to peel off from the wall. However intimately bonded with the mother, we are explicitly and implicitly separate right from the beginning. Such individuation agency has to be present from the start; it cannot be hastily added on when it is suddenly needed. Such pre-sited individuation process is integral to our survival.

Longing for unified consciousness

Our preoccupations with monotheism also state the longing for an unified consciousness from which to understand the pluralities of our experience. And in our literature, novels like Mary Wollstonecraft-Godwin Shelley's *Frankenstein* deal centrally, tragically, with the assembly of disparate parts into an integrated whole in the "man-created" individual.

Recent revisions of the 19th and 20th century Internalist Movement reinvent this model of division by therapeutically promising to escort what is not part of our (self-)awareness into awareness. Those who follow Freud's strategy, such as Jung, add different kinds of specificity of attention to this model, perhaps focusing more upon **Step 1**; though all are concerned with how to bring our re-discovered parts of ourselves together. From the Odyssey and Bible on, integrity has been the issue. Each commentator has added a note to the new and old chord.

I have found useful the understanding of the gestalt theorists, including Perls, who pay particular attention to the active binding agency which connects, not merely the recognition and definition of the, say, shadow side and the light related by Jung – the divided self. I think Jung's significant achievement pertains more to **Step 1** than to **Step 2**. For me, gestalt theory is particularly compelling because it is not so much concerned with the divided aspects of our human experience which unrecognized, need recognition, but with resultant states when the parts come together.

In fact, I find *e pluribus unum* to be the cardinal insight paraphrase of gestalt thinking, and I thusly approach the energetic which results in a transformed consciousness which I can directly sense – a left-right brain process if you will – where the center, the energetic site, Being, is discovered and confirmed. Somehow some – two – sides, if you will, become invisible, as if the particulate of divided narrative dissolves.

This vision is brought forward within the 19th Century dialectic systems of Hegel, but it goes as far back as Plato in the West and then some, not to mention the Eastern writings and meditational traditions. This insight, apparently arising (again) from the gestalt therapeutic tradition, implemented itself within my awareness rather suddenly, like an "Ah-ha" moment, one which I had been probably preparing for for years.

Mining the experience of the gestalt

I first encountered gestalt strategy directly when reading Perls and encountering wild-card therapists in the late 1960's, but my understanding did not become active and viable until, courtesy of a close relative, the Jungian analyst Philip Metman pointed out, that rather than focusing on the novel as the forbidden story of a dirty old child molester, it was as illuminating, perhaps more strategically so, to see all the characters in *Lolita* as aspects of a single personality.

There was plenty of evidence that Nabokov saw the same potential in the combinant figure of skewed dopplegänger Clare Quilty, who moves in and around the main action like an inner witnessing, demonic presence. Near the conclusion Humbert confronts and shoots Quilty multiple times to destroy the plural, embodied pattern in its clear, arresting form. And we know in so doing, he seals his own linked trajectory, only this time the pattern is not violently annihilated; in a more developmentally creative way, the pattern is brought to a characterizing halt, an arrest.

Like the best prisoner in the best prison, or the jury trial itself which sends him there, what has been slowed down to a viewable moment can now be perceived; and we get to see what the real success and real failure of the novel's sequence involves, significantly arrest itself. Within the novel's comic playfulness, its European self- irony, Humbert's arrest is long-overdue and devastating, not because readers enjoy or find distasteful having this come-uppance demonstrated in salaciously pre-disposed three dimensions; what is revealed is that the energetic pattern expressed in "exterior" narrative is interior and immobile, as direct and private and accessible as a milkshake.

Gestalt insight puts living hold on the held-energy pattern Nabakov demonstrates. We see to the energetic core of the immigrant dilemma, in which traumatic patterning will not be solved merely in the illusion of narrative embodied in some hapless American Dream. And that somehow, Nabokov records the blowing of the whistle on a basic, thwarted idealism (filled with fulfilling something, here anything forbidden), generated in Europe and projected upon, perpetrated, and collusively sustained within the seductive apparently innocent American social landscape. The line-ends of the railroad tracks curve upwards and back; and the trap of the novel is to focus on the forbidden narrative, rather than in the deeper revolution against authority sought.

Attending to the novel in this way makes it possible to witness the connections between the characters and reasons Nabokov writes about their intercourses as he does. Various proposals of self or identity transmute and configure in what turns out to be a commanding portrait about integrity serially declared in a coast-to-coast Road film. When confronting some agitated students who flagged down its humor and its perversity (the usual responses to the book), Nabokov questioned whether they were reading the story or the book. From a gestalt point of view, I have found *Lolita* is grief-ridden and relentlessly, unbearably sad – the saddest book I have ever read.

Examining *Lolita* with these insights, the book is not just about predation or erotic exploitation (all of demonstrative very legitimate contemporary concern, yet, I think, with very little current hope or signs for immanent restitution and prevention because it is so hard to focus beyond the abusive narratives), but about the encapsulation of a soul, demonstrated in all its complexity through all the characters, not just its main voice, Humbert.

In the surprising first seduction scene between Hum and Lo, we are able to witness the intrapersonal dynamic which might lead anywhere if it were to be expressed into the outside world by its carrier, a so-called individual person. Even though complex, it would not necessarily lead to bad behavior or disreputable "externalized" or "acting out" activities, including those which appear to do harm.

Regularly, the exteriorizing narratives with which we seek to explicate and resolve our inner trauma narratives don't (quite) match their inner, energetic promulgators; often the parallels are wryly subtle to the point of invisibility, and sometimes deeply comic or radically destructive, or glaringly overt. In our fundamentalistic simplicity we think that what is internal seeks to be expressed externally in a direct parallel way, and often it is; but we also dream and act in code. In Humbert's story, it is Lo's seduction reversal which highlights the novel's gestalt formulation and interpretation; the energy is unexpected and vector-contrary and, I think, can be best viewed accurately from a position of unified awareness.

Thus all the intercourses secure statement/depictions of how the embridging structure of so-called personality holds or does not hold together; their descriptions are significant for their primary informational function of this interior, not exclusively as statements of interpersonal exchange. Now we can be concerned with the intrapersonal structures they reveal, and it is upon some preverbal intuition of their intrapersonal veracity that we judge their appropriateness, both humane and artistic.

Ultimately, within the energetic of our neurochemistry, there are flows, not narratives, and when we ask the meaning of a symbol, we are usually setting a trap; for I think what specific symbols eventually lead to is a melting down or transmogrification of the symbol and its subtext meanings into pure and radiant energy. Viewed this way, symbols are attempts to narrate the energetic, which when detraumatized, flows evenly and without (and simultaneously with) differentiation, as a whole. And, like Little Black Sambo and the tigers, we have a chance to melt, digest, and return to Being.

The movement into realms of taboo events characterize this matrix, including the held-energy systems of traumatic memory. We discover limits which may or may not declare what is true within, as it were, the flow. The characterized taboo floats, as it were, on an inward sea, indicating direction, velocity, and size of the waves, but, much as we might like to think it does, it does not control the fluid out of which it rises. Being itself.

Despite all it can do, the symbol is ultimately powerless to its fate as is dissolving salt crystal in water. And often the narratives which attach like links in a symbolic chain describe the formulation of symbols themselves, including forging, immolation, and transcendence into pure energy: maybe there is only one Story and that is the story of the development and transmogrification of the symbol and symbolic thought. I think all this has to be noted before we can return with any wisdom to our usual discussions of symbols.

Implied unity

Just as we evaluate ourselves, we judge a book by its implied unity. We want the unity of ourSelf to be visible and declarable. Art, in its many manifestations, including particularly the energetic realms of painting, sculpture, and music, offers stability of stimulus experience with which to witness such unity. The painting remains on the wall, while we move toward and away from such a focal point.

Clearly we can be fragmented inwardly, and our activities reflect those partial fragmentations; even when the activity has manifest power in the real world (we dig a water well for some dessicated village), we can acknowledge that it has not been generated entirely by an inward scenario of integrity. We look to the saints for demonstrations of such integrity.

When we talk about multiple motivating forces behind a decision or gesture, we are approximating this understanding. I think it is the striving for this level of integration between internal depth and order and exterior action (not activity) which may characterize the so-called Adamic, American Dream. In a perhaps strange sort of way, it defines our pursuit of happiness and its achievement, problematic as its definition may be.

Accuracy maintained

The accuracy of wholistic presentation is maintained throughout *Lolita* – grotesque, comedic, and tragic to its ordinary core. We get to see beyond the possibly harrowing, curiously simple hapless narrative to the way in which narrative (here perhaps challenging, to put a point on it) declares the elusive immobilized energetic sub-text, in this case, its arrest. It is the arrest and the attempt to resolve its immobilization which sponsors, perhaps disastrously, the narrative sequence of the novel. The American highway grid upon which the desperate narrative is stretched enhances and forces the story's accommodation to its mundane, held-energy system center.

And as with all tragic literature, if we can witness the underlying disturbing pattern in slow motion, with all its parts visible and "sustained", it may be on its way out – predestined to appear as it may seem. Our victimhood, which includes projecting our unresolved trauma patterns upon a hapless world, may have its limits, a message we need to comprehend; talk about Good News.

As in the Oedipus plays of Sophocles, if we want the innerly-held pattern to transmute, we shall have to witness it in its deepest, perhaps initially most easily rejectable form (the narrative levels such as patricide, incest, and self-immolation). Then we get to perceive the ordinary stuck point beneath the abuse, or violation, and if lucky, we may heal – even soul-heal at the font of Being. We will have to address a world which includes shock with its heritage of resilience and sustained immobilization.

Written by a Russian émigré, the pattern revealed in *Lolita* characterizes so much of American spirit, filled with inflated immigrant idealism and its self-permitting goal of challenging authority and redefining authority in its telling and the linear sequence of its picaresque, Road-film structure. It contains an insight about the American ideal of creating a shockless world, or at least one in which shock's power is effective and quickly integrated into invisibility. No wonder critics have so actively discussed its importance as a window-portrait on American experience.

Aristotle

I had studied Aristotle but did not initially see how preoccupied with the gestalt (my view of gestalt) formulations of the tragedies he is. Traditionally (and somewhat simplistically) viewed, Aristotle perceives tragedy (tragic dramas) as imitating a serious action within a single unity of time and place; such action could be encompassed within a single moment, even, I have come to understand, significantly, within a single breath. This unity was later rendered by some French tragedians into a single time and place in perhaps a rigid, idiosyncratically fundamentalist way; they got caught in a fixed definition of the narrative.

What seems to me significant about Aristotle's definition of tragedy is that throughout, it consolidates around unity, contextual and the thing itself. Action is perceived not as fragmented but as single, unitary; and the drama which we would currently describe as narrative, is an imitation of a (singular) action, or of activity(-ies) perceived from the viewpoint of being single. Time itself is singular, in any way you might want to state it, such as that the "tragedy" takes place within the confines of a single day, or in the "real" time it takes to play out the theatrical narrative, or in some cognitive/emotional variant such as in our Biblical Time.

The serious action is "serious" because it "has" unity, integrity. Those actions which have this quality are the ones which we view over and over – to see what happens next, if anything. It is the moment when we identify (and judge) a President, for example, because we can see the integrity of his actions (and the list is short where this integrity is observable). It is the unity of time and place and action which makes it a serious action, or the dramatic imitation of such.

And it is significant because in that serious action, we can move past ordinary narrative, filled with activities, into pure radiance or Being. Our patterns dissolve, and we are rendered as radiant – in short, creatures of Being. The movement toward this (neurochemical) state is what is being imitated on stage through narrative. It is the empathic power of the audience member who absorbs and responds to the narrative nexus playing out in front of them which enables the triggering of a catharsis of the emotions involving pity ("How sad for Oedipus....") and fear ("If I can recognize the pattern at some level, then I carry it – I am the tragedy I am watching.").

I find action and serious here mean the same thing. Working with his equivalent of this gestalt insight, Aristotle does not say imitations of serious actions. Or imitation of serious actions. I think serious in this context means unitary, that which is perceived as having integrity, where the parts participate as whole, and whole is what is declared, sometimes in amalgamated and transcended particulate form. The Torah equivalent scan would be *righteous*. The Latinate root for integrity means that which cannot be touched, *i.e.*, fragmented or corrupted. Corruption here reveals itself in fragmentation as such: plurality, even rebellious or defiant plurality.

Plural is always understood within contexts of singularity and could be considered a way-station (on Via Dolorosa?) on the path to unity, unity being perhaps energetically prior to it. Historically, the monotheistic discovery of God as singular appears to have come after the theocratic perception of Ultimate Reality as being plural or polytheistic. But in fact, developmentally, both ends of the candle are lit, and we are best suited for reality delineation when we can move comfortably between monotheism and polytheism; and in that movement we can provide the opportunity for a consciousness which transcends both poles. And if we propose a God-strategy with both, we shall see that it mirrors our understanding of ourselves, which includes plurality and unity, even as we are "conceived".

The scan of gestalt understanding – and it has been demonstrated to be occasionally site-specifically identifiable in the brain – is one which keeps being evoked, in so many ways. However, the actual experience of gestalt awareness cannot be just rationally, analytically applied. It includes an altered mode of consciousness, one which can be perceived and sensed. Some would suggest it reflects a movement from left-brained consciousness to that of right-brain.

Transformation

Gestalt awareness moves us into a most important aspect of literature and myth, namely that of transformation. Aside from distraction and a certain level of enjoyment with diversionary narrative information sequences, classic literature is classic because it promises the description of deep, inward developmental sequence in its heroes, in the broad, unifying sweep of its stories, in its capacity to describe human experience from a unified point of view, equivalent to seeing all its aspects as parts of a single personality, in immobility and in mobility.

One well-worn definition of the epic carries gestalt understanding: a narrative of an entire culture expressed through the life of a single person/ character. We could add that we, as so-called individuals, express in the unity of our single personality our entire surrounding, encompassing civilization. And our ability to achieve and sustain this unity is a measuring stick for the idea of civilization itself; the parts are demonstrated to be parts of a whole, and in being so, characterize the problem of integrity: when the assembly of the parts "works", what does integrity look like? It includes civilization and civilized existence, even for the person standing alone, in the desert, on the sea, or on the Cross. And crucially, once achieved, what comes next? Matthew Arnold and Walt Whitman acknowledge this insight in their roles as personal embodier and articulator of their culture.

Happily ever after

This what-comes-next solution is what is narrated by the integration of the parts of a whole encompassed in children's stories which end in "happily ever after". The *animus* kisses, *i.e.,* connects – interfaces? – with the *anima*, and we see integration occur at an ultimately satisfying level. We know in real life that this moment in narrative can lead to complex after-situations which are not happy at all, but that does not remove the clear and settled, recorded moment, particularly as it relates to inward states. It is precisely in those unhappy after-moments, our brain, if it can, will refer to the pristine base line which has been clearly initially set down, in order to energetically stabilize.

These base-line moments accrue from synaptic repetitions between parent and child over time, and I like to think they consolidate into a single "fixing" moment when the predisposition toward generosity consolidates into happily ever after. In effect, this conclusion characterizes the positive sealing of the parental introject – to be applied over and over again, for ever after. From such neurochemical moment of completion, all further activity and action, including bad things which happen, can occur and can be conceptualized in the framing sense of that term.

We know that we can build entire lifetimes upon early developmental sequences which contain moments of such possibility generously fulfilled. Such satisfaction is an initiating historical referent point of clarity for human systems, a benchmark essential to stability. Our brain system refers to these moments of integrity to orient itself when subsequent information comes too quickly, or too randomly, too violently, or too perniciously.

While we can struggle with the narratives of children's stories, as we read them to our young minds, perhaps the sealing and storing aspects of "happily ever after" is the most significant part conveyed in the stories' narratives, one they all share. For example, the emotional content surrounding the Virgin Mary nexus consolidates and implants positive "happily forever after" mothering experience within social and personal matrixes which in real life may be more fragmentally held; its mythology can serve in such a benchmark function for many who experience personality and so-called exterior reality in disturbing plural ways. And we should not be surprised when complex trauma sites seeking resolution follow hard upon such an originating, could we say triggering, benchmark High.

One might suggest the *pieta* tradition contains such a (chronic) set of juxtapositions. But the encompassing Virgin Mary aura, hard as it is for some to rationalize, declares a substantial and cell-derived, cell-absorbed truth, that of a fully-resolved patternless and radiant energetic. Its partial and abusal applications in the real world notwithstanding.

My understanding is that the apparently distinctive initial parts of what will be a unifying or unified system (say, *animus* and *anima)* subsequently dissolve and amalgamate. As a new system, this fresh amalgamation then turns, or better, expands outward at a High, vibratory level which often sequentially reencounters further traumatic process in its encounter with the new system's environment. The sequence mirrors the moment of conception: apparently separate sperm and egg unite, and as separate haploid entities zipper and dissolve into a new transmogrified combination which now diploid, proceeds to confront its environment, including, significantly, the uterine wall. Hegel, take a number.

Garnerings

We face the fullness of the outside world from a gathered and sustained position of security and integrity. We then primarily duplicate our inner integration process as a so-called (inner) "Self" with a so-called (exterior) "Other." The psychoanalytic tradition has commented upon the complex ways in which desire and orgasmic fulfillment fire from a sequence of energetic "garnerings" which are usually hidden, except, notably, in socialization and foreplay.

These garnerings involve subtle energetic sub-systemic recapitulations, swerving, adjusting, making 90° turns, connecting and dissolving; and these labyrinthine reductions explicate into an energetic sequence beyond narrative elaboration. It is like the spin of atomic particles which gather momentum before they are finally fired down the accelerator's alley and hit/connect with some other density. The entire life of the system, its history and elaborations, recapitulates into a single moment, and the gestalt strategy addresses this "wholistic" sequence specifically.

And in so doing, it enables us to witness the crucial – for lack of a better term – moment, when the implied encapsulation of personality encounters its boundary(-ies) with the so-called outside world. The negotiation of a self-system which perceives itself as being one, with another One or Other, is what classic literature regularly confronts. And this intercourse is a crucial part of gestalt understanding.

We are interested to see what that integrated moment feels like internally, and what is evoked, if we can even see it, in our actions and in the outside world. The relentless exploration of *pas de deux* in ballet speaks to this relationship of one to two and the space between. There are moments, of course, when we can experience the energetic flow between two systems as one, just as we can comprehend our place in the world as a deeply unified creature energetically bonded and interacting amid relational fields; there is no outside/inside. We are participants in Emerson's Ubersoul; I am even the Ubersoul itself.

Then, if we are Moses, we perceive in clarity the Burning Bush paradox and immerse ourselves as at one with that environment. The Burning Bush paradox is followed mythically by a Second Shoe, which I shall call The Ten Commandments phenomenon, which speaks to an insecurity or prior trauma pattern which seeks narrative certainty – a sure moral error whose nature is further explicated in the Book of Moses: it is a mistake to anxiously render the energetic in stone, or to teach it with stone. From a gestalt point of view, the tablets, traditionally shaped in a brain and spine configuration, reflect not just the conveyed zapping wisdom of J..., but of the way we learn, the stages of learning: zapping, tablets, rigidity, then transformation.

We are in various stages of dissociation

Gestalt awareness reminds us mid-place in every narrative, that there is a single moment of unity within each narrative sequence, and within each moment of the linear, particulate narrative. Such awareness gives us necessary pause to take our bearings and to realize that we are in various stages of dissociation, and subsequently, of clarity. By proposing each portion of consciousness of each individual as part of a whole, and then extrapolating that wholeness upon the individual's place in the exterior world, we move ourselves into both a particulate and a unified consciousness. I find the gestalt strategy takes me to the edge of each "whole", where I await its dissolution into pre-conscious unity.

Here follow some samples I have discovered where this sequence is laid out with some clarity in poetic form.

The Demon Lover
This (here, Scottish/Irish) ballad goes back at least to the 14th Century.

"O where have you been, my long, long love,
This long seven years and mair?"
"O I'm come to seek my former vows
Ye granted me before."

"O hold your tongue of your former vows,
For they will breed sad strife;
O hold your tongue of your former vows,
For I am become a wife."

He turned him right and round about,
And the tear blinded his ee:
"I wad never hae trodden on Irish ground,
If it had not been for thee.

"I might hae had a king's daughter,
Far, far beyond the sea;
I might have had a king's daughter,
Had it not been for love o thee."

"If ye might hae had a king's daughter,
Yer sel ye had to blame;
Ye might have taken the king's daughter,
For ye kend that I was nane.

"If I was to leave my husband dear,
And my two babes also,
O what have you to take me to,
If with you I should go?"

"I hae seven ships upon the sea-
The eighth brought me to land-
With four-and-twenty bold mariners,
And music on every hand."

She has taken up her two little babes,
Kissd them baith cheeks and chin:
"O fair ye weel, my ain two babes,
For I'll never see you again."

She set her foot upon the ship,
No mariners could she behold;

But the sails were o the taffetie,
And the masts o the beaten gold.

She had not sailed a league, a league,
A league but barely three,
When dismal drew his countenance,
And drumlie grew his ee.

They had not saild a league, a league,
A league but barely three,
Until she spied his cloven foot,
And she wept right bitterlie.

"O hold your tongue of your weeping," says he,
"Of your weeping now let me be;
I will shew you how the lilies grow
On the banks of Italy."

"O what hills are yon, yon pleasant hills,
That the sun shines sweetly on?"
"O yon are the hills of heaven," he said,
"Where you will never win."

"O whaten a mountain is yon," she said,
All so dreary wi frost and snow?"
"O yon is the mountain of hell'" he cries,
"Where you and I will go."

And aye when she turn'd her round about,
Aye taller he seemed for to be;
Until that the tops o' that gallant ship
Nae taller were than he.

The clouds grew dark, and the wind grew loud,
And the levin fill'd her ee;
And waesome wail'd the snaw-white sprites
Upon the gurlie sea.

He strack up the tap-mast wi his hand,
The fore-mast wi his knee,
And he brake that gallant ship in twain,
And sank her in the sea.

Anonymous, Traditional

Here is a schematic of the poem:

Commentary on The Demon Lover

LINE	ORIGINAL TEXT	TRANSLITERATION	GESTALT COMMENTARY
1 2 3 4	"O where have you been, my long, long love, This long seven years and mair (more)?" "O I'm come to seek my former vows Ye granted me before."	A married woman greets her former love, long held in her heart, long gone away – for over seven years. Apparently he has not emailed her telling her what he has been doing, how much he has missed her, etc. He explains, "I have come to have you fulfill the promises, pledges you made to me over seven years ago."	His absence is narratively declared as seven years, but the time includes, more importantly, separation experienced in inner time. We have the same issue with Biblical Time and the seven-fold creation of the universe. I find this inner time strategy is the first to turn to – literal narrative is complex, badly reported, and for purposes of transformation, initially inconsequential.
5 6 7 8	"O hold your tongue of your former vows, For they will breed sad strife; O hold your tongue of your former vows, For I am become a wife."	She responds, "Stop talking about what was; that will lead to sad trouble." She repeats, "Stop talking about my former promises and pledges to you, because in the meantime (and because you went off), I got married to another man. How long was I supposed to wait around?"	The repetition may be stylistic to the ballad form, but it may also reflect the systemic urgency of the feelings the lover's return has generated. Can our inner historical process be brought forward, reappearing like a ghost, given the perhaps illusory sense that we have grown (past) where we were?
9 10 11 12	He turned him right and round about, And the tear blinded his ee (eye): 'I wad (would) never hae (have) trodden on Irish ground, If it had not been for thee.	In his disappointment, perhaps in a self-pitying piece of manipulation she is used to coming from him, he turns to hide his tears from her, and he says, "I would never have come back to Ireland (in this version the location is Ireland) if it had not been for my love and hope for you."	At some level, he speaks the truth, but he sets it in an easily misunderstood context, one she will reject, only later not reject. What drives her turn-about decision may have little to do with his reasoning.

LINE	ORIGINAL TEXT	TRANSLITERATION	GESTALT COMMENTARY
13 14 15 16	"I might hae had a king's daughter, Far, far beyond the sea; I might have had a king's daughter, Had it not been for love o(f) thee."	He adds, "I had the chance to marry very much up, but that my (sincere and truer than material considerations) love for you drove me back to you."	Passion is trump card here, and it often takes the priority trick within systems: "I just cannot help what you set off in me." Our human system experiences often unpleasant irritations which demand discharge.
17 18 19 20	"If ye might have had a king's daughter, Yer sel(f) ye had to blame; Ye might have taken the king's daughter, For ye kend (knew) that I was nane (none).	With the directness of a mature woman who can see from a mile away the perhaps guilt-tripping and manipulation from this old lover, she rejoins, "If you might have had a king's daughter but now choose me instead, you only have yourself to blame for making the inexpedient choice, because you knew I am not a princess."	There is some skewed logic here, basically reflecting some sense of values about love being more important than money and status. Curiously, here she argues obversely for his point, namely that at this level? Choice cannot be rationalized. She is on the edge of an unexpected decision.
21 22 23 24	'If I was to leave my husband dear, And my two babes also, O what have you to take me to, If with you I should go?'	But in some way she has been waiting for him. In a variation of the Seven Year Itch, perhaps the current husband and children have become tiresome (in some versions of the ballad her spouse is a carpenter). She abruptly counter-offers, "What is in it for me?"	As we enter erotic encounters, we sometimes "list" what is in our cluttered house before we give it away, or it is orgasmically subsumed into preverbal, pre-narrative states.
25 26 27 28	"I hae seven ships upon the sea – The eighth brought me to land – With four-and-twenty bold mariners, And music on every hand."	He promises her a good time in which she will feel special and probably won't have to do the laundry. He describes/hints at the erotic potential, full and omnipresent. "There is a richness of experience to be had with me," he claims.	The total system, characterized as man and women, is gearing up toward some kind of merged, narrative-obliterating unity.

LINE	ORIGINAL TEXT	TRANSLITERATION	GESTALT COMMENTARY
29 30 31 32	She has taken up her two little babes, Kiss'd them baith (both) cheeks and chin: "O fair ye weel (well), my ain (own) two babes, For I'll never see you again."	She capitulates and kisses her children good-bye (forever). She knows her going off will destroy the family. The pheromonal lure of the lover is overpowering, as is her memory of him.	The suddenness of this change speaks to risks of impulsive action. Interiorly, the shift is abrupt in an almost something-out-of-nothing way, even though this couple has had a history. The woman, being a mother, also has had an intervening history. Perhaps the children are perceived in the casual, dismissive way of fantasy. The social identity of the mother is dropped for that of a lover, spatially rendered as a crossing over.
33 34 35 36	She set her foot upon the ship, No mariners could she behold; But the sails were o the tafietie, And the masts o the beaten gold.	She goes with the lover, but all is not as promised; even now reality begins to set in upon her. But, the "environment", perhaps "bed", is well appointed, and they make good, even special love. What did she expect? Yet after all these years, he is still better than good enough.	There is an initiating interface here between anima and animus which is not smooth or predictable, yet a strong connection is still available. The system combines its parts not completely, but in a relatively good enough way.
37 38 39 40	She had not sailed a league, a league, A league but barely three, When dismal drew his countenance, And drumlie – grew his ee.	Three (days) out on this affair, things start to go south. The lover gets depressed and begins to show his darker, more depressive side. Something is wrong with this (commonplace) situation.	The system achieves a High, which for some moments is sustained, then cannot be sustained. Nothing gold can stay. "When" crucially notes the bridging connection between the achieved High, and its closely following narrative: of the lover's depression, now revealed. With the coinage of the prior High, the (gestalt) system – seen as a whole – also brings forth the next dissociative state (held-energy state) for resolution.

LINE	ORIGINAL TEXT	TRANSLITERATION	GESTALT COMMENTARY
41 42 43 44	She had not sail'd a league, a league A league but barely three, Until she spied his cloven foot, And she wept right bitterlie.	Within a short space of time, she perceives that she has been seduced by a devil or demon, and she weeps bitterly at her mistake. The bonding which initially occurs quickly leads to an elaboration. And rather than hold the elaboration to herself ("I have succumbed to a devilish experience. I have been foolish.") she blames her lover for the problem and scapegoats him: "You are the devil who is leading me astray and who wants me destroyed." There is no room for negotiation or of partnership in the tryst. She becomes encapsulated, or, perhaps better, her encapsulation becomes clear.	The narrative expresses the complexity of the energetic systemic situation. One solution is to scapegoat the lover and to demean him as a devil (with supernatural powers). But the systemic compression makes such characterization absolute, when in some ultimate reality way, it is not. The man is just a man. In the way that this is a dream or fantasy of let's say the abandoned husband, the narration describes a limitation to direct, ecstatic flow.
45 46 47 48	"O hold your tongue of your weeping," says he, "Of your weeping now let me be; I will shew you how the lilies grow On the banks of Italy."	He orders her, "Stop crying; stop elaborating in a self-encapsulated way. If you demonize me instead of taking responsibility for your own actions, and for our relationship, then this affair and the relationship is lost." Shifting her attention, he proffers, "I can show you so much that is exotic, right here within reach of [Interstate 95 here in Boston]. I have a lot to offer you."	The parts of the system are conflicted – this is the trauma site emerging further through the narrative in response to the original ecstatic (?) golden-masted High.

LINE	ORIGINAL TEXT	TRANSLITERATION	GESTALT COMMENTARY
49	"O what hills are yon, yon pleasant hills,	She proffers an appreciation of where she would like to be, at some distance from where they are. He tags this comment as not real, not something achievable. I see also his despair that if she does not see him (and herself) accurately, no solace or happiness between them is possible. Their shared reality must be equal and relational. She begins to fantasy a sweet place some distance from where she is (perhaps the motel room does not have a Bible). He hears her dissociation in this fantasy, rather than seeing where they really are (Boston's motel-lined Route 128), and who he really is and what he can realistically give her, all of which may be possibly accurate. He proffers, "Don't aim for Heaven; its fantasy will come in the way of our relationship, which, if you weren't so a-relational, could be plenty good."	One voice in the system understands, the other is impacted and encapsulated – all within a single system. We see the inner space between and the way in which the space is perceived as unbridgeable. If this poem is the abandoned husband's "dream", we may see that the separation evokes unapproachable held-energy systems.
50	That the sun shines sweetly on?"		
51	"O yon are the hills of heaven," he said,		The system has to declare the full history involved so inner permission to eliminate all narrative is achieved. These narrative alternatives may be describing energetic "spaces".
52	"Where you will never win."		
53	O whaten a mountain is yon," she said,	She becomes depressed, in response to the initial High, with her now-depressed lover. Every piece of the landscape shows itself impossible. "You are creating hell by your elaborations, for you and for me," he cries. Though not usual, there are mythic Hell mountains, and Dante has mountain landscape in Purgatory, suggesting climbing struggle. Perhaps climbing up is an hellish agony. The Hell here is the result of projecting our depression upon the outside world. She cannot see the "outside" world clearly, and so his cries are cries of existential despair. He has chosen a partner who is in this moment trauma-bound and is now stuck with her process which is incapable of movement. Throughout it may be useful to see that he is not demonic, i.e., intentionally, sadistically out to destroy her. He accurately predicts the truth about hell which is a state of mind.	A demonic, sadistic reading of these lines is shallow, I think. It turns the ballad into soft-porn.
54	"All so dreary wi (with) frost and snow?"		The poem describes the systemic problem of negotiating integrity vis-a-vis the outside world. The lover senses that the outside world will never solve the problem of integrity.
55	"O yon is the mountain of hell" he cries,		
56	"Where you and I will go."		The encapsulation and the narrative which expresses it becomes undeniable. A fine characterization of what we call Hell. It is a neurochemical, trauma-bound energetic nexus, a trauma "site", again perhaps held by not the lover but by the husband.

LINE	ORIGINAL TEXT	TRANSLITERATION	GESTALT COMMENTARY
57	And aye when she turn'd her round about,	She turns around to see him directly, and he now seems taller than before, to the point where his "posture" or "position" matches the environment of their relation-ship.	In gestalt meditation, we often get differences in scale as the developmental shifts turn and alter, subject and object reverse, and early, infantile trauma sites emerge for resolution. Like Alice in Wonderland, proportion follows moving emotional as well as physical scale, spatially declared.
58	Aye taller he seemed for to be;		
59	Until that the tops o' that gallant ship		
60	Nae (never) taller were than he.		
61	The clouds grew dark, and the wind grew loud,	The exterior natural storm describes the interior energetic turbulence, including lightning and woeful wailing, upward bolts of snow white lightning and thunderbolts upon the rough sea.	The energetic vision has a turbulence which may be that which initiates the appearance of shock as a holding mechanism.
62	And the levin (lightning, thunderbolts) fill'd her ee;		
63	And waesome wail'd the snaw-white (snow-white) sprites (upward, red lightning discharges)		We may be witnessing the equivalent of the turbulence of the juxtaposition between one deoxygenated held-energy system and another, prior to some kind of aftermath resolution (which the "poet" does not provide).
64	Upon the gurlie sea.		
65	He strack up the tap-mast wi (with) his hand,	The scale shifts radically, where she and the boat are small and the lover huge and demonic. The unreality of the story here perhaps speaks to his fury and pre-causal power. He is doing this because of what? Like God, is he punishing her for her abandonments, of her family, and now, emotionally of him, shown by her projecting upon him the power of a tempting devil instead of a human co-conspirator? Could he appear gratuitously sadistic, moving past causation – like a perfect storm? And he sinks her into the sea where she will drown and be dead? Or she becomes a demon like him, in some vampirish co-conspiracy? The ending is too catastrophic, too abrupt, too out of scale to be credible on any linear scale. Shall we give the ballader poetic license for the sake of a violent thrill?	The transition between one inner state and another is made ungracefully and abruptly, and the narrative "accounts" for it, but because of its irrationality, reveals the subject as energetic and trauma-bound. We are looking at the scale and distancing of dissociative process, which probably gains some kind of release, but not resolution. I see the suddenness and violence of the sequence here as cues to treating this sequence at some absurd level not as real, but as systemic, prior to engagement with the outside world beyond the self-system which holds these ecstatic and depressed sequences. It is a process which each partner of a couple must bring to their neighboring interface as they begin some (any) kind of intercourse, here characterized as an oxygen-depleting submersion.
66	The fore-mast wi his knee,		
67	And he brake that gallant ship in twain,		
68	And sank her in the sea.		

Cautionary narrative

The anonymous poem/ballad "The Demon Lover" [*Taken mostly from Cleanth Brooks and Robert Penn Warren. Understanding Poetry, Fourth Edition. Holt, Rinehart and Winston, New York, 1976. ISBN 0-03-076980-9. p 27*] starts as a cautionary narrative for young girls, and maybe their would-be boyfriends, or young, more experienced adults, warning against the lures of sensual and material distractions, positioned against the necessities of conforming, non-adulterous life. We see how past attachments can still be overwhelmingly forceful; and how passion can lead to errors in judgment. The alluring lover appears to become demonic and brings the wayward mother/lover to an extraordinary demise. But what precedes it is a conversation which takes place every day in the motels of America, as Nabokov, Updike, and others have tragic-comically illustrated.

Our heroine begins to feel badly about leaving her children for the earlier lover/seducer and projects her guilt-syndrome onto the occasioning, triggering male; yet she does not own her own role in the seduction. As long as she thus projects and blames him for her activity, there is no hope for the two, even though the lover can show her good times, "where the lilies grow."

The situation is not one of sustained mutuality, which might be successful, but of a solipsistic dead end: the feminine part is not (morally) capable to take responsibility for her vulnerability and susceptibility, and so the so-called cruel demon, sadistically, tyrannically, dreadfully destroys the boat in which they sail, sinking it and her to some bottom of some sea. What happens to him is not made clear. A sort of blunt, commonplace morality tale.

A gestalt point of view

Yet from the gestalt point of view, some other insight may emerge. What we see is an inward drama which proceeds actual sexual intercourse or actual intercourse with the outside world and which must occur and be dealt with if any relationality with that outside world, sexual or otherwise, is to be established. Within one proposed partner of this realistic intercourse are all the ballad's characters, the abandoned children, the long-lost manipulative lover, the distractable anima, the rage-filled, abandoned, and disappointed lover, the masts, the boat. All this narrative must be raised and played out, even obliterated or majorly set aside before real exchange can occur. The final moments of the poem declare the dissociative momentum which propels the partner into connection with the Other, a connection about which we, the readers, know nothing.

We have to give up our manipulations, our projections, our fickleness before reality in the form of the Other (who is ultimately invisible in this poem, right to the end, where we could begin to look for its appearance) can be engaged. In some sense, this poem is this husband's occasion. The parallel dramas we enact between ourselves and our lovers demand that we know these inner dramas of each other as personalities, but our goal, reflected in song and story, is not just to play parallel, but to meet reality face to face.

The space between ourSelf and the Other becomes the slope for our intercourse traverse, and the domestic abandonment themes prefigure what it can mean to be alone. Without a solid identity based upon wholeness, and the energy thereof, nothing real, no action, can occur; we are left abandoned in mere activity. Though amid all this activity, of course, real conception of a real baby itself willy-nilly could and often does happen.

"The Demon Lover" can be seen to operate, or better, demonstrate, three levels:

1. an ordinary cautionary tale for young women (and men) about seduction and its subsequent motel variants, how quickly the hormonal impulse subsumes into Second-Shoe complaints;

2. a description of inner narrative which is inwardly real but not actually happening in the three-dimensional world – the story does not actually take place between two mind-bodies; and

3. a perhaps hopeful vision of a somewhat dramatic, perhaps trauma-based violence which presages the successful transition between inward plural activity and outward action. This idealized intercourse is preverbal, pre-image-determined, but the sequence of the transition out of complex trauma-based emotional memories or statements (primarily abandonments) into real interaction is here obscured.

Activity here, encapsulated and solipsistic, is not the same as action, which includes declaring the relationship between inward and outward in some kind of hopefully successful explication which promises what is real and how reality can be intercoursed with, or better, into. To read the poem narratively, one has to revert to moments of poetic exaltation which do not make literal sense, including the size of the demon, the vision of Hell, etc. All image sequences are comments on the partner's limitations engendered by projection, and upon the system's power to face reality without being hampered by our use of projection. Somehow, we approach the threshold of encapsulation and its dissolution, including reoxygenation.

Two signals

There are two signals that we may comprehend in order to move to the energetic level of the narrative rather than rest with the linear story.

1. The transformation of the lover into demon demonstrates how projection is used to answer questions about agency ("Who or what is responsible here for the rotten situation we are in?") and here projection has an animation-cartoon feel about it. Our heroine elaborates upon her lover's impoverishment and turns him into a devil: "You are evil, a demon for making me do this bad thing, and you did not keep your promise." This is of course not entirely true; "the masts of the beaten gold" do occur. And the story goes along with her elaboration.

2. The violence. Here violence substitutes for a realistic resolution of the problem the (inner) couple faces: how do we recognize that love is more than projection? In fact projection is or can be destructive to a realistic encoupling. How the disillusionment phase of adultery, occurring in bedrooms everywhere, gets worked through is a piece of information young people and old might best be warned about.

The final violence is unreal and characterizes a resolution which does not allow for growth and knowledge; it is fear-inducing, even terrorizing. Like Santa Claus, it misstates the truth with a spiritual monolithicism which shocks but here, does not illuminate. The final scale of the ship and the bodies is infantile and skewed. We may be able to see the abandoned husband from this vantage point.

Yet because the imagery is unreal, it states the presence of dissociative energies which truly are seeking immanent resolution, in their most gigantic, oxygenless forms. The violence is a sign of activity, not integrated action – perhaps the longing for, or the move toward wholesome action, but not completed. As such, its appearance throws us back to reevaluate the entire poem, as if the ending forces us to get new bearing as to its overall theme or focus.

This rebooting can occur in close reading of any lyric or poem, where a single element does not fit with what we thought was happening, and we are forced to go back to the drawing board in order that all the parts of the system are accounted for; here the gestalt drive toward unity of conception brings us to a place where we are satisfied that we have understood the poem's meaning, the hidden gold of gestalt organization.

We have to assume that this is the way the holder itself experiences them; though narratively cartooned, the poem is honest, and honest to the patterns, all of which seek dissolving, reoxygenating resolution. Here we can witness the implication of gestalt embodiment, when all the parts dissolve into pure energy. The spine ceases to have separate segments; the angels, the energetic flows, climb up and down freely on, in, Jacob's ladder.

It is access to this inner resolution which brings us our greatest sense of strength, from which we have our greatest flexibility with boundaries and our best hope for not needing the ordinary ones. We cease to need the Ten Commandments because from this centered place, we would see no reason to violate its prohibitions, nor advocate its proscriptions. We would merely Be, and in Being so, in so Being, be righteous.

With the gestalt strategy in hand, we can see that all the narrative parts can be witnessed as aspects of a single personality profile: the return of the lost lover, the self-pitying manipulation betraying a not-true evaluation of the truth, making the impulse to abandon quite credible, the yielding to earlier experience, the abandonments – including of the children by their mother, the discovery that passion is short-lived, the guilt and demonizing of self and other, the shame, the violence which provides an abrupt boundary, on the other side of which in reality dwells another, waiting, unknown person. If this is the husband's self-soothing fantasy, or his foreplay sequence, so be it.

All these incomplete phases co-dwell within whomever it is we are viewing, and all the parts are seeking resolution into some kind of integrity. Each interaction with the other person who does and shall remain (always?) nameless presents the developmental crisis all people and all people within a couple situation face, married or not. How am I going to see past my elaborations, my projections, my encapsulations, to apprehend the person I am with (including myself)? St. Paul proffers, "For now we see through a cloud darkly, but then face to face. Now I know in part, but then I shall know, even as I am known." [*1 Corinthians, 13:12*]

The violence in "Demon Lover" is disturbing because the resolution is not complete. There is no slowing down the inward exchange, only a snapped mast and a sinking into the sea. That is the best this individual can offer – a panic-dominated, fear-engendered, possibly rageful, perhaps rapacious, and unobservable oxygenless outcome, or the prelude to new system balance.

Again, the entire ballad could take place within say the interaction between a person and themselves, or between two heading for bed. For either, the entrance into an action-filled intercourse recapitulates the surrounding encapsulations, which have to be forgotten or moved aside, for direct connection to be successful. The moves into this world could be seen as adulterous, abandoning, isolative, encapsulated, and demonic – initially.

A glimpse

However, the gestalt also offers a glimpse of what it would look like if we reach the door of our house and step out to greet our significant neighbor. We can see what needs to be given up, sensually, what developmentally is rendered invisible. When we truly resolve a pattern, it is subsumed into invisible and fluid capability, and from that neurochemical site, we can engage from what can be called an adult position.

The gestalt approach shows the problem directly and indicates what needs to happen and what needs to be observed, because we see the separation and abandonment pattern(s) in their relationship to a whole. This is real information, not just analysis. It returns us to the problematic cloud of dissociation within which we attempt to find ourselves, and it identifies for both adolescent and adult a commonality of identity and humanity which invites discussion and the conveying of truth. If this is not what literature and the study of literature currently does, it could.

Gestalt implies boundary

I think what comes next is two-fold. In plays, tragedies, when the dramatis parts fail to render wholeness, we are left with stage-strewn bodies and some survivors trying to pick up the pieces and carry on. These patterns could not be resolved in a self-generating and thus permanent way: lesson learned. When the patterns involute and dissolve, connect in wholesome ways, we are also left with a full emptiness, a freedom which is a sign of resolution which returns us to preverbal (in both senses of the word) witness of ourselves and our world. Politically, our stalemates, distressing as they are, are real and prefigure resolution, if we know how to view them.

As I understand it, the gestalt perspective always corrals and describes the interior, and its premise leads us to the implied gate of unknowing and Experience. The boundaries of the unity become interesting, even crucial, for they state the conditions of the whole which then, by implication, interface with other "wholes". This condition is perhaps early stated at our journey from fallopian tube to the placental wall, and it continues in various elaboration throughout our lives. As every gestalt form has at its center Stillpoint, so it also implies an edge. And it turns out that edge is interesting and complex.

By language and imagery, we are drawn into our energetic core which only slightly if at all commerces initially with the language centers of the brain. We are grounded by the universality of our experience, specifically demonstrated. And the goal of experiencing our integrity is perceived by its inhabitants as realistic. It evokes an inner silence of Being, beyond desire and attachment, beyond narrative and ordinary conscient thought. (And perhaps we could upgrade the word conscient to mean, to include this inner silence, rather than just feelings and thinking thoughts.)

At deepest levels, this sequence may be what it means to teach someone how to read. It initially begins with a primitive decoding; and it leads to complex unraveling, and ultimately to enlightened Being. At the center of gestalt forms dwells Stillpoint, the core site of pure Being, and language and narrative can lead us to this site, though often they do not. We become addicted to their enthralling specificity.

Poetry as meditation

Can all poetry can be understood as meditation? What we want from poetry is for experience to be set down in non-anxiety-influenced clarity. Wordsworth could suggests that experience can be recollected in tranquility, by which he could mean without shock, without anxiety which clouds our focus. This insight is something we can agree upon, and it will enable us to witness the patterns which determine us, which dominate and render us slaves, indentured perhaps, to the some-time past. Under these pre-conditions, can we ever know what the present looks like?

If we free ourselves from the trauma-fixated past, and from anxiety, a series of clear, simple statements will emerge, in ourselves as individuals and in our society (in customs, laws, iconographic art, etc.) The patterns get declared and here is our dialogue:

> "Why did you do it [whatever]?"
> "I was afraid."

and

> "Why do you hold to this view of yourself?"
> "I do not know how to extricate myself from shock."

Years of analysis may come down to these realizations. And because we are compressed, poetry often reflects that compression, both positively and negatively.

Sometimes teachers of literature are so captivated by the language centers of the brain that words have a magical power to them, capable of generating feelings and commitment; so from that they work their way down to sounds and word order, and expression which includes at their best, preverbal levels of understanding.

The elevation of experience through words clearly dominates our educational forms. Yet often the verbal territories become rarified in a way which appears arcane and without essential, neurochemical-altering, grounded meaning. Meaning is wherein we experience gestalting action, not activity. And yet we predominantly teach to the cultural test.

We can get caught up in the narrative of our sexuality, and the way the hormones discharge urgently within these partial systems, and sometimes lead to held-energy systems resolution; that is the promise. But this ballad, viewed with gestalt insight reveals the partial nature of our actual intercourses, our sexuality, to use a corrupting term, and shows us that we have understood only partially what we are doing. That this abandonment can occur while we are creating children in what appears to be overt, straight heterosexuality, or the somewhat newly-gained ground of homosexuality, is of course God's way of in ensuring propagation; if not socialization. It does not matter where you come from, or come to, as long as a child is the result.

The violence in the ballad speaks to the urgency of the oxygenless pattern seeking resolution, which under the experience of sexual arousal, may increase. What this ballad can illustrate (not because it is a great poem but because these points are illustrated within it) is that we misdefine our (sexual) intercourse, Self and Other sexuality by setting laws to it. Under the current rubrics now fashionable, we are invited, appropriately, I think, to see ourselves, and others, as on a spectrum of variations, as to erotic activities and predilections.

I see at least one other level of understanding beyond this current strategy. Poets, more than the philosophers, but they too, intuit this realm of consciousness, grounded in energetic dissolve and free-flowing movement in the brain system. It is the basis of our drive for freedom, individuation, and centered anxiety-free calm, hallmarks of integrity, a living breathing reality, of pure Being. Again, the angels climb and descend Jacob's Ladder, and they float above and below and through its chordate rungs.

A pattern which we can recognize

When we are discussing our sexual behavior, we do not want to exchange data merely upon shared narrative. "The Demon Lover" demonstrates a pattern which we can recognize, perhaps almost universal in its collected aspects of development therein recapitulated, but the intercourse only truly begins at the end of the poem, and somehow amid the violence.

Violence is a sign of the territory but also is sign of the dissociation seeking resolution, and beneath that, the energy, which classically in literature at least, exposes fear as well as excitement. And the promise of concluding the interfering patterns. We somehow bring, or better witness some part of us bringing the patterns to a halt. Of course, in real life narrative, such activities lead to real and retraumatizing results, with an entire history of human endeavor filled with futile and destructive behaviors wherein nothing is experienced or learned, and souls leave the battlefields of the bed and of the Somme hardly satisfied.

Our sexual intercourse, urgent as it presents itself, seems both natural and organized, when in fact we do not, perhaps cannot understand it very deeply. Its experience is preverbal, its seizure caused but hardly voluntary. Its completion, a lesson in organicity and dissolve which lives immanently in every moment, even in every existential unity. To use the term sexuality to describe this energetic is to be hopeful as well as limiting. Our instruction to youth can be through example, more than through rationalization. And, as trusted Others, we best may ask questioning youth, "What do you see?"

CHAPTER NINE:

MORE POEMS AND THE GESTALT

A Pattern Which We Can Recognize

What the gestalt insight – better, function or even capacity – shows us is that our activities are based upon, within, and above energetics; and it reveals an urgency to dissolve at every point the encumbrances of dissociative systems within us, their ununified, skewed and jolted carriers. We seek to return to the light.

Aristotle's definition of tragedy applies here, but from another angle, namely that we are tragedy, the tragedy we study, explicating itself as a series of shock patterns seeking resolution. We return to the goal of unity, our first diploid setting where we experience our oneship, Being. Tragedy is when the pattern that's destroying us has nothing to do with us; it's about the transmission of patterns across the boundary between Self and Other. Thus, haply, all interactions are projective and dissociative, until they are not. All identities are projective, until they are not. Each personal, tribal, national identity must return to God, *i.e.*, the unknown, not the known, *i.e.*, projective, *i.e.*, dissociative God.

In relationship, we marry our projections until we give them up and seek to see and meet the Other, not just the Other in Ourself, though that, too. There are a couple of corollaries as we approach this line between our energetic and the Other's. One question we, as trauma systems, do ask is, "Are you with me (us) or against me (us)?" We also ask, "How will we recognize ourselves and each other?"

And we establish diplomatic relationships which allow for trust between two wounded systems which contain held-energy systems, both systems seeking resolution. And we engage with the same reality when we decide someone is not a lover but an enemy; for all the good it does, our declaration of war might as well be written on a valentine: from a gestalt point of view, the same reality confrontation is at stake, and engaged.

Energetic boundaries and boundarylessness

The resultant "masochism" behind declaring war radically includes the insight that by seeking an enemy we are seeking to self-destruct. We might not have to go further than that. We can choose not to be someone's enemy. Every provocation will skirmish into police mop-up. Do we need to drop our imperialism, personal and national? Our international service to the world may be to provide stabilizing presence in order that the earliest "civilizing" traumata can resolve. And to that end we may narrate physical and social improvements but not confuse them with progress, which would include increasing appropriation of an internal, luminous center of Being – enlightenment.

The idea of Civilization has included at least two polarities: the collective gathering of objects, instrumentations, institutions, memories, and ideas serves the dissolution of trauma; it is what people who understand trauma do and are. Being civilized means having acknowledged the resolved trauma patterns and creating a world and world view which has a certain consciousness and resultant order arising from the freedom established therefrom.

Yet from this perspective, civilization is also the collective garnered trauma forms prior to their acknowledgment and resolution; civilization is both accomplished and pending. Thus civilization as an idea or set of experiences functions as a collection of energetic problems and their resolutions. With this understanding, if some nation or civilization nexus has a chip on its shoulder, or seeks to bully us, we can only turn away and refuse to play in that destructive native fashion.

In the history of World War II, for the Japanese, surrender becomes one phase toward assimilation of the chosen enemy. If you make us your enemy, one risk is that win or lose, you will end up absorbing us, and our ways. Is that the best thing for you? Crucial to the playing out of such trauma patterning in war is its ending. We may be surprised to discover that surrender may not mean saying ultimate uncle; it may be negotiable. For the Germans, who were used to past European war games, ending the war conditionally was very much a part of concluding it. From within a gestalt trauma model, however, there is a drive toward complete resolution of the held-energy pattern, including a dropping away of its narrative and the return to Being. This can be imaged as a place of energetic transcendence, and includes narratives of promised bliss, sacrifice, resurrection, solutions which are final, etc.

For the Japanese, surrender did not mean acknowledging cruelties; nor did it mean giving up industrialization, or its industrialists and their ways. Nor did it remove the authoritarianism of the gestalt formulation of a single personality incarnating an entire tribe – the emperor. Under MacArthur's supervision (a modified imperialism they were not unfamiliar with), Japan's business leaders resumed shortly as if the war and their unconditional surrender meant nothing. The top guys were mostly killed off, leaving the not-so-second-level industrialists, with a significantly modified political (and implied personality) structure.

In spite of these possible connections, it is hard to sense how civilization as an idea relates to trauma and trauma resolution. Certainly in the arts and architecture, major cultural achievements address inroads on the perpetuant, messy world of trauma; for Minos, the Labyrinth myth elaborates upon self-understanding, if in its earliest forms it did not promise or achieve meditational Being. It has been noted by some critics that the art historian Kenneth Clark's television-lectures on what civilization is ends up with Clark, in effect, declaring himself as the measure and template of the concept: "If you want to know civilization, look at me, its perceiver and embodiment: the (predominantly Western) civilized man."

Civilization involves defiance against the intractable impactions of trauma, and moderate freedoms therein; civilization fulfills and stabilizes the daily vicissitudes of resultant neurotic behavior. Civilization reflects and accounts for or shelves the experience of shock and promises situations of transcendence. Civilization meets and creates the necessities of life which sustain as well as divert us from the influence of shock.

If the gestalt perspective gives us partial access to the energetic of held-energy systems, can we view the artifacts of literature to help train us to see where to focus energetically to allow real transformation to occur in a sustainable way? In some manners, we have to accept the strategy that straight narrative levels of perception are not enough to warrant transformation; more has to be engaged.

We shall now turn to another, famous poem wherein I think these issues are enjoined.

Stopping By Woods on a Snowy Evening

Whose woods these are, I think I know.
His house is in the village though;
He will not see me stopping here
To watch his woods fill up with snow.

My little horse must think it queer
To stop without a farmhouse near
Between the woods and frozen lake
The darkest evening of the year.

He gives his harness bells a shake
To ask if there is some mistake.
The only other sound's the sweep
Of easy wind and downy flake.

The woods are lovely, dark and deep
But I have promises to keep,
And miles to go before I sleep,
And miles to go before I sleep.

Robert Frost, 1922

Here is a schematic of the poem:

Commentary on Stopping By Woods on a Snowy Evening

LINE	ORIGINAL POEM	TRANSLITERATION	GESTALT COMMENTARY
1	Whose woods these are, I think I know.	One standard narrative approach is that these woods are owned by someone who lives in the village, a neighbor whose ownership would be known by everybody in the village, including those owning land plots not directly adjoined to their home or farm.	From a gestalt point of view, the poem declares a dissociative truth. These are Frost's woods, legally owned by him; in this stopping moment, he loses "possession," and discards it as a strategy. We view an existential awareness of his own identity, separate from ownership, and his capacity to drop "ego" possessiveness of the world, including the property he is witnessing.
2	His house is in the village though;	There are some who would suggest the owner of the woods is God, but the placement of God in the village rather than out here in the woods seems problematic: God is everywhere, not just in Its Self-Concept, which could be an idea or point of focus of social thought we might experience in a (village) church or in religion.	The above gestalt strategy reveals this line sequentially appropriate, not paranoid: who would object to someone looking at their property, unless they assumed such behavior strange and a sign of trouble ahead? Yet what the poet seeks is interior permission to watch. Perhaps here there is some recognition of dissociative process.
3	He will not see me stopping here	Why is this line here? We are not in the town or city where stopping outside someone's house for a time might bring the police.	The division continues, between the issue of property ownership and the place of Stillpoint as a confident replacement of that owning grid. Wherein do we get the permission to watch, particularly in our dissociative awareness? This is a significant "permission" issue which takes us beyond ordinary witness.
4	To watch his woods fill up with snow.	This is the main narrative goal, restated and elaborated.	There is nothing more really to do here. In the meditational place of near Being, we can only watch.

LINE	ORIGINAL TEXT	TRANSLITERATION	GESTALT COMMENTARY
5	My little horse must think it queer	The animal may "express" the concern of its owner and, if you are intuitively connected with horse intelligence, its own, namely that this is an unusual, odd – out of regular parameters – situation. Grammatically, the author grants that it is the horse's concern, not necessarily his. He is merely describing what he knows his horse does (and thinks), though his understanding may have a projective quality. Even in this descriptive moment, Frost's persona strategically includes being separate and empathically linked to the horse.	The animal part of the system notes the oddness of the activity. We are entering what for Frost, as a narrator persona, is perhaps uncharted territory. Even if we own the land itself, does that give us permission to watch it? Or even see past our usual perceptual preconceptions to some more essential truth? Can we move through Pollan's default mode network toward a greater Innocence, and sustain it?
6	To stop without a farmhouse near	This seems an ordinary landscape description. The sense of trusting in the moment involves a decision which the horse does not process; it's cold and its cues are set off: let's not freeze out here (is my driver asleep or dead–or has my watch stopped?)	The meditation successfully takes the narrator (voice) into the possible center of a trauma site, with the perhaps ancient risk of death, of freezing. Possibly we are witnessing an arrest of the narrator's consciousness process. At some level, this Second Shoe may be what the High of witnessing anticipates.
7	Between the woods and frozen lake	This seems an ordinary landscape description, a differentiating siting, as it were.	Here is an energetic landscape, including the frozen lake of traumatic process. Frost pauses between these two crucial sites. Brain scans for Stillpoint. The inciting High is the decision to stop, already a central position within enlightenment process. Enlightenment here means successful dissolution of the held-energy system, so that clear vision can be achieved.

LINE	ORIGINAL TEXT	TRANSLITERATION	GESTALT COMMENTARY
8	The darkest evening of the year.	"The darkest evening" suggests the December Solstice, a turning of the relationship of earth to sun. The night, whichever, is the darkest, a reminder that we are in cold, rarified mood frame. We may be at the cusp of dissociative process, just prior to a lightening.	By stopping, or trying to stop, the temporal environment triggers the as-well dark trauma site, darkening into even, shall we proffer, black. Here Frost narrates in approximate form the held-energy system below or within the pristine natural landscape.
9	He gives his harness bells a shake	Frost's scan reveals some deoxygenation, some turbulence.	The system cannot easily sustain the watchfulness mode; this apprehension is interior and somehow is warranted from the outside as well. The "horse" knows that it is sensible to realize day is ending, and that brings winter risks best avoided.
10	To ask if there is some mistake.	The system is communicating challenging held-energy.	There may be some apprehension of where this free moment is taking its "holder". Right from the beginning of the poem, we are aware of apprehension about whether or not we can do what we are doing.
11	The only other sound's the sweep	The energy is experienced as soft and unthreatening. We are at the peak or center of the meditation.	This is a breathscape, carrying us deeper within, somehow without anxiety – even soothing; a return to the generating High, experienced in breath.
12	Of easy wind and downy flake.	Parallel to the exterior landscape, the energy is light and free – a high. The energy is soft and unthreatening. This is the peak or center of the meditation.	This is as close to pure Being or Stillpoint which, in this poem, Frost attains, and he describes it accurately within the surround of a traumatic environment (within), cold and dark and frozen, and juxtaposed to the woods, with which he no longer identifies. The triggering occasion drops away, and we are in new inner territory, wherein there are no recognizable ego-possessive markings.

LINE	ORIGINAL TEXT	TRANSLITERATION	GESTALT COMMENTARY
13	The woods are lovely, dark and deep.	The meditation is on its way to conclusion. The situation is summarized.	He holds the glimpse of reality for just moments, a High which is soon interrupted by the appearance of trauma patterns as well as "reality".
14	But I have promises to keep,	The transition is from isolative Being to one of Heran, relational reality.	The issue of promises include social reality but here describes the time transition between the witnessing High, and its Second Shoe, the completion of some trauma energetic, here narrated in the form of obligations.
15	And miles to go before I sleep,	The persona is tired, somehow aware of further moments.	The transition word "and" reveals the comfortable transition to another level of awareness.
16	And miles to go before I sleep.	The line repetition, which some readers have suggested, correctly I think, that sleep equals death, means the simple turn toward home, the village, and bed suggests that the promises will be kept until the life, a place of New England responsibility and care, is ended. By repeating the line, the camera dollies back for the long shot, of a widened horizon. Frost playfully criticized this perhaps death-wish interpretation: "The poem has nothing to do with death;" but at other times he admitted to the theme of immanence which would include death as a part of his concern, if not actually wishing for the end of promises in a life which included a lot of bad, tragic stuff.	With gestalt awareness, the repetition is a way of acknowledging-capturing the elusive importance of the transition within the self, between the High and the triggered trauma. In this sense the poem is classically American, and part of the meditation tradition designed to interiorize the High of the New Eden. Setting off into new territory, the promise is that the new settler will have the strength to master the corrupt and unresolved (European) patterns of dissociation by careful witnessing, not only of the exterior reality, but of the interior reality, which process also can be witnessed. In "Stopping," we see the interior forms gather toward and at the doorway of intercourse with the (tragic) world.

Juxtaposing

In Frost's "Stopping By Woods on a Snowy Evening", we have a tranquil meditation, juxtaposing two worlds, the village and the woods. The village is equivalent to the world of Hera, responsibilities and social commerce – promises. The woods are the world of an almost-stilled Zeus, moving quietly, filling, but basically in hover mode. We have slowed down the anxiety ("He will not see me stopping here"): we are in a slow motion phase.

Frost encompasses both mind-sets, if you will, and links them with the hard-edge ordinary transitional word "But" ("But I have miles"); what we wish for him is that he could have both worlds in some less abrupt way: "The woods are lovely, dark and deep, / And I have promises to keep." We could have the world of Being and the world of becoming and doing, not strictly juxtaposed. But in the poetic syntax of the poem, too many "ands" turn the finale away from such kind of possible grace.

From a gestalt point of view, each part of the poem (holographically?) states something about a whole personality, the woods, their owner, the witness, the horse, the harness bells, the snow, the frozen lake, the village, the wind. The most prominent aspect of this perspective is the persona of the owner of the woods, the narrator. They are his own woods ("Whose woods these are"), and in this moment he does not connect with the world of ownership, which is part of his village persona.

Here is a potentially socially radical insight. Perhaps we can tolerate, even abandon the idea of ownership in the meditative moment, even when our animal nature of habit shakes against the cold surrounding Stillpoint. Frost raises the question of what we are permitted to witness, even simple snowfall; this question perhaps frames an inward process which is not merely the purview of poetic awareness. We are negotiating toward a rare, unrepressed inner freedom.

For gestalt understanding, the fulcrum of the poem may stand at the conjunctive word "But", and it provides us a vision of both Frost's moral limitations, and his hopeful rendering of the pattern which needs smoother energetic resolution. It coincides with a Frost tendency to word-play, here at the spelling of "woods", which can be rendered "woulds" as plural subjunctive ("Whose woulds these are, I think I know"); the poem becomes a more direct, even playful statement of procrastination, moral (theological) resistance, postponement; and the focus upon Stillpoint, at the center of all gestalt systems, wherein there is no movement, no restriction of movement, no need for movement.

Still stopping

Frost describes the still center of his meditation, but he can hold it only for a while – it cannot stay. The system brings forward patterns for resolution which are stated as promises, which means unresolved patterns which can be resolved, *i.e.*, promises filled. My guess is that Frost does not have a firm sense of how those patterns, now evoked in stillness, will resolve. The ones of darkest evenings, including depression, have not. The fadeout for me is that rather than staying longer in the cold (the cold a sign we may be near the bottom of the traumatic pattern, but not out of it), the harness bells are given a shake, and Dobbin starts movin' again.

Throughout all the commentary about Frost's implied death wishes and the like, we can remind ourselves that he reports (variously) writing the poem on a hot summer night when he roused in the middle of the night (or shifted gears having stayed up all night writing another poem) and almost trance-like (fatigued), conveyed the poem to paper. He is the recording secretary of energetic process, and as artifact we can do with the poem what we do, just as he has done. His comments may help us arbitrate its meanings, but we are the holders of these poetic systems patterns: any systems we can recognize are ours; and the best Frost could say in response to our musings is, "I merely set the patterns down. Some times I can see issues of balance and consistency and even meaning, and sometimes that results in editing changes. Often I cannot see what I write. Often, witnessing involves going toward a deeper than usual level."

The ending aspires to a dissolve, within the return to Heran world realities, including the linguistic capacity to voice and keep promises (a statement about the future) in time. From a held-energy system perspective, Frost approaches the High of Stillpoint within a system which is dangerous, isolative at worst, cold and frozen, not to mention lovely. He can find Being even amidst the cold and apparently tranquil landscape, but his concern with witness involves a question of loyalty. Which can he sustain, Being or the held-energy systems which are coming forth for resolution in the form of promises. Why ask for more when we already have enough? Here may be a New England accommodation toward trauma resolution.

One more point. If Frost as poet and persona, sees the possibility of witnessing the Stillpoint of Being by stopping his active, distractive mind, he may intuit such an arresting High will trigger the death-like cold of the held-energy pattern adjacent to it. He anticipates a meditator's existence, where the productivity and life-sustaining vocation may be challenged because he cannot fully integrate it with being recognized (or recognizable – "he will not see me") and paying his bills. Like his horse, he is stirred by native anxiety, and there is in the system being described both the longing for solitude and the inner inability to sustain it.

He may be on the edge of held-energy systems awareness without the reassurance that such a viewpoint has a resolution, one he has been seeking for a long time. Perhaps he sees the way in which his writing is about the held-energy systems with which he is living – a kind of skewed and simultaneous and subjunctive projection upon the real (outside) world of narrative and image and situation. And that the resolution of the pattern must take place at the energetic, not just at the narrative level, including the development of recordings of this relationship in writing poems, which so far hasn't quite worked to bring the patterns into resolution, even at his age.

He comments upon this issue in, among others, his poem "After Apple Picking." The gestalt becomes not just a concept but an experience which may separate out the trauma from its current attempt to declare itself upon the current moment. Frost may find the task too difficult, the solitude too confounding, the image in arrest not sufficiently indicating where to focus. "Stopping By Woods" might thus become a vision of subtextual randomness, wherein solace is sought, idealized, and thwarted, and the search is avoidant; Frost goes on for miles until he sleeps, without holding, even knowing, the Being center, approached from trauma's gates.

The realization of death may carry traumatic import for Frost; he knows a lot about hard-scrabble New England life and death. The recorded longing for cessation which accompanies insight about Stillpoint seems clear enough, as is the New England hardiness which gets up after pausing to go back to work. As poet, however, his deeper concern may be about the lure and danger of Stillpoint. Stillpoint triggers forth some next near-death pattern in which life is involuntarily "coerced" by shock to survive. Separating this crucial sequence out (a poet's task) may reveal a sense that Frost may not personally be able to sustain the freedom which comes from trauma resolution, a freedom hinted about as singular, devoted, and isolated ("He will not see me stopping here"). There is too much romantic detail and presence of others for Frost to give himself that freedom. His imagination, which takes him so, so far, also restricts his sense of Being. And can't be stopped.

I know it will seem as if I am proposing a Trauma Energetics reading upon this old and beloved text – way past ordinary exegesis. But increasingly, I find that the discovery of the energetic and its symbolic declaration in narrative is not limited to psychology or psychiatry; it has been a purvey of poets and thinkers who examine human experience since the beginnings.

The sequences are simple, yet because of their shocky weight, they are also formidable. Someone who sees the source of the patternings from which his poetry arises and sees the possibility of resolving them into silence, and radiance, may ask the crucial question, "What follows resolution?" Frost may be offering the traditional hardy answer, at the expense of deeper healing, deeper vocation, and deeper discipline.

At some point, he himself proffered that he forms the last two lines of "Stopping" because he liked the first and couldn't think of another line, so he repeated it, and it sounded good to him. An important, I think, idea.

Plural to singular

To encounter the movement from plural to singular, from *pluribus* to *unum*, is revolutionary and at times thrilling. It is like finding a legitimate, uniquely brain process, for it takes us to a sense of our power to discriminate reality within the reality which appears so variegated, even fleeting. The movement between singular and plural and back again renders an encompassing perspective, a bicycle we can ride.

In order to approximate the state of Being, we can reduce ourselves to a focal point of awareness, of the present tense. Where we begin with a (cognitively approximated) mass or density, signaled by a single word, what we find is a series of unexpected levels of differentiated experience: vanilla, chocolate, strawberry, pistachio. When we look at human experience, we discover that adolescence extends far beyond and to other levels of depth than has been heretofore perceived. As a result, we notice segments and sequences which may have been experienced in the past, but not elaborated upon. As a culture, we give ourselves permissions for young people to experience different levels: openly witnessing, our definition of what is possible changes and enriches.

An important aspect of the scan of anxiety is that therein appears to be no Stillpoint visible or manageable; trauma determines. The way out of this "illusion" is by stopping, or attempting to stop the process, establishing Stillpoint within the experience of the brain. The discovery of silence, both inner and outer, is crucial and characteristic of this energetic task as is the tolerance of witnessing reality in its manifold layeredness: gazing and ruminative.

If we can eliminate anxiety from our current experience and from our memory, we shall be able to see to the Being center which we seek to know. All roads lead to this Rome. And, to be witnessed, Being must be slowed down, trauma dissolved and integrated, for this to happen. This is no mean accomplishment, for most of the time, we cycle through the patterns and repeat them, perpetuate, be predator upon, rather than experience something serious and new.

Frost takes us into the problem of stopping, and shows us why we cannot rest, or rest for very long. The integration of the (ultimate) site of Being with the rest of our turbulent trauma-intruding is iffy at best. And for Frost, it suggests a vision of spiritual rest which is like sleep, which it is not.

What do we get to when we get to Being? That's our goal, particularly if it is hidden. But the stillness it supposes seems like a stopping or an arrest, even though that is not it. But the Stillpoint also allows us to see reality clearly – why not? And with that mind-set, we can see the anxiety which surrounds most of our activities and our perceptions, not our actions, which, latterly, are few.

Then we can see the layers we have not witnessed or been able to apprehend even in the most rudimentary ways. The time of war expands and particularizes, the time of assassinations expands and particularizes, the time of adolescence expands and particularizes, the time of orgasm expands and particularizes, the time of cancer particularizes and expands. Empowered by the ability to bring each particle into its wholeness positioning, we can go further, go subatomic, go God.

Being radiates, distributes evenness throughout the system, raises and sustains Higher vibratory states, mellows and intensifies, clarifies to awe. Pausing, systemic stopping, may take us closer to the judgment-less destiny.

The Insusceptibles

Then the long sunlight lying on the sea
Fell, folded gold on gold; and slowly we
Took up our decks of cards, our parasols,
The picnic hamper and the sandblown shawls
And climbed the dunes in silence. There were two
Who lagged behind as lovers sometimes do,
And took a different road. For us the night

Was final, and by artificial light
We came indoors to sleep. No envy there
Of those who might be watching anywhere
The lusters of the summer dark, to trace
Some vagrant splinter blazing out of space.
No thought of them, save in a lower room
To leave a light for them when they should come.

Adrienne Rich, 1986

Here is a schematic of the poem:

Commentary on The Insusceptibles

LINE	ORIGINAL TEXT	TRANSLITERATION	GESTALT COMMENTARY
1	Then the long sunlight lying on the sea	These first lines set the context for the significant (social and personal) gestures to follow. The image has the sunlight placed upon the sea surface.	While there is possible wordplay echoes of "lying" and seeing, the context is one of "baked" relaxation and preparation for a transition to another state or states of awareness.
2	Fell, folded gold on gold; and slowly we	The sunlight falls as the day is concluding. "We" initially means a minimum number of four individuals, two couples.	"We" encompasses a complex system which, as gestalt, may be reducible to a single person, or a single moment within a so-called single person.
3	Took up our decks of cards, our parasols,	The beach day has been one of traditional, structured – and unstructured – pleasure and relaxation,	
4	The picnic hamper and the sandblown shawls		The parasols and shawls may suggest some of the party are, during this time, women.
5	And climbed the dunes in silence. There were two	a sun-numbed recreation at the seaside. One of the couples,	The poem hinges here into a division of activity, two and two.
6	Who lagged behind as lovers sometimes do,	most likely lovers, peels off from the other couple	The separation is graceful and sequential. There are no "scenes". Brain narrows its focus into pairs, four into two, two into one.
7	And took a different road. For us the night	heading for a loving occasion separate from the homeward-bound couple, for whom getting to bed and to sleep is the primary objective, not trysting. Their road is seen as "different" from the first couple, moving	Here is the narrative pivot of the poem, where the parts are declared as separate, while the ensuing elaboration on that difference clearly indicates a parallel and deep understanding of the whole by the narrator's voice. This is the energetic fulcrum of the declared problem of the poem, the finality for the first couple or individual calling itself "we", as they conceive the night. This line is the first plank of the juxtaposition created in the poem which contains rigidity as well as accommodation, and, later, ultimately, crossing-over compassion.

LINE	ORIGINAL TEXT	TRANSLITERATION	GESTALT COMMENTARY
8	Was final, and by artificial light	into the confines of the civilized, electrified beach home. The indoor couple thus concludes the day, isolating somehow from the recalled intensity of experience of passion, projected upon the second, outdoor couple.	Here is declared the separation of the two couples, two aspects of a single personality, the one based in Heran stability, the other, Zeusan (see line 10).
9	We came indoors to sleep. No envy there	The first couple comes in to go to sleep. They are perhaps a more settled, older couple (or have been a couple for a longer time), past the enthralling lure of erotic neurochemistries of the younger (?), urgent pair. They have their satisfactions well in hand, not envying the wandering lovers. The expectation of feeling envious is presented and dismissed, perhaps realistically, but indirectly, the lovers still remain the focus of the author's awareness, and	"No envy" expresses both the truth and its denial, a compromised acknowledgment which restates the first occasion of the juxtaposition (see line 7), with its tone of certainty and finality. As involving an held-energy system, the narrative is reversed: the sensuous High evokes an apparently stabile fixed, and artificially lit (trauma-site-apparent: final) accommodation to ordinary reality. We may witness a serious interface which most poets might not think important; but, with Rich, I do. The transitions, the implied and declared boundaries, the specificity of delineated and differentiated reality become vividly poetic because of their implied gestalt process of unification.
10	Of those who might be watching anywhere	who are described in general terms as they love, a witnessing process shows the power with which that system forces itself to center stage, juxtaposing with the High with its finality and no-envy positioning. There is a bluntness here which may be a hallmark of residual shock and is referred to in the title. And like Frost's "Stopping", there is some special sense of witnessing – what is being seen and by whom?	Here passionate and ordinary coexist, without judgment or repression. There is no personal specificity, but the lovers, like lovers everywhere, are witness to a more universal process, specific and casually arising out of a dark field of happenstance awareness. There is no anxiety in their witnessing; nor in the narrator who witnesses their loving imaginatively. From a gestalt point of view, the self may "divide," and there is a residual sense of plurality to the process of witnessing. Here, I think, for whatever reason, the poet is isolating the imaginative vision in order to recognize the ahistorical quality of orgasmic experience. She is also hinting at some trauma-determined opaqueness in the system. The repeated two-ness of the poem evokes a (gestalt) longing for oneness: amid the separations with which the held-energy system (artificial) is characterized as simultaneous with the ecstatic.

LINE	ORIGINAL TEXT	TRANSLITERATION	GESTALT COMMENTARY
11	The lusters of the summer dark, to trace	which includes emblazoning passion (lust), watching some,	Tracing here suggests a witnessing but also the participating following of
12	Some vagrant splinter blazing out of space.	falling star blazing out of space, a vivid and compelling image which includes shooting stars as well as love-rapture and orgasm, experienced as a wandering seizure occurring like something out of a nothing and spacious context, both important and not so important in the universal scale of things.	orgasmic experience, again "some" indicating its universal nature, which comes upon us in some way surrenderingly and, ultimately, unwarranted; and while amazing, is also randomly selective and, curiously, impersonal and not site-specific, or perhaps site-obliterating. The interface of the High and its emerging trauma site coming hard upon becomes the focus of the poem, narratively reversed as they seem. Poets take ordinary situations and demonstrate special ways to focus on them.
13	No thought of them, save in a lower room	While the thoughts of the home couple ("We") about the lovers have already occurred, rather vividly (and perhaps not so final?), the lovers are set in a distanced context, not as an occasion for arousal or mirroring, but more matter-of-factly dealing with helping them,	The division is restated, setting up the final bridging gesture of the narrative. "Save" is a somewhat old usage, evoking a past which may have been repressive (in the old Christian, or for that matter Jewish world, such lovers might not be witnessed or helped out). The lower room places the light (in the mind-body) "below". It is an ancient, classical division between upper and lower, which shall be connected and healed. Mythically, the lower room may refer to the Easter sequence where Jesus conducts his Last Seder. The possibility of envy is again addressed through a distancing statement which sets up the final gesture, which
14	To leave a light for them when they should come.	with the aid of a (lower room) light, to find their way in the dark, so safely and directly, they can come home.	is one of empathic compassion, juxtaposed wryly with the final word wordplay. It may also be read as a wistful view of the perhaps "non-experienced" disconnect between the High and its immediate neurochemical aftermath. The finalists help, as best they can; and, with gestalt perspective in hand, we may sense that within our neurochemical limits there is more to reality than we can grasp.

Two worlds

In her brilliant love sonnet "The Insusceptibles" [*Adrienne Rich. Collected Early Poems 1950-1970. W.W. Norton, 1993. ISBN 0-39-3034-186*], Adrienne Rich similarly juxtaposes two worlds, again the Heran grouping of regular, sleeping commonplace reality, and the Zeus realm of passion. The latter is characterized as beyond sight, potentially disorienting, lusty, and passionately orgasmic: "vagrant splinter blazing out of space". Apparently, there are a minimum of four characters, the two who are lovers, perhaps newer or younger, and the older, first pair, who do not respond explosively to the evening ("For us the night / Was final").

As in "Stopping", the Heran world is one of electric light domesticity and security of daily schedule, and the Zeusan awareness is the natural world of passion, which operates universally and "anywhere"; it is limitless. The boundaries between external and interior are relatively secure in both "worlds", yet within gestalt concerns, the question is how are these two worlds reconciled? Unlike the "But" abruptness of Frost's combining, I can see Rich's narrative as a moving statement of empathic compassion; the two realms of awareness are allowed to co-exist. The older couple leaves a light at home when the lovers, disoriented by post-orgasmic bliss and the dark of night, should have to find their way back to the beachhouse where the four are staying.

Another reading, perhaps simultaneous with this one, is the somewhat hidden appearance of the trauma site which appears after the sensuous High, though it is narratively staged as precedent. Maybe Rich does not know which comes first; the thing she is describing is systemic, and sadly dissociative, with a mere thread of light connecting both neurochemical stages. She does identify the dissociation with the crucial shock-referent words "final" and "artificial" and "envy".

Erotic and mundane

Yet here may be a transition between the erotic and the mundane which is also wholesome, grave perhaps, mildly wry, knowing, and generous. There is no irregularity to envy, if there might be some, and of envy; the older couple is satisfied and satiable. Or perhaps, reading the title in a dark way, they can only be hospitable; they are (hormonally) invulnerable to passion;

they just need their sleep. Somehow there is satiability in the system. Or paradoxically, separating out the erotic simultaneously shows how quickly dissociative trauma sites coexist with our passionate involvements.

The lovers are also insusceptible to the world of regularity. They separate out from a perhaps judging and mundanely structured existence. As a system and a gestalt, the working out of the accommodation between the two basic modes – passion and order – generates a viable inner security which makes the issues insusceptible to corruption and influence within a single personality. Furthermore, if this poem is historically formulated within a so-called lesbian sensibility, it encompasses the deeper issue of accommodation within two modes of experience, order (finality) and passion, rather than at a more superficial level of judgment, including judgment against lesbian or against general sexual experience altogether.

If the characters are all women, they give each other permission to experience the night. If the characters are mixtures (of gender or of gender types), the same permission is given, personal and social, juxtaposed to a world which can and does repress sexuality, no matter of what variety, at the expense of witnessing a deeper, more organic truth. The ball is in the reader's court as far as assessing how much gender-bending can occur between people and within a single personality: I find the quarry pool is complex, multi-vectored, and very deep.

There are two levels to the significant and recurring boundary issues raised by this poem. If the boundary is energetically experienced as strict, absolute, final, and insusceptible to influence, the one side with the other, that is one kind of boundary. Any chasm-crossing bridge which follows is the beginning of a blend which may be difficult to sustain because of traumatic patterns emerging hard upon such a triggering High.

The other kind of interface, and one which is beginning to occur in this poem, is energetic and radiant, not apparently fixed. This boundary is enlightened because it provides a significant trusting strength in the face of repressive arbitrariness which for example instructs a two-year-old brain system, "No means no." If we are enlightened, we can move beyond ordinary understandings of separation, and our inner reaching from one attitudinal mode to the next suggests this is the mistake-less direction or capacity we may grow into. As involuntary seizure, the orgasm may partially model this radiance, but as we know, orgasm by itself does not necessarily bring about total sustained psychodynamic and characterological transformation. It may merely report this presence and possibility.

The important line, "For us the night was final" may reflect an historical pattern of adjustment *vis-a-vis* sexuality and coupling, perhaps repressive, perhaps not. The entire system presents itself, but may not come to a boundaried edge of pattern completion, wherefrom the patterns dissolve into boundary-less radiance. As noted, this transformation is what the orgasm promises, but frequently does not sustain; we are momentarily transformed, but we detumescently return to ordinary Heran realities. Thus the off-rhyme of the last couplet is I think deliberate, with the implied slang spelling of the word "come": "come" means to "come home" and to arrive, as well as here, to pheromonally, hormonally, seizurally complete. This is a resting place, as conclusive as the older couple's "final" night; it celebrates the importance of the neurochemistry of orgasm – it cannot be ignored until it is ignorable, *i.e.*, integrated. Its blazing climax and cessation are grounding moments, encompassing Zeus and Hera. One is reminded of Shakespeare or Donne who similarly link slang words to the transcendent sacred, the mode of description appropriately carrying the dissonant as well as the harmonic. Rich's final line takes my breath away.

One further point. There may be only one functional couple in this double pair, and what we can see with the help of gestalt insight is that the passionate and the ordinary can compassionately co-exist, within one couple or within one person, even though one portion seems thoroughly "domesticated". Or division between people or groupings involves a tolerable, "good-enough" repression, called boundary itself, though the very idea of boundary is complex and often contains paradox before it evolves into radiance.

The political and social implications of this (neo-Freudian?) vision for ordinary society may be profound; the potential for strict repression ("For us the night / Was final,") serves nothing if we close our eyes to our experience of love and of passion. To compassionately support that latter environment even from a place of satiation no longer involved is a wonderful goal and, as Rich shows us, is inwardly quite possible. Furthermore, if we view the poem as a meditation/description of potential traumatic resolution, wherein the held-energy system coexistingly appears separate from the (dune and night-obscured) orgasm, the intercourse is taking place by the older couple (or the divided self), separated out from the passion and hidden Other, whose joining with this dissociative shock-intrusive state is accommodant and stark, but hopeful, maybe.

Armed with the flashlight of held-energy systems awareness, we can view the poem as holding both time-zones, both breath-zones, in compressed juxtaposition. Which comes first does not quite matter, but their simultaneity does. The poem is written as a description of an inner state of partial resolution. With full resolution, perhaps there would be no poem, only preverbal radiance; and/or the achievement of the poet is to lead us up to the pattern site where we can experience the movement into Being.

The light, though artificial, as the transmitter of information, may be an initiating step up and out of the disorienting dark. It provides a focal point upon a social and personal (and universal) gap – a perhaps gerrymandered transition – which, usually insusceptibly invisible, we can see. No healing will occur if we don't witness the dissociative, insusceptible pattern at this site-specificity. Having hung out with the pattern as long as she has, Rich means business – the business of seeing the entire pattern resolve. And the last word of the poem has the last word.

a man who had fallen among thieves

a man who had fallen among thieves
lay by the roadside on his back
dressed in fifteenthrate ideas
wearing a round jeer for a hat

fate per a somewhat more than less
emancipated evening
had in return for consciousness
endowed him with a changeless grin

whereon a dozen staunch and leal
citizens did graze at pause
then fired by hypercivic zeal
sought newer pastures or because

swaddled with a frozen brook
of pinkest vomit out of eyes
which noticed nobody he looked
as if he did not care to rise

one hand did nothing on the vest

its wideflung friend clenched weakly dirt
while the mute trouserfly
confessed a button solemnly inert.

Brushing from whom the stiffened puke
i put him all into my arms
and staggered banged with terror through
a million billion trillion stars.

E.E. Cummings, 1926

Cummings' poem elaborates on the Jesus parable of the Good Samaritan as follows:

From King James Version, Luke 10

And behold, a lawyer stood up to put him to the test, saying, "Teacher, what shall I do to inherit eternal life?" He said to him, "What is written the law? How do you read?"

And he answered, "You shall love the Lord your God with all your heart, and with all your soul, and with all your strength, and with your mind; and your neighbor as yourself."

And he said to him, 'You have answered right; do this, and you will live."

But he, desiring to justify himself, said to Jesus, "And who is my neighbor?"

Jesus replied, "A man was going down from Jerusalem to Jericho, and *he fell among robbers*, who stripped him and beat him, and departed, leaving him half dead.

Now by chance a priest was going down that road; and when he saw him he passed by on the other side.

So likewise a Levite, when he came to the place and saw him, passed by on the other side.

But a Samaritan, as he journeyed, came to where he was; and, he had compassion, and when he saw him, he had compassion, and went to him and bound up his wounds, pouring on oil and wine; then he set him on his own beast and brought him to an inn, and took care of him.

And the next day he took out two denarii and gave them to the innkeeper, saying, "Take care of him; and whatever more you spend, I will repay you when I come back."

Which of these three, do you think, proved neighbor to the man who fell among the robbers?"

He said, "The one who showed mercy on him."

And Jesus said to him, "Go and do likewise."

Luke 10:25-37

Here is a schematic of the poem;

Commentary on a man who had fallen among thieves

LINE	ORIGINAL TEXT	TRANSLITERATION	GESTALT COMMENTARY
1	a man who had fallen among thieves	A man who had been attacked and abandoned by thieves	The story is easily identified with the initiating quote from the parable of the Good Samaritan (*Luke 10:25-37*), see above.
2	lay by the roadside on his back	lay at the side of the road on his back	The beginning of a hapless, hopeless portrait of a passed-out drunken, marginalized man.
3	dressed in fifteenthrate ideas	dressed in the unstylish clothing, probably of a down and out streetperson or its intellectual (dishevelled, disorganized, not current) equivalent	I find this inclusion of "fifteenthrate" crucial to the development of the final movement of the poem. Fifteenthrate means not first rate by a long shot. Cummings compresses the words for emphasis, including perhaps self-satirically: raw life continues to overwhelm his poetry, which barely catches the essence which eludes him when he paints with words. I see in this rendering Cummings' strong spiritual drive.
4	wearing a round jeer for a hat	wearing an unfashionable and provocatively defiant (lower-class) hat.	There is some sense the man is wearing a hat which defies the abuse and humiliation which as a "wino", he would experience from people on the street who see him and who judge his decidedly unfashionable self-presentation.
5	fate per a somewhat more or less	The background for this sorry, probably chronically repeated scene, is now wryly explained. As if by a force as grand and inevitable as fate, the drinking begins without intervention by the man or by his environment. The use of "per" lends the story a quasi-official, quasisatirical tonus. We join the narrator's pleasure in telling us a narrative which we see and think we understand.	In traditional approaches to addictions, non-addictives may say that the drinking is a sign of characterological weakness, remediable by will and faith. With addiction, there may be a deeper alliance to a masochism which seeks resolution sequentially but never structurally, institutionally, within the psyche.

LINE	ORIGINAL TEXT	TRANSLITERATION	GESTALT COMMENTARY
6	emancipated evening	This phrase is an euphemism for a drinker's "emancipation," echoing its determined and addictive nature, far from freedom and far from the vividly revolting portrait to follow.	Bergler writes about psychic masochism which creates patterns of denial in the form of defensive addictions. For the chronic addict, the proclaimed freedoms are anything but that.
7	had in return for consciousness	Again, the clinical or refined reporter's diction, soon to be contingent with repulsion.	By the elevated word usage, Cummings satirizes the degraded situation so the reader may assume a superior attitude, which will be radically reversed at the end of the poem.
8	endowed him with a changeless grin	"Endow" is a high-falutin' term for being knocked out, either by the drink or by the mugging thieves. The grin is involuntary and a sign of the depth of violation the poor fellow has received.	The parable exegetics usually focus upon the victim's experience of violation, not on his initial, pre-mugging vulnerability. Cummings knows the complexity of addiction and victimization.
9	whereon a dozen staunch and leal	Again, the arch syntax obscures and reveals the parable's lesson. A group of citizens, upright and loyal ("leal" lends a tonality of old-time Scottish-Celtic values, soon to be forgotten). Cummings trusts the common people to reveal themselves as shallow, insensitive, and prone to rationalize away humanity's suffering.	
10	citizens did graze at pause	These "citizens" (ironically labelled) act like cows or sheep, pausing to view the human disaster.	
11	then fired by hypercivic zeal	Then internally fired up by having to do something more important in the service of society, as a defense against the hopelessness and degradation of what they are witnessing as well as their unwillingness to get involved.	
12	sought newer pastures or because	They seek other places to "graze", or because – a nicely consistently ironic rhyme with "pause" –	Cummings juxtaposes the refined and the vulgar.

LINE	ORIGINAL TEXT	TRANSLITERATION	GESTALT COMMENTARY
13	swaddled with a frozen brook	There is the locked momentum of cascading debasement, swaddling echoing positive maternal (Biblical?) support, here now absent,	
14	of pinkest vomit out of eyes	which climaxes here, including the visualization of the details, anything but poetic (how many poems have these words in them?) The victim's eyes are	
15	which noticed nobody he looked	disembodied and dissociated, dangerously fixed, the following phrase	
16	as if he did not care to rise	rationalizing, denying his desperate unconscious state.	"Rise" prepares us (theologically, certainly spiritually) for the movement and serious action to come.
17	one hand did nothing on the vest	The camera moves across the scene with some sense of sadness, perhaps absurd delight of schadenfreude.	Cummings is visually vivid and his focus precise.
18	its wideflung friend clenched weakly dirt	The syntax is reversed as is the decency which is being challenged. The mention of friend, disconnected, separated and weak, echoes the abandonment theme of the parable.	The use of "friend" as in that of a helping hand, here weak and absent, is, I think, deliberate. It echoes the initiating question of the parable.
19	while the mute trouserfly	The hapless groin, silently covered and exposed, indecent,	
20	confessed a button solemnly inert	paradoxically, religiously, declares the stasis of the moment, comic and tragic.	

LINE	ORIGINAL TEXT	TRANSLITERATION	GESTALT COMMENTARY
21	Brushing from whom the stiffened puke	With an arch, arcane sentence formulation, the narrative continues to repulse as the hero, the "I," begins to relate to the grotesqueness of the recognizable yet impossible situation.	Cummings capitalizes "Brushing" to signify an important shift in moral focus. The gesture is compassionate, as is the careful correct usage of "whom".
22	i put him all into my arms	The narrator (here identified for the first time) takes up the entire victim, and cradles him in his arms, perhaps evoking a pieta or early parenting trope while keeping significant distance with the perhaps objectifying, distancing verb "put."	Throughout his career, Cummings does not usually capitalize "I", thereby reminding us of the danger of ego-and self-grandiosity, as well as how naming something as complex as oneself by the word, or letter, is potentially a fool's errand. If we are going to bring serious moral attention to some experience, we at least must take "ego" out of our reckonings.
23	and staggered banged with terror through	He staggers carrying the burden he has just picked up, taken on. We know from the parable, that he is the Samaritan who will supervise the healing and enhancement of the life of the put-upon bum. This is a terrifying responsibility; it has none of the shallowness of what precedes it in the poem or in the usual readings of this parable.	"Banged" refers to the heart-knocking terror which may come when we take responsibility for someone else, or, in this case, also of ourself, including the (our) viscerally offensive, detailed attributes.
24	a million billion trillion stars.	In a spiritual vision, he moves a huge distance, to the ends and beyond of the universe, to the limits of existence.	The parable describes the social truth that we can help ourselves and the world when we follow our heart's compassion for those who have been afflicted. But here, Cummings does not make the victim merely inconvenient, airbrushed, as it were. Here the victim is addictively self-destructive, and chronically so. The pattern is absurdly unresolvable, which magnifies the task of taking responsibility for the suffering in the world we witness. Responsibility is in the details; it is particulate. And from a gestalt point of view, the victim is the "degraded" self of the Samaritan himself. As poet, Cummings continually faces the limits of what he is doing, the ways in which language and syntax are "fifteenthrate" in comparison with the truth he attempts to record, or respond to, or convey to an often language-confounded audience.

The bruised "self"

From a gestalt point of view, the victim is the bruised "self" of the Samaritan himself. As poet, Cummings continually faces the difficulty of what he is doing, the ways in which language and syntax express but also conceal the spiritual essences of his – our – experience. As an artist who paints as well as writes, he is aware that his "ideas" are fifteenthrate – here perhaps clever – but for a straddler of both the verbal and the non-verbal realms, they hardly match the task, which I consider to be for him relational, spiritual awareness.

The traditional lesson of the parable is that we wisely follow The Golden Rule and take on the difficult care of others – as we would be taken care of. Our reward will be the spiritual expanding of our vision beyond the ordinary limits of personality, tribal affiliation, identities, and categories; herewith we can glimpse the universality of the humane application/response to the question, "Who is a friend? What is my relationship to the suffering of my fellow man?" With The Golden Rule in hand, we may approximate the preverbal state of Being. The Golden Rule becomes the first door we pass through from Being to the manifest outside world.

In the history of the spread of Christianity, it was the universality of the applications of the essential spiritual insights, traveling from person to person as well as most significantly within the individual – the equality of the energetic characterized by gestalt insight – which had tremendous direct challenge and appeal. Here, in Samaritan, we have a demonstration of the problem of responsibility stated within the Hillel rabbinical tradition "If not us, who; if not now, when?"

If we perform acts of compassion but we are not compassionate with ourselves, we have missed an important point about action and integrity. And our misunderstanding may compromise our real experience of righteousness, no matter how good we appear or do. Integration occurs when we go the extra, universal mile, here with ourselves, not the easy, or easily given to, or easily supported self (Self). Essential throughout our world cultures, The Golden Rule has an obvious social meaning, but it also has a shadow side. We do to others what we do to ourselves, which includes abuse.

Because we are in traumatically-founded stages of dissociation, we convey our patterns outward, until we do not; then we may experience a high radiance integrity of Being, which can socially manifest as compassion. Jesus is watchful about this final stage of soul transformation and enlightenment, something that his audience in its self-righteousness and rigidity – dissociative defenses – might have trouble recognizing, much less manifesting. It is sometimes hard to be friends with ourselves.

It is easy to conclude our Good Samaritan meditations with what I could call sentimental good-doing; and those who read this poem might have difficulty rationalizing the ecstatic star vision Cummings concludes with with ordinary good behavior. Yet the dissolution of sentimentality means seeing that the usual reading of the situation, no matter how gratifying or important, may repeat an underlying trope, which can include a masochism within the person experiencing the compassion.

Edmund Bergler claims that our "unconscious conscience" is more horrid upon ourself than the worst villain: if we did to others what we do to ourselves, we would be put in jail. And he proffers that we are engaged with this function defensively, until we are not. Cummings makes the victim and its condition repulsive, as if the usual understanding will not show us the real situation and the underlying factors involved when we do good as a defense. In our process of help, we may have the possibility of reworking our entire relationship to this sado-masochistic "superego" within ourself: we put him all into our arms.

Though so far as I know not an alcoholic (nor a non-ambulatory street-person) himself, Cummings sees the repetitions, in his writing as well as in the unthoughtful, unmindful, humanly dissociative environment; and, son of a sermon-delivering minister of integrity that he was, I think he wants the repetitions dissolved, concluded. His love poems traverse such dissolution. I see him wanting the entire system, including the agency of judgment, reworked. Then the transcendent truth can be witnessed, our freedom experienced. Repeatedly, his poetry shows us the problem and often intimate solutions.

Finally, Cummings inhabits a world tragically limited, where coming together with another person, delightful and satisfying, may be rare. Prejudice and ignorance are the rule. When, as it were, there are two people in the room, they are both flawed by traumatic holding, by dissociation. If this is the default, then coming out into a clearing into the space between the two is a possibility, if not the (only) task both face. Watching the trauma sites dissolve is ultimately (erotic and) sacred, and transcendently ecstatic. I think Cummings' father would understand.

Gestalt strategy

One of the pleasures or satisfactions of gestalt strategy is the universality of its importance. It reminds us of the systemic development of situations we are observing. In Snow White, in the disintegrative aftermath of escaping the tyrannical, toxic, life-threatening stepmother, Snow White seeks refuge with the seven dwarves and duplicates the mothering process which has abandoned her, and she restoratively becomes a good mother to the dwarfs. Simultaneously, she recapitulates aspects of herself (sleepy, bashful, etc.) representative of a whole. She remothers the seven attributes of her self, in small-adult forms, the beginning of her maturity. Though losing two mothers (good and wicked step-), the good mothering pattern within her can be relocated and transferred to other situations.

And, as has been pointed out, the cruelty of the step-mother is probably an infantile elaboration on abandonment, not the fact of the real mothering, which may include extraordinary devotion as well as ordinary life with flawed benefits. Perhaps like the Garden of Eden, we approach the mother from the back door of memory, then based upon this historical process, we re-elaborate upon her (and Eden's) characteristics in further encounters within the world.

In "The Wizard of Oz", there are numbers of gestalt forms, but among the most significant is the five-some who dance down the Yellow Brick Road: Dorothy as the nominal head, the three divided (self-proposing) selves, and our natural animal part, the unconditional dog Toto. The system has to confront the flawed humanness of the Wizard, express the sadness underneath the vicious and lonely Wicked Witch and resolve into unconflicted unity.

In "Hamlet", the important bedroom scene with mother and son [*III.4*] demonstrates the integration problem of the developing adult. As he hormonally matures, teenage Hamlet comes into an awareness of his parents as real people, not just as idealized icons. The double aspect of the father, ideal and wonderful, and his replacement, the power-hungry, queen-lusting murderer of the ideal image or introject. Hamlet holds both portraited aspects in his hand and asks his question of the Queen, "How could you go from this to this?"

Seeing the father in both ways needs to be held together in the child before he can accept the responsibility of becoming an adult; and this integration is personal and inward. Interestingly, Gertrude does not answer her son with, "I do my best to see my husband as a whole person; knowing what you now know about yourself, what's your best shot at the same problem? After all, you're heading to be his royal successor."

Parenthetically, *Hamlet* seems all about gestalt awareness and its place in adolescent identity. At its core, Hamlet addresses primary concerns about being alone ("Now, I am alone."), about self-destruction ("To be or not to be"), about hypocrisy (Are you honest?") and holding twin realities simultaneously ("but yet I could accuse me of such things that it / were better my mother had not borne me" – he knows he is potentially Claudius as well as Hamlet Sr.), all of which are part and parcel of our move into unified adult consciousness and identity. That the narrative of the tragedy is incomplete, with only Horatio and Fortinbras as the surviving elements of a toxic system ("something rotten"), says something about Shakespeare's limitations as well as his mastery of the problematic processes of developmental integration.

In Orson Welles' film version of "The Magnificent Ambersons", there is a similar bedroom confrontation between the son and his mother about the two versions of the father. Here the mother stands up to the tyrannical, bullying son and says that both versions (Wilbur, the legitimate husband, and Eugene, the concealed lover) love, have loved her. Strictly speaking, Wilbur is not included in the love trajectories of this interpersonal system. George, the encapsulated son, confounded for perhaps the first time, says, "But you're an Amberson (you can't participate in such complexity – where is the faithfulness which I require to have a stable home?)."

"Yes, George, I can," the now-rising Isabel replies, and George, deflating onto his mother's bed, responds, "I don't know, Mother, I don't know." It is an Oedipal moment of some power and vulnerability. By contrast, it throws Hamlet's pyrotechnics into an hysterical light; Hamlet's anger and vengeance are avoidant, which Shakespeare has illustrated by the "incorrect" killing of the manipulating "diplomatic" and apparently desire-limiting father Polonius, yet another father. In *Hamlet* there are six father killings, including the final one, Hamlet's – as father to his own self, the self-creating self.

The gestalt allows us to see that the murder of King Hamlet is infant internal and follows the laws of infantile internality. Like children's stories, by power of an increasingly myelineated nervous system, the idealized good mother is killed off or dies and is replaced by the reality-based wicked stepmother, another stage of our understanding of our mother's position and power. If we are to grow into (and past) our image of her, the primal image of the mother must be transmuted. The Ghost of King Hamlet advises his anxious son about the emerging mother imago, "Leave her to Heaven." [*I.v.86*]

The Odyssey

Gestalt forms can be approached in closeup subgroupings and long shot overviews. Don Quixote and Sancho Panza, Holmes and Watson (and Moriarty and Mycroft), Abbott and Costello, Tonto and Kimosabe, The Marx Brothers, The Three Musketeers (significantly 3+1), King Arthur and the Round Table, The Hardy Boys, Jesus and his disciples (?), Astaire and Rogers – all illuminate.

The *Odyssey* demonstrates a full gestalt as the Odysseus portion goes around the world, while simultaneously at every point in every day of the ten-years separation, Penelope characterizes a pattern of weaving and unraveling her father-in-law's shroud, which activity keeps developmental issues at a point of *stasis*. Both parts are concurring in the course of the same (each) day and together make up the whole; which Homer, and we, do not bring together until the final stage of the narrative.

If we were to dramatize the *Odyssey*, we would split the stage and one side would show the itinerant picaresque life of the hero, with his accompanying plural Seamen. The other side, Ithaca, would demonstrate the loom, Penelope, and Telemachus, with its plural Suitors. From a gestalt point of view, both sides declare themselves simultaneously; it's like patting the top of our head while rubbing our stomach. What happens to Odysseus away, occurs simultaneously day for day, in Ithaca, with its repeating advancing and retreating patterns.

I always wondered how Odysseus would lose so many of his Seamen in one episode after another, and yet he always has Seamen. For me, the answer is in the gestalt substructure of personality described by the Odyssey. The hero has plural forms, just as Penelope has plural suitors. The praxis does not take place until the relationship between the many and the singular, between activities and action, is made manifest. Odysseus returns singular, disguised as a beggar. With the help of his son Telemachus, he strings his old bow, closes the door locking the suitors in a singular space, and he slays the plural forms of self which are threatening to decimate his estate. As unitary, he now addresses Penelope.

Again, the ten-year return of the traumatized warrior could take place with Odysseus literally already at home in Ithaca, the narrative being an inner accommodation to his dissociative state which takes a decade of inner time to resolve. The significant sequence of the epic becomes then the point where the repeating pattern, quite visible now, floods itself into completion. The next moment after the resolution of the trauma is the mind-set of unknowing and the unknown.

Only when the humble wandering beggar part, now unitary and without his associates, driving toward gestalt unity, returns to slay the plural aspects of himself, the near-overwhelming suitors, that some further action/movement can occur. Odysseus reunites with his son and wife, and then after a time, is able to meet the future with full strength, walking inland (inward) carrying an oar on his shoulder, waiting until someone asks, "What is that for?" We thus understand what it looks like when we are in the site of enlightenment: our questions are basic and simple, generated from beginner's mind, as it were, a full explication of the relationship between Innocence and Experience.

We move to a new level of consciousness where enlightenment is possible and immanent. We can see what we are looking for, in simple complexity. The final mind-set of the *Odyssey* takes us to the edge of implied encapsulation raised by every gestalt form, to the doorway of our personality house, from which we can confront openly an unknown and unknowing Other. It is a restatement of beginner's mind or its equivalent – and it is past judgment.

This gestalt insight does not mean that we can only have singular identity; colloquially, we can be and are plural, at many levels. It is just that when in dissociative process the two modes become separated or a-relational – as wide apart as the Mediterranean Sea – that trouble can be discerned. The inner space between the two modes begins to interest us and initiates the healing, integrative process. Prior to this twinning site, we are in isolation, prone to solipsistic elaboration and a resultant inability to witness reality.

Like Oedipus, whose past is significantly characterized as separate from his present, the reunification process is immanent and painfully necessary, as the Oedipus portion declares: "I must know it all, / must see the truth at last." [*Sophocles. Robert Fagles, translator. The Three Theban Plays. Penguin Classics, 2000. ISBN 97801 40444 254. p222, 1168-9*]. Can we comfortably move from our plurality to the unity of gestalt insight easily and without obstruction? Gestalt strategy encompasses this insight: both poles, if you will, fire simultaneously, and without both poles firing simultaneously to anchor us (if you will), we pull crooked.

Plato's "Allegory of the Cave"

One of the most significant Western texts is the Allegory of the Cave, from Plato's *Republic* [Plato. *The Republic.* Benjamin Jowett - translator. Dover Thrift Edition, Dover Publications, New York, 2000. ISBN 0-486-41121-4. Book VII: p177-183]. Here identified is the life-objective of enlightenment. I find enlightenment in this text and elsewhere means attachment-free consciousness with the resultant clarity in perceiving reality and experiencing our human place within that. I also think this state of Being is concomitant with what has been termed Beginner's Mind; it is pre-Edenic.

The Allegory contains a linear narrative which begins with Prisoners facing a cave wall upon which images are cast.

> Behold! Human beings living in an underground den, which has a mouth open toward the light and reaching all along the den; here they have been from their childhood, and have their legs and necks chained so that they can not move, and can only see before them, being prevented by the chains from turning round their heads. [*Republic, p177*]

One Prisoner is released from his shackles, turns around and for the first time sees that the images [he] had thought were ultimately real are in fact produced behind [him] by a fire and puppeteers holding objects whose shadows are cast upon the cave wall.

This turning process of truth-garnering continues in some sort of repetition until the Prisoner finally exits the Cave and perceives the outside world and ultimately sees the Sun as the Source of all things.

Currently, I have tried to accommodate to what I find are the crucial elements of the Allegory by ordering its structure in the following way.

The Allegory divides our (summary) confrontation with the environment/world into three parts:

Position 1. The Prisoners in the Cave, facing an eternal (damnation, as a spiritual equivalent) characterization as victims of illusion; its equivalent is trauma-induced dissociation. They do not comprehend where they are. And

Position 2. The transition from **Position 1** to **Position 3**, the movement of the Prisoner upward and out. In terms of garnering, garnered insight, I find this middle part the most interesting.

Position 3. The world above (outside of the Cave), which characterizes our inner state of achieved enlightenment, of Being. When we are outside the Cave, we can see what is true and essential; we are "masters" of reality, though mastery here implies a relational-with, as opposed to dominion-over mind-set.

As Prisoners, once we realize that there are hidden (and interior) constructions which move and titrate our presumed, imprisoned experience, we turn from our enchainment and by various cognitive, developmental, structural, abstractive strategies move up the Cave and out to witness the form of all strategies, the Good. The Good is a kind of resting place beyond doubt, beyond paradox, where Being is experienced as *the* point of arrival as we attempt to master reality and its apparently multifarious, plural features. I find that we must remember that Being is a neurochemical state as well as a meditational site, and that to convince our primitive, survival brain that this place in our experience is of some, if not essential significance, and that we can "lose" it, is not easy. It may be part of Plato's awareness as salesperson of this enlightenment as well as how to frame this discipline to a distracted and distracting (self) environment that he terms it The Good.

> Whereas, our argument shows that the power and capacity of learning exists in the soul already; and that just as the eye was unable to turn from darkness to light without the whole body, so too the instrument of knowledge can only by the movement of the whole soul be turned from the world of becoming into that of being, and learn by degrees to endure the sight of being, and of the brightest and best of being, or in other words, the good. [p180]

In its gestalt unity, Being encompasses and transcends plural and singular. **Position 2** characterizes the transition period between ordinary narrative forms of awareness and our perception of the energetic, which allows us to perceive our purest information as radiance, the Apollonian sun – mirrored in our interior energetic as Source. This is **Position 3**.

Perceiving the Sun as the source of our human experience is an idea we still hold to, in more astrophysical detail; we acknowledge that the earth and all its glories come from the Sun. Though now we would be interested in wherefrom comes the Sun. From a meditational point of view, inner light emerges when brain takes out its fixed trauma held-energy forms which prejudice and limit our experience.

Socrates begins the Allegory

Plato has Socrates begin the Allegory with what I call **Position 1**, wherein individual "Prisoners" are living nominally ordinary lives based upon the images they see on the wall of the Cave, in fact shadows cast by objects held by "puppeteers" who move invisibly in front of a fire. The Prisoner-individuals are imprisoned by chains so they cannot turn around to see the causality of the image-phenomena cast upon the wall. This portrait is one of dissociation, or unconscious process. As has been noted, the Cave situation structurally duplicates our current experiences in the spaces of movie theaters. We Prisoners watch the narrative screen/wall of the Cave.

Position 3 is the goal of an achieved level of awareness for brain systems process moving toward enlightenment, the state of pure, unattached Being. If we ask ourselves, "Whatever on this planet are we doing?" Plato's answer could be, "Moving toward enlightenment." My sense is that this goal is embedded in our cells, which at their optimum yield the capacity for full "self-knowledge" – both in performance and in awareness, at whatever level.

The movement toward enlightenment has an enflowering soul momentum; the gestalt problem is how to bring the two states, **Position 1** and **Position 2** together so this goal can be accomplished.

Incidentally, or not so incidentally, I think the "soul" refers to our first and compelling awareness of ourselves as unitary, at conception; this conviction orders and remains as the guiding principle for who we are, no matter how many times and how many ways we subdivide. When we talk about soul, we are talking about this organizing principle/entity, our (zippered) unity. Though embryologists may have differing estimates about real-time between the zippering and the first division, inner time for our first cell may be mythically quite flexible and variant.

It may be important to acknowledge that embedded as it is in the larger vision of The Republic, the Allegory serves to bring a rubric for training of leaders for society, in the case of 5th Century BCE Greeks, an aristocracy of spirit and intelligence. It would seem this enlightenment stuff is not for the masses, any more than Athenian democracy is for the masses, though the masses are effected in a direct and trickle-down way by enlightenment in their leaders. Only a small proportion of males are given the vote.

Yet it may need to be stated that people of all sorts who read the Allegory come to the realization that it describes the human condition, not just an elite class of men. And as a potential, its applicability densifies into every living person. And in a democracy of whatever scale, the person who votes needs to be enlightened, if the vote means anything; every vote-caster plays a leadership role. To lead and to guard for the common wealth, the person in charge must account for what all parts of the society experience and be able to resolve the emergent issues by envisioning the society as a whole in some way that individuals are whole.

The painful turning

Initially, Plato describes the painful turning around of the **Position 2** Prisoner and the way it initially discovers how the images are caused. Facing the images on the wall, then facing the fire behind, the Prisoner approximates/ senses a twin reality which is resolved with causation: that causes this. The Prisoner perceives the fire light originally behind it, which dazzles its eyes; but it becomes acclimated to the new complex reality of two time-senses: its imprisoned, immobilized state, and the opportunity for movement. We are transmogrifying from the dissociative two-dimensional consciousness of shock-induced compression into three dimensions and human reality.

Generally **Position 1** has been seen to characterize unexamined ordinary consciousness, which then gets challenged – and transformed.

In terms of held-energy systems, **Position 1** can be understood to describe the impactions of trauma which determine and fix our perceptions of the truth, inner and outer. In this portion of our be-shocked chemistries we cannot change our perspective; we are locked in, and we *create* social relationships with other similarly-bound creatures, setting standards, witnessing achievements based upon an imprisoned consciousness, trauma-based and memorialized.

As Pollan notes, recent research about the so-called default mode network suggests that much of our perception of the world is primarily predetermined by our library of the sensed past and that we dip into only a very little of fresh stimulus, only the smallest bits of triggering "exterior" information to get through the day. Much of the illusory nature of our perceptions comes from the fact of projection of these earlier evaluations and sensations upon the current real world. We run our engine of awareness upon the tracks we have already laid down.

Somehow, however, a deeper structure becomes cognitively, energetically available, and the Prisoner turns around – the equivalent of 180° – and is confronted with a twin, apparently contradictory reality: **Position 2** is now more fully understood, as is **Position 1**. We could argue that until the turn,

Position 1 has not been understood at all. In **Position 2**, we are at the site of juxtaposition, wherein one reality integrates with its "paradoxical" opposite, a transition initially difficult, painful, yet ultimately promising movement and light.

Position 2 describes the transition of Becoming into Being. Because Being may be considered beyond ordinary historical awareness, it is also the point where historical consciousness becomes active, because it enables a true understanding of causality, which is tied to light, and is (therefore) energetic. It (re-)sets an inner priority of the soul-movement toward light.

I think such movement tells a lot about birth and death process as well. Prenatalists like William Emerson suggest that when the birthing baby's forehead confronts the mother's sacrum, it must radically turn its head to the left or right, and in doing so, as a spinal reality-information, it acknowledges the mother as a creature of life and death as well now as her baby. The child is given permission to live and to die, as is its mother. We move, progress as straight, and we turn.

Why begin where Socrates does?

Though the Allegory has a narrative beginning, what I find interesting to ask is why begin where Socrates does? What, psychodynamically or energetically occurs just prior to the vision of Imprisonment? The Imprisonment has all the qualities of a trauma form, an held-energy system. It characterizes the shock memory as a rigidity, an immobilization. There is some realistic functionality maintained, for the prisoners converse, evaluate: though it resembles death, we are not dead yet. So the **Position 1** (Prisoner's) Vision bridges ordinary social dissociative process with the original sponsoring shock neurochemistry, which is more frozen. And the Prisoners do not complain of their limitations because they do not see enough of their condition to know them.

What happens before

Plato, with Socrates, does not tell us how we get into **Position 1**, our Imprisonment. He only shows that it is possible to depart from our immobilities. What happens prior to the Imprisonment must include some higher vibratory state, which triggers or prompts the appearance of the site(s) of impaction. Even to see the chains and fixed gaze which Socrates describes is an achievement; a resolution process has begun. If we cannot "see" the pattern, we remain victims of it and its default position in our presumptive narrative: the curse of so-called unconscious process. From a TE perspective, we might begin our meditational focus with the Prisoner's chains or the blinders.

The Allegory is a sequence which describes an healing process, ending with a clear mind and reality-based, unattached state of Being. This sequence applies to the individual as well as to the social awareness of communities of individuals. Perhaps paradoxically, Becoming, with its implied vector of neurochemical and energetic movement, is moving quite simply toward Being, and moving is quite simply resolving into Being. Becoming settles down, expands, and rests, only not exactly. Amid stacks of defenses and illusion, Being is real.

As the system "heals", adjusts to the new realities with a concomitant reduction of shock, the movement is slow and, though arduous, basically steady. Plato does not parse a back and forth movement as the Prisoner moves up the floor of the Cave to the outside world, but he accounts for it.

> And suppose once more, that he [the Prisoner] is reluctantly dragged up a steep and rugged ascent, and held fast until he is forced into the presence of the sun himself, is he not likely to be pained and irritated? When he approaches the light his eyes will be dazzled, and he will not be able to see anything at all of what are now called realities. [p178]

As the held-energy system gains oxygen and movement, gradually **Position 1** becomes more peripheral. Brain scans upward. The trauma site is reduced in its shadowed fixity, and it is replaced by increasing light, of the fire (including inflammation?), and then of the ordinary daylight; and finally the direct sunlight itself. All of this movement is energetic, and, if you will, spiritual. As healing sequence, it is a journey of the soul, toward Source, as witness and participant. Our journey-sequence restores the priority of the soul, an instrument of light.

We could suggest that there is only one "movement", from **Position 1** to **Position 3**, and that the upward journey to the top of the cave and beyond is a function of the repetition of the initial pattern. In TE sessions, we note in circle-forms, like stars (a gestalt assembly of repeating points), that they are often made up of recurring patterns, sequentially declared, and our objective is to perceive the pattern in its most simple aspect. Sometimes we get movement from observing only one of the points of the star.

The final characterization of **Position 3** is about Being, a contemplative state approximated by Stillpoint. Informed perhaps at least by our natal experience, we become creatures of light, which is something we have intuited about ourselves long before. We are our trauma until we are not.

The next step

With Glaucon's prompting, Socrates acknowledges that individuals achieving this state of awareness will have difficulty living in the "real world" of trauma-based dissociative consciousness, and of Becoming. They will be ridiculed or worse, by those who cannot fit these enlightened "souls" into their cubicles of understanding.

In addition, Socrates acknowledges the necessity of mastery of both aspect/realms, that of energetics as well as practical three-dimensionality; as evolved: "here they must be made to descend again among the prisoners in the den, and partake of their labours and honours, whether they are worth having or not." [p181]

From a therapeutic or even humanistic standpoint, the goal of integration means the juxtaposition of the impacted trauma sites with those portions of the neurochemistry which are "enlightened", *i.e.*, those portions where reality can be perceived as light. Plato indicates that the process of enlightenment may have breakthroughs, but that there is a continuity of attention which must be prepared to embrace the juxtaposition between two body-time states, **Position 1** and **Position 3**.

This returning connection

It is this Prisoner-returning connection which signifies gestalt understanding, for the portions of the self which are imprisoned must find a means to turn around. This is not a mere political activity; it is the basis for righteous, serious action. But as a combinant identity, the philosopher-king means gestalt, namely that the two elements must coexist in order to bring our human systems, both three-dimensional, external social, and internal personal, into balance; all devices – images and discussions and rationalization – bring us to the crucial site of Being, which transcends cognition(s) and words.

We could suggest, with Plato, that The Republic is directly concerned with justice, and has a lot to say about failures and successes; but as the idea of justice includes resolved paradox, so one could endlessly pursue the apposite poles of such paradoxes. Justice implies unitary resolution, and Being is experienced as without paradox. At some point the idea of paradox separates out from the experience of paradox, just as the idea of justice separates out of the experience of justice. Both experiences are foundation hallmarks of serious action.

Grounded in a gestalt understanding, the famous Allegory reveals a vision which is developmental and evolutionary. It is about healing, and it is tragic in structure, based as it is on an initial characterization of shock, and its offspring, projection. Energetically, it is preceded by a not-mentioned "High", which triggers the appearance of the so-called beginning Imprisonment phase **(Position 1)**.

It shares a similar structure with another "myth", the Garden of Eden, which posits an idyllic state which triggers the appearance of the Fall. I think both sequential narratives enter the trauma sequence from behind, as it were, not frontally; the idyllic beginnings are added on, almost by implied extrapolation, because we are immersed in the aftermath of the sequence and do not (yet) see its connection to the precedential High. Only Plato/Socrates does not describe the initiating High at all. Except if you start at the end of the Prisoner's initial journey, seeing the Sun as the Source of all things.

The problem of addressing the unlocking of the original trauma as it is currently held includes the fact that the holding trauma site is not stored in the straight narrative sequence of how the occasion originally happened. Its unlocking includes factors of multiplicity, fragmentation, elements scattered all over the floor or bouncing at the ceiling. Each fragment probably holographically contains the whole story, but for defensive purposes, these pieces need other, often invisible and lightning-fast linkings-together.

Given the universality of this Cave pattern in us as humans, it is not surprising to have its template superimposed upon issues surrounding birth and the development of consciousness. With Eden, we enter the states of Fallen awareness with a necessary but easily misleading narrative about agency and causality, which ignores the centrality of shock as a formative, brain-transforming (and brain-saving) experience. In the Allegory's Imprisonment, we get the second phase of the process, not as it occurs in real time, but in the sequence of inner time awareness. These two time sequences are often confounded, to put a point on it; for the individual, the inner timescape takes us closer to the controlling dynamics of our suffering and thus to its resolution.

Addendum:

I find the assembly of "The Insusceptibles" exemplifies this Allegory problem in narrative. The winning invisible-like scan of the lovers sets off the domestic but also traumatic framework of final, artificial light, which helps, even civilizes, but at an ironic cost of an held-energy system not yet resolved, insusceptible to transformation, no matter how closely juxtaposed with the lyric High. We are at the threshold of (be)coming.

CHAPTER TEN:

THEOLOGICAL CONCEPTS AND ENERGY

Important strategies

I have noted before that there are important concepts or strategies for understanding our human experience which tend to cause us to stumble. And to seriously argue about. Illuminated by gestalt and developmental insight, I think they can and should be simply decoded. My approach is to see that the energy patterns described in so-called religious dogmatics are word-prior and preverbal, and essential, and true. The words and narratives used to describe these patterns and states of awareness may be sites of hazard – by their holders, prone to distortion, rigidity, and even arrogance. Historically, war and destruction have been triggered by these words, while the essential energetics remain untouched, unexamined, ignored, and (otherwise) simple – and, interestingly, usually something hard to disagree about.

1. The concept of God

God is a gestalt word-way of approaching the intelligence and order – or not – of ultimate reality. The order characterized by the word God (and its courtly train of attributes) can be denied, seen as void, as something we cannot know, and as a strategy for bringing unified focus to humans who ask the question of Ultimaticity, including Source.

One hidden subtext for talking about God, perhaps useful, is for determining whether individuals have acknowledged the (perhaps primary narcissistic, developmental) task of recognizing that there is something beyond our so-called self, often, usually, more powerful than we are. By extension, the awareness of Ultimaticity – what is finally true – is a real question and includes the significant realization that there is a superceding more to Oneself than one supposes. And retrospectively, there is powerfully more to us than what we commonplacely experience.

"Do you believe in God?" can be a coded inquiry related to this Other awareness; and one optional response might be, "Belief is not the issue. Personal knowledge and engagement with the problem of Ultimate Reality reveals the possibility for greater, deeper personal focus. With some increasing accuracy, I may be able to tell you what I know, not what I 'believe'; and it would be nice if you did the same for me."

I find proposals of monotheism pretty much are stretched pretty much on a frame of polytheism. By characterizing God (or Its allied names) as unitary, gestalt insight is present. In fact we dwell in fragmentary levels of worship – God of the BMW, (God of) Mammon, God of College (Admission), God of Power, God of aesthetic moment, of intense feeling, etc. Our sense of sanctity scurries amid neurochemical preoccupations, and to bring a unitary frame of reference from which to witness reality may be more difficult than it initially appears.

Using the term God, or Its equivalents, often reveals the gestalt drive toward some singular unity of consciousness, usually against a background of plurality, or multifacetedness. Thinking projectively, if we are one, reciprocally, God may be one. If we are plural, we may engender a polytheocracy. Or we may propose apposite functions (such as a triune, triangulating God) in order to clarify the problem of discerning the nature of ultimate reality (and its cohort, truth).

For the plural self, acknowledging a monotheistic structure may be a helpful way to balance some aspect of its interior, even to the point of life sacrifice. And the reverse could also be true. How do we carry these concepts seems to be the central, not often asked question. When we subscribe to articles of faith, even though everyone in the room is saying the same words, the individuals not only apply them differently; they store them in varying proportionalities, as it were, in different rooms of the many-mansioned House of Self.

One useful variation on knowing God is that it cannot be done. The Unknown God truly stands wherever but cannot be approximated by mere human creatures; our intelligence is not that subtle or accurate, and it is prideful (not to say grandiose, not to say silly) to think it is.

Concomitant with this strategy is that God is beyond inconsequential human cognition, beyond words, hence it is deeply dangerous to name G- . Aside from being reverent in the face of what is truly awesome, here is an awareness of the paradox/error that by naming something, we understand it; when by naming something, we are perhaps significantly and predictably limiting our active understanding. This task gets particularly risky with something as complex and simple as Ultimate Reality.

The alternate strategy is that we are, somehow, God's creatures, and albeit imperfectly, we partake of Its divinity, maybe particularly through consciousness. As a Genesis-style injunction/permission, God could say, "Thou shalt understand Me as I understand Myself – with all the ironic rights and privileges affixed thereto."

As Source, God is the terminal point of causation concerns, both cognitive and energetic. And thus God resolves paradox, including the paradox contained in the idea of beginning. Such God is beyond cognition. It is as if there is a permanently impenetrable wall, against which we project our menial understandings of ourselves and the outside world. Even as our understandings increase in subtlety, the wall always moves back, not necessarily in a cruel way.

2. Incarnation

This focal thought declares the relationship of spirit to matter. When we die, we cease to move, and so, *post facto*, we who witness death in other people acknowledge that something has departed – some electromagnetic life force – has ceased to be present. Thus retroactively, we presume that what has departed is spirit. Then we must be a combination of spirit and matter, for matter is what remains after we die. People's experience of spirit may include witnessing the fluidity of our electromagnetic fields, viewed from within. Current energetics awareness about atomic forces which make up "matter" may challenge radically the traditional apposition of spirit and matter.

For dualistic thinking, the combinant model works rather wonderfully (and has for a long time and for a lot of people), for we can somehow witness the movement, the densification, of spirit into matter, and perceive ourselves as being both, in various ways and densities.

This visibility may amount to a trick of consciousness; or it may include a deeper sense of presence for the individual who meditationally attempts to achieve such a state. The idea of incarnation provides a grid upon which to describe the resultant movement as combining spirit and matter: two into one, a gestalt formulation. As a strategy, it allows us to see, perhaps even measure, the dynamic relationship between soul and its densification into matter, a movement, not a (cognitively) static appearance or manifestation.

3. Soul

The Soul is the over-riding, omni-infusing organizing principle of what we are, including traditional dualistic strategies of mind and body. Soul is delineated within, at least, the first moment of Conception, when we are a creature of a single cell. We transmogrify from Haploid to Diploid, and that commanding sense of unity never leaves us, no matter how many times we subdivide.

It is this energetic cellular memory and intelligence to which we refer in all subsequent transformations and elaborations. Because it organizes our material incarnation and its varietals, it has been considered beyond time, hence immortal. As Soul, we incarnate, we densify. Soul tends to be singular, as in "My Soul" – not My Souls – "doth Magnify the Lord". Sometimes the recognition of Soul is juxtaposed to the Body, as in "I love you Body and Soul", which means a full integration of the incarnated being, not just mind and body, which, in some usages, sort of means the same thing.

Colloquially, Soul, or having Soul, may suggest awareness of or reference to this deeper, non-superficial, non-dualistic, integrated sense of Being.

4. Being Chosen

This concept includes the singularity of identity, both energetic – physical and spiritual – and psychological. It is part of our selectivity: out of stardust, we are singularly "chosen" to become and to be. Everyone has this chosen fate, not just those who feature it on their menu. Chosen brings with it a certain mandate of consciousness, which in application is hard to maintain. In Buddhist terms, from this awareness of individuality, related to Ultimate Reality, we may move into sainthood. Sainthood usually means exceptional spiritual integration; it can also refer to everyone – just walk a mile in another person's moccasins, and you will see the perfection of their complexities, sustained and completing.

The celebration of this chosen lineage can easily run amuck, in egocentric, even socially aggrandizing strategies; but all indicate a link of consciousness between so-called Self and Ultimate Reality. Being Chosen carries the seeds of self, which includes both grandiose levels of awareness and the crushing of that grandiosity in order that the connection with Ultimate Reality be maintained. Linked to Lord of Lords, King of Kings, and similar formulations, being Chosen challenges earthly positions of power and governance (often tyrannical), to indicate a spiritual hierarchy from which political force cannot threaten or distract our allegiance.

Furthermore, Being Chosen, as a wordplay, might suggest that Being and Chosen are somehow, parallelarly identical. As noted above, Being is difficult to characterize, because Being is pre-verbal and energetic. We cannot see what it is made up of because it is ultimately pure, ineffable radiance. But somehow Chosen belongs with the task of framing Being, perhaps conveying the *gift* of life itself in our specific incarnation of that selective gift. It implies a sense of Other, and of Source.

Each selection of the new Dalai Lama, perhaps a choosing, includes a developmental narrative relating to former-life patterning. It is a model of understanding about what we bring to the world at birth which influences each member of Buddhist-related traditions.

5. Virgin Birth

Virgin Birth is a development site and a spiritual truth. No child is born in real time without sperm and egg or its cloning, DNA equivalent. But our own understanding of ourselves as created creatures goes through a number of stages which include literally denying the agency of the father; not to mention our attempts to probe the cognitive mystery of creation itself.

Variations upon originality or how we come about:

How do we come about?

1. Like Topsy, we just growed. Our experience appears as a something-out-of-nothing, perhaps without a cause for which we are the effect. Its current cosmological form could be the Big Bang – shall I name

it – myth, and often the way we hold experience is as an aftermath of some Big Bang variant.

2. We are self-creating. Like the Godhead, there is no precedent for the Uncaused First Cause. Yet in time, we develop and create ourselves, and our world, by ourselves; brain synapticises and resynapticizes. And we eat our spinach and grow into a Big Person. This preverbal conviction (sometimes called the autarchic fantasy) gets challenged by the first person in our infant world, Adam – the mother – whom we, as God, have created in a something-out-of-nothing Virgin Birth way. (In Genesis, that we are shaped from the chemistry of the earth, though poetically stated, is literally true.)

Only the giantess mother does not always obey or anticipate our directives, and in some significant, dissonant ways proves to be substantially powerful. We will not give up the (valuable) self-creating-self conviction or insight, but if, in our mother-challenged grandiosity, we cannot have it to ourselves, we shall give it to her: she created us, in the same self-creating way we think we create ourself. (I am indebted to Edmund Bergler for this insight sequence).

Here we have a conviction collective which adjusts closer to the truth of how we come about (we literally come from the mother's body) while maintaining the somehow important idea of our self-creating self. And the "doctrine" of Virgin Birth expresses this insight complex, including its elaboration/add-on of the Holy Spirit, which also is a spiritual insight that there is something seriously and causally, transcendently energetic about this whole process of self-creating self. Virgin Birth is prior to the understanding that a third "person" in the room is involved in our creation, traditionally and mythically called the father. For some, the Fourth Person in the room is G– .

I was present at a psycho-analytic conference in the 1980's where it was belatedly acknowledged by Freudian Oedipal-complex-driven insight holders that in order to solve some complex developmental sequences, one had to focus on the dyadic, triangulating relationship of child to the good and the bad mother, a three-post pattern which was then conveniently re-expressed in a kind of rescuing way in the famous Oedipal triangulation of child, mother, and father.

Here, the father takes on the good (or bad) side of the problem, leaving the mother with the remaining portion of the child's dualistic mythology. The attending analysts called this "new" level of apperception the pre-Oedipal Mother, an insight somehow devotedly utilized for millennia in the insight nexus of the Virgin Mary, though those at the conference did not acknowledge/recognize the connection. Emerging clothed in an analytic lineage (which included many earlier psychoanalytic musings), we reinvent the wheel. After centuries of misapplication, it is hard to recognize what truth the Virgin Mary nexus actually contains. It describes a developmentally rich sequence, and with some accuracy, it charts strategically significant early infantile elaborations about perception.

A therapist who worked for years on her relationship with her sexually-abusive father once reported that she could not get a handle on the "Oedipal" pattern until she contextualized it historically as an extension of the preexistent pattern (of exploitation – and abandonment) with her mother.

One additional perspective. The Virgin Birth may record a dissociative sequence wherein causality itself is denied. There is a skipped sequence in the lineage, which voidy omission is characterized in reverse formulation as perfection; and many individuals who have stumbled on the Virgin Mary insight cluster pick up but cannot hold or frame the intellectual (and spiritual) thing(s) being described. So they dismiss it.

From a gestalt point of view, the declaration of various positions around the question of our singularity, our individuation and unitary form, drives us closer and closer to the truth, which may be materially very specific, even gene-manipulatable, but which rests upon the premise of Virgin Birth, just as the created universe in Genesis is a virgin birth, as are both Adam and Eve. The gestalt strategy invites us to juxtapose and combine both realms, Virgin Birth and material, astrophysical reality to coexist within our dual, single brain.

All science may be seen as meditation upon the nature of Ultimate Reality, and our perception of a created world paradoxically implies Virgin Birth, as does the awareness of the perceiver. Recently it has been so easy to dismiss the power and rightful place of this complex idea because apparently it has not been taught or absorbed at anything but the shallowest levels of understanding.

The gestalt strategy takes us from narrative to an energetic understanding of relationships between the parts, and the places where those relationships have a strong bridge, and also to where the bridges characterize impasses, or appear severed. It is spiritual in its direction, though not religious – shall we save our religions for politics and sociology? Gestalt consciousness is at least always interior, and its premise leads to the door to unknowing and to experience, including with the Outside world. As differentiated consciousness returns us to Being, the gestalt movement leads us to the energetic, to a sense of the brain in process, not just being led along.

Even more intriguing might be the possibility that Virgin Birth as a strategy attempts to account for how we grow and sustain our self as creatures, through cell division, a something-out-of-nothing process that gives birth to each next moment in our development and our lives. We may focus on the trembling divisionary line, which potentially catastrophically, as cancer patients know, yields us from our first single cell identity into two cells, while remaining one entity.

As declarent of the nature of source, of beginnings, Virgin Birth may also refer to the default mode network and its synaptic underpinnings as we "create" our understandings, consciousness both old and new. And these understandings include and color those focusing on God and Its Virgin Birth.

6. Holy Spirit

To this insight nexus is added the overall energetic of creation which "causes" human creation itself, a mystery perhaps felicitously approached contemplatively in the paradoxical juxtaposition of Virgin Birth with the reality of DNA, sperm and egg. In this meditational, koan-like understanding, there is always a third, energetic presence, or entity; or better, the entity of the Holy Spirit is a characterization of a transcendental, limitless energetic reality always present, in every moment of Being, including Creation.

The use of the Holy Spirit as a phrase or code image takes us into the realm of the energetic, particularly from the cognitive and materialist understandings in which we are prone to live and think. It is often employed like an aside or trope, offered to establish the energetic amid distractions, as a reality and as the priority reality, the determinator, not the usual instigating suspects contained in narrative.

7. Son of God

We are all children amidst and within an actionable part of (U)ultimate (R)reality. This insight should not be transferred and isolated to a specific individual, except to each and to everybody. We carry the "divinity" as a part, or even as a whole, of what we are. If we envision Son of God this way, we are half person, half God (or all person and all God), and to project this process upon a single individual in historical time for anything other than trying to get a sense of clarity about our own perfect soul-identity (our divinity) is to risk turning a spiritual, energetic insight into political or social agenda. It cannot be done; yet this distortion occurs all the time. One has the feeling that its positive use has been proposed as an apposite shield against the all-too-manifest real-life tyrannies of kings, caliphs, and lords. Its voice wryly, defiantly notes, "There is a higher power than you, Your Highness."

The Eastern traditions recognize many individuals who carry this insight-capacity – clarity, if you will – at an energetic level which often results in exceptional changes – of state, of personality, of physical well-being. These people are identified as saints, and the West has elaborated on this universal insight as best it could. The actions of Sons – and Daughters – of God mindfulness demonstrate a distinctive humility and moral acquity. They are exceptionally spiritually and energetically balanced creatures of humanity.

Its misuse: by projecting onto the mythic hero/heroine (itself our projection of ourselves) a distinction he/she him/herself, as an enlightened individual, would not employ, we obscure and even obliterate what is essential here. Our humanity includes our divinity, even though we carry both aspects of this gestalt form haphazardly. Traditionally, in the East, upon greeting another person, we bow and they bow in mutual recognition of the divinity we all carry. The Other is the Buddha; as are We.

8. Tragedy

Aside from its commonplace meaning of a dreadful and irremediable accident or occurrence, tragedy is a "technical" literary term applied to some imaginative texts, particularly serious plays. The history of the study of what makes up tragedy includes a lot of early psychological rumination, particularly about dissociation and projection. For the purposes of this commentary, tragedies (the plays) are narratives which delineate trauma energetics, or patternings.

Diagrammatically, these stories and situations take us to crucial interfaces where there are immobilities and de-oxygenation (the stories can include suffocations, hangings, and death). We witness tragedies dramatically performed in the theater, and by our internal mirroring of the performance we are witnessing, we respond in a complex way, including, according to Aristotle, experiencing a catharsis of the emotions involving pity and fear.

By such a process of dramatic imitation, connected to the way we take in information, we work through a narrated trauma pattern, and we leave the theater feeling cleansed. I think this insight is what is behind Aristotle's definition of *Merope* as *tragictatus*, most tragic, because its story describes a mother who is about to destroy an unknown young man whom, just in time, she discovers is her son – and he is saved. The narratives of Pinocchio and Frankenstein illuminate this parental hazard. Seeing the pattern may allow us to resolve the pattern without projecting it upon external reality, including thereby catastrophically.

In the tragedies about the sacrifice of Iphigenia by Agamemnon, a stalemate begun by her father's arrogance is broken by a restatement of the original violation of life – the sacrifice of the pregnant rabbit; the ultimate meaninglessness of the Trojan War can be witnessed as based upon an error or *hamartia*, here about the nature of reality and the reality of nature. Better for the kings of Argos to have remained in Diana's windless immobility. As with Abraham and Isaac, with devastating consistency, war involves the sacrifice of children by parents – and what is sacrificed also is our hold on reality, our own and that of the world around us.

Tragedy's narratives deal with the basic experience of projection, where we heroes, as agents, project our insoluable (held-energy systems, usually bestowed from the past) patterns onto exterior reality in order to resolve them. We count on the outside to help us somehow with our inside. One part of our error is that we don't acknowledge where the patterns come from (or when). As humans, we take compressed two-dimensional deoxygenative patterns and rather than perceive that we can internally get them to resolve, we disastrously attempt to three-dimensionate them by projecting them onto or into a three-dimensional outside, external world which sort of resembles the pattern.

Some irresolution is mirrored, or we think it is, in the real world. Our *hubris*, or pride, amounts to assuming that our view of history and reality, taken down or enscribed, we feel, with accuracy from the outside, in fact is the same as that outside reality, with the same rights and privileges thereof. In tragedy, we confront our self-creating selves, which usually have to be modulated, transformed, or re-constructed as from dead, or immobilization.

In the story of the impossible-to-untie Gordian knot, there are two strategies for achieving the solution: 1. Remaining with the impossibility through many attempts at possibly pious, physical intervention. And 2. the Alexandrine move, whereby Alexander takes his sword and slices through the knot, and resultantly gains the rule of Asia. Will that suffice for Alexander?

In the tragically-informed modality of TE insight, a third proffered solution is through focus, to have the shock-inspired held-energy system of the knot untie itself. The possible result may be elimination of projection as we restore the capacity to confront and embrace Being.

A question which may next arise is about scanning. Which narratives express the trauma pattern, or held-energy system patterning itself, most clearly? I think this is important information. As individuals we scan our own process; as agents of culture, we collect and discriminate about what images and narrative images take us closest to the black point of impaction, the trauma sites. And overall, which images and narratives account most deeply for the problem of trauma resolution? The Oedipus cycle? *King Lear*? The Labyrinth? *Prometheus Bound*?

One of the narrative finalists is the (Judeo-)Christian myth, whose spiritual insight is importantly supposed to be grounded in the life of a real man (thank God); and the Crucifixion itself declares a view of the after-moment of pre-windshield shock as experienced from within. That this story, begun in Eden, reveals a resolution pathway locating it in the *tragictatus* category, as do the Oedipus plays, most importantly in *Oedipus at Colonus*, and in Aeschylus' *Oresteia*.

When dramatic tragedy is allowed its full run, or better, extension, it can be an agency for healing, for it brings brain to its opportunity for resolution. Its happy ending amounts to the acknowledgment of projection and projection's destructive power, which has been thus felicitously thwarted. But in order to accomplish this goal, the tragic narrative must traverse the most difficult energetic interfaces and impactions.

Shakespeare's *The Winter's Tale*, Aeschylus' *Oresteia*, and Sophocles' Oedipus plays demonstrate these movements and positive outcomes more vividly than, say, those tragedies which end pretty much in disaster. Our historical preoccupations with the narratives and their qualifiers, such as high-stature characters, I think can be perhaps misunderstood in the social sense of aristocracy being the only place tragedy occurs. The tragic process including its resolution actually can occur at all social levels, with every individual. What counts is energetic movement from within the place of held-energy systems, black and de-oxygenated and usually invisible. That the High-stature characters fall reveals at least the matter-of-fact sequence of the appearance of trauma sites following some energetic High, in everyone, prince and pauper.

When Aristotle defines tragedy as an imitation of a serious action, there are a number of ways that can be interpreted or focused upon. Here, the tragedy (the enacted play) is a narrative, and as such imitates an energetic patterning which leads to radiance, not on stage necessarily, but in the hearts and minds of the spectators. If effective, it triggers a resolution of the narrative in the particular spectators, who themselves have narratives which "imitate" traumatically generated held-energy systems. I have already presented further insights about tragedy in other parts of this book.

9. Eden

Meditationally constructed, Eden initially appears as a neurochemical state prior to traumatic shock. It can be backed into, as in a wish that we could be free of our current muddling attachments: so what would that "prior" state amount to? It can be an apposite (positive) statement of what we are not. In Eden, we are non-dissociatively stressless, somewhat timeless, deathless (not death-stung, death-preoccupied). It incorporates the neurochemistry of pure Being, and, if recovered from the position of corruption, of Enlightenment. It "duplicates" or "imitates" some infantile and probably uterine states, wherein may be sensed a remarkable dovetailing; there is a dovetailing congruence between the outside and the inside of our blastocyst entity-ness.

Eden is fantastic, in that it cannot be sustained, even in corrupted form, without the mechanism of shock, which shock process in reality is in our systems as a potential agency right at the beginning, prior to conception. Eden looks very much like Being, yet Being now in relationship to the exterior or Other, World. God places us there. And developmentally, Being's pre-shock, gestalt-unified perfection is memorized and referred to probably in every moment of our life, now felicitously set in its harmonious context. Eden herewith is the site of our grounding, and it bears the unconditional hallmarks of the 23rd Psalm. The fact that we explicate this site mythically suggests that it is not a given for everyone in every part of our individual systems; it needs reinforcing where we are in dissociation. But it is covalent in every moment of our lives.

Though (at least) three-dimensional, Eden is curiously a-historical; death-awareness and with it linear time, has not yet wheeled into place.

We await the introduction of shock. Our formulation of Eden thus can be seen as a retrospective attempt to explain how we arrive in the difficult, trauma-beset Present, the post-Fall After.

What happens, and it may not be accurately accounted for in this Edenic sequence, is that we discover we are off balance, and brain assumes it has done something wrong, or transgressive. What the Expulsion from the Garden of Eden describes is the dissociative aftermath of a world of shock, in which bad things happen, and from which chaotic catastrophic world we are rescued by shock in order to survive.

And/But in some important cases, the shock-memory does not melt away, and we are left East of Eden, which includes residually the perfection of the Garden plus the introduction of shock, which itself brings dissociation, and off-centered (and synaptically encrusting) positioning.

From this point of view, the eating of the Apple is a narrative add-on and is easily misleading, because as well as Eden, shock (and traumatic holding) is what we are, until we are not. The abruptness of the lesson of Eve's transgression seems to be extrapolant, perhaps an elaboration of a future lesson plan, two or three chapters ahead of where the class is.

Eve's "error" locates a sequence of Self and Others and identifies the earliest experiencing of eating with prohibition, all of it narrative and defensive. The cultural damage done, both to women and to men, from the Apple sequence and our elaborations upon it, can hardly be faced; and I hope it is possible to lift off its obscurant surface, which seems deceptively clear, and try to witness perhaps a deeper reality. And I am not the first to attempt this, particularly recently. How to focus upon Eden's essential truthfulness is the problem. We know something is odd about the story because basically there is nothing wrong with Knowledge and nothing wrong with eating apples. The Biblical narrative elaboration is clearly that, an elaboration. And linked to prohibition.

First person

If the mother is the First Person, Adam, and we come out of its body, we, the Child, are Eve. And in the uterine and post-uterine blurring of Self and Other *vis-a-vis* child and mother, the Mother is also (first woman) Eve, and somehow, perhaps later, we are also (like) the First Person, Adam; in fact this sequence describes some pre-natal then natal historical progression.

With the awareness of the disconnecting process of shock, we are confronted with a phenomenon that the world invites a new process into the Garden; and we are drawn into a new level of cognition, of good and bad, which must be accounted for. Eve's transgression is both accommodating to this transition and in narrative, totally defensive. We are the problem we are aware of, only there is no way to approximate its scale except through narrative, and linear time, which reveals and conceals the energetic, and developmental reality.

Shock, at the center of the trauma mechanism, occurs as a rescuer, and we could imagine a revision of the Eden story which would account for the true inner experience of shock sequencing for even prenatal beings. But the elaboration upon a world which interferes with and interrupts us could include citing the mother for bringing us into it and for sharing the same mortal fate as ours. As noted elsewhere, some prenatalists suggest this conjoining convenes when the natal infant's forehead confronts the mother's sacrum (miraculously named) and must turn in order to survive, *i.e.*, keep going down and out – and taking a strategically significant sort-of angled leave. From the straightness of Heaven we bend to survive – our humanity depends upon and is characterized as a turning.

So if we witness the Eve and Serpent sequence in isolation, as it is presented, we may view how our trauma sequence is distorted by narrative which accounts for the appearance of narrative itself; it is a description and a defense, filled with clear injunctions and rebellions, apparently vivid and causal, not dissociative and chaotic – a condition or awareness which the original crisis may have incited or sponsored.

The crisis described in the Temptation counters the original Genesis proposal of order and sequence, with only a (cursory) mention of void, for example. This Edenic account is at our core, closest to Being, not the memory-infecting sense of time which is illusionarily sequential; that is not how we experience it, and the narratives, including Eve's, significantly may take us away, rather than toward our core.

With snake-like, enabling conspiritoriality, we are abandoned by the very life-preservers which are thrown to us; and this action duplicates the dissociative heritage which shock matter-of-factly engenders. In order to parse this sequence, we may have to disengage all its important parts – eating, being eaten and swallowed (food disappearing), mother, parent, forbidden and forbidding, abandonment, permission, knowledge, spine, crawling, shame, even God, for golly's sake – to begin to see what the Genesis narrative is attempting to do; and in fact what it (currently for the most part disastrously as we hold it) does.

Our temptation with the Temptation is that we will accept narrative as way of approaching the chaos, the overwhelm, of the initial trauma. Such narrative, the Serpent's seduction of Eve and her succumbing, promises the things which we will eventually manifest when we have worked through the trauma site – causality, evenness of occurrance. When done correctly, we see the events as God sees them, even with compassion. The Temptation delivers this "explanation" with clarity so that presumably, even the chaos and shock will have observable sequence; the Temptation sequence is as much of a promise, and in that, perhaps somehow reassuring. The divine is ordered, no matter what chaos has demonstrated itself.

Eden describes cell systems

Furthermore, Eden describes cell systems with fully operant mitochondria and Golgi apparati, which spin in time and in dimension, and in a world potentiality which includes shock, right down to subcellular levels of existence. When in illness, our bodies are dissociative, the drive toward restoration of Edenic vibratory states can be profound. Also, it is marked and recognizable in our understanding of homeostasis.

Within this rubric, shock appears to be an intruder, the primitive brain serpent spine, but even though it is sudden in its appearance, it is sequential; and this (often initially invisible) sequence, engendered often in sudden crisis moments, can be slowed down and viewed in recovery meditation or, if lucky, in various forms of therapy or prayer. We have to stop our current forms of activity and cognition to energetically watch the woulds fill up with no's.

Shock and the trauma mechanism introduces us to an abrupt sense of historical time, perhaps more vertical than linear, which counterbalances with Edenic sequencing, which in some ways may have no linear order. While crucial for sustaining our Being center, shock disrupts our natural initial sense of Being's orderliness; and we blame it rather than accommodate to its often apparently obliterative power. And besides, how and by what trigger(s) is the shock mechanism evoked? And its memory reevoked?

Why do things happen in Eden?

If Eden is a rough approximation of Being, why do things happen in it? Timeless and curiously asequential, Eden often seems like a state of becoming or doing: Adam delves and Eve spins. One answer is that the myth is not refined; it is an approximation of what is later differentiated. Or it reflects an infantile awareness which extends from Stillpoint outward into narrative and, ultimately, death. It includes Being, but it does not stay there. We would have to look at the beginning of Genesis to see Being approximated, yet even then, we quickly move into the narrative of God: God carries the verbality of narrative and of doing and becoming. While Sartre opines, "Being is prior to Essence," though curious-sounding, here, Being is prior to God.

Eden then, could be understood as the hard-to-maintain awareness of Being dwelling in and through narrative. Perhaps paradoxically, Being is separate from the seductive attachment of narrative, yet narrative is how we begin to understand. Being incarnates into narrative, and Eden provides the (unreal, deathless) vision of seeing what that would look like, before shock and the moments, exterior and interior, which engender its appearance; that these moments are chaotic provide an important place to focus.

As best as I can figure it, the neurochemical energetic sequence goes: Being, Eden (incarnate Being), dissociation (set as a possibility because of our trauma mechanism and the sword-like cutting-through quality of shock), East of Eden (the actual post-shock experience of dissociation in the self-cluttering of held-energy systems). From East of Eden, we can take the bus to Salvation, which returns us to Being. All these phases are working simultaneously as an inopportune gestalt; in myth and therapy, we start with getting brain to resolve the traumata and see what clarity emerges out of that.

I think we approach, even establish, Eden always from the rear gate of dissociation; later, we recreate – re-extrapolate – its frontal entrance. Perhaps our meditations should focus on how Adam and Eve enter or are placed in the Garden; as infant God, we create (discover) the world, then we are "put" into the Garden, which we have generated, synaptically made. The Garden implies boundaries and unity of place, so that the gestalt function may appear very early in our consciousness. Or it may be an extrapolation from the present back to past levels of consciousness.

Trauma, Temptation, and Eden

The point of origin of the trauma memory is identified by two simultaneous but not necessarily related functions. One is our memory recognition in the past of the time and manner when the pattern sets in, in Peter Levine's term, $[T_o]$; this is the moment of the car crash, when our chaoticised neurochemistry is altered by (life-saving) shock, and held. It turns out that while this memory may aspire to originality ("Now I remember what really happened."), over time it becomes encrusted through repetition and bias and has to be considered a corrupt text.

Let's say the Edenic myth proposes four brain moments:

1. Being and incarnation, prior to Temptation;

2. The Temptation and its shock-inducing moment (the Fall);

3. The presence of shock remaindered (the Expulsion to East of Eden);

4. The return to #1 (implied in Redemption and Salvation).

We are either in a relatively pure state, in a crisis, or in an aftermathic impure state, seeking resolution. And finally, we are resolved.

In order to clarify the starting point, I have suggested five Positions.

1. Being

2. Being incarnating into, with the World (Garden of Eden) prior to Temptation;

3. The Temptation and its shock-inducing moment (the Fall – something interruptive, chaotic occurs and appears to conclude; shock rescues and holds us from obliteration).

4. The presence of shock remaindered and the dissociative timelessness of held-energy system (the Expulsion to East of Eden);

5. The return to #1 (implied in Redemption and Salvation).

We are in a pure state of Being, in a crisis, or in an aftermathic impure state, seeking resolution. And finally, we are resolved.

The Edenic myth's examination of the trauma mechanism is both complex and simple. We are talking about experience as noted from within, as well as from without. The achievement of narrative itself is significant, for what it accomplishes is a structuring of experience in a linear time sequence, which internally may not be experienced as (con)sequential. And while Being is in (linear) time, the inner experience of Being is transcendent, beyond time. Our confusion may be between the transcendence of Being, and the timelessness of held-energy systems as they characterize our consciousness.

When we are in the aftermath of the Fall, we are both in the memory of Being and its current corrupted present, which includes a different kind of timelessness, the timelessness of shock and poised movement – immobility. The binary nature of consciousness might propose we are either in purity or out of it, in full oxygen or in compromise.

The insertion of the Fall "Occasion" intuitively proposes a sequence, a "reason" for the transition between Before and After, and it proffers a directionality toward "healing" and restoration or resolution. This healing is positioned across the chasm of dissociation, in which the usual markers of time and space are suspended, in which there is no time.

Through this timeless sequence, the myth elaborating the Fall identifies the importance of the Mother and of eating and of spine and of consciousness of right and wrong, but as an accurate description of the trauma process, it is only partially helpful. In Genesis, we do not see the chaos of the shock Incitement; the "explanation" is all a little Disneyfied. Though in fairness and tribute to Disney, when chaos does appear, it is rendered in animated, preverbal, preconceptual, energetic ways. When Snow White is about to eat the poisoned Apple, her mouth opens, affixes at the apple, and the camera turns away. The next image shows the poisoned Snow White fallen on the ground. The camera is high above her body, which is lying face down, her head and face turned.

Misused

Though Genesis is highly ambitious as narrative – it is moving in on something essential, crucial – we have seen how easily The Fall is misused, in its literal interpretation; huge amounts of prejudice, anxiety, and damage have occurred or attempted resolution within its Gates. If as a reader, you sense that I am superimposing this trauma template on the Garden myth, and that there is no connection between traumatic process and Original Sin and Eve eating the Apple, you will sense the dissociative distance I am describing. The Edenic myth is approximate about a most difficult inner experience, compounded, confounded, characterized by dissociation.

Some people are concerned that Eve, identified as woman, is the designated driver in the Temptation, and that historically women resultantly get the bad press. I think that the story locates when these issues come to awareness as being in relationship to the first person, now the mother (as female), prior to the father. That we cross over from Self to Other, what's hers is ours, ours hers, generates a gender-bending swamp, which traditional sex-role identities propose to drain by simplification.

The Fall proposes a description of the crisis, a narrative, if you will, and in so doing, it reveals the potential falseness of the narrative, of narrative in general. We experience our need for narrative to negotiate these traumatically exposed voids and perhaps most significantly chaos, but narrative is not the same as the energetic truth.

And if the narrative obscures the chaos, the myth is flawed; we will have trouble finding out how Before becomes After.

The fourth function is the present neurochemical fulcrum which unlocks that memory. It is this second point which brain guards against scanning, yet finds continuously disturbing; this is our experience of being accident prone, wherein once experiencing the trauma, we keep trying to re-solve its held chemistry until it resolves; and in disguised and overt ways, we repeat the initiating situation as a means to that end. Addiction. It is the activation of this point in our neurochemistry which is now understood as therapeutically strategic to trauma resolution. Post-traumatic stress disorder is an example of this. We could call the first memory the Original Memory, and its dissociative patterning the Second Memory.

A word about gender and gender identity

With all these crossover moves between Self and Other, and our identification with and not with the Mother, our initial, formative energetic experiences of gender are complex. Over time, what rises to the surface of our awareness is a hormonal drive characterized by flow and impediment, at least traumatically determined or trauma-site inclusive. The energy is perceived as manditory and imperative, though with time and experience, various phases of the substructure of our energetic history emerge and refine. To come to a statement of *straight* and *bent* may be the way we experience ourselves, but with time and perspective, that statement, inner and outer, is the tip of a profound iceberg.

We can quickly move past a so-called heterosexuality into a bi-sexuality, or move beyond these shallow labels of sexual identity. Within our moves toward orgasm are fragments of historical self which occur so rapidly or invisibly that to presume a firm statement of what we are or what we prefer in preludey moments is highly suspect, even arrogant. Our announcements about our sexualities are easily dismantled, sadly proffered toward a certainty-monstrous and monolithic system of anxiety socially perpetrated; when people complain of being sexually abused, it might be in this realm of declaring (and being recognized as certain) identity that (all) people experience.

The energy behind our sexual movements is deep, flowing, and not always with firm concluding objectives, even though we achieve orgasmic cessation to the turbulence. To make that cessation the endpoint of our declaration of sexual identity – how we get there and with whom – seems, to state the problem of identity centered in Being – at best vague. Will we determine the spawning salmon by the apparent endpoint of its journey? God has created a way of preserving life which involves our whole personality and physical organism. Is it lucky to have the appearance of a single channel for release? Perhaps, but at what cost to our deeper awareness of what we are.

10. Salvation

Salvation is a code concept for traumatic resolution and all that that entails; Enlightenment is found within its realms. When we are primarily or even secondarily immersed in traumatic experience, we know that something is wrong, or better, incomplete. Our brain confounds by being clear and then not clear: we dissociate and are dysfunctional, suffering, neurotic, not clear, in illusion, whatever. We are prey to our incessant addictions and wasteful repetitions.

Salvation as an insight for both Eastern and Western thought brings forward the information that there is another state which can be achieved, free of traumatic purposivity or impurposivity. This "state" has a clarity and a positive foreverness about it. Movements made from within this centered, centering chemistry have an anchored wholeness about them, radiantly sited and in their way absolute and appropriately invulnerable. If we are ducks, we are ducks who comprehend and understand who we are.

We are told that certain focal heroic archetypical figures can bring with them Salvation: Hercules, Jesus, the eagle, for examples. Belief in these creatures' healing powers, albeit a complex process for each example, appears to help dissolve the toxicity, so that existence is clear and unafraid. Herein, herewith come relief and cessation.

By contradistinction, the world prior to Salvation carries the held, suddenly-installed memories of shock "mechanisms" incited to support a human system's survival, and such a world, internal or external, contains dissociative patternings, including violence and the held-energy systems hallmarks of eternal abandonment or damnation. We might propose that the eternality of Hell is different from that of Heaven: the first has containment and shock memory and its implied – and immobilized – historicity within it; the other – Heaven – is outside of time, spacious, and limitless, and, crucially, shockless.

And difficult to sustain; such a High vibratory state usually triggers the appearance of further traumatic patterning, and now our consciousness is dwelling within a shock-present system. And the characterization of Hell includes its endless bliss-cancelling appearance as the next trauma configuration lining up for healing after some High of Heaven. To all but the most experienced (including Job?), Hell's presence, this sense, is cruel. The removal of illusion sites – impactions – is narrated in both Buddhist and Hindu incarnative strategies as well as Plato's movement toward embodying the Good.

As I see it, historically, Salvation has remained within the corral of religious elaboration, tied as it is to our understanding of Ultimate Reality and our projections about that. As with other developed, even exploited insights, some think Salvation may need to be weaned a bit from those structures and institutions which have abused these insights in part because of their promise to bring relief; and frequently religious systems were the only lineages which appeared concerned with trauma suffering. They have identified the torment and as often have fostered it, often in the moment when they were attempting to bring resolution (see The Inquisition, and some current systems of psychological and spiritual transformation).

What needs to happen

Salvation as a way of framing the problem of existence may need to shed its sanctimonious garments and return to matter-of-fact healing, the secular redress of patterns of distress hopefully proffered by increasingly technical focus (neurochemical, physiological, psychological, spiritual) upon trauma and its elaborations. This does not mean that religions can stop paying attention to human suffering, but that institutionally they can recognize the developing expertises of psychological-humanistic, neurochemical understanding (primitive as in fact all these realms of focus may be). The best of both worlds already recognize these cross-over positionings, though so far apparently there is no unified strategy which actually works for all trauma-bound memories.

One could suggest that enlightenment (and the Enlightenment) secularizes and capacitizes the more theological idea of Salvation. Or concurrently, that Salvation indicates a clear state of (mindfulness) which precedes the historical appearance of, for example, Jesus and reaction to him by centuries, particularly in the ideas of Plato and the Buddhist meditators. This mindfulness is characterized by silence, stopping, witnessing, and devotion to relating to Ultimate Reality – reality.

Will it be I who will take on all of history, including the portions bequeathed to me through my parents, siblings, my congenital peers, my genes and my environment? How can these important others in time be expected to master the cruelties, the abandonments, fostered by actual experience and by energetic transmission? The task seems overwhelming and impossible. As has been known, Jesus on The Cross becomes a meditation upon these issues of karmic proportions. Can we take on the illusion contained within our commonplace sense of history drip by drip? And let it go, or better, let it self-dissolve?

11. The Christ

The Christ can be understood as a (verbal) concept/word expressing or characterizing a very high vibratory level of human consciousness, capable of being measured, with probably high serotonin content, leading to or expressing, embodying enlightenment. I think it carries a similar position to other transcendental modes of awareness, such as Buddha awareness (*bodhisattvan*), or Moses viewing the Burning Bush awareness, and certain Zen and Sufi states, Plato's The Good, and the like. We can often recognize its presence by the heightened sense of empathy and compassion and non-attachment which marks the person who carries and expresses Christ energy.

Its misuse is manifold, including identifying only one person of the past who holds (or incarnates) the energy, and he having lived a long time ago (though, according to the myth, he, and the Christ energy, can and shall be re-evoked). This strategy conceals its developmental truth, namely that all infants "contain" this energy, but through trauma, have it immobilized (crucified, dead, and buried), and apparently destroyed. In this sense the figure who has been The Christ and is no longer, except in a spiritual content sort of way, narrates what as infants we have all gone through and still contain within us as potentiality. We are traumata awaiting resolution: Christ energy immobilized, awaiting resurrection – sometimes declared as the Second Coming, to be manifest, delivered out of its immobilized latency in each of us.

The Second Coming as an idea centrally expresses the understanding that we are in dissociation until we are not. At the return of our accessing the Christ energy or centeredness, we shall be reunited with the segments of ourselves which have been cubicled, split off, whatever. In this centered place of Being, time is experienced non-sequentially, ahistorically, if you will, though we are walking through narrative time as well.

A preferable reading of such individualism might demonstrate that accessing this consciousness, one must be able to individuate to early prenatal states which are expressed ideationally by the co-relational pre-natal terms, "Only Son," "Only Begotten Son (or Daughter)", and "Son of God," all of which as prenatal creatures, from conception on, we embody, we incarnate.

Its misuse can be to project this crucial aspect of our development by attaching extravagant elaborations (King of Kings) to surround and protect the insights carried by a mythic hero. Which in the case of Jesus, he himself reportedly stated just the opposite: he was not the only one to hold the energy (he saw ancient tribal precedents); and his movements were not miraculous (as illustrated in the story of his Temptations) but were rooted in the reality-based understanding that The Kingdom of God (a neurochemical potentiality) exists within each person and is crucial to its development; the Christ is the marker of our development, right from the start. This is a spiritual potentiality, not a material one, though one could argue that it must be, and is, integrated in the material world energetically.

One side thought. By characterizing the spiritual hero as the only individual to encompass Christ energy and only once, and in the past, brain may be able to access the dissociative path to its own trauma sites, also involving one individual and also in the past. Otherwise, the task is so wholly energetic that its resolution is easily lost sight of in the apparent randomness of brain process. Unless we have narrative strategies, it is often hard to know where to begin.

For someone who as a person carries himself with transcendent awareness, the code term "Son of God" is a statement of his fulfilled transcendent awareness, not just a matter of the fact that we are all God's Children.

Another comment. When we seek the Christ energy, in the form of knowing the Christ (Jesus), one question is "Where can he (it) be found?" This question is always asked from the position of dissociation, wherein the black of shock obscures the Christ energy and its evolvement into the Light of Being. The rest of our story is fine – our Christ energy is moving and interpenetrating our neurophysiology quite nicely, thank you. We don't even know it is there.

But brain scans for the sites where it is not, the trauma sites, and it pleads for Salvation in these deoxygenated positions. Nothing else matters, the issue is crucial. All longings and calls for Redemption and Salvation arise from dissociated memorials whose essential characterization is movement, or essence, immobilized. No wonder the preachers promise relief in the meditational figure of the crucified Christ. Meditationally speaking, that appears to be the next step. We await The Messiah whose configuration will be a gestalt, a unity. The Messiah is the helpmate toward integration: as the Messiah is one, so we are one; and sociologically we are one. If applied with wry irony, The Messiah takes us to our Crucifixion, our impactions, from which we may ascend to Being.

12. Sins

Sins can be understood as narrative signs of dissociation. They occur once the trauma sites have been set in, often because of external patterns of dissociation transferred energetically by parents and society. Other forms of post-traumatic stress occur because we fall off a bicycle at the age of two, or get stuck in the birth canal. For the grandiose self, which is and is not responsible: time comes too early, cause and effect too difficult to evaluate.

We are crucified onto our own incomprehensibility. So the unraveling historically of the cause of some uncomfortable, even disastrous effect, has two stages. Stage One: the initial memorialization of some shock pattern. Stage Two: the attempt to resolve it and to preserve it. Sin has its own mythology, too often attached badly to bullying, perpetrating authorities, within and without each individual. With this in mind, sins can be viewed as propositive defenses against the deoxygenated cores of held-energy systems.

13. The sins of the father are visited upon the child

With the child's perceptions of the parents' helplessness, when it knows things could be different but aren't, then that empathy can lead quickly to a dark place of endless suffering: a place of Hell. As Dante proffers, Hell is filled with commemoration of unresolved held-energy systems. And once these sequences have been perceived, there is an historical consciousness which emerges, and one can see that starting with the iconic first person – a place of presumed beginnings – the sins of the world are the held-energy systems of traumatic patterning. And in their energetic invisibility, often they seem invulnerable to change. The karmic tradition demonstrates this phenomenon as old former-life patterns continue into the present for resolution in the here and now; and in the process revises and expands our sense of what the present moment, and with it, history as we know it, entails.

Confronted with a life-mandating empathic substructure, where we can comfortably and interestatingly move between ourself and the (uterine) world-environment, our infancy includes significantly learning how to discriminate energetic sensory-data coming our way. This task involves individuation powers between mother and child and includes learning how to conjoin, amass, to ignore, and to excrete. It also involves developing a platform for a secondary capacity for sympathy, a modified empathic mode.

Empathy includes the division potential of experience into Self and Other, such that Others are in fact others, not merely Self. This differentiation is an important strategy for limiting sense data, particularly at the deepest levels. We may start with everything seeming the same, in and out, but very soon, we are what we sense as different from. Of increasing importance is the thin chorionic tissue which – always present at some edge amid the landed blastocyst on the Mars Womb surface – will neurochemically separate us, critically, at birth, when the placenta, our buddy, peels off the uterine wall.

In the sensibility of the pregnant mother, there occurs a quickening, an awareness of the presence of an identity separate from the mother's baseline experience. In church myth, this quickening consciousness is expressed in the Annunciation of the presence of the Savior to the pregnant (Virgin) Mary. The myth declares a confluence of creation and originality as well as the (legitimate) grandiosity of the organic miraculous.

The mythic awareness of the Mother here does not include her being an active, sexual part of the creation of the infant; while pregnant, she is the Virgin, perhaps here a projection of the child's experiential "innocence". In some forms of regressive therapies, consciousness of conception and its surrounding circumstances becomes important to the dissolution of some held sequences.

In our empathic mode, one thing we do is to take on the parents' patterns; and we absorb them because by proximity, these patterns are ours, or they might as well be: we have to deal with them. They are in the room. I think it may be useful to propose that we first understand them empathically; then sympathetically, including at preverbal levels.

The other neurochemical level of sin transmission comes through the genes, where proclivities, tendencies, and physiological structures unfold. But to lay the blame for troubling sins, as opposed to deformities, to some Ibsenian syphilitic father is not the way this insight is usually meant. What is being noted in general is that the apple does not fall very far from the tree, through habit, imitation, mirroring, and training.

Another way the sins of the father are visited upon the child is through history, energetically and with words. Behaviors are reinforced by discipline and indoctrination. But again, this transmission is basically energetic and takes place invisibly, and we as individuals are left with insoluable patternings which come from the parent. My understanding is that the reason the patterns persist into the next generation is that they don't belong to the designated carrier/initiate. They originate from before.

14. Take on the sins of the world

The significant related corollary to the visiting sins of the father is "He takes on the sins of the world." This means that the infant absorbs the patterning from the parents, and later of the environment. Specifically, our bonding with the parent, by necessity and choice, involves an identification with the parent as an older version of the infant. It is the trusted escort. There appears to be a sequence where this absorptive sequence turns from necessity into choice, a crucial insight developed dramatically in what we might call the Crucifixion meditations.

A note. The phrase "take on" has some complexity. How do we take on the sins of an Other? One is by mirroring or imitating, another is literally absorbing across the Self/Other boundary, as in our uterine experience. Another is by a sort of memorization by rote; we are exposed over time. Another is by genetic transmission. Another is by attitudinal indoctrination through history, custom, and ritual. The final one, related to the second, is that we take on the sins by violence or insult, as in perpetration.

There appears to be a swamp-like phenomenon wherein we and the mother appear the same, though differentiation is always present, though not crucially mandated as later on, particularly at birth: what's hers is mine and vice versa. We take on her world because we are the major part of it as we experience it.

Empathy and metaphor

There are crossover sites, recorded in poetry and dream and music, when the Other takes on human qualities, and vice versa. In E.E. Cummings' poem, "Spring is like a perhaps hand" spring is compared to a human hand. The similie implies a differentiation, whereas a metaphoric treatment would involve more of the crosssover mode. As readers, often we are being linguistically escorted into the boundary-less territory of the pre-natal energetic.

Not surprisingly, the same insight applies to God, where we are God, as well as creatures of God, embodying God in our creatureship, in our ultimate reality. Both applications are developed linguistically from this sensate experience of blend. In this crossover mode, where we move from similie to metaphor, poems regularly mixing these features or initiating this premise are taking us back to the differentiation sequence which may be incomplete, or not.

In Dali's "Un Chien Andalou", his shots of the woman and of the man radically and scarily as well as funnily, portray the movement between Self and Other; a crossover which extends to the identification of the viewer with that which is being viewed on the screen. The artist is showing some efficacy, as he demonstrates the reality of the territory, perhaps its earliest stage. It is this level which brings or evokes empathy, though before, it is not self and other, nor Self and Other.

Out of a volume of blur – a developmental wash, if you will – emerges a platform of empathy, upon which Self and Other correspondingly play. It may be for a moment, it may last a lifetime. Here is the chorionic line of individuation. From this sea, there is a magnet-like focusing which draws infant brain toward resolution into firm objects, Self and Other, mouth and breast, if you will. As meditating adults, we can sense that decision to trust a world which is both plural and singular, the retaining of "We are the same" with "We are different."

From this mix, we may see the development of connection with the Mother, her importance as clarifier and point of stability; out of plurality, her oneness stands out, and we do too. In a similar way, when some supervising priest "regresses" its converting future "believer" to this crossover level, the importance of the singular gestalting form of Jesus becomes evident. Recapitulating and transmuting the old system of imperfect introjects, Jesus importantly becomes the Only Lord and Savior, a magnetic meditational focal point through which the power of the gestalt to take the plural and form it into the singular is manifest.

In like manner, our decision to use words and link them reflects our understanding of the energy they describe, and words become focal points of similar saving magnitude. Though we may not hold these words in our system without anxiety. When we hold these words without anxiety, they function as "symbolic" and organic, relating back to their energetic source without encumbrance or elaboration. They are distortion-free.

The heroic "saving" mind-set

A possible reason for the heroic "saving" mind-set is that as infants, we are learning how to discriminate and locate and maintain our center. We want this for ourselves, and we want it also for our escort. Here are the beginnings of relationship and compassion. Some theorists propose that we desire a clearer parent because we need the clearer parent for better parenting for us. Others intuit that we want the clearer parent not only for ourselves but for themselves. I ally with this latter position, which prefigures adult relationality with the parent, who is more realistically perceived and witnessed. Yet can we have both?

The initial intra-uterine wash between parent and child begins to have boundaries, at the chorionic level, at the umbilical severing, at the newborn's ascent up the mother's body, and the subsequence separations of time and space. Self and Other becomes an axis of understanding, with an implied inter-wash provided by the energetics of empathy. "I know you because I sense what you are experiencing. And I do that because we are the same." I think it is these formulations which lead to Aristotle's definition of tragedy as being an imitation of a serious action, leading to a catharsis of the emotions involving pity and fear. Imitation implies a Self and Other construct.

The patterns don't change

But, as I have discussed elsewhere in this book, the parent patterns do not change. They do not change because they are absorbed from their carrying and transmitting parents, to whom they are dedicated in the same way as our infant is dedicated to them. We end up picking up both the positive energetics (experienced as direct, clear freedom) as well as the held information systems of traumata installed generations before; rituals and tradition occasion such pattern transmission as well as often the promise of their resolution.

Our task can be to integrate and absorb the information in digestible, non-incapacitating form. One useful way is to "return" the impacted pattern to the parent, and to advise the receiving parent to do the same. Again, I surmise that the reason the patterns persist is that they do not belong to the carrier, so the carrier has no informed way to bring the pattern to the curbside for the recycle Green-people to pick up and appropriately dispose.

15. He dies for our sins

At the core of the idea of dying for someone else's sins (or better, holding patterns) is in fact a cultural-personal memory of something we have done, namely observed that people absorb patterns (including ours) and take them in with the conviction and (what becomes a) moral-emotional goal that we are ready to die in order to help the persons we love from being in agony or danger.

Maternal love has this significant quality, so we may adopt it in learned form from the mother's energetic; our mother could and will die to save us from whatever. Some prenatalists, like William Emerson, suggest that as the infant's head confronts and navigates past the mother's sacrum, the issue of life and death is manifest – the mother can die and will die and so will the child: our gift of life includes the fact of our mortality.

Children (including, I think, infants) feel this transmitted conviction intensely, and the die-for-sins strategy, contrary to being an obscure, arcane, or inexplicable theological side-order, is in fact a developmental understanding about childhood, particularly infancy, which we seem to forget rather often, yet it matters very much. It is crucial to our discovery/experience that there is a Self and an Other. And that the Other can die – even when they are trying to help us out.

Concomitant with this ultimation is the awareness that we die. Our held-energy system(s) prefigures, or perhaps better, imitates death, as well as the insight that within the held-energy systems of trauma lies a code of restoration, and more, the promise of full-functioning cells. For some, the Resurrection promises that this radiant core can be reactivated and the shock residue dissolved. Using this model, set within an historical grid in which the present represents (imitates?) a completed expression of the past, it is possible to propose that "belief" that the crucified Jesus (a crucial description of traumatically held-energy systems – but not necessarily the only one) has died for our sins can bring about a transformation of our current (ahistorical) held-energy systems: here is Salvation, if there ever was one.

Furthermore, as preachers worry a lot about when traversing this mythic slope, the factuality of these forms, their pervasive influence in our development, the truth of resolution is not a matter of faith or belief, or hope; one could easily get stuck even in fundamentalism, attempting meditationally to generate and achieve these alchemical states (as true).

Also, the discovery that such Salvation, or trauma resolution, is demonstrated in the narrative particulars of the life of Jesus may lead to an understanding of how the pattern resolution is to be achieved; this means that the resolution could be triggered by anyone holding similar points of focus. This understanding should not be a secret. In the Christian tradition, there is a concern built from this understanding that in order for the rubric to work, one has to acknowledge Jesus as one's only Lord and Savior. Perhaps obviously, this strategy carries both truth and error. From a gestalt point of view, our ducks (including the Jesus part) have to be aligned within the system of Being in order to invite the desired transmutation. This gestalt strategy repeats our selection in conception as "only begotten", "Son of God", the Chosen One. The error can lie in a limited delineation of the nature of the spiritual hero; the Jesus who transmutes is hardly comprehended. Just as the historical Jesus (the actual man, if there was one) only recently has begun to emerge in commonplace dialogue in very limited ways.

A nexus

We take on the sins of the world, but sometimes we don't explicate what those sins are and in what ways they do us in – until they don't. It seems this strategy is preverbal in nature, and the literature indicates this and art indicates this because in these "narratives", for the most part, Jesus is still a non-speaking child. There are of course exceptions where speech balloons arise from Baby Jesus's mouth, or he makes adult benediction gestures with his hands. We also recognize that people appear to sacrifice themselves for other people, including soldiers, doctors, mothers, policepersons, fathers, sons and daughters in the military, etc., literally and psychologically-mythically.

As I now understand it, the phrase "he dies for our sins" narrates an energetic nexus, or complex grouping of ideas/experiences. We take on the sins, the traumatic holding patterns, of the parents, and discover that we share in some sense the responsibility for their resolution. We discover that sins can be transmitted. And ultimately we discover the grandiosity within this mechanism; and we have to give this grandiosity up. No matter how strong the emotional connection to the world is, the grandiosity must "die", *i.e.*, the pattern must transmute. This understanding, of course, is the major part of why Good Friday is called good: shock immobility, and its two-dimensional literal and compressed narrative is leading to transmutation into three-dimensions – and invisibility.

We also learn that our capacity for empathic understanding is thwarted by too early adoption of this strategy, when we become flooded by this intergenerational input. Sometime later, we also may realize that if we live with these patterns, this "mechanism" destroys us. Beyond loyalty and thereby remaining close to our parents, there is no compensation for some (most, all?) patternings, and they must be energetically, vectorally returned as the sins of their parents, to apparently at least three generations back. But, as above, because the same mechanism is operating in the generation before us, where the parents as children have taken on the sins of their parents, the patterns are endless, and are endlessly reduplicated and impossibly re-revisited – until they are not. In a perhaps curious way, time, here emotional time, is a significant part of our understanding of three-dimensional awareness.

Abraham sacrifices Isaac

The story of Abraham sacrificing his son Isaac demonstrates these issues. Under Ultimate Pressure, Abraham is convinced that God wants him to kill his son, a primitive animal response and one which helps mother bears guard their young against the predatory father bear. Somehow, Abraham comes to the insight/conclusion that he can "sacrifice" a nearby ram stuck in a bush, and God – some inner and outer "voice" – will be "satisfied". For some analysts, this insight shift is the beginning of symbolic thought and of civilization; it certainly seems to be a sign of muting – repressing or transmogrifying raw aggression.

For the infant who contains this story, we can witness a modification of its aggressive nature and the beginning of humane and decent social living. The insight works two ways, outwardly in socialized behavior, and inwardly, in our sense of intelligent playfulness with inner forces. The power of this sublimative strategy means that the internal narratives do not have to be acted out (upon), but that satisfaction of the brain-tyranny can occur in substitute ways. Direct narration, outside and inside, can be transformed, even dissolved; thus activities contain layered and complex understanding. It is like the night-mared child being told by its mother, "You've just had a bad dream. It did not really happen."

In the same way that the ram/lamb substitutes as way for transmogrification of sins, so, the myth illustrates, Jesus substitutes for us. The inner voice which is being stilled here says, "You have sinned, you should die". Or, currently, "Your traumatic, shock-retaining history has permanently separated you from Ultimate Reality." Like a fantasy portrait sequence of the Virgin Birth, we transfer what we tyrannically thought was ours onto another persona as a way of keeping the useful concept of sacrifice viable.

We shall sacrifice the hero – only he chooses to be sacrificed – for all of us. There is a reduction of agency in the image and fact of his surrender, and it speaks to the infant's surrender to the patterns and to their resolution. We substitute sins for self, and substitute self for self. Projection and imitation of held-energy patterns flourish in this mechanism.

The idea of sacrifice occurs as a strategy for disposing of or concluding held-energy systems. It presumably concludes the urgent movement to the surface of dissociation of patterns and narratives which do not apply to the present; they obscure and confound Being.

There may be two things

So there may be two things, at least, happening here. One: the recognition of narrative layers of understanding, including the basing of activities on their symbolic meaning – and that symbols can be (sacrificially) dissolved. And Two: that sins, as narratives, can be dissolved into new and releasing (of obsessionally stalemated) neurochemical configurations. The salvation or redemption formulation seems to take on the following sequence: "This pattern does not belong with me, Mother, nor does it belong with you, nor does it belong with Granny, from whom you got it." This strategy is different from substitutional sacrifice.

For the infant, there is the experience of the mother's total devotion to its life, the experience of sacrifice if you will, which mothers carry and convey, right from the start. This understanding is now transferred to the infant itself, the spiritual hero. The two-way-street-ness of the capacity to self-sacrifice, as it were, is a significant developmental place, setting the child deeper into the world of adult and relational experience.

That the hero can or does choose the new role seems to me significant. That the resultant neurochemistry comes out all right in a transformative way is significant information. It is a little like learning how to hold your breath under water; we work against our survival "impulse" and find we can do more than we thought. The death of the hero and with him, the death of the grandiosity and the unmoderated use of empathy, we are somehow saved from our sins. That of course is a fantastic, infantile structure. And imperative in its meaning, both magical and real.

We know that the therapeutic presence of another who is empathic changes some trauma patternings, though one might argue that that is a sometime thing. But true empathic understanding provides an externalization site which allows us to see the Other and Ourselves realistically and with realism; the brain restores itself to its original purpose, which is for each cell, each individual, to complete fully, a curiously democratic, even reiterive Protestant ideal, if you will. We could think of it as a blooming.

According to the myth, the compression of the crucifix – and its narrative the Crucifixion – is expanded in the days after its Occurrence, and the Assumption, in spiritual time some 40 days later, entails the re-siting of the energies encompassed and acknowledged in the death of the hero.

There is something about dying for one person's sins – like a policeman, at risk to himself, rescuing a drowning boy – and dying for everyone's sins, which takes us into the plural, the grandiose and infantile objective, which includes child-like understanding of the nature of love. It also provides narrative grounding, as Adam's wounded and wounding role – heroic– is served by Jesus and speaks to the child's understanding that there is a transmission of patterning, and that it has to start somewhere. If it starts somewhere, it ends somewhere.

There is contained in the idea of dying for someone's sins a grandiosity and an over-the-top gestural scale which, though developmentally true to our earliest experience of the mother and to our sense of worthiness in our survival, is exceptional. That God would agree to such a sacrifice returns us quickly to the drawing board as to where do we get that idea in the first place. There is a complex spiritual and developmental combination plate here, set in neo-poetic jargon.

To this can be added the parental sacrifice of its young, God of Jesus, Agamemnon of Iphigenia, indirectly King Marke of Tristan, and huge sections of enormous blood-shedding in emotionally driven wars such as the American Civil War and the World Wars of the 20th Century. The rhetoric promises healing with the survivors; the child (son) is dedicated to bring healing to the wounded parent (father).

Some prenatalists observe that in the sperm journey toward fertilization, perhaps millions of brother sperms die in the task of sending one (or more) into the egg(s). They draw a prefigurative parallel to the monstrosities in war, where, for the Cause, hundreds of thousands are "sacrificially" slaughtered and slaughtered.

16. Perfect sacrifice

Each child takes on an historically-bequeathed pattern but cannot resolve it. Here is a boundary problem, because we think the pattern is ours, when it is not. Then the parent may reject our attempts to resolve the pattern. The parent "says", "You are not enough to solve my problem (any parent's problem). The alleviation of my suffering is beyond you and your presence and your heart-felt desire that my agony be different." Here is a loss of agency, perpetually foisted upon the Christ Child. And perfect sacrifice restores the relationship to the love-wounding father (or mother) so that it is ok not to be enough to solve the parent's pattern: with this realization comes a regaining and modulation of confidence within the infant.

Again, the reason the parent cannot solve the (whatever) problem can be that the parent is tied in allegiance to its parent's allegiance to its parents' parent's trauma sites. Laocoön-like, each child is betrayed by its distracted parent, whose priorities are elsewhere and beyond reach. One starts to look for an "ending" or "solution" to this nightmare, invisibly conveyed lineage. Here are notes from a TE session.

> Energetically, the meditator sees that the form has penetrated her chest like a lemon slice, so what needs to happen is it is lifted out, and a separation can be experienced and transmitted.

The questions "What needs to happen here?" and "Whose pattern is this?" are both requited. The reason the pattern cannot be excised is because it doesn't belong to the person holding it. Here, the Christ child taking on the sins of the world can be experienced as a developmental curse, and it must be resolved.

Sacrifice includes significantly the objective of trauma resolution. That is its promise, and it involves displacement and representation. When people object to the death of Jesus and the inflamed, obsessional reverence with an event which may seem sadomasochistic and is rendered sacrificial, they may be sensing that what is significant about Jesus' position is not the surrender, as a prelude to an entry into the black of Good Friday and the reformulation of the neurochemistry into light at the base of Good Saturday. The vision of the Cross brings us to the epicenter of the trauma site, with its unresolved 90° angles, and this site as a site of contemplation will not "work" within agonizing surround. Perfect sacrifice might mean complete dissolve of the pattern, not its violent destruction. In this sense surrender would describe how the pattern, terrible memorial as it is, must be completely viewed without anxiety.

It is confounding for the child to sense that its parents are more (irrationally) loyal to their parents' absorbed patterns than they are to their own child, itself. Allied is one of the assumptions which parents profess: "My child's life will be an improvement over mine." Yet the confoundment mitigates as we understand our own absorption of the sins of our parents who remain loyal children in the same way our grandparents were to their parents' child-loyalty. It is a kid-loyalty bonding thing between generations.

We also know that the darker version of this strange realm contains the truth that some people die psychologically because they have not been able to remove themselves from the influence of others. Grounded in the rampant green fields of empathy, it is not a sacrifice we would think real or immutable. Or worthy. Yet I think it occurs and is not recognized as such.

The idea of a contract or covenant with God however can appear ludicrous; while the energy of this syndrome is not. It falls into an axis of Self and Other, and the experience of empathy, which is compounded when the child-body is separated from the placenta and the mother (yet miraculously, the relationship is sustained in a new – resurrected – way and elaborated).

17. The Crucifixion

Aside from the complete and sad irony of a very good, enlightened person, an individual man, being destroyed by tribal, societal, political, militaristic imperial suppression, ancillary insights about human experience soon rapidly cluster around this renowned event within the first three centuries after it presumably occurs. As spiritual hero, Jesus is basically non-violent; and in this case, non-violence loses politically, but ends up with the social, political authorities of the later Roman empire acknowledging they had got it very much wrong (while continuing to manifest and support violence and "power over").

The "King of the Jews" commentary at the top of the Cross encompasses a revision of what it means to lead, and it shows both to Jews and not Jews that the spiritual hero supercedes and is the destination point for the culture, not political aspiritualism. The resurrective aftermath of this text for the Hebrews, and one which both "believers" and non-believers fall into, is that this nexus is traditionally discerned as a question of belief, when it is merely a statement of spiritual fact. If we could site it, the subsequent separation of Jews into Christians, and Gentiles, and Jews might be seen to rest on errors of understanding – misunderstandings – perhaps nothing more. Not anything we would disagree about. That would be the substantial irony.

The third "irony" is that Jesus, precocious and supported in Buddhist practices, wherein he is thought to be an highly-evolved *bodhisattva*, returns to his home where he is both understood and not understood. His higher vibratory state (non-violent, psychodynamic insight and master of some inward sea), brings forth the cultural traumata (brutal, isolating, cruel, ironic, abandoning) just waiting for a narrative to hold their resolution. And here we may see how the scapegoat is always an inherent, incipient leader, and vice versa.

If we hadn't had an historical crucifixion to mobilize this insight, we would have had to invent one; culturally, evolutionarily, it was time for the next phase of understanding the patterns discovered by the Jews and the Buddhists, precursors to so-called Christianity. Throughout the known world, a series of enlightened thinkers and spiritual adepts appear in the first BCE millennium; there is something in the water. A civilizing momentum demonstrates in the West with the perhaps mobilizing focus initially enabled through the Book of Genesis and its collective meditation. But its spiritual foundations very likely lie eastward.

The Crucifixion is mythic, and psychodynamically illustrative and perhaps can (only) be understood as such. Otherwise it reveals a social chaos in which we are never understood and wherein primitive fear powers over – prevails – as we are merely, annihilatively, casually and painfully destroyed. This happens a lot. With its strong Buddhist substructure, the Easter sequence involves the transformation of consciousness wherein the trauma site, initially graphically characterized as a cruciform with four juxtaposed 90° angles, upon which a body is forcefully immobilized – shock systems be advised – finally dissolves; and radiance is relocated and finally re-expressed, in an adjusted spatial (right-left brain) and administrative, executive functioning hierarchy ("he sitteth at the Right Hand of God the Father Almighty").

The Cross itself captures or locates a confluence of right angles, the hardest energetic line to smooth out, closest often to the epicenter of traumatic process and itself a declaration of shock, created and creating. Energetically, the Cross states what shock can look like, and the figure affixed to its form is how it retroactively energetically senses, once in the memory. It is the pre-windshield sign of arrest.

The crucified Body disappears

The crucified Body disappears. Meditationally, the Body, and the dualism which it often characterizes, disappears as the energetic becomes precedental. This is a spiritual fact and a reality worth noting. The psychosexual interpretations of this insight nexus significantly include the fact that it is three women who discover the empty Tomb, a container with no body in it.

Jesus (and on the Cross) might be viewed as a gestalt of the Jewish tribal tradition, referring to its intimate relationship to Ultimate Reality and to the social traumata within Hebrew lineages. Again, is there reason for disputation about these spiritual, energetic issues?

If adeptly held, the Crucifixion reveals the traumatic compression and its resolution destiny at an alchemical level. But most of us, Jews and Christians, and Gentiles, and others, cannot hold its explosive and liberating truth in trustworthy fashion; because what it describes is at the heart of traumatic dissociation. At best its application as insight (and flashlight) is a slow drip, a vaccination which millennia later is still "taking". And for its explication, the resolution destiny strongly depends upon the Buddhist focus on removing the attachments which cause our suffering.

The danger of the Cross as image and meditational focus is that it, like other strategies, can bring us very close to the nexus of our potentially healing center, but in our dissociative enthrallment, it can become addictive, both revealing and concealing the truth.

No matter the frequency of Crosses in our awareness, the sequence is not easy to visualize. Because it is a literal narrative with a symbolic, energetic (sub)text, the figure of the spiritual hero on the Cross both reveals and conceals the truth being explicated; beneath and within the surface, narrative image, lies the energetic. I wonder if the bait and switch quality of sacrificial substitution itself may have something to do with the continuing draping of Jesus's loins. It certainly motivates the need for a perfect sacrifice, because otherwise the whole strategy could be seen as corrupt: symbolic substitutionality could let us get off scot-free, never having to reset the initiating aggression nor our tyrannical supervisory judgment function of response, or learning. We would never experience our true, liberating transformation.

Additional Crucifixion commentary

Narrative of the Crucifixion myth (which is true as spiritual and energetic reality – it did and continues to happen) allows for the trauma sequence as we experience things post-traumatically. We have the High – Palm Sunday, the celebration of the Jesus neurochemistry at the Last Supper, with portending ominous clouds on the horizon. What follows is a portrait of the crushing mechanisms which bring forward the Crucifixion portrait itself. In the Easter sequence, these elements are spread out in a political and human sequence, whereas mostways, the compression of the Crucifixion occurs suddenly, or invisibly: suddenly the trauma pattern is on the plate from which we are eating.

I think the historical elaboration of why or how Jesus ends up on the Cross could be seen as a "false" narrative, similar to the Temptation of Eve. It is an attempt to fill in some level of causality where the central insight is the sequence High, followed by patterns of impaction and compression. Historically, the reworking of this sequence has been fraught with meaning for millions, including those who have died concerning its interpretation and framing. Somehow, someone is accountable for this deeply influential and profound pattern sequence; but I think it is not the usual suspects.

Let's remember that there are two levels of trauma, the first implantation of the synaptical sequence, and the later attempts to influence the pattern or for the pattern to resolve. These get layered (and confused), so that the attempt to get to the truth below the narrative is quite legitimate, similar to finding the Original Sin or the point of initiation of the First Trauma. This is the point we have to get to to enable the primitive brain to spring itself out of the trap of unresolved trauma. But our understanding of history at the narrative level obscures or commingles with the energetic reality within and below, and it is that reality which must be addressed if we are going to line ourselves up for the alchemical change we seek.

Often in ordinary therapies, if we are lucky, narrative and energetic levels combine, reducing our suffering to tolerable levels. By making the narrative historically site specific, we aim to achieve this developmental sequence, and the church mythologists have "uncovered" Stations of the Cross to indicate some emotional sequencing; how effective they are in bringing Enlightenment is a question. Overall, as one "recovering" Catholic said laughingly, "We have focused on the Body, not on the angles of the Cross; we have been focusing on the wrong thing." Well, maybe.

The death of Jesus on a cross includes real perpetration against a real person: we tend to lose our focus, and the nails and the blood are real. This is a tragic and befuddled weekend, but the overall sequence as elaborated by spiritual insight is *tragictatus*; it demonstrates, perhaps crudely as we currently hold it, a viable completion of an energetic problem initially recognized in the West perhaps by ur-Hebrew mystics.

18. Aging and trauma

One way toward characterizing our path to Enlightenment is to suggest that the process of clearing out traumatic patterning becomes increasingly difficult and also more simple. We get to identify the trauma sites with greater skills, and we experience these sites' dissolution: we know more of what freedom means, and we seek to live in the light.

And the remaining sites, or their ruins, continue to plague us and are reflected physiologically and synaptically. Our preoccupations become less grounded in reality and are more clearly signs of decrepitude and illusion; the narratives of our dementias and lesser disconnects state the original traumas sites cast in stoney black from our earliest times. The problem of clearage remains as it always has, amid rigidity and dissociation grounded in shock.

19. Judgment Day

Judgment Day is a sequential and consequential sense of time, and it expresses the longing for returning to a state of Being. All the projections upon this focal point, including bliss and gnashing of teeth speak to dissociative process, or the wages of such. Perhaps we need to recall that at Judgment Day, all further judgment ceases. We are restored to pure Being, wherein we now, only partially dwell. How ready are we for such change?

20. Miracles

First of all, creation can and probably should appear to us as miraculous, that is awesomely (ultimately) beyond our ordinary human understanding. When we perceive and understand creation's workings, down to the subatomic substructures, the reality of creation remains marvelous, and thus over time we contract and enlarge our understanding of the word or experience of miraculous. At the tiniest and grandest levels of creation, we may know how things appear to happen, but do we know why things are the way they seem to be? To affix the word miraculous to this level of not understanding includes an appropriate sense of wonder. It also may help us renegotiate our sometimes tyrannical relationship with Ultimate Reality.

In religious lineages particularly in the West, the term miracle is used to describe an occasion when our expectations for reality are expanded by a sense of extraordinary process, usually positive, beyond what we are used to; usually we don't call the Fall of Constantinople miraculous. In the Christian tradition, the stories of miracles are used to validate the belief that by performing them, Jesus was (the) Son of God and hence a clear someone to pay notable attention to, to learn from. He maintains a translucent focus and spiritual positioning which enables him to have especial and supra-inclusive dialogue with Ultimate Reality.

In fact, as far as we can glean, Jesus spoke against miracles, *i.e.*, against defying the laws of nature. His responses to his Temptations show a firm understanding and alignment with the real world. As a developmental stage, the Temptations reflect infantile grandiosity coming to grips with oxygen and gravity, and as lessons, they are good models for the modified spiritual hero we might become. They refine what we can be looking for or at, as opposed to things more fanciful.

What can we say about the so-called miracles of Jesus? They can all be explained or better, framed psychologically, psychodynamically and their gospel reportage corrupts and is corrupted by individuals, both speakers and listeners, who want to present, in baby-step ways, the experience of belief and faith to a gullible and dissociatively resistant audience, which incidentally, after centuries, continues to thrive.

The problem up for examination is then not to disprove the miracles as miracles, for their underlying truthfulness is still true. Rather, they are ways of seeing what the spiritual hero brings to situations which reflect a special level of consciousness which is connected to spiritual enlightenment or transformation. What Jesus brings to each situation appears to be an understanding of clarity with reality, which he relationally calls the Father, and what happens when you align yourself within that alliance as a child-like follower. In the aftermath of the miracle situation, Jesus and his followers see the event as instructing in a new level of consciousness in relation to Ultimate Reality.

From this special, relational point of view, we follow the directions on the package and then special things happen ordinarily, things which might not have happened if we focused elsewhere. Inner, spiritual transformation has an alchemical effect on our mind-body, and our sense of what is possible in the most important ways is expanded into the realm of the awesome. Interventionist, the world then is incipiently miraculous; we merely have to just not know it but also to understand it. Then the truth emerges in its potentiality, in its always-present actuality.

Twenty centuries later, Vimala Thakar reiterates, "Knowledge is not understanding. Knowledge is useful, but it is a burden. Understanding however does not accumulate like knowledge. It is a function of being. Knowledge helps us organize the world, but it is memorized." In the default mode network, our perceptions are largely predetermined, both helpfully and not. Understanding comes when the dissociated held-energy systems within that network dissolve, and we can see clearly.

Apparently here there are two levels to our predetermined consciousness, the neurologically regular, and the held-energy systems. That they might overlap or coincide would be a problem of differentiation for the experiencer of these modes. The regular would be ordinary easefulness with tasks: we do not have to reinvent shoelaces and windows to tie and open them; or to talk about them. They reveal themselves in synaptical sequencing full of color and transform regularly into light. The held energy-systems are shock-bound, addictive, repetitive, and characterized energetically in black – frozen, blocked, and deoxygenated. Shock leaves markers.

What then perhaps is Jesus preaching? Through his sermons and often koan-like parables, he prepares his listeners to listen in a transformative way: watching the energy directly, not just through narrative, takes its place at the table, and alchemically, we are invited past our regular and trauma-strewn consciousness toward the much harder apprehension and dialogue with reality.

In the film The Gospel of John [*Visual Bible International, 2003*], which heavily follows the so-called original text, I think we see dramatized a particularly clear presentation of this historic and spiritual transformation. What the young visionary rabbi is suggesting is possible is a kind of attention (in our current jargon, perhaps, mindfulness), a movement through and past of ordinary awareness to a different way of experiencing things.

At this extra, meditational level, Jesus is discovering the Father, and that the Father is separate from the Mother. As the movie dramatizes, his pronouncements, as well as his actions, are exciting, yet people, including his followers, do not understand, and of course that includes the establishment rabbis and the priests, and the rulers. These latters observe a ranting, charismatic seer who is evoking responses in the populace which enflame them into magical thinking, one of the risks of belief and to social order.

Somewhat unlike the parables, Jesus's demonstrable miracles are duplicatable and explainable from gestalt and Buddhist insight, both of which Jesus has access to, by experience and by intuition. If we have a chance to see the miracle events through these perspectives, we may be able to see them accurately; and we will not quarrel about the reality being described.

Apparently, what Jesus does is set the mental stage for transcendent integration which is desired by almost everybody, and the rabbis, concerned with the inflammability of the populace, perhaps rightly, want to order and control. They do not want to join him. In fact where recorded are the rabbis or rulers in his presence who convert? St. Paul, one of the resisting establishment, who finally understands the toxic nature of projection, changes in major ways, but not completely; I find his enlightenment significant and partial.

So it may be easy to see the threat Jesus's presence characterizes, and, attempting to re-establish order and safety, perhaps correctly, these civil and military individuals respond to it at the political level which the Romans (and the oppressive Roman dominant presence in the lives of the Jewish communities) provide. A resultant historical question is how could anybody assassinate a fundamentally good man, not to mention a non-violent spiritual hero? Somebody or some people, should be made to pay for not seeing the truth.

In the death of Jesus, we have a confounding double aspect which has confused us. The narrated killing of the man Jesus, though different, runs iconographically parallel to the killing of or suppression – the repressive thwarting of Christ energy, Christ consciousness. Many times, the individual who carries such high vibratory states with some vividness gets killed (and yet the spirit lives on) see Kennedys, MLK, Malcolm X, Lincoln, Itzak Rabin, Jesus, some Old Testament prophets, etc. To say that the Jews are responsible for the death of Jesus has been politically manipulative, for it is the Romans who are the literal murderers; they have the power, though not the imaginative, spiritual understanding, to stop the Crucifixion. The political gesture of getting the crowds to vote and the entrapped rabbis to conspire is a Roman crowd control ploy obvious to those who are caught in the middle of it, including the victim. As is often opined in sermons, most of us would side with the authorities and the scapegoating crowds, as we now still often do.

At the historical levels of narrative, it may be argued that it does not matter who kills Jesus. Or whether he dies or survives. The story is very ordinary at many levels, repeatable and predictable. The judgments made are matter-of-fact and contemporary. In a sense there is no (new) lesson to be learned here: crowds are crowds, magistrates are magistrates, and scapegoats scapegoats. And these problems of authority continue to rankle, often in catastrophically morbid ways.

If you want to say, I don't like the patterns you are pointing out, and so I object to the Crucifixion, yes, of course. In the first three centuries after Jesus's death, some begin to stand up against the aeons-long tyrannies and demand to sit at the front of the bus. Yet the victimization and scapegoating prevails throughout the subsequent centuries with only slight movement toward the obliteration, better, letting go of such phenomena. If you add to it not only Jesus the man, but the figure identified as a creature of higher consciousness, then it seems all the worse, but as Jesus reports, "They know not what they do." We are talking about wholesale, rampant, perpetrative dissociation. And if we project our own trauma upon others, why kill any Other?

One further question, terribly elaborated upon, has been whether the Jews as a social tribe entity kill off not only one of their own, but more significantly the Christ energy, and the answer is sort of (repeat sort of) yes and so does everybody else, by factor of the held-energy systems we institute and preserve. We are all administrative victims and perpetrators of the perseverence of memorized shock and the truth it conceals. Until we are not.

But this insight makes the narrative of the death of Jesus become something else, an add-on healing subtext which for centuries has been working its way to the surface, to dovetail with ordinary political understanding. It makes the death of Jesus a statement about trauma and its influence and primacy in our lives. Until we can contextualize its presence in our ordinary dissociative consciousness, it makes the death miraculous, hence, paradoxically, our focus on the literal event. I think the descriptions of the Holy Week and Easter phenomena are filled with cross-over focus between the literal man and the energetic embodiment of traumatic process.

The post-death Resurrection is confirmation of the spiritual truth which takes over the telling, namely that the fixed patterning of shock which survives energetically throughout variant narratives, can (be) dissolve(d) at the energetic level, with resultant transformation of personality perspective within each (any) individual, and without. This fact Jesus understands, particularly when he notes, "The Kingdom of God is within you."

Thus, Jesus knows this neurochemical, developmental potentiality, and his miracles are ordinary and not counter to mindful existence. Each occasion records the bringing of people into an altered state, at best usually from magical thinking into a true apprehension of the (sacred) transformations which occur and can occur when observed with luck and with some skill. And yet the miracle experiences get transformed quickly by those who are nearby witnesses and turn to tell others about them.

For example, the storm with Jesus walking on water to save his disciples is the equivalent of a Buddhist meditation, an altered state that transforms the momentary attachment to anxiety into a calm perception, gravity congruent, of reality. The group of apostles get anxious together – stormy – and then the technique, courtesy of their teacher, comes to them, and it works. The storm subsides as inner violence is replaced by affiliative comfort and centeredness. We can hear Jesus saying, "OK fellows, when you are experiencing inner turbulence, let me show you a meditational strategy the monks taught me in the East. They call it Walking on Water, and here's the sequence; it's at least about attachment." And later, separate from their teacher and in despair, they try it out and, applied, it works, in some crucial way. But the transformation of this truthful strategy quickly gets obfuscated by errors in focus about literalness by those who preach his life and gospel; with friends like these, Jesus does not need enemies.

How to share with others of the practicality of Jesus's vision. As Jesus tells stories, so his followers teach with parable, disguised as historical narratives upon which there is, through time, elaboration. They conjure up an image of a storm at sea and of Jesus's energetic consciousness transcending the storm, in effect, walking on water. This story, literally true in the energetic, meditational sense, corrals magical thinking coupled with a sense of surrender, perhaps yielding into an altered state of awareness in the brain of the hearer, perhaps not. The usual suspects of narrative, literalness and logic, are held differently, as is narrative itself. If the death of Jesus means the death of holding narrative in a different way ("Oh Death, where is thy sting?"), then its apparent loss returns us to our dissociative selves, without hope for transformation at the neurochemical, alchemical levels.

Ironically, I wonder if self-proclaimed Buddhists may be as susceptible to this brand of culpability as are those orthodox or fundamentalist strain holders, and there is a mystery as one peers past one's presuppositions inwardly viewed, asking for answers to questions like "What's is next?" and "What happens inside and outside?" And being able to roll into this form of believability, transcending the ordinary without collapsing or floating upward, is a skill, not to mention an acquired taste. And hard to sustain.

But the miraculous as experienced is not magical, it is manifest reality, grounded in reality. It depends upon the transcendent being manifest in the real world, with real flesh and blood; it contains the alchemical truth. And it can be approached through reality, which in ordinary terms is as transcendent as we could wish. It can be approached and joined by mindfulness, if you will: as special kind of mindfulness.

How we hold the miracles, and the miraculous, is the important thing: what we focus upon and do not get distracted from, once we absorb the initial narrative approaches to the problem of consciousness transformation.

21. War and trauma

Thoughts beyond the regular thoughts: War and trauma are carefully linked. Wars occur according to the sense of too much density and compression, related to territory, inner (including deoxygenation) and outward. When the lebensraum is experienced as too limited, as carried by the leaders in their personalities and trauma patterns which move them to leadership. Then there is a choice to fight, and to sacrifice. To die or to kill, both expressing gestalt insight. People die for various ideas, reasons, but I think it might come down to compression and territory, as held. Beneath that are clusters of traumatic patternings pushing forward, crowding forward, for resolution. We are promised: here is the freedom from to which we all aspire.

But in war, the freedom is a predominantly head-banging, violent strategy, doomed from the start. The men who choose to surrender their lives, site their lives at the ground are partly suicidal, fixed, and oxygen-depleted, as are the leaders and populaces who sanction them. Again coming out of a limited sense of space, inner and outer.

There is also a cultural territoriality, where people encounter their trauma patterns. And the patterns seem to be insoluable; and they drive us mad and into a do-or-die resolution: we invite some cowboy to hit us on the jaw, to knock us past our current consciousness.

If we are full of crap and can't get rid of it by ourselves, we pick a fight. Our hope is that we shall conquer the inner turmoil by projecting on another our own impasses. And graciously mirroring, they do the same. Thus choosing the enemy has to be done carefully. We have to line up ourselves thematically with the Other, whom we shall destroy or be destroyed by.

War has a number of pausing, surfacing points; and one, crucial for the frontline soldier, is when he sees that the war means nothing but destruction and chaos. He is alone without any supports. He faces Ultimate Reality which includes meaninglessness, see the movie "Platoon", Crane's *The Red Badge of Courage*, and Melville's *Moby Dick*. It is a point, often heretofore experienced, of supreme individuation, wherein we face retraumatization.

The battle set is not the battle chosen. The game plan moves to a point, when the battle is joined and then all hell breaks loose, and what follows are standard, recognizable tropes of rescue and abandonment. Here World War I is just like World War II, as is Vietnam and the American Civil War; and the Battle of Waterloo. Locked in prewar traumatic patternings, we promise ourselves greatness, but concomitantly we deliver squalor and death, wherein nations and cultures are eliminated, the survivors left carrying old unresolved trauma and new.

War prunes, war occurs to prune. But the held-energy systems are maintained in those who survive, until they do not. And they may not die, even though their carriers, their embodiers, do: in children, historians, in cultural memorialized identity.

War obviously creates trauma, in my uncles, in my friend who loses his hearing because he stands too close to a shipboard cannon, in my great-grandfather who survives the Civil War.

War tries to be decisive, provide a final solution to held-energy systems which will not obliterate under violence; but only by careful, watchful unwinding and dissolution. And accountability.

22. Loss of Faith

Often we confuse loss of trust in religious tropes and institutional perpetrations, often tyrannically applied in early childhood, with loss of spiritual experience and its allied openness and self-reliant inner experience, spiritual and energetic. Leaving the church or the temple or mosque is not the end of the journey, by any means. Our capacity to know and to understand still remains.

23. Developmental Bible

Perhaps the most important reason for the sustained Bible lineage is that it contains poetic and descriptive statements about our developmental history as cultures and as individuals. If the states of awareness were not accurate to these neurochemical and psychodynamic stages of existence, I suggest we wouldn't be interested in them. I find it intriguing to approach these tradition-saturated texts as presentations of stages of infantile and early childhood cognitive sequencing, and, here, of course, of identifying trauma and its central place in our consciousness. That these events are in some way true, and literally true to the reality of energetic awareness makes sense; the truths and observations are fundamentally true, though people who read them as literally true in fundamentalist exegesis often obscure the deeper truth they contain.

24. The Father

The traditional tropes about God the Father suggest God is like a creative father, and we are Its children. God extends and limits our capacity because God may be code word for Ultimate Reality, and that we know is true. It is our neighboring truth, that which we face inwardly and outward as we open our door and step outside.

Freud renews this insight claiming that for the child, the father is the door to the exterior world, an alternative to the imbedded dyad of mother and child. In the Gospel of John, Jesus walks around talking about achieving this level of understanding and how he has a loving, anchoring relationship with the Father. Implied may be that he is beginning to move out from the developmental immersion with the Mother, and he finds an inner energetic strength by responding directly and lovingly with the reality outside himself and inwardly dwelling within.

Our hope for Messianic rescue at some levels may be universal, and certainly in early experience we know about messianic truth of being saved in our upbringing reality as well as implied abandonments in its portfolio and our sado-masochistic elaborations upon these separation experiences. And the stories about him indicate Jesus knew about this human feature and its boundary issues, including those for whom such deliverance is a form of attachment (see Lazarus and Mary Magdalen). He seems to have been surrounded by individuals who were susceptible to, even addicted to its strategic misuse. In this sense, like a good, helpful theologian, by vocation, the Messiah will take us to the Father edge: to the knowable, relational, now Unknown God. Even that helpful strategy also will dissolve into our embodied righteousness, with, and then without the Iconic God. What we are left with is a realistic, humane, and potentially miraculous perception of ourself and our immanence in the universe, the universe within as well as the universe without. Our attempt to master this vision with words and regular cognition is doomed to partial success, but fathers and mothers are our first teachers toward garnering this early conundrum.

25. Hell and Satan

Hell can describe the reality of impacted dissociation as it effects our living lives. It site-positions the pain and torment of trauma-initiated conflicts and stress patterns, which, because present but often unobserved, or apparently unobservable, show up or are characterized as being below ordinary consciousness. Would there be any illumination if we were to characterize Hell as above, not below? Or somewhere deep in some auric field of the spine?

Some of the difficulty is cognitive/linguistic, wherein we remain confused about the nature of what our narratives do within our awareness. We hover and determine at these narrative levels in the hope that they are describing the deeper organizational energetic realities, including the immobilized and immobilizing black, at the almost center of our trauma sites. Hell describes these apparently impossibling, unresolvable, ineducable conundra, and our sado-masochistic elaborations upon these immobilities. About the inner experience of shock memory, Hell can appear eternal, outside of regular time, but it is not the eternality of Heaven, altogether outside of shock.

Satan can be understood as a gestalt personification, the personality narrative of our organizing of traumatic process, which, because of the held-energy systems and their black includes at times unrelenting, invisible torment. Possibly appealing to the narcissism of the observer, Satan is a characterization of the aspiration that personality can control the appearance and disappearance of the trauma sites for resolution; and of the hope that ego surrender may take the novitiate deeper into the possibility of significant, experienced, neurochemical resolution, if that even can be recognized. While Satan is acknowledged as an enemy in order to marshal emotional forces toward his defeat, the actual "defeat" of (seductive) dissociation is more likely experienced as gradual, silent, subtle, and real. Hope emerges then as a sign of movement where there was none.

Because Satan arises out of brainscapes of shock, Satanic systems promise a reality of personal narrative and in some cases vitality, but the realms of Satan are basically not real – not that they don't "exist"; I think in some way or other, all Satanic myths recognize this often overlooked aspect of their nature. Insofar as trauma is resolvable and is like a floating (and apparently fixed) island, then all dissociation and dissociative neurochemistries are what Buddhists would term illusion; the worlds of Hell and Satan consciousness are separate from reality: essentially, we are creatures of light.

Satan helps dramatize what has been (enablingly, I believe) narrated as an historical bargain, which offers and shelters the intensity of fight and flight adrenaline at the expense of radiance and stabile oxygenation; the fires of Hell are resultant systems' inflammation. What we are talking about is the relationship between held-energy systems and the core radiance they contain and conceal.

On some Faust-like level, it seems as if we can control or participate in the maintenance of the held-energy system, surely a portrait of hope as well as of damnation. If the held-energy system comes forward for resolution at, say, ten times a second, we may have an opportunity to slow the pattern down, even by observation support its melting dissolution because there may be visible gaps within its otherwise impenetrable surface. But the initial appearance of shock in our system is not voluntary, nor, initially, is the residue of its influence. Devil's bargains and contracts (covenants?) include demonstrations of denial, based upon deoxygenation.

As administrator, Satan does not suffer the agonies of his community (shall we venture family?) of damned (and pluralized) souls; but as emerging docent of dissociation, and as Hell's source, present at its creation, his development is characterized as in rebellion to Ultimate Reality, against God, a denial of catastrophic traumatic chaos, which itself is apparently forever with us. Insofar as the shock "apparatus" saves our integrity and our existence, there is no eliminative solution for its crucial presence in our life, nor reason to seek one. What is significant is that once established, the held-energy system may be dissolved or resolved back into radiance and Truth. In some cases, we do not know by how much.

When someone says to us, "You are going to Hell" – as if this destiny will come to us as we die – we may best proffer that we are already in Hell;

it is not a future state but a current neurochemistry awaiting being brought forward. Hell is not the future; it is in the unrealized, dissociative present, and it is always here, until, significantly, it is not. As dissociative process, Hell forms can disappear – sometimes in the twinkling of an eye – within human, and interior, vision.

26. Evil

Scientific research has demonstrated that brain self-scans at least 10 times a second. Its scans include the black, coming forward for resolution (we want "it" out), and simultaneously denying access ("It is too dangerous to go in there; not enough oxygen."). In our efforts to resolve this memory system conundrum, we shall sort-of recreate something which should not happen in the first place, contained in the memorialized trauma site. Our narratives of behavior and feeling states run parallel to the energetic, and often they seem to express these held-energy systems directly, sometimes catastrophically.

All our trauma sites might be seen as spindling on former sites, so that there may be one (original) which sets all subsequent sites; in crisis, brain does not have time to reinvent the access to shock as a saving grace, but uses the old, first (and successful) one. Because the subsequent shock areas get associated with apparently different (narrative) situations – and I figure the key factor here is deoxygenation – we can think we are solving the core trauma, the way to freedom (salvation), when we are merely substituting narratives.

This ruthless trajectory might be related to an individual's elaborational sense of a comprehensive and malevolent force. Like being on a diet or addiction recovery plan whose proffered strategy never works for very long, or at all: something persists, no matter how earnestly we attempt to bring it to resolution, directly and indirectly. We characterize and name this persistence, including thus its cruelty; there is a gathered empowerment which intentionally does not appear to want to help us, innocent though we are. We repeat the original occasion, only this time (again and again) we surely can remove the initial toxicity, the energetic immobility.

A woman who smokes cigarettes regresses to her prenatal experience of her mother smoking. Initially she experiences no problem with the black in the pattern; everything is fine. Then she notes, "I know my mother loves me, but this is killing me." The pattern dissolves, and afterward she reports no desire to smoke. Or to be violent with her step-daughter. As an adult, each time she lights up she has been addictively repeating the initial prenatal and unresolved trauma in the "hopes" she will solve its puzzle.

The attempt to deepen our connection to this process includes characterizing it as demonic, and our subsequent efforts confirm its ineluctable nature. It becomes, or consolidates cognitively as evil, and then all sorts of elaboration on that characterization occur, all recapitulating the problem of the held-energy systems, including perverseness, sadomasochistic perpetrations, occasions of individual and universal abandonment – the usual suspects. Approached through narrative, these only indirectly address the problem of shock and the held-energy.

Dissolution of the black is a problem of history and our elaboration of synaptical, neurochemical sequencing. The elusiveness of siting and witnessing – no shovels or pushing will remove evil – may be due to the stacking of the trauma sites, one upon the other. Their accompanying narratives may help, but they often hinder the attempts to get clear (achieve salvation) by seeking narrative interventions when brain apparently has to take itself out of memorialized shock, previously invoked.

Evil describes a natural process of self-understanding by primitive brain, only the characterization of evil prompts disastrous narrative applications in the form of revenge, dunking, torture, genocide, murder, and manifold other perpetrative processes. Following some amalgamatic recognition of the labyrinthine nexi of trauma systems, evil as a process includes the objective to clear the mess by intention. Yet attending to the black on its own terms may be different, for, when successful, it may lead to movement at the deepest levels, with resultant restorative energy and hope.

Evil as a concern may be a defense. Evil as a concept – even corralling conviction – promises a synthesis of approach, finding the Original Sin as it were, something which will give us an appropriate focus at the appropriate depth, to enable us to see our painful experience as a whole. It promises us clarity. When we personify it, we may think we are getting closer to our own experience, and to the fact that evil describes something about what is true about us at this uncomfortable, suffering level. Again, this singularity may be a contrarian defense. And we may experience evil when we sense a conflict within us between so-called Good and Bad.

Historically there have been many approaches to the problem of evil – its evaporative skin and holding power. We can dramatize it and bring the energetic of it into narrative form. But as in Faust, using it to gain control over our experience, including pre-verbal, is a bargain for, but not the reality of, Being. To conclude the sequence, we must return to primal areas including sensate chaos, love, and disappointment: early trauma around separation and betrayal and our elaborations upon these shock-inducing experiences. The experience of evil often has a defensive, compressed quality about it, promising liberation but delivering somethings else. Somewhere in its vine-jungle lies the non-judgmental fact of shock, energetically brain-sited in black.

27. The scan

From our experience of P.E.T. scans, we know that as brains, we self-scan at least 10 times per second, 24-7. All voting districts report their local evaluations, and they intercommunicate and adjust. We can witness our scans and find ways to transform them.

Our total systems are conveyed within time modes which may pay homage to linear sequential clock and calendar time, but not really. Even though these exterior measuring sticks become increasingly subtle. And we try to superimpose them upon our pre-verbal experience. Or to find the present moment within ourself, optimally a place of Being, and subsequently, its offspring, enlightenment. Each temporal moment matches and does not match the energetic occasions within. Our attempts to link our inner (subjective) experience with exterior measured time may help us to bring discriminative focus to these scanning data, including feelings and thoughts; but I find there are significant dangers here as well.

Our scans can be differentiating, so that our sense of real time can include distortions of personal experience or augmentations of the same. As we discover what is real in scientific terms, we know that as organisms, we function at subatomic levels as well as at levels of organ and body organization within an environment which describes time in millions of years. Alchemically, we may be able to witness the densification of spirit into matter, including at sub-molecular levels.

Each time we renew our study of our experience, we discover scans can be divided, as with pointillism, or with microscopy. Aristotle recognizes the concept of the atom, and now we witness the Higgs boson. If we have the instrument, we can perceive subdivisions. One corollary of this particulate experience is that at conscious levels of our awareness, we are synthesizing information about ourselves and the world with only a surface, probably truncated awareness. Perhaps by definition, Ultimate Reality is always discriminative; God is in the detail.

Our primary scan mode we might call developmental. From conception on, certain objectives have to be achieved before the next flowering stages can evolve. Our DNA sets up the sequence plans for all parts to arrange, complete, and blossom. Then, a certain homeostasis indicates all systems are operating within a functional productivity, out of which the next phases emerge. If the map is incomplete or askew, anomalies, distortions occur, even to the end point of death itself. In order for the organism to survive, a great deal of variability and substitution and crossover and holographic potentiality apparently needs to be present.

Part of our arsenal of support potential is the mechanism of shock, featured in our surviving overwhelming sensate and physical input. Such occasions, sudden and slow-drip, immediate and historical, can leave coded, memory-residue of the experience which have been termed here, held-energy systems. These are recorded and then scanned at the energetic level in black, as compressed, deoxygenated, and dangerous to approach. They run by rules which can be thought of as trauma scan, always coming forward at 10 times a second into systemic reportage in terms of physical, emotional, and behavioral commentary. We are systems seeking completion. Trauma thus may compress our sense of developmental sequences; its distortions can be held in the cells and their systems, leading to neurochemical vulnerability, inflammation and disease.

This is particularly true when we first approach the scans pertaining to our trauma sites. When, somehow by meditation and magnified focus, we slow down scanning of inner time and space heretofore compressed and anxious, we can begin to sense for a deeper balance and can comprehend Stillpoint and void, included in states of consciousness called Being. The knowledge that there are sequences of scanning focus and experience which can restore balance in trauma-skewed systems is what much of culture, religions, and therapy, are about. Overall, we could call these civilization levels scans, with variants which can be acknowledged, developed, and even enjoyed.

Our renewed discovery of these scans' divisionability includes the clear consciousness of pure Being, as well as mastery of the physical exterior world. Within these divisions are the awareness of trauma's influence on our capacity to see, and to see reality. Each division potentially carries us deeper into our reality as individuals and as perceivers of reality which task is subsumed in the concept or activity of God. Within our quest about God lies a recognition of trauma's distorting function as well as our desire to know the clear truth. By perceiving our scans as well as our viewing of our scans as transformable, we enlarge our knowledge as well as the possibility of experiencing Being and understanding.

Our scans involve emotional experiences, the inward sequence of feeling and cognitive states of consciousness. These are variable and, from the position of Being and Stillpoint, can be considered often as altered, even alternative states which can amalgam into experiences of personality and identity. And our interface with the world, which includes "real time" as well as other people.

When we use language from one scan sequence/realm to describe an other, or to pin our preverbal experience to the posterboard of serial time, we can get anomalies such as Methuselah living 900 years. These "thoughts" may very accurately describe an emotional or developmental-cognitive truth but not one which matches calendar time; our vocabularies get stressed when we use the same words to describe differing aspects of consciousness. Clocks and their time may affect us, but our inner experiences of consciousness as demonstrations of the (preverbal) scan are beyond ordinary time. Sequence and space imply time but not minutes and years. TE takes brain reportage of sequence and finds its characterizations are spatially rendered, at least.

We might string these truths within what has been called Biblical Time: very true and very not true. They may describe cognitive development and sequence with greater accuracy from within (which is fundamentally true in terms of our inner experience of time and scan); including the conviction that what is coming into consciousness is fundamentally true, as true in its way and perhaps more accurate to our inner experience than scientific external reality as described.

We are creatures of the scan, now recently expanded to include subatomic realms as well as universal realities. Essential to our scanning are the vocabularies we use to explicate where we are in the time/space scanning spectrum. Crossing over between one system and another may bring confusion. Our syntaxes threaten to break between Biblical fundamentalism and Darwinian insight reality, for some, an untraversable slope.

What we have discovered is that consciousness can refit itself as it probes each of the layers of existence and can move from infinite spaces within and without. Each layer has its truth and so states it; it is the integration of these points of view which becomes of interest, as we discover vertical unities among all the horizontalities. And our so-called subjective experience includes our preverbal scan, before we can understand words, and before the Word – not the beginning, but surely the start of, something.

Asking someone which part of their scans they are speaking from or about, would imply a dialogue in which power over would not be the objective. Seeing parallel attributes to reality descriptions would be the goal. I have often thought that it would be interesting to set endlessly disputing theologians (and somewhere they are real troublemakers) to be locked in a room until they could take their differences and resolve them into a deeper synthesis wherein there was no disagreement. They could not leave the room until they had achieved such understanding. They would have to reach out in empathic glory: "You do it that way? Of course. We do the same thing in this way."

CHAPTER ELEVEN:

LITERATURE, ENERGY, AND DEVELOPMENT

Objectives for literature

Traditionally, the study of literature, informal and formally in schools and religious institutions, provide cultural benchmarks for discussion and recognition of what we would now call psycho-spiritual and relational wisdom. At best, the texts studied over the centuries consolidate and refine the essential questions which thoughtful (including reading) people ask themselves about life and experience. The texts provide examples and points of focus on inner and behavioral experiences which might bind otherwise random and disperse populations of individuals left to drift on the compass of our own insight, presuming we have some.

There have been at least two major "literature" objectives. 1. The recognition and validation of current administrative social systems; and 2. The recognition and validation of personal psychological and spiritual development. Strangely, these objectives have often come to be characterized as practically at cross purposes.

With the peeling off of psychological understanding from its original theological, mythical densities, additional perspectives can be rendered. Here are some examples.

Ran and *King Lear*

What story are we watching? It is probably not fair to call *Ran* a version of Shakespeare's *King Lear*. According to the background history of *Ran's* development, Kurosawa preplans his story and then discovers later its parallels with Shakespeare's version of an aging king dividing his kingdom. What we have are mildly parallel mythic narrative clusters of relationship and sequence, basic and archetypal, expressing universal domestic, family values.

In *Ran*, the Japanese medieval war-lord, the Great Lord Hidetori, bequeaths his full territory to his first son, which at least from European feudal practice is the done thing. Within the European tradition, the later-born sons will be assisted into independence by the eldest brother, or they will take predetermined roles, like careering in the military or the church. These later children might see the system as unfair to them, as the natural, bastard Edmund, of *Lear* rails against his brother Edgar's legitimacy; but systems are systems, implemented by families as well as institutions.

Ran determines the inheriting children as sons, not daughters as in *Lear*, and this difference does not alter the shared family problem. Kurosawa revises the initiating premise of *Lear*, which is the kingdom must be divided three ways in order to prevent posthumous conflict and vulnerability. No Philadelphia estate lawyer (or consulting cleric, for that matter) could devise a better strategy, even though holding to the tradition of primogeniture could be demonstrated as equally satisfactory toward serving the same end. Both strategies have been used, sometimes with peaceful success, sometimes not. The gender variation between the two dramas does not change the fundamental dynamic of the story which is about inheritance.

One deeper lesson of *Ran* and *Lear* is that the parent/ruler/child cannot control outcomes – he cannot predict them, nor can he prevent his becoming the apparent victim of his own maneuvering. From a gestalt point of view, the parental "inheritance" gets visited upon an internally divided recipient (there are plural children); already fragmented, the child cannot accept the gift, if it be that, in clear, direct untrammelled receptivity.

Both versions show the ruler's "madness", when he confronts the fact and the illusion of self-creation. Both show his subsequent movement into a different world view, more compassionate, more lyrically lunatic, more realistic, and, in *Lear*, more brain-balanced, even wise. My colleague Jeanne comments that she never has been fully convinced of Lear's heath transformation, and I can see her point; it is too facile, and perhaps there should be more blossoming evidence of how he gets to his illumination and of his sustaining the compassion revealed in the storm scene. Or his aftermath pillow talk with the blinded Gloucester. But the culture which teethes on *Lear* has regularly argued for the transformation as real, and realistic ("undo this button"), and one which values enlightenment over status. When push comes to shove, the social systems and the identities garnered around these status-derived identity values are seen to be pretty flimsy, particularly by those in power who have clearly bought into their strategies.

What I think is important is that the children argue about the parent's inheritance, as we seem to have to. We need to be shown that we do not share a single parent; the occasion of sibling rivalry obscures the reality that the parent is different for each child – each child evokes different parenting style and information; in these matters the "historical" passage of time and sequence count. The parent as a uniform and consistent fiat-issuing authority is another part of the parental image; but we children want it both ways – we want to be treated equally and as special – with a parent who tailors its behavior and expectations to our unique needs. And because of dissociative process, these needs vary and contradict and compete within the family and family inheritance system. The parental gift cannot be singularly and efficiently shelved by those who receive it.

Primogeniture

The developmental issue which the primogeniture strategy attempts to resolve through its tradition is, in Freudian terms, obversely Oedipal. The first child gets the complete inheritance, with the other children falling away from that position. The first child inherits the possession of what is the parent's to give, with no sharing. In such developmental sequence, the child has to learn that it has to share its mother with the father. In a strange sort of way, Lear is radically challenging the primogeniture order (perhaps because he has only daughters?) by dividing his kingdom into three parts: each child gets to rule, but within a domain aegis reduced in size by two thirds from the original.

Furthermore, we may see here the infantile brain consolidating through memory function, integrating the first gift with second and third occasions of giving, each of which may be different. The afternoon feeding is delivered into a different context from the morning one; and therewith we can narrate the synaptical sequence which establishes not only continuity of memory but continuity of self, supervening the vicissitudes of variation in the accumulating lineage of feeding occasions. We are the first child and the other children.

Furthermore, from birth and maybe before, the infant is accommodating to the fact that the seen mother (post-natal) is both the same and different from the apparent hegemony of the uterine system. There is some focus-intensified process which establishes a differentiating awareness that there are two people in the room, even though the system appears to be one. In some therapeutic meditations, clients have discovered that the narrative they are subsequently left with includes crucial confoundments over the question of whose pattern this is. More of this later.

Cordelia

Some part of Cordelia holds onto her specialness with her father by challenging, in the name of sincerity, the link between love and social (feudal) order. Often, her loyalty is seen as honorable, the child whose feelings (true and real as the boy confronting the emperor's new clothes) cannot be manipulated. But the challenge she represents has been already set forth by Lear himself, who destabilizes the system in the service of avoiding posthumous sibling rivalries. This theme is re-elaborated in the conflict between Edgar and Edmund. The idea of a developmental meritocracy where people get what they deserve screens the inevitable developmental wounding, passed as it is from parent to child: there are limits to the power held by both members of the dyad, giver and inheritor.

I also find a corollary set of insights pertaining to *Lear*, namely that Cordelia does not understand the initiating context of her father's desire to be told he is most loved. This opening scene of the play satirizes the oath of fealty, which was a necessary and complex and not always adventitious, often potentially contentious contract between lord and vassal. You placed your vassal hands between the hands of your lord and accepted his protection in return for your rents to him from the land you were using. Though *Lear* takes place in pre-Stonehenge times, its Elizabethan audiences, and ours as well, know about loyalty contracts of gangs, and families, and landlords, and governments.

We are in a court where fealty procedures are the norm, and they presage in the family what must occur for the society to be organized around the king, the lord of lords, the don of dons. If the daughter opposes the father openly, so can one of her father's vassals, or maybe not. Like the wedding ceremony wherein the spoken vows emotionally extend to those already married in the witnessing congregation, Lear's reminder that "Nothing comes from nothing," is addressed to his courtiers as well as to his daughter.

Perhaps not unlike her father, Cordelia is perhaps adolescent and narcissistic in bringing the family dynamics, with herself as favorite, into the court. With no wife (where is Queen Lear? Is she The Fool?), he can prove that he can attach to someone in a tender way, and this capacity might be an essential political subtext in court, though some courtiers might find it unkingly. In mafia myth, the don is kind and doting as a father, but an abrupt killer as he faces the outside world.

Lear's emotional move is essentially political; he is teaching his daughter about a serious point in ruling; whereas Cordelia's focus is predominantly personal: don't ask me to gush in order to get. This discrepancy shows her inexperience, as well as her winning potential courage when she stands up to her dad for the best family reasons: paradoxically, she is holding onto a father who is heading for death. His exile of her is "deserved", confounded by his aging process, and curiously self-isolating; in this first scene, while France stands up for Cordelia, no one really stands up for Lear, not even loyal Kent. By their behaviors, Regan and Goneril align themselves realistically with Lear's political world.

Furthermore, Cordelia is unprepared for Lear's initiating move, and being graced by his love, she instantaneously takes on the leadership which Lear has already forfeited. She opposes him and immediately she becomes the wise regent, in the way that when parents flounder, children stand in for them in the best ways they know how.

Ran

Ran takes some of the feminine, perhaps defensive deceptiveness and power-mongering of Regan and Goneril and explicates this modality in the characters of Lady Sue and Lady Kaede. We see flashes of the Japanese female hatred and contempt of the male and associated male samurai values which put women to some side while being trapped within the system as well – as in the third and fourth tellings in "Rashomon" and echoed in Western texts such as "Who's Afraid of Virginia Woolf?".

In both dramas there is the reverberation of blinding, but in *Ran* it is an outright assault on a victim prince, not a full-scale, and in someways ungrounded vengeance, as with Gloucester.

The *Ran* Fool, perhaps transvestite, has a feminine streak which gives his insights irony, as well as perhaps some warmth to the emperor's bed. This may be implied in *Lear*, but the essential role of the Fool as amanuensis and serious commentator on the king's process is located in both versions. The marriage-like intimacy of understanding between Lear and his Fool has been acknowledged.

The figure of Kent is retained, someone in the court, not of the family, who is loyal to the king; but he is killed off in *Ran*, whereas in *Lear*, now facing death, he supports the surviving order including after the death of the king.

Ran is visually saturated with images from battles, which comment on the scale, destructiveness, and implied futility of warring, whereas in *Lear*, we rarely see such epic scale. Particularly affecting is the contrast of the Great Lord in his gown, bare legs vulnerably exposed, standing madly amid huge destruction, or descending the palace stairs, as an Oedipus might after self-blinding.

In *Ran*, the fallen leader is visually juxtaposed to landscape and ruin in a way that only the poetry of *Lear* can identify – we do see Lear as a creature of nature with Gloucester. However, a sparse production of *Lear*, such as the Brooks/Scofield one, suggests that the scale of the theater can be tuned commensurate with the narrative content of the play and in terms of psychodynamic meaning, supercede cinematic images.

In *Ran*, there is no parallel subplot like that of Gloucester's in *Lear*; even the showdown fight between the brothers Edmund and Edgar is amalgamated in *Ran*. They kill each other off as rivals as do Goneril and Regan, including the sexual competition between their wives over Prince Jiro.

Ran gives us exquisite film shots, landscapes, costumes, effects, whereas, though a theater piece, *Lear* renders definitely more emotional complexity, substance, and intimacy. Both handle the storm scene about equally well, though Edgar's role as poor Tom may not be so much a problem of Lear's disintegrating world as the blind Prince Tsurumaru's condition is a direct result of the Great Lord's silverback behavior.

In both versions, we witness the pathos of the king's dilemma, but in *Lear*, the dilemma is more explicated, and we see him move into wisdom which is humane and extrapolatable to all members of the audience; whereas in *Ran* that is not the final touch. There it is more what a fool a ruler is, one who assumes he is something special, someone who creates an empire leading to his own demise. Lear's learning is paramount in the Shakespeare version, whereas I do not experience it as important in *Ran*. It is more the revelation that the Great Lord is a fool than that he realizes it and gains wisdom thereby.

Does Lear learn?

In the concluding anxious gestures of the Great Lord in *Ran*, we are focusing on his inability to be psychologically resourceful; he is antic (frantic), merely surviving. We see those who want to protect him do so not because they love him, but because they are trained to protect and sustain the Great Lord. The cultural order of which they are a part demands their loyalty. Perhaps the fact that this film comes out of post-Hiroshima Japan, where the Emperor's role in establishing and maintaining a collapsing empire was and continues to be shielded, is an important context from which to view Kurosawa's perspective here. Witnessing the personal and up-close portrait of the Emperor, including seeing his naked leg and thigh, may place a particular challenge upon a post-war Japanese audience which until 1945, was never allowed to look directly at the man, who was considered divine.

I think the key to *King Lear*'s power, and one which *Ran* does not achieve, is the developmental one, where the parent asks for forgiveness from the so-called abused child for the abuse that parent has perpetrated (if only by sharing). There are some plays which allow us to see this archetypal interaction, but not many as cataclysmically framed. Lear's "Come, come, let us away" speaks to a transcendent view of parent and child, mutual spies on the facile, prepossesing conventions of court and society. The passions of preoccupying politics are reviewed within a context of mutual reality-shaping and of reality-observing. The tragedy is based upon a simple lesson.

Without the usual intentionality, our aftermath, Monday-morning sharing between parent and child is everything and the best sign of healing within the family system and within our so-called self. The goal of a meditative detachment is paramount here, shared, past blame, by both parent and child; here is emotional maturity, enabling us finally to perceive reality, wherein self and other are tuned toward some essential equality.

Christian application

To carry this developmental place of healing one step further, in the Christian myth, this same theme is worked out, built as it is upon the Expulsion from the Garden of Eden. As children, we absorb, "take on" the environment, in particular the graces, but also, the traumatic patterns of the parent. Parents are abandoned and wounded, specially imperfect, and as their children we want to see them heal, not only so they may be better parents to us, but so that they may be more whole persons for themselves – so that as their children, we may see what integration looks like, and learn. Our individuation process promises this as a reality which we can achieve and exemplify, significantly in our dialogue with these important, role-providing adults. This is the inheritance into which we can live (with) and grow, and it can be the basis of our experience of loving another person.

Yet our parents do not heal, not in the place wherein they are stuck. And we offer ourselves as the perfect instrument of their self-justification; we shall justify their existence and make everything better. And when they in effect say, "You, my child, even you, cannot draw me away from a priority which surpasses you, a loyalty which is revealed in my errors, including parenting errors," we can feel (be?) crushed. Our self-regard (let's not call it narcissism here and confound an already subtle territory) hits a wall whose consequences to our own ability to love are usually severe and debilitating.

Of course the critical and strategic irony is that the parent holds the same destiny *vis-a-vis* its parents, and this fundamental limitation (because it iconically transfers in time through personality and generation, the trauma pattern – or the fact of trauma itself – can be described as sin) is thus passed from parent to child with only occasional glimpses of progress, *i.e.*, trauma pattern cessation. We even come to worship the pattern and its repetition. Yet it is the endlessness of this cycle for which we seek permanent conclusion, the war to end all wars.

It is this very inability of the parent to shed its parents' patterns, to know what to do with them and the information they contain, at the heart of much inherited traumatic process, which makes the parent (ambivalently) loyal to the wounding past and distracted: the patterns appear apparently forever, even sacred. Yet while as children we know these patterns seem immortal (after all, they are dissociative, timeless states), as souls we know they are not.

The endless repetition of these *error(s) perpetuale*, simple in their basic structure, is what we seek rescue from when we seek what the clerics call salvation. And the Christian myth identifies, I think correctly and powerfully, though in a barn-door-as-fly-swatter sort of way, that this cycle is resolvable, and that it has something to do with the transmission between parent and child, mother and child, father and son, Father and Son, if you will.

All the talk about fitting sacrifice of the son speaks to an incomplete resolution carried and narrated by the Hebrew myth, which identifies, again in a barn-door way, the trauma sequence and its implementation through time and generations. It is a karmic insight and well-worth its price. That at base the entire structure is linked to the loss of oxygen for the primitive brain is hard to focus upon, yet my sense is that this is a major part of a way through.

The Christian myth focuses with varying degrees of clarity upon this sequence, but it includes it in the centrality of its spiritual hero, Jesus, who carries his identity as an energy state or mode of consciousness, called the Christ, or enlightened (often "anointed" – oxygenated and dynamically oxygenating) one. And as he "dies" and reformulates in transformed formless form, his death is proposed as the completion or perfect sacrifice, a final solution to the endlessness of traumatic pattern transmission. When will it all end, and what will the end look like? Is a meaningless death (or perhaps better a death involving some colossal misunderstanding) enough to characterize the random, inappropriate transmission of trauma patterns which seek resolution intergenerationally?

The question is "What will stop the traumatic, retraumatizing pattern which is wordlessly transmitted from generation to generation?" Poetically, the church proffers the figure of Jesus crucified on the Cross as a sacrifice which will do the trick:

> All glory be to thee, Almighty God, our heavenly Father, for that thou, of thy tender mercy, didst give thine only Son Jesus Christ to suffer death upon the cross for our redemption; who made there, by his one oblation of himself once offered, a full, perfect, and sufficient sacrifice, oblation, and satisfaction, for the sins of the world; [*Holy Eucharist. The Proposed Book of Common Prayer. Episcopal Church, 1977. p334.*]

Within this prayer are contained coded identifiers which locate the trauma phenomenon as well as the specific sites. The first and most important is the Cross, which has four 90° angles symmetrically juxtaposed. The second point also describes the positioning of the brain as it is overwhelmed by the trauma-inducing overstimulation, as of an accident. The third element is the idea of sacrifice, which suggests not only the surrender of the ego identity in the moment of crisis, but also the way back in to the trauma memory if we really want the memory and its prolonged effect to dissolve and the radiance (oxygen) restored.

The fourth element in this prayer includes the idea that this entire mechanism is true and a true part of healing, God-given, if you will, to be approached gently and with tender regard, not bullied through as in the initial experience of the intruding trauma it might be. Not all trauma is sudden; we must include slow-drip toxicities, including uterine ones, as well as automobile accidents, though there may be a point of cessation wherein the brain numbs – the straw breaks the camel's back, which appears to be final and sudden.

At base, the prayer and its accompanying ritual confirms a causal relationship between the trauma mechanism being evoked, and its ultimate resolution: if we experience immobility such as being nailed to a cross, our identification with that moment enables us to return within that moment to a reworking of the bad situation back into radiance. The brain is satisfied by the reappropriation of the crisis, and armed with its most difficult-degree points, in a complete and satisfying way restores itself to balance. An oxygenating, high serotonin elixir occurs and transforms what has seemed to be dead back into living vibrancy.

As a matter of fact and of strategy, the pattern of blocked energy ends with each individual who takes on the sequence as it is perpetuated in him or herself and watches and enhances the dissolving of the pattern, which melts, dissolves into the air (see the ceilings of many Baroque churches) or the sea (see The Sphinx). The vision of the end of the world is encompassed in the end of certain incomplete levels of awareness which Buddhists call illusion. Then we are reunited with our fundamental Being and can apprehend Ultimate Reality.

In the Christian rubric (to me this formulation, as the clerics lyrically, hastily, phrase it used to sound like impenetrable poetic, religious gobbledegook) we are redeemed by the occasion of the Christ energy and are reset in relationship to the parent (or parent God), whom we can then (again) approach as blameless equal ("No cause, no cause." *King Lear* 4:7:78) to the task of perceiving Ultimate Reality. Parent and child unite within this task ("who's in, who's out"), free of the grandiose iconism of family positioning and its deep wounding, for and by parents and children:

> *Lear:* No, no, no, no. Come, let's away to prison.
> We two alone will sing like birds i' th' cage.

> When thou dost ask me blessing, I'll kneel down
> And ask of thee forgiveness. So we'll live,
> And pray, and sing, and tell old tales, and laugh
> At gilded butterflies, and hear poor rogues
> Talk of court news, and we'll talk with them too—
> Who loses and who wins; who's in, who's out—
> And take upon's the mystery of things,
> As if we were God's spies. And we'll wear out,
> In a walled prison, packs and sects of great ones
> That ebb and flow by th' moon.
>
> *King Lear 5:3:8-19*

As noted above, such integration is envisioned mythically in the story of Jesus, the gifted, grandiose Child, and it is a valuable inward-based insight about our inner reality and our relationship to our exterior situations. And it is dramatized with some clarity in *King Lear*: we get to see and hear the tonality of reconciliation, at least for some moments.

One problem with Shakespeare's endings, as with the brain sequencing he describes, is that with the exceptions of the late romances and the comedies, once the High of trauma resolution is achieved, brain offers further patterns up for resolution which crowd out and even appear to destroy the clear moments. For the big five tragedies, I find Shakespeare has no superior insight to conclude this sequence except to pick up the remaining healthy fragments and sweep the stage clean of its remaindered tragic debris.

Both *Lear* and the Jesus myth give glimpses of transformation in response to the way in which we inherit ourselves, through genetic sequencing, energetic aurae, and traumatic patterning: all perceived and unified at the energetic auric level, where if we do not learn at this level, we learn nothing. Thakar proffers the distinction between knowledge and understanding; it is the latter which makes our difference.

Even the abuse is energetic, though it takes the form of direct, unconscient assault and debilitating violence. In the Christian myth, the transformation as envisioned is sustained through some kind of surrender. There is a personality, even metabolic fulfilling restructuring which is possible, given our immersion in the trauma pattern.

What we see in the history of the use of the complex and often misunderstood term *tragic*, is that it contains some often unknowable and unknown, preverbal force driving our human systems, social and personal, toward energetic resolution. By all means – activities and addictions, relationships and social securities – we seek dissolve, and to experience the moment after.

Addendum:

One further point, about which I comment more extensively elsewhere in this book. For the client meditating upon its energetic interior, there are patterns which need to be acknowledged that clearly belong to the pattern, crucially carried by the mother, who transmits them in the placental "blood" and then through its "mother's milk". If we ask whose pattern of held-energy this is, the answer sometimes wrongly is, "Mine and mine alone." Upon reflection, it turns out it is the mother's. And where does she get it, from herself? "No, it is from her parent, who is similarly determinedly stuck."

The parent gives the good stuff, but frequently in the intensity of especially caring devotion, she gives also the confounding questions for the child to solve. The child takes on the sins of the world in the maneuver. The reason why the child receives this crucial information is that the parent is the not just the parent but is the sins-absorbing heroic child to its parents. Thus the importance of studying the history of transmission; at some times because this offers the chance for resolution.

And it can appear that brain will accept the sins and transform their nature, including the historical cultural sins and abuses which belong to the "culture". We can see this in the Seder formulations of tribulation, as well as the abuses of the church in Protestant sequencing, or the status of immigration in the United States where the myth coats the abuse of the native Americans who occupied the land, and in a sense belonged to it before European immigrations destroyed their occupation and their civilizations. We do not really know how these Indians occupied the land, stealing it from what others. One ultimate result is we do not "belong" here, no matter what the Civil War bleeding into the ground has done for the sense of guilt which can be transmitted from parent to child, often obversely, from sea to shining sea.

The problem of whether we can be set free and by what sequences includes the important strategic inheritance questions, "Whose held-energy pattern is this?" and "Where is it gotten from?" The resolution seems to go backwards at least three generations before it evens out, if it can.

I have one savvy client who reports to me, "You ask me whose pattern is this, and I don't even understand the question. It all seems mine." If he can return it to the mother, and say, "Not only does this pattern not belong to me, it does not belong with you – the sequence goes further back." One wonders what the subterranean vicissitudes of ancestor worship might entail using this strategy. Knowing that the patterns come from the so-called past, is a crucial insight, and until the child is able to master the idea of past, present and futures, including beginning, middle and end, there may be limited significant development, moral, emotional, sociological, or political.

CHAPTER TWELVE:

GESTALT IN LITERATURE

Conrad

The gestalt insight gets well-explicated in the works of Joseph Conrad, including "The Secret Sharer" and "Heart of Darkness", where the journeys are inward, and lead to energetic discoveries of some import. In the former, two sides of the self meet, two aspects of self-understanding are held in juxtaposition until one side, understood by the other, can be dropped away to swim for freedom, whatever that may be.

In "Heart of Darkness", we see the movement up the energetic stream of the spine (two rivers – the Thames and the Congo – a dissociated state) to the source, wherein the trauma pattern (Mr. Kurtz) is characterized, first as bestial and iddy, and soon thereafter, as immobile (*i.e.*, dead). The vision for an individual attempting such a journey illustrates that civilization, as self-characterizing dissociative states, will barely support such an interiorization transformation. Our spiritual journey begins with clearing: the discovery of trauma and its holding power. Next we focus (learn) and watch while our primitive brain reshapes and dissolves the traumatic holding. In the trauma-free zone we have established, we can then confront, experience reality without bias or trauma-determined anxiety.

The Secret Sharer

It is not exactly that we have given narcissism a bad name, but I am not the first to realize that we misuse the term "narcissistic" when we refer to skewed, and predominant, overt, and probably over-determined self-centeredness. The foundation which the term narcissism encompasses is developmentally legitimate and necessary, one which begins at least at conception. When we start off, if that is what we do, we are the Center of the Universe, the Only Begotten Child, the Child of God, the Chosen One.

It seems clear to me that if we put words to the energy of communion which we experience and are as sperm and egg meet and combine, these are the phrases which come to mind; and most myths and religious carriers of myth refer to these "ideas" or preverbal, energetic convictions, in one way or another. They are a locus each of us has always known, our first unity, to which we refer from each moment to moment throughout our lives, every time we perceive ourself as an individual. That we are comes amid unity, derived from parts.

This energetic focus, which occurs within a plurality of energetic fields, we eventually sense and call self, and self is combinant with the emerging declaration of our bodies as separate from, first the mother, and then with that, the world. Our personal big bang is a place which explicates and elaborates, there being nothing new under the sun: everything we are is merely unfolding explication of our initial moment. If we knew enough about that initiating moment, we could know our unfolding as we know the unfolding explication of a rose. Or the universe.

The sequence of separation and return, of individuation and merging, occurs in radical ways and continues to unfold, even perhaps shall I say it, evolve, throughout our lives. We have separate time, and then we return to the social mix, whether that be the family, the classroom, business, a friendship, our marriage, or within aspects of our plural and unitary self. In addition to being *The* Center of the Universe, we also discover we are *A* Center of the Universe, one of many; we are relational, condemned and liberated by our relativity. For many of us, the extension of this insight lies at the core of tragic experience.

When fulfilled, if only for moments of our neurochemistry, the process stated in the problem of narcissism, the defining of self and self in relationship to others, has the balance of the 23rd Psalm, complete with support from outside and inside, the awareness of self and the ultimate, through world:

The Lord is my shepherd, I shall not want; he maketh me to lie down in green pastures. He leadeth me beside the still waters; he restoreth my soul. He leadeth me in the paths of righteousness for his name's sake. Yea, though I walk through the valley of the shadow of death, I shall fear no evil, for thou art with me. Thy rod and thy staff shall comfort me. Thou preparest a table before me in the presence of mine enemies, thou anointest my head with oil, my cup runneth over. Surely goodness and mercy shall follow me all the days of my life, and I shall dwell in the house of the Lord forever.

Here we are in devoted harmony with the devoted environment, and we interact with it with charm, skill, justified confidence, depth, gratitude, and humility. In this Psalm state, we can ask for what we truly need: we do not ask for more than what society would call our fair share, yet we radiate a generosity of spirit, plentiful, unstriving, and empathic. In this chemistry, we may not generate envy.

Friendship

Relationship is one of the narrative grids upon which these energetic sequences can occur, and Joseph Conrad's "The Secret Sharer" [*quoted here from Joseph Conrad. The Secret Sharer and Other Stories. Dover Thrift Edition, New York, 1993. ISBN -13: 978-0-486-27546-8; ISBN-10: 0-486-27546-9*] illustrates not only the phenomenon of friendship but of its significant subtext, which explicates the psychological fulfillment for our individual and collective "self".

Amid a tumultuous, perfect storm, Leggatt, chief mate of the *Sephora*, initiates the life-risking reefing of the ship's remaining sail, thus saving the lives of his 24-odd shipmates. Reefing here means tying down and thus shortening a portion of the ship's one remaining sail so that it does not tear away and thus keeping some forward trajectory to an otherwise mortally foundering ship.

In the midst of this ultimate activity, a disgruntled, perhaps drugged, neurotic Seaman brings forth his masochistic personality traits at the worst time. While everybody else is ready to convert, as it were, he insolently challenges Leggatt, generating an adrenaline-incited engagement (a struggle) with him which both acknowledges and distracts from the reality of the storm with respect to souls facing how lost they (we) truly are.

In deepest frustration with the intractability of personality, even in the face of death – why should we be surprised? – in the pernicious absurdity of non-conscient impaction, Leggatt strikes the (mutinous?) Seaman, who strikes back. They wrestle and punch, and Leggatt throttles this shipmate as the waves overwhelmingly inundate the ship. Ten minutes later, Leggatt is discovered with his hands around the now dead Seaman's blackened neck. As a so-called murderer, he is put into custody, from which he eventually escapes, swimming until he reaches the rope side-ladder of a nearby other ship whose new, inexperienced Captain, the narrator of the story, is, uncharacteristically, on watch.

Naked, Leggatt initially appears spectrally, surreally headless in the phosphorescent dark water out of which he emerges. And in a few statements, including the existentially depressive, "What's the good [of going on any further in this life]?" [*Dover, p87*], he establishes immediate conscient, even-tempered rapport with the now-rescuing Captain, who clothes him in a pair of his own pajamas and hides him in his stateroom. His initiating conversation reveals a composed, clear person who knows who he is and where he is. Quickly, he develops an intense, secret relationship with the youthful Captain (Leggatt is a couple of years younger), who recognizes Leggatt as his double.

Leggatt is perceived as ultimately self-possessed, a strong soul [*p88*], someone worth trusting. His identity as murderer is a chance, provoked thing. Conrad reveals the intimate bonding of understanding which occurs under forbidden circumstances, and readers may sense an erotic aura between the two sharing men, who co-understand each other in a fundamental way. While Leggatt somewhat dismisses the worthiness of the Sailor he has killed, both men are saviors, Leggatt of the *Sephora*, the Captain of Leggatt.

Cain

Leggatt refers to his problem as of inheriting Cain's lineage; thus Conrad contextualizes Leggatt's sin of murder; Leggatt, a minister's son, reports the initial connection probably thought by the Sephora captain's limited, Bible-bound wife. He delivers his understanding as a throwaway.

> She would have been only too glad to have me out of the ship in any way. The "brand of Cain" business, don't you see. That's all right. I was ready enough to go off wandering on the face of the earth – and that was price enough to pay for an Abel of that sort. [*p92*]

The way Leggatt phrases it, the allusion to Cain and Abel may be not entirely parallel to what he has done; he renders it as a cultural tent peg which may or may not apply; something you could use if you found it useful. It is only what the Captain's wife says, take it or leave it; and in a way he takes it on. But as with any intepretation, the not only intelligent but wise person may know that understanding is not merely cognitive or analytic. Coming through the entire experience, Leggatt might reply, "Brand of Cain business – you dont know the half of it."

Yet Conrad has raised the issue as a way to illuminate the pathway to and away from personal experience, now socialized. And I think the lineage of the myth of Cain and Abel has much to say about Leggatt's experience on the Sephora.

With Cain as the world's first murderer (and fratricide), the Torah myth quickly establishes the capacity for humans to murder even (particularly?) relatives; some instinctual, developmentally early impulsive aggression is recognized, and it is useful to recall this potentiality when confronting other human beings. The Bible mythically sets this precious and expensive insight very near the start of everything. In fact, it could be seen to characterize a crucial developmental transition into human experience.

In the story of Cain, we are told of the brother who is envious of his sibling's connectedness with, for lack of a better term, life. As with pre-Apple Adam, God favors Abel, while Cain has to work for his own more arduous, slimmer pickings, or at least he thinks so. Out of jealousy and theological frustration, he ups and kills Abel, then avoids God's inquestion, "Where is Abel your brother?" with "I do not know. Am I my brother's keeper?" Countless homilies have opined that, yes, we are our brother's keeper and should not kill him, to boot.

Cain is subsequently thrown out into the world, but with a mark on his forehead indicating that the world must not take direct vengeance upon this (first) murderer. (Maybe we can merely blackball his application to the club.) And because this myth carries karmic intentionality, we are all Children of Cain, traumatically, karmically, bound to Cain's destiny as envy-prone creature/killer.

In terms of individual awareness, the story reminds us of our primitive, reptilian brain and the somewhat iffy nature of civilization and civilized behavior. Right under the surface there is the possibility of uncivilized activities, and it is not limited to families. When we look in the mirror or out of the window, we ignore our Cain lineage at our peril.

I think one moral pivot of the Biblical story is Cain's plea to God, namely that because of what he, Cain, has done, he will be hunted down and destroyed: "My punishment is greater than I can bear." One can imagine Olivier delivering this line with a momentary insincere cast of his eye. God's second intervention is one of compassion for the sinner, reducing the eye-for-an-eye level of social interaction, to one of sustained, civilizing but not intolerable guilt and a certain (spacious?) hopefulness for the individual who violates "God's Law", thou shalt not kill.

But it is not exactly God's Law; Cain's sense of sinfulness is acknowledged as an inner perception, elaboration, if you will, of an already trauma-compromised system. Cain's past, which we never hear directly about in narrative form, is included in the dissociative sense of dissatisfaction and envy he carries. We are already out of Eden, including a tendency to "act out" in violence, and to perpetrate self-violence in the form of a cruel conscience. Why does God create creatures, who, unlike snakes, feel so badly about themselves? Here, the myth indicates, is a situation which needs intervention, from without; or from a liberating acknowledgment from within an higher order or higher consciousness.

Our inward psychodynamic economy is thus sustained against an early childhood tyranny of conscience which would (self-)destroy the system; God's (here, That which is beyond Self) mitigating intervention takes authoritorial precedence over what we do to ourselves. It is this perhaps arms-length perspective that gives rise to the legal systems we endure. As with Abraham sacrificing Isaac, an intermediary function (increased nerve myelination and with it, cognition?) of the control of raw human experience, including at childhood, becomes the foundation of an accommodated social vision which adjusts and modifies our human absolutism and its rebellious, tyrannical offspring, fundamentalism.

How does Leggatt's trajectory mirror, fulfill, and comment upon the Biblical myth? In some ways, I think, very little. Because for one thing the (Abel) renegade Seaman is not enviable and God-graced, but rather a disconnected, alienated being. In his exchange with this Seaman, it might better seem that Leggatt is the Abel to the Seaman's Cain. The violence on the Sephora has an irritability factor missing from the Torah myth. In effect, as he kills his brother, Cain says, "Your exalted (balanced) presence drives me crazy, and I am getting rid of you in order to quiet my soul." Envy seems to drive Cain to eliminate his "rival" for "God's love". It might be that the Seaman's provocation would amount to, "Your exalted presence is driving me crazy, and I am provoking you in order that you blast my already challenged soul." In Conrad's "version", the parallel roles in both stories somehow reverse.

What interests me about this story about violence and killing and redemption is that the killing of the Seaman occurs but is not premeditated; and it occurs within a flood of seawater which threatens both lives in the de-oxy-genating embrace. In the Torah, we see the entire interaction, from Cain's strike to Abel's fall. In "Sharer", we see the results in the black, throttled neck; the killing is impulsive and, in an aesthetic and moral sense, mindless.

For a mythic commentary on killing, the Sephora incident reveals a level of what we might call madness which impulsively defies rationality, even motive. And Leggatt acknowledges this in his casual, uncharacteristic dismissal of the Seaman's worth. As a commentary on the Cain/Abel myth, the Sephora incident shows killing itself to be invisibly crazy, no matter who's involved. Heading into the mystery of murder, I find the Conrad story may take me deeper than the Torah's.

In any case, we can draw the complexity of Leggatt's situation into a nexus-like ball, having to do with the killing man, and swim him toward the over-hanging ladder of a sister system. As in "Heart of Darkness", it is as if we have two spine systems, created by dissociative process. Leggatt demonstrates this killing problem for the Captain's boat "system" – he is taken on board surreptitiously with a history which interferes with and augments the present – the Captain's uneasy new leadership of a ship, a system already staffed and experienced. From a unifying gestalt rubric, Leggatt must be accommodated or integrated into the present; what he is includes significant success and significant error, and we are always bringing divided process into unitary wholeness. It is perhaps our deepest motivation, as fundamental to us as its acknowledgment of a monotheistic god.

One problem of history or our attempt to understand through historical sequencing is that "The Secret Sharer", not unlike other Conrad stories including "Heart of Darkness", demonstrates how what is raw becomes, somehow, civilized. Or what appears civilized contains a turbulent, even violent, often unknown or unacknowledged subtext. Marlow's floating "pause" on the River Thames has within its setting sun settling down, the life and death of Kurtz, apparently separated in time, sensibility, and geography from the rivered London – but not. Dissociation, as in Cain's response to God's query, appears to be the bridge between what has happened and what is open now. And our definition of civilization must include the savagery its formalisms outright suppress, and, with Freud's insight, sublimate. Marlow is a commentary on, a variation of Mr. Kurtz, ego-maniac, libidinous (and surrenderer) such as the latter character possibly is.

More interesting, perhaps, is to see the entire story of "The Secret Sharer" as a direct double of the story of Cain and Abel, this time with the killing as background, and the resurrection of Abel as the second venture to "solve" the impass declared by that killing. The transition between two aspects of self, or better, of our neurochemistry, the divinely connected Abel – our Edenic Adam – which inner state triggers the dissociative trauma site (Cain) to move it aside, is sudden and in the original story, violent. The replacement of Abel by Cain is easily perceivable as a fratricide, and yet it may be useful to posit that it is Abel's, not Cain's story.

Cain (our Cain portion) abruptly substitutes and dominates personality consciousness. This part of the chemistry must be readdressed on different terms, so that what is wounded is healed and the trauma-less Edenic vision restored and embodied. Cain is post-Edenic Adam, lost from God by dissociation; the narrative appears sequential, but the history is vertical, spindled upon the initial *praxis* of the story.

It is the Captain's discovery of this redemptive aspect of self which must be somehow integrated in order for the boat, ultimately without wind and thus direction – not a perfect storm – to move. It is this vision which Conrad leaves us with at the story's end, and the sequence of delivery means that a recreation of the clear, free Abel, is where Leggatt is heading, this time from a platform including "non-innocence". Is it a transition which can be made, observed, and sustained?

As long as we understand the story of Cain and Abel without gestalt insight, we may shallowly polarize our understanding of ourselves and not see the dynamic role of each portion in the Torahic story. Here Cain is the trauma-site in a system captained by Abel, coming forward for resolution. Within the current framework of Conrad's story, neither parts kill or get killed. The invisibility of Leggatt's throttling encourages us to see the exchange in its irrational, heat-of-the-moment suddenness, closer to the real interaction of portions of our psyche upon the emergence of trauma held-energy systems as they make invisible the preceding and triggering (Abel) High.

The tragic error for the individual who experiences this movement might be that of striking out against the (any) triggering situation, identifying it as the cause which must be obliterated, rather than staying with the interior integrative pattern which somehow must be dissolved. The projective exteriorization of the pattern sets off a sequence of mirroring violences which is unnecessary, and meaningless, and truly crazy. In this sense all (subsequent) Abel/Cain violence is misguided and all rationales about it conceal a void at its core.

Abrupt transition

The transition between the pure Abel consciousness and its trauma held-energy system "brother" raises the question of what, if anything, we can do to restore our decided innocence, knowing what we now know. The interface between Innocence and Experience may be experienced as a gradual, rather than abrupt transition; even though inwardly, we often experience the one-two punch of traumatic process invisibly and as if brutally.

The brutality comes from the initiating situation which promulgates the appearance of shock. One minute we're High and pure, the next moment we are in a morass of abandonment and irresolution, as if punished. As noted above, we could consider the appearance of violence in stories, particularly involving relationship, not as violence itself, but as a screen concealing our deeper insufficiency about transitioning.

In "Sharer" our longing for Initial Innocence includes danger risk which accompany deliveries, and in the process, the Captain and his ship are reconnected, embodied. There is the successful surrender to the deeper force of the land-wind. Conrad's Captain bestows the resolution of freedom to Leggatt (and to himself), but Leggatt carries the memory aura of punishment with him. Perhaps this is the best most mature humans can do with traumatic process and the issues of historicity it raises. How short of Nirvana are we?

Urgent dissociative process

If we suppose that the present contains the ever-present potential for connecting to Ultimate Reality (which we are already a part of), then the study of the past becomes the recording not only of those important successful moments in the lives of individuals and groups, but of the failed moments when the striving for the truth is not envisioned or realized, when the trauma sites seeking resolution predominate and sustain against dissolution, as they do. And because they take the held-energy forms they do, it is no wonder that much as we think we learn from history's lessons, we don't. After all, these lessons arrive wrapped in urgent dissociative process, itself a process we hardly comprehend, immersed as we are within its encolding embrace. And as well, we have not yet gotten around to setting standards for public and private evaluation of "achieving" reality.

The historical past emerges often quite suddenly in the form of (karmic) held-energy patterns demanding resolution through the current narratives of the obvious present. That this present includes Ultimate Reality, the truth, as well as a *tabula rasa* aspect which allows full-scale projection of the patterns upon the material of life is both hopeful and ominous, if not condemning.

Here we can see the myelination synaptic process as it multiplies and confederates, both within and without, a sense of openness and freedom which cannot be addressed and experienced as potential without an already evolved neurochemical potentiality in place. Though our understanding of the interface moment of these two apparently different modes, Innocence and Experience, may evolve when we ourselves can differentiate it, both are present right from the beginning.

We live in the curse, with the curse, of irresolution. In the presence of held-energy systems, the past (or better, the only aspect of the "past" which matters) is only unresolved traumata, until it is not; and the speed with which the high vibratory states of connection with ultimate reality sets these systems in motion is enthralling and daunting. We do not have time to acknowledge where the past, in these forms, comes from. Demanding attention, they are constituted of memorized, memorialized, deoxygenated (or transpositioned oxygenating) shock.

In "The Secret Sharer" the past comes on board naked and complex and fully descriptive of the installation of shock on the occasion of sensory chaos; and it is hidden in the present until it is delivered. The bonding between Leggatt and the Captain is intimate and built on the problematic psychological economy of dissociation: the Captain repeatedly acknowledges Leggatt his double; and as such the payoff for Leggatt is the experience of "equality" otherness implied in what we could call empathic understanding. In this somehow, the narcissism resolves and completes; and Leggatt swims away and out into an invisible future. Here is a model of both personality and of history and our understanding of it. That of history which emerges in the present is usually unresolved stuff; otherwise the resolving past appropriately dissolves like oar prints in the water of the sea.

"The Secret Sharer" characterizes the essence of the problem of the present, both for the individual and for a culture which moves, sometimes, conscious of the aura of the karmic, irresolute past through which it swims. We can observe its structure vertically as well as horizontally, so to speak. The issues of the story recapitulate what William Emerson might call uterine implantation trauma, wherein as blastocyst, we land – a living, conscious at some levels entity – on a Mars of responsive and not so responsive intelligence. This occasion is also congruent with the moment of Annunciation, when the maternal system acknowledges the initiating presence within of its "double".

Immoral juxtaposition

Leggatt rationalizes the murder by degrading its first victim: "miserable devils that have no business to live at all" [p89], and in Leggatt, we see the immoral juxtaposed with the heroic. In his defensive way, he here reveals a moral incompleteness. In retrospect, Leggatt realizes that in a court of law, he will not get sympathetic support from his captain or shipmates whose lives he has saved. Extenuating circumstances or "fit of temper" [p89], temporary insanity or self-defense will not be applied in this situation. What needs to be legally "repaired" is the rent in the sail of trust between authority and those under its command; and, on the firm ground of courtroom land, society will opt for the security of simple trust.

The crucial moment is when, ultimately fatigued and extraordinary, abandoned by his immobilized captain, Leggatt first strikes the provoking Seaman; he is dangerously human in his striking out, as if there is a direct connection between what the Seaman says and himself. He could merely identify the Seaman for who he is, a toxic ball of trauma seeking resolution through projection, and allow him to be, for all the good his provocations do anybody.

Here is a tragic insight, and Leggatt provides a head-banging strategy in response to the Seaman's proffered impaction. We could argue that the Seaman invites such a response, on the line of "Somebody knock this pattern out of me." We see this often-expressed strategy in plays and movies where there is a lot of heroic and anti-heroic punching of the body and of the head. And my intuition is that rather than wanting to kill the man, the savior Leggatt would rescue the hapless Seaman a second time if he were falling overboard.

Hamartia

We may realize that the realistically even-minded, strong-souled Leggatt would probably agree to stand trial if it were fair and took into consideration the exceptional circumstances. After all, he was provoked, by his confounded captain and by the Seaman. His primary error is in initially striking out, not in the subsequent murder. Whatever the Seaman says, Leggatt takes it somehow personally, a deep moral error or *hamartia*. Such a person merely responds to provocation because they contain parallel held-energy systems, also seeking resolution through a shared narrative; that's how we (always incorrectly?) establish who our enemies are; it is called picking a fight. From a position of enlightenment, we have no enemies.

The Seaman who has seen what Leggatt has accomplished perhaps feels guilty about being saved. Or he cannot find his way to expressing gratitude. Or he proffers his worst pattern to the hero with "Here, Savior, now save me from this." In Christian myth, the Hero is thanked for his exceptional goodness by betrayal and crucifixion. But Leggatt, a parson's son, has lost faith in the system's ability to respond fairly, non-dissociatively, and he, I think, correctly anticipates a conventional hanging. He is dispensable to broader social objectives. Hence he, like other Conrad (anti-)heroes such as Lord Jim (and Kurtz?), jumps civilization's toxic ship.

What does the Seaman say? We know Leggatt "loses it", it being his civilized composure. From my own experience, I think it must be like my occasion with Thomas (not his real name), when I was twelve. I had spent a summer with this difficult, immature, and demanding, easily scapegoatable boy, befriending and supporting him when everybody else in our group avoided or shunned him. At the end of the summer as we were saying goodbye, he accused me of not being a friend, that I did not like him, that I was somehow the opposite of what I saw myself to be; and in a furious response to this core misunderstanding, I pounded his shoulders (I was sitting behind him) with all my might, to the rageful point of badly injuring my arms and wrists.

The "dissonance" arrived at my door: all I had done for this fellow was for naught; that he did not take in any of my kindness or compassion with which to reduce his obvious toxic, wounded spirit. Perhaps a bit older and more insightful, I could have dropped back and seen the pattern in a different way, asking Thomas a few psychologically discriminating questions, and then even-handedly separating, which may have been Thomas' deepest concern.

But I struck out at the impossibility of the defensive sequence, with a sense of my failure to make a dent in his self-destructive pattern. About six years later, I found out that soon after this summer journey, he was a drug addict (he may have been one already), from which over years he recovered to the point of being a drug counselor, or maybe did not. And then he knew me not.

In addition, Conrad has an ultimate, overwhelming wave come over the boat, submerging the two men, locked in a mortal embrace. Ten minutes later, they discover Leggatt with his hands still around the dead Seaman's neck. As a narrative of the way our brain processes experience, the image is provoking and in some ways cognitively suitable. Conrad specializes in explicating the relationship between the fluid and often chaotic nature of the sea and the Seaman, as personality, which survives its bottomless terrors.

Our consciousness of self, if we can presume to call it that, survives within and floating upon a sea of neurochemistry which we can hardly appraise, much less consciously control. Again and again Conrad returns to this to me wise and sufficiently deep perspective about the nature of human experience and the way we talk about it, particularly when we describe our "history". We are humbled by our continued posturing, even apparently noble activities in the face of how little we know how to captain our ship of and with personality. Buddhists would caution about the illusory nature of the ego, or of self.

Furthermore, the image demonstrates the application and aftermath of shock. Amid a disorienting, life-threatening sensate flooding, brain seizes and holds life energy in a locked position, which the brain system reads as oxygen-depleted and dead. In fact the whole fight sequence intuitively describes how in response to chaos, from without and within, shock occurs; and its aftermath must be dealt with. Shock is instituted under extreme and "violent" conditions. As Conrad narratively frames the problem, how much are we to be held accountable for the further perpetration of shock and our shock systems, radical and destructive as they seem, after having saved us?

Peter Principle

Additionally, we could suggest that the story confirms the Peter Principle, wherein as chief mate, Leggatt seeks to administrate in order to complete a pattern wherein he does not understand leadership; his trauma brings him to a point of violence duplicating some earlier moment of vulnerability and shock coming suddenly forward for resolution. Can he, or any leader, be held responsible for this part of his/her process? We can see the connection between shock resolving and violence, perhaps, probably, the echo of an earlier shock-inciting sudden moment. At any level, competent leaders will illustrate their trauma sites by their eventual incompetency.

In the gestalt of the story, there is a layering wherein the first version between two men ends in murder and death, whereas the second version, slower and more differentiated, allows for Leggatt's deliverance. Both versions are part of the single personality system Conrad is describing, and we get to see how from earliest developmental, maternal if you will, cues, resolution is possible. There is a parental (uterine) abandonment – Archbold, the captain of the *Sephora*, becomes dysfunctional – followed by a premature, violence-surrounded rescue of the ship, followed by a retraumatizing killing off of the trauma-ridden, hapless Seaman. Mythically, killing the Seaman will not do; he will return until the pattern he characterizes is understood.

Captain drawn closer

Rather than judge – and thereby distance himself from – the man who has murdered an ordinary seaman in violation of the laws of the sea and of humane order, the young Captain is drawn closer to him, probably witnessing his action as understandable, a sign of Leggatt's humane sanity, not his asocial insanity. The Chief Mate's amazing courage under enormous stress is worth protecting and even honoring; and certainly his life is.

The correspondences between the two graduates of the same training school become intimately shared, to the point where both Leggatt and the Captain know he cannot continue to hide the stowaway, and what he represents (including the Captain's love for Leggatt?) for much longer; the secret relationship must come out. He must deliver him unto his freedom, at some considerable risk to the ship, which must come dangerously close to the land in order to give Leggatt a fair chance to survive. From within the layered gestalt, healing love emerges.

I find crucial points in the story consist of Leggatt acknowledging to the Captain how grateful he is that the Captain, a little bit older than he, has understood him:

"But of course you [understand]. It's a great satisfaction to have got somebody to understand. You seem to have been there on purpose." And in the same whisper, as if we two whenever we talked had to say things to each other which were not fit for the world to hear, he added, "It's very wonderful." [*p107*]

Parting

Their final, whispered parting is intense with suppressed emotion and physical gesture. And the Captain delivers Leggatt to a new freedom which includes Leggatt's vulnerability, for as killer he carries the curse of Cain, and only the Cain mark, not always seen, often forgotten, will protect him from a world which may not see what he has done or could do.

God's protective mark is energetic, if you will, and it is carried aurically by Cain so that he does not invite brutality from the outside world which subliminally, invisibly reads his past and is triggered to scapegoat him. We read others and are read by others at this "invisible" level, and when our traumata are resolved, we present a radiant and porous presence which at some level protects us from duplicating the original crisis, inviting others as it might seem, to perpetrate the pattern we are declaring as ready to be reenacted, hopefully resolved.

Nor has Cain the humility to explain everything, particularly to an unempathic ear, including his own. This realization is behind the exterior surface of self which, as children of Cain, we all set as we stand before another person. We know our flawed, defensive natures and in good moments, acknowledge them in ourself, and in the person we face. Through our mythic, karmic historical lineage, we enter the world as innocents against a backstory in which we have already killed, dwelling in the shocky aftermath of trauma patterns, to which we desperately pledge allegiance.

The insight about our killing nature accrues and sharpens over time, culturally and individually, and it raises the question, "With what face can we face the world?" What is the nature of our innocence? In prenatalist mythology, there are those who suggest that as the surviving, fertilized egg, we have already killed off weaker sibling eggs in order to be first in line for conception. In "The Secret Sharer", Conrad's Captain sees the killer "energy" as being of the same force which sustains Leggatt's capacity to save the Sephora: "The same strung-up force which had given twenty-four men a chance, at least, for their lives, had, in a sort of recoil, crushed an unworthy mutinous existence. But I had no leisure to weigh the merits of the matter–". [*p102*]

In the way we hold our held-energy systems, also, we know we "kill" our highest vibratory states through dissociation; our potential is rarely fulfilled. This formulation answers the continuing diversionary question, "Who killed Jesus?" The proper question could be, "Who kills off the embodier of the Christ energy?" and the answer is, "We all do, even now, in our maintenance of our dissociative states."

The separation also includes a hair-raising maneuver which takes place in the fierce, silent darkness near the island Koh-Ring (some allusive wordplay here). The energetic vision is of an immense and fatally threatening black density which resembles energetic trauma sites within each of us. In the dropping off of the double or divided self, the engulfing black is terrorizing, until the Captain's white hat helps guide its owner into safety. A unity is (re-)established.

This parting action is a deliverance, in the way all births are, and they occur where attachment and identification yield to love. But the love is not just love of self, or of the double; it recognizes at some deeper level the organic necessity, the implantation of individuality and separating destiny, in spite of equal weight in our conviction that we are not separate.

As noted before, some prenatalists opine that there is a crucial moment in our birth when our forehead confronts our mother's sacrum, and, to continue getting born, we must turn our head to left or right; we cannot go straight ahead (*i.e.*, back and down). Here we learn that life has turns, and that we can turn. Theorists proffer that this task includes the lesson of mortality, that we are entering a world where mothers and children live and die – turn, and therein we receive permission that it is ok to do both. And as with "The Secret Sharer", mother (ship) and child move dangerously close to catastrophe to survive and explicate individuation.

I think this myth/moment lies in the same territory of Michaelangelo's renowned *Pieta*, where Mary appears to be younger than her adult dead Son in her arms and lap. No matter what her age, no matter what his age, the Child Mary delivers is the Child who (will suffer and who) dies. It is the sacrum moment and essential to the differentiation for both which is now occurring; and the sacrum moment is not the first prenatal occasion when this issue is laid out for energetic and psychophysical explication.

"The Secret Sharer" re-characterizes this deliverance realm, and it reveals the potential for dissociation, the separation of self from itself, a separation akin to killing, but critically not the same; and the story describes the thrill and complications of reuniting. The narrative begins with a first-pass explication of life and death individuation between self and other in its murderous, compressed, dissociative form: the impossible storm, the rescue, the fight, the strangle. The capacity to induce and partially survive shock, in partiality.

Like an individual who discovers a society-shame-filled secret about itself, the secret being very true, perhaps carrying deeper truth than the individual initially supposes, or could be reasonably expected initially to see clearly, the secret must be held somehow until the system can integrate it into its day-to-day existence. We know of this truth currently among so-called gays "coming out". Or alcoholics ("Hello, I am Tim, and I am an alcoholic." "Hello, Tim."). It takes time for a new platform to be rigged to contextualize radical personal insights which include this new element of the present, now, too quickly, becoming the past as well. The problem of historicity again raises its head within often timeless, trauma-bound paradoxically ahistorical energetic moments.

Captain Archbold

Parenthetically, the bonding between the two lead characters is challenged by Captain Archbold, of the *Sephora*, who visits and inspects the boat wherein Leggatt is hiding. Conrad reveals Archbold's lower-class (? – "I am a simple man") prejudice against the Conway-educated Leggatt from the very start. Leggatt has a resourcefulness of which he, Archbold, is the definite beneficiary, yet he refuses to acknowledge Leggatt's savior role in the storm and his own desertion of responsibility. Both Leggatt and the narrator share a privileged past, one which gives them, or assumes to give them, the ability to live past the rules; and ultimately to ignore them in the service of a higher purpose, namely the rule of (group) survival. This entitlement may obscure the real *hamartia* which is being outlined: Conrad's riff on the source of violence.

The story ends with the separation being acknowledged and resolved in spread out evenness. Impossibly near the shore, Leggatt swimming toward an unknown fate involving, paradoxically, a curse (the new information of enduring shock) and freedom, the doldrummed boat picks up a land-wind and finally moves; and for the first time, its new captain becomes united with his ship.

> The foreyards ran round with a great noise, amidst cheery cries....Already the ship was drawing ahead. And I was alone with her. Nothing! No one in the world should stand now between us, throwing a shadow on the way of silent knowledge and mute affection, the perfect communion of a seaman with his first command. [*p113*]

The entire gestalt is characterized fulfilled, expressed, and with it, the ship is turned. I find the mixture of activity and surrender – the immobility, the black, the danger, the hat, the swimmer, the land wind (the breath) – assembling in sequence, profound. At the heart of this serious action, or *praxis*, perhaps the only action in the whole story, is empathic perception, wherein narcissism is not surmounted or surpassed, but where it is fulfilled and resolved. Unresolved trauma interferes with the evolution of narcissism, in its dissociative function masking and mirroring the tasks of integration of information, both internal and external; until it does not. Again, the only significant move is that which brings trauma sites into healing dissolution and thus enables serious, *i.e.*, integrated, non-tragic integrative action.

The effect on our collective history of these actions is that most of what has been described in histories can be perceived as merely activities. Or the way they have been framed does not allow for viewing them except in dissociative terms.

In the Christian rubric, the one significant action around which all time-keeping is organized encompasses this historical agenda, namely the death and resurrection of the Christ – an energetic reality – not necessarily co-existent with the death of the man Jesus. In the poetry of meditations on the meaning of the Death and Transfiguration of Christ, we hear the preoccupations with Only Begotten Son and Complete and Sufficient Sacrifice.

For some practicing Christians, history becomes personal and universal, the explication of a (the) single unprecedented moment, which encompasses and discharges the apparently fixed and tragic nature of the present. This moment is filled with the time-bound configuration in which dissociation thrusts itself forward for dissolution, for resolution. Until this move is incorporated into cultural awareness, there is no future worth calling it future. Within this rubric, we turn to discover we are ignorant in a dark age whose scale we can hardly measure; barbarians, we have only just begun.

Let us recall the separating lines in the classical gestalt forms of mermaid and centaur and apply them to inter-relational body systems and the space between. The line between us creatures at the skin or at the outer limits of our auric energy field, and with other people (or better, the Next Individual) characterizes the site of separateness from which empathic sharedness begins to vibrate and radiate; this development, crucial to our understanding of history as the site of recalled merging and separateness, is ultimately a happy place. And this "line" is what Conrad narrates in "The Secret Sharer". If we were to deliver a visualization of this phenomenon, we would animate the separate characters, Leggatt and the Captain (and including, crucially, Archbold), who would both fuse and intermingle. Any overt sexual explication would merely hint at this energetic: the experience of empathy would allow for the dual flow of separateness and merged perception, a distinct solving solution.

Battle of the centaurs

The battle of the centaurs around the top of the Parthenon narrates the ambivalence of the struggle, built upon the difficulty of mastering paradox. And the images of men fighting with centaurs propose, I think, a subtext to the occasion of war, wherein the line of separation is perceived as a strict and catastrophic division along which trenches – as juxtaposition of two forms of similar consciousness, a division instilled and confounded by dissociation – we wrestle with the burdens of incompleted narcissism. Perhaps this is obvious.

What "The Secret Sharer" concludes with is a vision not only of healing, but of history and our place within the present. The Captain takes on a complex view of mankind – naked, flawed, traumatically bound and heroic – and locates it secretly on board his "ship". And we have a gestalt which characterizes the human condition as well as the (often secret) love relationship between men. Beneath the secrecy and passion, if you will, lies a chemistry which begins energetically in a perfect and dreadful storm, chaotic and threatening, wherein a connection is toxically sought and resolved in killing, not kissing. (Is Judas nearby?)

In versions of trauma resolution, the juxtaposition of two allied but separated forms of awareness allows for primitive brain to reoxygenate the oxygen-deprived realms of memory; and this reoxygenation, structural and organic, I have discovered, often cannot be intentioned. It is not a simple matter of aiming the life-conveying garden hose into the empty, parched container. The container itself must be structurally, historically retuned, otherwise the water coming in will not be held (and appropriately distributed) by the container. Apparently, held energy must be held in order to resolve itself.

Thus the gestalt of "The Secret Sharer" can be seen as containing a commentary about dissociation and its resolution. One part receives, holds (understands), and finally releases the other part, its double. One might argue that all fractions or characters within gestalt formulations are "doubles", awaiting understanding and deliverance. Or that with the appearance of doubles, we have entered the hard-rock land of trauma and dissociation – and the complex landing of the blastocyst on the uterine surface. In this case, Conrad begins with order radically challenged by overflowing chaos, wherein violence in the form of a maddening and deadly struggle, mirrors and attempts to stabilize (intentionally?) sensuous flow.

In a pre-liberation sensibility, such turbulence would have no order-restoring expression. The fulcrum of the *Sephora* fight would involve sensate overflow, incapable of erotic discharge. From a men's liberation point of view, a different kind of permission needs to be granted in order that new synaptic connections can prepare for new insight and new action.

Paradoxically, the vision of erotic discharge currently in contemporaneous time also is incomplete. Only briefly can we sustain a new sense of connectedness, wherein the bound memory of violence and chaos is confronted, endured, and dissolved. In current web pornography, the culturally frozen patterns are often reworked or from the start eliminated in order to achieve permitted entry into some non-catastrophic, ecstatic present.

Note

One final note. As I have taught "The Secret Sharer" many, many times with adolescents (all of whom have been in various forms of intense therapy), I have recently found some students, girls and boys, opining that they think Leggatt should go back to stand trial, even to be hung as a murderer. This counters my own tendency to give him a Conrad's chance; I am as enamoured of Leggatt as is the Captain.

But as I take their viewpoint on, increasingly I focus on Leggatt's flaws, his judgment/defense about the worthlessness of the Seaman, rather than his "owning" the irrationality of his behavior. I see this as characterological, to give him some slack in the face of his efficacious perfectionism. While a bit off the point in its application to the Sephora situation, the moral problem of the story of Cain and Abel is illuminating because Cain is bereft from having already abandoned God; the burgeoning superego proffers no mercy, though it presumes itself to be in place to civilize the individual. Therein lies a contrariness because we revolt against its arbitrariness and are prone to violence which we were supposed to be frightened away from.

The letting go is what brings us past the violence which we have engendered toward others and toward ourselves. Without leeway, we will continue to perpetrate violence which we project onto the outside world. From within.

The more I dwell with this story with my students, I am forced into specifying in detail what Conrad, perhaps cursorily, presents: for hidden within the story are crucial moral moments of perspective which the students/readers use to ground their own evaluations of it. Currently, when they look at the relationship of Leggatt and the Captain, they want to evaluate its sensate, even sexual components, and we confront the limits of Conrad's sensual sensibility. Is he describing something which in his time, was unspeakable? Yet the fundamental issues between the two characters are properly, respectfully, transcendentally explicated; the intimacy and trust between two men are declared. Conrad is a humanitarian, for he uses a perhaps jimmy-rigged situation to show how the parts of the self get realigned toward a place where action, not just activity, can occur.

CHAPTER THIRTEEN:

GESTALT IN LITERATURE: GODOT

Waiting For Godot

In Samuel Beckett's play *Waiting For Godot* [Samuel Beckett. *Waiting For Godot*. Grove Press, New York, 1954. ISBN 0-802 1-3034-8] we may see the wages of dissociation visited upon a traumatized child and get a glimpse of what its healing dissolution might look like. The play can demonstrate how a victim perhaps of abuse can wait for a relieving intervention which never arrives, or can anticipate a vengeful God who, in some fashion, may further perpetrate abuse.

Two bums, Vladimir, called Didi, and sometimes Mr. Albert, and Estragon, called Gogo, are poised on a bare stage, with only a single "tree" visible against a barren land and skyscape. They talk about what they are doing there, and they say they are passing time, waiting for Mr. Godot, who actually never arrives. There is a ritualized quality to their repetition of "waiting for Godot", usually following the concern voiced as, "What are we doing here?" After a while, Pozzo and Lucky appear, and there are further discussions about how people and situations are controlled, including the supposed master/slave relationship this latter, tattered pair are in – Lucky is the apparent, designated servant and Pozzo, cracking a whip, orders him about.

After they leave, a Boy appears, announcing to Didi and Gogo that again Godot will not be coming this night. As Godot's goatherd and apparent go-between, the Boy does not seem to be the same Boy who came last night, and he is challenged by Gogo and protected by Didi. The Boy leaves, taking

Didi's message to Mr. Godot that he, the Boy, has seen the two bums. Soon afterward, the act ends as follows:

Estragon: Well, shall we go?
Vladimir: Yes, let's go.
They do not move.
Curtain [*p59*]

With variations, a somewhat similar sequence makes up the second act, and this has led critic Vivian Mercier famously to offer that *Waiting For Godot* is a play about nothing which happens, twice. But for many of the play's witnesses, what that nothing is becomes the problem which the play addresses. This theme about the nature of nothing, and its corollary, the boredom aligned with unresolved waiting for something that does not happen, is picked up, for not the first time, by the academic, intellectual, often left-brained establishment in colleges and graduate schools after the play is first produced in America in the early 1950's. For some, *Godot* is the essential play of the 20th Century.

Waiting For Godot is deceptively organized, centering upon the inability of brain, somehow "divided" from itself, to re-engage, center, and to heal. The theme of a divided chemistry is stated at the play's beginning when Didi reminds Gogo about the image of the two thieves flanking the crucified Jesus: one is saved, the other is not. Perhaps in response to our human desire to reestablish holistic covenant with God, this Christian myth reports that Ultimate Reality is dualistic, creating salvation winners and salvation losers, as in separating goats from sheep – a story concerning dualism at least as old as the parents of Cain and Abel. While dualism implies an equal sharing of two entities, like hot and cold, I am not sure the term applies thusly in this play.

Within a gestalt interpretation of *Godot*, wherein all the characters can be considered aspects of a single personality, we are conjoined in the process of the play in reverse psychodynamic order, similar to the way we encounter our own traumata. We experience our traumata in their dissociative configurations in the present. Only upon reflection, or because of suffering, do we escort ourselves back to these dissociative states' historical, generative point(s) of origin, and this, we discover, is not so easy to do. From such perspective, we live in fact in two coexistent internal time chemistries, bridged by the function-problem of, for lack of a better term, memory. And, as creatures, we have sought to describe and to focus upon these aspects of our human nature.

Moment of trauma induction

For much of Western culture, the moment of trauma induction appears to be recorded mythically and historically in Genesis when we are cast out of Eden. The Church has identified the causal moment of the Expulsion as the Original Sin, and contrary to inappropriate usage over centuries as an insight, this strategy reflects the awareness that our current "sins" or errors are dissociative, and that they rely for their shape on an historical First Sin, or Error. Eden's story is essentially a karmic strategy, and, rather dramatically, it still applies, and on two levels.

On the personal level, each of us creatures experiences Our First Trauma, or Original Trauma, and we are thus introduced to our two-stroke, or binary engine, Being, and, let's call it Off-Being. Every subsequent crisis evokes the same shock-synaptic solution (or fan of solutions), the one which got us through crisis the first time. Thus, at some level, all subsequent traumata functionally are the same; they spindle on our First Response/Solution to the First Crisis.

More importantly, as survivors (thanks to shock's life-saving attributes), we can view the transition between Being and Off-Being and begin to characterize that transition as a way of viewing the installation of the pattern which we end up being stuck with.

Why should we be worried about any of this? Well, we make what we call mistakes, and often we see ourselves in patterns which we try to stop, but, just by saying, or thinking, "Stop!", we can't. We try to get to the base of the pattern in order to solve it, to reduce what turns out to be our addiction to crisis-related adrenaline, or willing our repeated lack of oxygen to re-engage from Off-Being to a purer state of Being. If someone asked me about my pattern-resolution process, I would say, "That's what I am doing all the time."

We have various levels of awareness of this problem, some of them immanent, some of them more covert. But after a third "divorce" – and we do not have to ever have a divorce to experience divorce – we know we have a problem. The question is how to establish handles on the spicey (black) meatball so that it can be worked with and dissolved, or concomitantly resolved at the deepest levels.

The point of entry into the trauma memory matrix cannot always be sensed, or controlled for. Suddenly we are overcome with an old and disturbing state which may be linked to the original situation by narrative similarity to our present one. Or we are in therapeutic regression, and saying we want to recover the past, it is not "available" until we somehow turn a corner and there it is. Or, over long periods of time, in psychoanalysis, we deliberately experience "transference", its obvious and its not so obvious forms.

Whatever. Expressed in Edenic longing, we are moving toward Being, toward Enlightenment, toward a resolution where we can have a Covenant with Ultimate Reality. And to do that, at some level we have to experience the pattern as both in and out of current time; just as the pattern(s) is coexisting in our current time, as Being and Off-Being. At times we are cruising for a narrative which approximates the energy of crisis and shock impaction, maybe even so basic and universal that it describes the First Trauma or Original Trauma. Wouldn't that be the cat's meow. We would then have a handle on the pattern, now (we realize this after months and years of repetition and obsession), beyond narrative.

In the recovering-Jew aspect of Christianity, the later, refined elaboration of the Fall in the Crucifixion demonstrates how the radiance of our personal, universal Christ energy is cast into immobility and black. It is part of the Christian (re)examination of traumatic process that the Body is powerlessly nailed to the Cross, a presentation of some spinal, perhaps meningeal process in dissociation; this is the moment of shock cast by and into our neurochemistry, and we are pinioned to it. For most of us, it is this kind of experience, having its antecedents in prenatal trauma configurations (or absorbed patternings from historical transferring), which determines our sense of time, personality, and history, until it does not.

The second application of this insight is social, and tribal. We discover that there are other people in the world who are doing the same thing, attempting to complete unresolved, trauma-determined, shock nexi. And at the societal level, there are groupings which experience collective traumata and which pass on the collective patterns to individuals through recognition and membership identity; and they seek national, or tribal destinies whose narratives are full of resolving or more importantly, the possibility of resolution of traumatic nexi.

For so-called neo-Jewish Christians, the crucial description of the chemistry of traumatic response is the Cross. Everything moves toward and away from this image; all things, including history itself, can be understood within the nexi which Christ on the Cross embodies. In *Godot*, Becket's variation is pivoted upon the Original Sin and its subsequent elaboration of the Cross. It becomes interesting to see how the single moment, including Being and Off-Being, can find different elaborations, though the moment is always the same, and it is both explicated and black blind.

Back to Godot

In *Godot*, our radiant Christ energy is not flowing but held; and this trauma memorial is characterized by two flanking, muted, and derivative forms, Didi and Gogo, repetitively polarizing into a duality which at first witness seems futile, endless, and boring. In response to crisis-inducing shock, brain apparently can divide into dualistic functioning and ideation. And with Didi and Gogo, here is the zone of dissociative, shocky chemistries where ordinary three-dimensional time means nothing, where, in a surreal and radical ordinariness, we find no sustained integrity. It may also be the place where, as currently understood, and as experienced from within, prenatal consciousness develops.

Though characterizing these chemistries and attributes as bums and cartoon abstracts, in *Godot* Beckett describes a universal human movement, beyond social and aesthetic caste. In its artistic representation in the play, the duality expressed by our two common men, Didi and Gogo, is eternally rendered as tramp, so that within a degraded, essentialized context, the two sides conduct a dialogue, whose underlying immobilizing *stasis* never resolves.

Praying to God

When looking at a play with gestalt glasses, the question for me becomes who or what part of the play holds the pattern, expressed through plural characters, in its most comprehensive, unitary form: in traditional dramatic parlance, "Whose play is it?" In *Hamlet*, it is the survivor/witness Horatio's play (with Fortinbras). In *Cyrano de Bergerac*, it is Roxanne's, or DeGuiche's, not that of the main heroic figure of the title. In *Waiting For Godot* also, the play is held not by the characters who dominate stage time. Rather, the play "belongs" to the Boy who reports on the direct experience and nature of Mr. Godot. This means that all that precedes the Boy's appearance can be circumscribed as dissociative and set aside as we watch the encounter between the Boy and his "voices", Didi and Gogo.

While children are being raped or beaten or abused by their caretakers, they often later report praying to a God for relief and cessation, but in the moments of abuse, sometimes lasting years, God never comes. In "A Child is Being Beaten", Freud posits that actual abuse may not occur for infantile elaboration of ordinary limit-setting, for example, to be experienced for a time as abuse. Or we Christ Children absorb the abusive patterning from the historical past as a portion of our "karmic" or social-karmic inheritance. "That's life," we are told. Some prenatalists have proposed that some reports of later sexual abuse are rooted in birth trauma, not in subsequent, actual parental or adult perpetrations.

An abandonment configuration may be included in all trauma memories: God arrives in the form of shock, to rescue our systems from destruction; but God does not come forth to anticipate and obviate the situation wherein there is a necessity for shock in the first place. Within the trauma moment, the sense of guilt (*Did I?*), shame (*Pozzo - Pot So*), relief and love (*Lucky*), and fight or flight (*Go go*) chemistries mix and cluster, and in those moments of terror and compassion, grandiosity and humiliation, pain and crisis, our young brain is prone to memorialize in dissociation.

The Boy reports to Didi and Gogo that his shepherd brother, not he, is beaten by Mr. Godot. If we ran into such reportage within a therapeutic setting, intuitively we might want to include the possibility that there is no brother, merely a proposed dissociated fragment of so-called self; the polarization already has occurred. Within the genius of its holographic, hovering, float capacity, our neurochemistry fractionates into "plurals" in order to maintain parcels of integrity in the face of perceived or actual annihilation. This annihilation can be physical and/or energetic. This capacity to transfer function from one fragile, downed portion to another enables us to develop and to survive from moment to moment. (see Abraham sacrificing a ram instead of his son Isaac).

In the tranquillity of recollection, the after-storm chemistry of trauma initially has revealed two pairs of conjoined voices, Didi/Gogo and Pozzo/Lucky, which achieve no lasting resolution satisfaction. By their very dual, paired nature, they never will. Salvation occurs within a deeper sense of unity, of a radiant chemistry wherein we pass from belief into knowledge, the full knowledge of Being. Constant within all our action, this energetic knowledge is not expressed verbally, so that in all dramatic dialogue, we know we are compromised, away from our silent, Being center, which we often may call God and identify as unitary. And understanding may follow knowledge.

If we think of Didi and Gogo as, say, the first part of the Boy's "dream" (in one production utilizing Beckett's specific staging directions, he appears to be in pajamas), the second part involving Pozzo and Lucky is a sado-masochistic elaboration on the same theme. We see further down the brain stem, as it were, this elaboration terrifying in its duplication of Beckett's initial pattern, yet somehow offering hope that something can be done, through a vigorous and totally ineffective application of intentionality. When Pozzo and Lucky appear, we see how in retraumatization the pattern repeats, and we see brain's attempt, through the haplessness of authoritarianism, or, in a curious way, fundamentalism, to control or discharge the pattern. The interactions of this couple prefigure the Boy's mentioning that Godot beats his brother.

Pozzo and Lucky are ventures in getting clear, and the cognitive-behavioral approach to mastering dissociation is something we all try out. With reward and punishment we attempt to objectify our traumatic process. In his tumultuous monologue in Act One, Lucky powerfully expresses the connection between non-verbal and verbal centers of the brain, but the connection cannot be counted upon. Servant and master, master and slave, get mixed up, the roles reverse and tumble as they do in real life. As they do within our single and momentous chemistries of brain.

The final encounters of each act describe the chemistry/state of the Boy, and the Boy reports fear, but no sense of integrity. Though the Boy speaks as one who has direct connection with Mr. Godot, the connection is ineffective — perhaps, dare we think it, spurious. And the various "Boys" are not the same Boy, even though they appear to be. Can *Godot* be Godot's play?

Importantly, there is no volunteering by the bums to help the Boy out with his potentially punitive Godot, who comes in some form, we might suggest, perhaps every night, to the Boy and to his "brother". From what we see of Didi and Gogo, they might intervene in the beatings, but they are stuck where they are, themselves characterized as waiting as is the Boy. From this perspective, the presence of the characters can be seen as the interventions themselves, distracting from the beatings, expressing and staving off confrontation with the repeated despair about continual beatings, or a world which contains that possibility. *Waiting For Godot* embodies, characterizes despair, but it may rest on a most sincere platform of idealism.

The person who administers the abuse also carries the possibility of its cessation, at least at the most obvious levels of three-dimensional experience. There is no talk of an all-forgiving Godot, because the consequences of trauma linger, and in some cases are apparently irremediable. As a world consciousness/culture, we have just begun to address trauma resolution with renewed intensity, and we cannot be sure about its hardwiring nature.

The person who administers the abuse also carries the possibility of its cessation, except when the victim/recipient masochistically elaborates upon the abuse, as we are wont to do. Getting the initiating Other to stop punishing the Self is an important start. But getting to the initiating point in the punitive Other's punitive inner system so that they do not project it outward onto the (another) Self is yet another beginning.

Thus Godot's name carries four possibilities: the Godot who beats and the Godot who stops beating, and the Godot who concludes the entire pattern, the trauma memory as well as the instigator of shock, *i.e.*, the Savior who restores us to Being. In the play, the first is still somewhere apparently off-stage – maybe beating the "brother" – and the second is in the paired form of Didi and Gogo, who reassure us (the Boy) that their reality replaces (can replace) what is really going on, which is traumatic and unfathomable. This position duplicates the theological conundrum about God's love creating a world which includes evil.

Beckett is raised by an apparently loving, even gracious father, but if that is the case, his father's compassionate oasis does not preclude the son absorbing, even by obverse default an Irish, or mis-applied "Christian" desert surround which brutalizes and conveys suffering within a beating world. Didi and Gogo express a defense against this pattern which seems to be permanent, yet is really temporary: we are waiting for Godot. What seems to be a filler aside – "Why are we here? We are waiting for Godot" – hides a universe of suffering. And because their intervention is temporary on behalf of the Boy, who is waiting for the second, or even the third Godot, with a perhaps smile, we could propose that the reason Godot does not come is because he is off-stage, perhaps waiting for Didi and Gogo. Or the Boy.

The fourth Godot is the Godot who abandons. Because he never appears to us, the audience, nor to the characters, except perhaps to the Boy (and this is not certain), we wonder why we have to wait. Significant to their position as a proposed, wishful defense against the trauma memory, to Didi and Gogo, Godot never arrives. Where is the Messiah, First Coming or Second?

Beckett demonstrates how brain in dissociation narrates trauma seeking resolution at every point. For if Godot comes, someone may get beaten. Or a choice, a separation between Didi and Gogo, will be forced. Or the initial polarizing event will be re-engaged. Or we cause the accident to happen again. From brain's, and the Boy's position, this must not happen, for to reenter that shocky chemistry will bring deoxygenation and suffocation, signaled here in the text by suggestions of suicidal hanging from the spine/tree. Shock in trauma takes our breath away.

Nor will Godot come this night to aid the Boy with his adulty, partialized fragments, but we can anticipate him "surely tomorrow". Waiting for Godot successfully, perhaps superstitiously, holds off the trauma memory, and from therapeutic experience, we know the play's dull boringness is a sure sign of trauma patterning underneath. Is waiting another form of stopping?

And for the time the Boy is with Didi and Gogo, the beating Godot does not show up because he is still beating or about to beat the 'brother". While the play reiterates that strategy as defense, as a distracting, even charming couple, they are flimsy; Didi and Gogo's "waiting" indicates a system which seeks full resolution of the trauma, which may have nothing to do with "beating". The psychoanalyst Bergler might opine that the entire play is an infantile elaboration on separation by the child from the mother, including the above plural, contradictory aspects of the mother who "abandons". Beckett's father may be great, but as perceived (and not showing up), his "mother" may be something else.

Crucial signs of change

The system the play describes is retraumatizing, and there are few signs of movement, though these are crucial and, I think, real. The first comes at the very beginning of the play when Gogo removes one of his pain-inducing shoes, an act of self-relieving, self-soothing, which in therapeutic terms counts as some progress. Gogo's shoes do not fit, and as the play slowly elaborates this theme, they signal how healing can be registered within small and subtle changes.

Being able to bring the self-healing capacity of brain to bear within our timeless dissociative chemistries is of crucial importance. Which of us can not be interested? Here is an apparently clear example of cause and effect, where pain is generated by the shoe; not the strategy one can easily use from within a dissociative neurochemistry.

It takes an entire act for Gogo to remove his other painful shoe. Actors who play this role know its physical awkwardness, and it is a sign of getting clear that his hobbling state is finally replaced by Gogo walking on two bare feet. This may be the most significant action, or *praxis*, of the play, and it stands strongly against our initial superficial judgment that in *Waiting For Godot*, nothing happens, twice. In fact, rather than being disgruntled at the repetition, we have the opportunity to orbit the Boy's pattern slowly, perhaps to witness it for the healing "first time".

Act Two records this change in spinal shift: the tree has sprouted leaves; and Gogo's shoes are not as much a problem for him as they were. We can accommodate to the pinching qualities of narrative when we discover how we can bring relief to ourselves. The deeper part of the shoes motif comes when we discover that while our energetic core can be sensed in narrative, in dissociation, our core is not the same as narrative. "Being is prior to essence." Our experience-organizing souls float through and within narrative, and we, whatever that is, can be distracted by narrative's compelling, often apparently necessary detail. Yet no matter how enthralling our incarnation, when stuck, it is because in the densified neurochemistries of trauma, we have forgotten, or are blinded to the fact that we are, also, energetic; in some people's term, that we are spirit.

The importance of Gogo's shoes is not initially obvious, perhaps because our literary mind-set is distracted by Beckett's commonplace framing of the problematics of self-healing. And those seem to be all Gogo and Didi talk about. Only after some contemplation can we see the kabuki, or Zen-like compressive and expansive qualities which Gogo's taking care of his suffering feet come to stand for. "Oedipus Rex", "Agamemnon", and the Crucifixion carry foot gestures with similar import, and each views the same problem from alternate vantage points. Yet all these examples establish benchmarks for measuring our progress toward enlightenment and wholeness.

The critical feature of our dissociative process is that in dissociation while we are always seeking resolution, we also are always retraumatizing. In the moments near the end of Act One, we see how and why it is difficult making the connection between the Boy and his plurals.

> *Estragon*: (*forcibly*). Approach when you're told, can't you?
> *The Boy advances timidly, halts.*
> *Vladimir*: What is it?
> *Boy*: Mr Godot . . .
> *Vladimir*: Obviously . . . (*Pause.*) Approach.
> *Estragon*: (*violently*). Will you approach! (*The Boy advances timidly.*)

What kept you so late?
Vladimir: You have a message from Mr. Godot?
Boy: Yes Sir.
Vladimir: Well, what is it?
Estragon: What kept you so late?
The Boy looks at them in turn, not knowing to which he should reply.
Vladimir: (*to Estragon*). Let him alone.
Estragon: (*violently*). You let me alone. (*Advancing, to the Boy.*)
Do you know what time it is?
Boy: (*recoiling*). It's not my fault, Sir.
Estragon: And whose is it? Mine?
Boy: I was afraid, Sir.
Estragon: Afraid of what? Of us? (*Pause.*) Answer me!
Vladimir: I know what it is, he was afraid of the others.
Estragon: How long have you been here?
Boy: A good while, Sir.
Vladimir: You were afraid of the whip?
Boy: Yes Sir.
Vladimir: The roars?
Boy: Yes Sir.
Vladimir: The two big men.
Boy: Yes Sir.
Vladimir: Do you know them?
Boy: No Sir.
Vladimir: Are you a native of these parts? (*Silence.*)
Do you belong to these parts?
Boy: Yes Sir.
Estragon: That's all a pack of lies. (*Shaking the Boy by the arm.*) Tell us the truth!
Boy: (*trembling*). But it is the truth, Sir! [*p53-4*]

Intervening upon this boy-threatening moment, Didi asks his buddy in reproachful horror, "What's the matter with you?" but for a moment, perhaps we may glimpse the narrative form of Beckett's personal trauma, the one which essentially informs *Waiting For Godot*. In this moment the pairings of Didi/Gogo and of Pozzo/Lucky are established as equivalent, and Pozzo's whipcrack echos through both pairs, as well as through the Boy, who knows Mr. Godot beats the Boy's "brother".

We see an "abusive" – perhaps Irish, or in Beckett's dissociative pathos, French – authority person, or its mythic equivalent, for whom no intervention, by authority or perpetrator or by child victim, can bring the pattern and the narrative through which it seeks resolution, to a halt, to a stop, to an arrest. For the Boy, the paired proposals of adulthood standing before him promise a rescue station duality, but not the unity of salvation. In trauma energetics process, his Third Eye has been compromised, and he cannot recognize what is energetically true both within and realistically true without.

Living well is the best revenge

Does it matter whether Beckett himself was abused by being father-beaten? Or did he witness something he feared but could not understand ("the two big men")? Is *Godot* projective flotsam from Becket's Jungian psychoanalysis, or artistic slumming in the ghetto of depression, not even his own? His biographers may respond variously. But such narrative description of the energetic he describes is universal and does not require evidence of a specific pants-down stropping, or worse, to be real.

Currently, with clients, I find that one strategy for a long-standing resistant pattern is that the pattern cannot be excised or brought to the curb for recycling because the pattern has been transmitted from someone else; it does not belong to the individual, who thus has no resources to decode the "foreign" pattern. The reason it persists is because it does not belong.

Nor, as early Genesis illustrates, is the father the only way by which the trauma pattern gets transmitted. Even Freud, who showed concern for the Child Being Beaten, sensed that the curbing of sacred eros does not have to be directly violent to set us into the traumatized inward violence of self-abuse. There may be a point in all trauma resolution, no matter what the crisis, where our held pattern narrates something like *Godot*.

Waiting For Godot is about transmission between generations, between the old and the young, of information about experience. And our initial experience of being beaten may come to the surface around ordinary masturbatory discoveries, or, more likely, much, much earlier in the developmental sequence: as we discover what is permitted to relieve and be relieved, and what is not. In short, we can find what shoe, or hat, or garment suits. Self-removing an instrument of suffering is an action of considerable self-soothing magnitude and may be the first move toward realizing, from a dissociative, impacted state, that we are energetic beings – and free.

Our seeking for a narrative cause for our suffering may have within it elements of seeking revenge, hunting down our victims turned perpetrators. As dying Laertes proffers to dying Hamlet, "The king's to blame." But I think this kind of vengeance occurs not merely to stop the perpetrating agent. Rather, it is because underneath our vengeful machinations, we do not know how to stop the retraumatizing pattern as it is perpetrated into and through us. Or let's narratively blame it on our First Messenger – and feeder. In developmental terms, our Christ Child comes to save the world and then gets stuck with the patterns hurled upon It, the sins It takes on. And because the energetic pattern expresses itself through narrative, we keep hunting for its cause and cessation in narrative, sometimes fundamentalistically applied.

If the held-energetic trauma pattern could dissolve, then we would consider the narrative, with its attribution of blameful agent, if not also cause, less consequential. And we would still curb the perpetrators, but not in the way we now do. Living well is a best, an only, revenge against abuse; it is the only internal signal that the held-energy pattern has conclusively dissolved. But, as addicts know, living well cannot be faked, nor does the pattern stop just because we imitate a good life, or collusively create or enable forgiveness. Attempting to conclude some patterns by changing only at the narrative level ultimately succeeds only some of the time.

Learning how to occasionally relieve suffering is so important to the sufferer, victim and perpetrator. Yet Beckett shows us the living well of trauma resolution is the something more and different which must also happen. *Godot*'s second act takes us through the pattern again, with some significant alterations. Pozzo is now more appropriately himself, *i.e.*, blind and unproud, and lucky Lucky is mute. And the tree has leaves, though their energetic vector is ambiguous. We are closer to the core trauma and can witness the energetic pattern with an inner vision which had been formerly blocked. Nothing is not going on here.

Brain contemplates its dual forms

Brain contemplates its dual forms: "We can still part, if you think it would be better," Vladimir proffers at the end of Act One. More clearly at the end of the second act, the following reiterative, clarifying exchange occurs:

> *Estragon*: If we parted? That might be better for us.
> *Vladimir*: We'll hang ourselves to-morrow. (*Pause.*) Unless Godot comes.
> *Estragon*: And if he comes?
> *Vladimir*: We'll be saved. [*p109*]

If Gogo and Didi were to separate as they here envision, for the Boy, whose play it is, separation would be only for a neurochemical moment; but that moment would be an oxygen-less, suffocating chasm through which brain does not yet know how to pass. Then the energy described in the *Godot* system would regroup into an unity, or toward some other phase in the sequence toward integration.

What we hope to see is the dissolution of the duality, of the predominant two, four voices of the play, in some simultaneous, completing way. Then the Godot, at least the part holding Godot's promise of resolution, will occur, and the Boy will be free, and saved. The system of which the Boy is the central part will be transformed and the underlying trauma will be resolved; this is what it means to be "saved". This salvation is an ever-present reality, characterized by Ralph Waldo Emerson as essentially protestant and democratic and ensoulfully individuating.

But Becket shows that while there is some relief, and brain has begun to recognize its torment, the pattern has not been resolved. There is a significant difference between relief, release, and resolution. In the most telling moment of true righteous anger in the play, in the first act, Didi/Vladimir demands of the Boy, "You don't know me?"

> *Boy*: No Sir.
> *Vladimir*: It wasn't you came yesterday?
> *Boy*: No Sir. [*p54-55*]

In dissociative disconnection, brain cannot regain a sense of time, with time's ordinary embodying beginning, middle, and end. And, as with a quickly forgotten dream, the Boy barely acknowledges the narrative of Didi and Gogo. And who can blame "him"? I think this moment is the second, and clearest statement of the healing crisis *Waiting For Godot* describes. And we who have lived with Didi and Gogo for too boring long, cannot initially comprehend that they could not be seen: for we see them. Yet that is the dissociative truth, the truth about dissociation not only in its craziest forms, but in its everyday mundanity. And the dissociative chemistry is carried not by the pairs, who turn out to be dominant but strangely inconsequential, but in the gestalt form of the one, the Boy.

To escort brain to the place where it can begin to examine its retraumatizing chemistry brings it to the threshold of profound enlightenment. Passing from characterization into the silent, still state of Being, the multiplicities of personality, Didi and Gogo, Pozzo and Lucky, and the unlucky Boy would dissolve into an unity of radiance, carried holographically somewhere between, within, and without all five (plus – significantly – one) dramatis personae. We anticipate this perhaps mystical sequence because we have seen important and subtle beginnings of the change process already. Though repetitive, the second act, overlooked by the occasionally(?) leafy tree, reveals a shift in our perspective on our held-energetic alignments and how far we are from experiencing a beginning of motion at the shocked core.

In the retraumatizing aspect of unresolved traumatic process, we return again and again to a narrative in which we tell us that we are waiting for some intervention, the rescuing, or perpetrating, Godhead, which, for reasons at least neurochemical, in that timeless apresent moment, like the mother who abandons us for a time, never comes. In resolution, however, the four plus one characterizations would no longer be necessary. Enlightened, we could face a gracious, unknown future energetically based upon a pre-verbal knowledge, of Being; not, as Beckett concludes *Waiting For Godot*, with a known future cognitively based upon the dissociative certainty of belief. And from this knowledge, we may achieve understanding.

September 24, 2000

Chapter Bibliography:

Samuel Beckett. *Waiting For Godot.* Grove Press, NY 1954. ISBN 0-802 1-3034-8.
Edmund Bergler. *Curable and Incurable Neurotics.* Liverright Publishing, New York, 1961. Currently ISBN 082361092 and 978023610926, 978023610921).
Ralph Waldo Emerson. *The Essays of Ralph Waldo Emerson.* Belknap Press, Cambridge, 1987. ISBN 0674 267206.
Sigmund Freud. "A Child is Being Beaten, A Contribution to the Study of the Origin of Sexual Perversions". 1919 Int. Z. Psychoanalysis 5 (3), 151-72. 1920 International Journal of Psychoanalysis 1. 371-95 Transl. A + J. Strachey.

"Ein Kind Wird Geschlagen" Beitrag zur Kenntnis der Entstehung sexualler Perversionen 1919 Int. Z. Psychoanal. 5 (3), 151-72.
Modern Critical Interpretations Samuel Beckett's Waiting For Godot. Edited and with an Introduction by Harold Bloom. Chelsea House Publishers, New Haven, 1987. ISBN 1 55546 058 5.
Peter Levine, Ann Frederick (Contributor). *Waking The Tiger: Healing Trauma: The Innate Capacity to Transform Overwhelming Experiences.* North Atlantic Books, 1997. ISBN 155643233x.
William M. Redpath. *Trauma Energetics, A Study of Held-Energy Systems,* Barberry Press, Lexington, MA, 1994. ISBN 0964-7730-07.
Trauma, Explorations in Memory. Edited, with Introductions by Cathy Caruth, Johns Hopkins University Press, Baltimore, 1995. ISBN 08018 5007x.

Videotapes:

Beckett Directs Beckett, Waiting For Godot, University of Maryland, College Park Visual Press, Cameras Continentales. 1990. Smithsonian Institution Press, Distributor. Directed by Walter D. Asmus, based upon the mise-en-scène of Samuel Beckett (with a Beckett relative (?) as the Boy).
Waiting For Godot. Directed by Alan Schneider. Produced by Jack Kaney. Applause, New York, 1997.

CHAPTER FOURTEEN:

SEXUALITY, ENERGY, AND SPIRITUALITY

Letter To Joshua

A letter (written in response to a therapist's request) to Joshua, 16, who reports he has had great sex with women and now is attracted (also) to men:

Dear Joshua,
Here's the deal. Or better, here's *a* deal. If we hang out long enough with our active sexuality, fantasy and experience, we start to get to know a bit about the territory, both inward and as we face the world, including for you, its (probably now central) place in your mind-body – your character and everything else. And we may want to know more, including where sex begins; maybe because we think we know where it ends.

For you, apparently, the "ending" parts – for surely orgasmic sex teaches us about important sequences of beginning, middle and end – have led you to increase the range of possibility with whom you can experience them: first with women, now with men. Against a social grid of predominant apparently heterosexual preoccupations, our society appears to be turning a corner to allow alternate forms of expression, including same-sex coupling and relationships. Throughout history, these alternatives have been implicit and explicit, as have the prohibitions, sometimes disastrously implemented, both for so-called heterosexuality and homosexuality.

Being able to experience the crossing over (and there are interesting questions about how you are experiencing this) as you apparently are, may mean that you will be able to take another step in understanding yourself, who you are and what you can experience. Aside from being careful with yourself and your partner(s), you may be able to take yourself into expanded ranges of responsibility and hopefully, depth and wisdom.

First, the emergent hormonal sequences toward men can be framed by traditional psychological literature, including that this new phase shows a deeper pattern in you which has been set off by your success with women; more confident and experienced, your system is taking a deeper cut. And one question might be, will you feature this new entrée on your menu? Will it become your predominant focus? I think these questions may not have to be answered right now; in some ways they are premature, and they are a bit off-focus. You may find it preferable to follow the hormonal trails without this kind of supervision.

New flexibility

One question which this new flexibility may raise, and one which may support your explorations, is about what we experience as sexual desires themselves. Where do they come from? Including procreation, what do they serve and how can we participate (or not) in their nature? We can begin by asking when do we start to be aware of our sexuality, and to be sure, that's interesting. The more we have orgasmic sexual experiences, including masturbating, the more refined we may become about our sexual history. We may see that our current adult intensities are set within synaptical sequences which were laid down right from the very start, including prenatal, infantile, early childhood, as well as so-called karmic, and cultural grids.

If we (you) are seeking support for the important new inclusions in your daily – I assume hormonally preoccupied – life, we may want to go further; we may use our experience to meditate from within our current inside about whether we can see to the heart of our drives to connect, with ourselves and with others. In trying to manage these rampant forces and energies within and without, can we see to the center of them, if in fact there is a center?

At your age, sex already is at the center of your consciousness; could it be *the* center, the way to experience wholeness and satisfaction, for all the parts of you, including your thoughts and your body? People with more experience may suggest that there are modifications to this universal plan and orgasm has its place in the pantheon of worshipful sites, but from your experience, it is most likely preoccupative. It dominates until it does not. And one way toward controlling sex's urgencies is to cum. It is the responsible thing to do; as well, learning how to express these forces in non-orgasmic ways, including non-toxic sublimation, is important.

Learning how to pleasure ourselves is a lifelong task, as is learning how to pleasure others and with others. And orgasmic experience is a rich place of consciousness and awareness, as you already know; it is always the same, and it is always different. Like a good rainstorm, it clears, or can clear the air. And some of the best times can be in the afterglow, when our mind-body may approximate states of Stillpoint (no movement, no need for movement, no restriction from movement) and Platonic Being, and associated relationality. Because the extended seizure leads to after-pleasure, our system is telling us we are doing more or less the right thing. Though we also know that achieving the orgasm may be at the expense of another person, something not the right thing.

If you can do it three ways (with yourself, with women, and with men), do the three ways have similarities: in your sexuality awareness, do they group into one unifying sense of direction? And does our sexuality have a single initiating site of generation?

Point of origin

Is there a point of origin from which to understand our sexual experience(s) as somehow unified, all of a piece? Let's say we see a set of hoses discharging water all over the lawn in different directions, but they are all hooked up to a single spigot. At some time in our understanding, and desire for the economy of focus, we want to head for the spigot, the source. Can we attempt this with our sexuality?

Getting to the place where we can be contemplative or even objective about the realm of so-called sexual experience takes inner time and experience, and meanwhile, we are battered and seduced by our own inner and outward experience which can happen very fast as well as very slowly, signposts appearing and disappearing like the smile of the Cheshire Cat. We are talking about consciousness and awareness, as well as synaptic firings, here. Sometimes it seems like we are threading a needle in a turbulent haystack in the middle of a storm.

If we can find the source point of our sexuality, the initiating position of our desire to discharge, and discharge in the direction of another person, with another person – for the pattern-originating hormones tell us to – we shall find that at the center, our sexuality has a lot to do about a general energy which sponsors a self-soothing crisis, a kind of special seizure, like a sneeze, which is benign and which basically causes us no harm, and, for a time, may make us feel better, calmer. And if we don't take responsibility for it, for discharging it when it builds up, we feel uneasy, even distressed, even sick.

To know clear, full-bodied orgasm is something which people experiment with in kundalini, tantric, and other meditation studies, trying to intensify and experience completely the inherent ego-dissolution involved with that activity of surrender. If, like young spelunkers, we attempt to look into the source of this hormone-driven power, we may locate its general, Zeus-like nature, polymorphous and powerful. Like water, this energy appears to be fluid and flowing anywhere: as everything, Zeus does everything with everyone, and if he does not like the form we are in, he transforms us, and himself, until the energy is met and discharged. He turns the reluctant nymph into a tree and as the wind, he engages with her.

But with-in us, Zeus, the playboy with everything, is married to Hera, who expresses our concomitant need for a more structured view of experience. We can be rutting around, going off into the bushes with everyone, including the bushes, which is what we can experience when we internally scan our self-awareness. Amid this sensate flood, we need some anchoring stability to raise and sustain children and ourselves, a constant hearth which is not impulsively outreaching everywhere, including within ourselves. Amid this fluidity, we need regularity of schedule and location, and constancy of those we love and who love us. These two forces within us can appear contradictory at times; the marriage of Zeus and Hera is usually uneasy.

Furthermore, like the building of the first transcontinental railway, our brain experiences itself as both the creator of its synaptic tracks and the train which rolls upon the established rails which it itself has brought forward for newly laying down. We need the rails, and we need the beginner's mind wherein we are facing the setting down of new track – actually, I think, allowing the new tracks to set themselves. I think William Blake refers to this phenomenon when he writes about the relationship between Innocence and Experience: apparently paradoxically oppositioned, we need both aspects of awareness to function.

So, like other learning experiences, our sexuality can have two modes, the familiar, and the innovative, and gradually as well as suddenly, we become aware of how to generate orgasms in various situations, both internal and external; we can sense when we are horny, and when we are satisfied. We enjoy the familiar and known paths, and we can sense if there is newness. Too much of either, and we become bored or afraid.

So all our comments about our sexuality refer in some way to this tracking grid, and they give us the sense, even the confidence that we know something about ourselves in this realm. However, the older I get, the more experienced and innocent I become, the less I think I know. Knowledge is one thing, experience with understanding is another.

But the history of our sexuality, including significantly our orgasmic experience, though cyclic and in some ways very familiar, may be hard to get accurate, sustainable information about. This condition complicates looking into the source of our sexuality, so we don't have to carry a restaurant guide to tipping each new bill: we merely have a common principal – (now) 20%.

Center of our being

When we look into the center of our Being, we can locate not only a huge quiet Stillpoint, but sequentially what follows from that fully-sufficient state of Being is a perhaps equally huge desire to experience in other ways, including to reach out and to express. As our brain matures, we relate to others "outside" of ourselves, and we experience desire, wanting to interact intensely with an "Other". This wanting may significantly involve connecting parts of our Self with other parts of our Self. Our "sexual intercourse" may be with the world, with individuals who walk beside us, but it also involves importantly Self integration.

Just like desire itself, the objects of our desire in the world of the Other are polymorphous and multilayered in intensity. We desire women, we desire men, we desire all sorts of things, and when some of these are odd or forbidden, we need to validate the Zeus truthfulness of these "object" choices, prior to Hera's structuring, which is not only external – what is legal – but also what is internal, what we can live with. I find the internal challenges substantial and crucial, and I will try to explain how this veritude is true.

For some of us, desire means that we can walk down the street and sense other people's energy(field) and respond to it. We have an awareness which comes from our monkey brain: we need to know at least who is friendly, who is a threat, what is possible as we move through the jungle.

For example, we can respond to men and women, including sexually. No big deal. If, drenched in our desire, we approach a woman, her and our energy systems connect, even apparently blend, yet we can discover there is a space between us which we both can serve. If we go up to her and ask, "Will you please come with me into the bushes?" or a variation of that, we may be happily met, or we may get our face slapped, or arrested for (unwanted) assault. A set of small, polite (and important) cautions suffice very well here.

The same with men

We can do the same with men, with similar results. And we may discover that there are steps between approaching and merging – and not merging – which can and have to be taken, for others with whom we play, and for ourselves. We may not feel comfortable with a slambam sequence – or we may be.

If we go even further toward the Zeus source of our Being, we may discover that our so-called sexual desire is located simultaneously, overlapping, and adjacent to a strong spiritual sense of ultimate reality. Why should we be surprised if we encounter this combinant, deepening aspect of our experience and awareness?

Or be surprised if during some spiritual practice, like praying or participating in some apparently chaste endeavor, it suddenly turns into something erotic, wanting expression and climactic discharge.

Those of us who have strong spirit/erotic desires can have sex with anyone (usually not with someone under age, for at least a number of Hera and developmental reasons – the key word here is having sex *with*), and we discover the longings for men or women, and their parts; in society's eyes, these end-sites make us definitionally heterosexual or homosexual. And if we chronically choose to be sexually intimate exclusively with men, that is socially determined to make us nominally homosexuals. That may convey something about our synaptic firings, the apparent tracks upon which our engine of awareness rolls. But as you already know, once the genie is out of the bottle, it may be hard to control. The more scattering information is too important to suppress or to ignore.

Usually we can locate ourselves along a spectrum between exclusive heterosexuality and exclusive homosexuality, though keeping accurate and honest track of our inner sexual experience may be more problematic than we initially think or know. Having indicated our place on a spectrum of homosexual and heterosexuality, it turns out we have not said very much. And, I think, we are not the best reporters about these apparently most intimate aspects of ourselves; because we are always on a potential learning curve involving Innocence and Experience.

Crucial to our (apparent) choices of Other may include attempts by our brain to link up with not only others, but with parts of ourselves, including very early, resolved and unresolved trauma sites which may have virtually nothing to do with the Other person, except that the Others trigger our own inner desire for inner completion. In Synge's *Playboy of the Western World*, the young female lead states, "The heart's a wonder," and the complex irony of this truth draws her increasingly to a world of emotional loss and maturing isolation. At some tragic point, our emerging priorities may lie with the inner patterns requiring resolution, not with the nominal welfare of our lovers.

Finding out

Here is what I have found out about the dangerous game of gender-naming or categorizing. Even though the longings which we recognize may occur toward one gender, there is a limiting, perhaps destructive simplification involved in setting ourselves into one category or another, because then we cannot see reality, our reality, the reality of us in the world, which is more liquid, and, paradoxically, more focused.

In a strange, even sad way, naming something already takes us away from the reality of what is named. Within any specific embrace which we have, how well can we know the lightning-quick variations which occur? You are butch, he is fem, he fancies s and m, you are into 69. At moments, he is frightened by his full (homo)sexuality, you are not in the same way. Or at the same time. What is he doing when he is sucking you off – what and who is being served? It quickly becomes a very varied field, hard to approximate in language, even awareness; even though you both "conclude" in orgasms. Maybe what the two of you then are doing together is concluding.

We come up to someone and ask, "Will you do such-and-such with me?" only the problem is that in that moment, they cannot be with us in that way, even though we (and they) have lined up all our ducks in a certain attractive order. Or, in the next moment, they can. Or, even more likely, we have misreported about ourselves and continue to do so. Here the problem of relationality becomes clearer and more important to be clear about. Imperfect reporters of ourSelf, imagine what is happening when we are in a room with an Other; with only one Other. With our Self and our own inner Other and some separate, neighboring Other.

And we will be satisfied in a self-contained, even solipsistic Heran way (by golly, *we* know what or who or how we are attracted), but the spiritual drive to experience ultimate reality in a personal way may remain, and there may be frustration because while we are dancing our pre-determined sexual steps together with our so-called partner, no real communication may occur; it is merely old-track (Experience) ritual.

Or maybe our portrait(s), when looked at close-up and slowly, changes. Some aspects of our plurality of Self immanent themselves in ways not initially anticipated; within its electrical aggrandizing, knock-about or streaming seizure storm, orgasm sometimes appears as confirmation that we are "one" person – *e pluribus unum*. There are parts to the sequence firings, but at the end of the orgasm, we don't usually say, "I am all these reporting districts (and here are the election results)". We say, "I have cum", or "I am finished."

And there may be some comfort in ritual. But the deeper, energetic longing to know and interact with what is real remains unsated. Though we think of sex as being as real as it gets, our cultural feedback indicates it is full of stratagem and masks. We may cross into the gay world from the straight, getting points for our courage, but we may carry our snail-like shells with us. As someone who is crossing over, or maybe better, adding, it will be interesting to see what your brain finds different and the same, between men and women, if you can evaluate your experience at that level.

As if this complex dance toward alignment were not enough, if we achieve some vibratory High connecting with someone, we may soon find ourself curling up and withdrawing, or showing stuff to our partner – and to another part of ourself – which comes out of left field (linking another part of our brain?) and seems bizarre; this is the Second Shoe of trauma, where, following the High, our brain offers up its worst old memories and irresolutions for healing in the holding embrace of our partner. I think this embracing phenomenon may be the ultimate "reason" people marry: in a sustained way, to be held and to heal and to hold our partners in their healing. Such holding also occurs in non-overtly orgasmic ways with varying sorts of friendship; and, often problematically, within families.

So having experienced great sex with women, and therefrom you may know something about your sexuality, you are now taking on men, including more directly your relationship to your own so-called manliness. Finding a partner to explicate this information, to unravel our complex sexuality, may not be easy, but the early steps may be.

We can suck and be sucked, kiss, caress, and penetrate in various ways. We need to sequence the openness we achieve toward our own tolerance and that of our partner, which requires vigilance and passion, connection, and noticing where there are no connections. There is something exhilarating about the feelings, the talk and sounds we can make, the moves, with another person in this intimacy. This brainscape includes liberty and freedom, founded upon honesty and self-examination. Over time and experience, old, ancient patterns come through us into the interface between us and our "lovers", and I find these sequences are very important.

What we offer up

While it may appear the same with men and with women, our makeup – including our evolving, growing maturing – may favor one set of experiences over another. But I give myself this caution: When we as men are being overtly homoerotic, we may be offering up some aspect of our "heterosexuality" to, or perhaps better, with our male partner. And he with us. The sharing will not just fall into masculine and feminine aspects, as in who is on top or who is the bottom, who is giving, who taking – the usual constructs.

In moments throughout our erotic sequence, we will reveal or express one thing, then another, moment to moment. The dance between us and our partner will be relaxed, intense, polymorphous, and site specific, even though it occurs between two men. The same goes for our connection as men with women, as you may have already discovered. It might be interesting to take a moment and characterize what you have already learned with women, if you dare come to some gender generalization (and I think there may be excellent reasons to resist such a gender generalization venture).

And if we seek to witness our source point with another person, we may see that our identity is organic and does not rest on *any* particular things or possessions or achievements or attitudes. There may be a delicate playfulness and freedom to be discovered here.

At our center we may find a Stillpoint, and from that voidy center, all relationality will somehow, paradoxically originate, and occur. Some positions, some objectives, some "Others" may seem more congruent than others, but the neurochemical, synaptic slush-slosh out of which our conscious identity is garnered is profound, and we are not a mere accumulation of our merit badges, trophies, or our diploma achievements. We are the lake and the hand holding the sword arising from that water, and the sword, and the water, and the witness of it all.

And cumming with another person may both reveal and conceal underlying assumptions about permission: authority, individualism, and coupling/merging, holding and letting go, not to forget freedom and surrender, which can give us assurance about our ability to ski these oft-times slippery slopes. The gestures we make or we permit to be made are the tip of an iceberg (I think that may be too cold an image – and nowadays we know icebergs melt), frequently the end result which we identify as our longings or our proclivities.

These recurring positionings of desires often contain traumatic residues, sequelae seeking resolution, developmental pauses which expose but also bind our synaptical sequences which are partial. And I find these partial positions ultimately do not satisfy and lead to feelings of isolation and despair. The good connection includes not only temporary hormonal release but may leave us with a sense of completeness which is individual and social; we have done the right thing for ourself and for, and with, another.

But as so-called heterosexuals, or homosexuals, or bi-sexuals – whatever – these identities have traveled far and wide from the depths of our neurochemistry and personality to resolve synaptically into the supposed clarity of our consciousness, which it is interesting to presume is always coming late to the party we call our Self. In our sexual moves, we revert to instinct and predilection in the trust that such gestures will work. To bring urgencies to satisfying completion.

But usually

But usually we do not see how these elements are attempts of our brain system to resolve something, some early conflict, some not-understood pattern wherein the erotic energy seems to unlock something, and we are carried away by the reflex activities of orgasm. Watch your orgasm sometime and see the energetic explosion as the brain recalculates its process, crashing and sequencing over mountains and voids and finally settling down. It's like the electromagnetic demonstration zapping off at the science museum.

If we realize that the end of achieving orgasm may be very important, and our bodies tell us that it is, the lead up to it is complex, and to say that the end of the game is what baseball is about may be how it feels in retrospect, but it is not the truth. Listen to people who know their experience in this way and then ask yourself – are they heterosexual or homosexual? Increasingly, the question will seem preposterous and presumptuous. Other details will emerge, will seem significant, and the narrative of gender will seem only a beginning to a long accountancy of what happens when you are in someone's arms. You may find yourself developing a new vocabulary to describe what you witness and experience.

Furthermore, even though we are created by orgasmic conception (or its test-tube equivalent), how our parents get there is a question. And we know from divorce courts and therapies that we can create children and not be sexually happy, adjusted, congruent, honest, or connected. And in some sense, thank God for that. And we know that orgasm can be seen as the organizing conclusion of all that proceeds it, but what we come to value, no pun intended, is intensity and clarity, and centering, which may take us way past our current levels of dialogue about our sexuality – into a new world of straightness, real and beyond homosexuality and heterosexuality.

Through the orgasmic chutes, our repetitions declare problems and issues wherein feeling centered can bring us a sense of being sufficient and whole. We measure our experience upon this rating – the mistakes we make, the corrections, the sense that in the storms of our sexualities, we can safely let go with deeper freedom and trust. Maybe here we can seek accommodation to old psychological systems and to establishing their true proportionality and their celebrations and their demises.

The ultimate goal

For me, the ultimate goal seems to be, somehow by immersion and increasingly profound letting go, to achieve witness of what we are, what we embody, the sacredness of our systems, and we as individuals can and should encourage each other to do that either with them or as a more distant witness.

So-called heterosexuality is hardly a uniform category, and if the life force is involved, it is most clearly roiling and without encumbrances. Particularly when we are young adults, it comes at us, through us, like a locomotive or tornado, carrying everything away with it. Like passing harbor buoys as we begin to sail out onto the sea, our socialized discussions about our sexuality rarely acknowledge the depth and size of the ocean. Some religious and spiritual practices will enhance this understanding, though often society expresses more of Hera to its congregations than of rampant, rambling, rutting Zeus; but he is always here, somewhere.

Likewise, so-called homosexuality can be a can of worms, full of contradictions, etc., more confusing perhaps, because historically it has been forbidden to look at for so long. There are entire galaxies of prohibition and denial within its maze. In "Angels in America," AIDS-ridden Roy Cohn tells his doctor he is not a homosexual, even though minutes before and minutes after their meeting, he is going down on one of his legal assistants. In a complex way, both aspects are true.

Even though Roy goes down on someone, who knows what that act entails? He might see it as an issue of power and self-assertion, even an empowering revolt against aeons of repression. Ultimately Roy is being, not doing, and then all categories are called off; and the reverse might be said about doing and being. Ironically, he may be at his most "heterosexual" in these moments; straightness then means connectedness, centeredness, not the gender of the partner we have chosen – or has been chosen – to discharge the energy with. I prefer this definition of straightness. If someone asks me the usually aggressive and limiting question, "Are you gay (or straight)?" if I can, I answer, "With you, no," or "With you, maybe yes." And that's just for starters. I want to know what they want to know and why they want to know it.

If we have had experiences with men and women, we may not be able to comfortably locate the center of our sexuality with either gender as the traditional determinator. This is both initially lonely, and reassuring; we are participant and witness of our process. In the olden days, the Greeks would say, "Zeus entered me and expressed himself through me." Or Venus. I am a channel for the hormones, and as I enter that neurochemistry, I become the drive itself. And lose my so-called ordinary identity. I am both more and less than I think I am or can state something about with any meaningful accuracy. I am the tracks and the train; and the air between the wheels and the rails.

The paradoxes contained in consciousness are enormous, and confusing, and confounding, and traumatizing, because culturally we have viewed, and not viewed this homosexual territory. If someone were to suggest that you head into the homosexual cultural territory, for starters filled historically with dead bodies and thwarted, crushed spirits, and massive annihilations, they might say, "You're putting your head in the lion's mouth; you'll never get out of that jungle; you cannot find clarity there." But that is not true, any more than saying as you head into the world of so-called heterosexuality, "Don't go there unless you have to."

Take a breath

Better to take a deep breath and look at your own process and how it responds and initiates with others (if you can). Notice how hard it may be to find your center no matter what company you keep; agents of focus and scatter, your hormones will have their way. You might choose partners who are similarly brave, whose personal values of integrity and honesty and emotional intelligence are what attract you. When apparently drowning in a sea of drives and feeling states, why rush to the raft of ordinary conversation about sex? I find the definitions we share about our so-called personal experiences are often preposterously, profoundly shallow.

Can we locate our observant Self and seek an observant Other? Can we find out about the deeper companionship: observe our consortability? Notice how you negotiate boundaries – the ones which need to be maintained, the ones which need to be dissolved. I know people who self-describe their process and never get below or above a certain level; like talk-show guests, they confess and conceal at the same time.

Same goes for heterosexuality, though the engendering of children makes people think we have all been doing the same thing when sperm connects with egg. Well, yes and no. At this deeper level people are more alike than not, but few of us confess the journeys of our pre-coital varietals, even to ourselves, much less to our lovers. This killing field is too loaded with shame, and guilt: somehow we have not gotten God's plan right, no matter how hard we have tried. The world of sexuality is filled with thorns from the present and the past. There are same-sex couples who are clearer than many so-called heterosexuals; once entered, clarity is the game, not with which hand we hold our racket.

Intimacy with other people includes trust of Self as well as trust of the Other. Increasingly we hear that there are clear trails in the jungles of closeness, and you may be able to hear, or witness couples whose understanding of themselves and each other seems transcendent. Hang out in proximity with these rare individuals. Ask them what they value in themselves and in their interactions with others. What grids of Innocence and Experience are they forging, are they noting? How much creativity do they embody, even, perhaps especially, when their brainscape is out of their conscious control?

Our brains revise

As before, over time, our brain synaptically tracks in new experiences, seeks them. But also enjoys ritual and repetition; the old Innocence and Experience bit: can we have one without the other? Gradually, our brains revise and clarify gestures and movements on the way to and often including orgasm, and what shows up are both restorative experiences where we can envision bringing healing to ourselves, and the patterns, some not so easy, which need revision: the held sites usually cluster surrounding abandonment – of and by ourself and of and by our Others.

What I find tragically ironic, is that the patterns which we do not like and want out – but they refuse to leave our house – are best approached as foreign to ourselves. If they do not leave – and thus represent some stuckness – it is *because* they are patterns which do not belong to us. In some variation of empathy or forced-upon necessity, we have picked them up from our parents, or our parents' parents, or the culture. Compassionate as we thus have been – we think the patterns are ours – we are stuck with a sequence our brain cannot decode enough to get the pattern out of our house and to the curb for the collectors or recyclers to take away.

This whammy is particularly toxic in regard to our sexuality, so basic to us (so we think) and to our identity. So we may be cruising in an addictive way into our heterosexuality, or our homosexuality, and find over time, such apparently free cruising has nothing to do with us. Under such elaborations upon anxiety and adrenaline, we who are going down on men as men, may not even encompass or experience our own homosexuality, if we even come to seeing it that way. The same realization occurs with men and women. And the current spate of radically accessible pornography will take us into this no-person's land, to feigned intimacy as well as to occasional portraits of truthful interaction or portions of interaction, ritualized as they mostly are.

In many cultural forms, we are being trained in rarified discrimination, and there are lots of people who don't like having their game called. They read for doing, not for Being, which initially can be experienced as something else altogether. I wonder if this realization might be a part of what activates the so-called terrorists who are so sexually and physically abusive; the histories of their educations are filled with violence, rage, and fright.

What is interesting to me is that for the present you may have a clear sense of your attraction to women and now to men. Because our social context is changing, and this new information of possibility is occurring throughout the webbed world, you may have an early shot at clarity about some aspects of your sexuality because it includes clearly many sites upon some (overt) spectrum. You may be able to embody a sexual sense of yourself as having choice and straightness most people may intuit but rarely achieve, or sustain.

Having achieved such a High, you may experience white-water "Second Shoes" of trauma sites within yourself or your partners which need to be dissolved so that the deeper reality, your deeper, straight (in my sense of the word) reality, may be observed and preserved, or more dynamically, sustained. And you may trigger responses in yourself or Others which will reflect something about the past, not even yours, but not about the present. As you rework the old historical dragons of homosexualities and heterosexualities, the permissions and impermissions, you may become more disciplined as you sustain your own clearing in the woods. That you achieve some clearing in your woods seems very important to the issues I have been discussing. Freedom includes voting and not being socially enslaved; it also includes this inner freedom.

I sense you may be setting out upon a developmental sequence which I never had, or at least at your chronological age; though the passions were (probably pretty much) the same, the context was restrictively toxic. We were expected to find our own, very private way through these mazes, supported by public good intentions as well as prevarications (polite word for denials and lies). The potential for nailing one's sexuality (or some aspect of it) clearly, without ambivalence, is of course, an adult project, but it occurs within the context of an inner environment which is barraged by countervalent winds.

Crucial here is our ability to see our own system and how it operates, how we shelve our experiences, how we juxtapose and burnish and exclude and recapitulate stuff. Usually, we are more fragmented, less aware, in some sites crazier, if you will, than we think, even with our often rebellious servant, our rationality. And the ideas or belief systems, the values we "hold" are not just like those who speak similar word sequences. Theirs is a different world, separate and maybe similar, though as we know from marriage and friendship and family, often barely.

And the so-called ordinary sexuality itself becomes only a narrative upon which the deeper maturities within us are expressed and not. Our hope is for growth and movement in our capacity to steer our ship, counting on each new synaptic folding-in sequence to lead us to what has been called enlightenment or, theologically, salvation.

Even now, with the supports you may find in the big world, the inner journey remains individual, the tasks of clarity paradoxically similar. Singing the homosexual note with straightness, without anxiety, may reveal a great deal to you which will enlarge your sense of who you are and who you are not; it may escort you to Being, a crucial state of awareness. That is certainly my hope.

What our so-called sexualities may reveal to us is that we are more independent from the world than we think we are: like initially having the private responsibility of masturbation separate us from the more public world of our parents and society.

And as a result, we may have a different view of authority, enabling us to ask authorities, "What is authority protecting, and what is it discouraging? How strong and weak is its voice? How in touch with the deepest longings and sources of our self, and selflessness is authority; and where does it get its authority to be authority?"

And by challenging the authority of selfhood itself, which challenge is in part founded within our attractions leading to and past orgasmic experience, we may come into a deeper, more satisfying, realistic view of what we are.

Sitting shiva

On a visit to Dallas, I encountered that a 40-something man, deeply involved as an elder in his Orthodox Jewish community, preparing for a divorce, set in motion after his wife discovered some gay pornography on his computer. It is reported she feels betrayed, because he did not tell her this was part of his story when they met and were married. Her rage may be predictable, but given the weight of the taboo against homoerotic experience, the man perhaps has jimmy-rigged an internal compromise which is understandable and human. Now he is pre-suicidal.

As a young man, this husband may not have carried the homosexual level of his neurochemistry in the same way then as he does now. And as boys we were trained not to take this part of ourselves as significant – except to relentlessly stop it – hence our sometimes hope as men that it will go away.

For some, inwardly being allowed some developmentally crucial experience may be a one-time thing; evolving, the brain aligns around the perfect experience and shelves it appropriately. Our mothers may be imperfect, but we can assemble the memories of their full sufficiencies, enough to measure and carry on our life. We know how the perfect moment looks and feels, and we return to that memory site millions of times, especially during the subsequent bad ones.

For most of us, there is some void lodging in our erotic sequencing so we repeat the sensual experience, including its traumatic subtext, but never Experience and thus conclude the prohibitions, permissions, whatever, contained in our synaptical firings. Our orgasms pronounce, "We are the sufficient justifiers of the continued Self and other abuses." This postponement happens in so-called heterosexual and homosexual encounters, again and again. Just ask our mindful adults.

Given our current understandings of human sexuality, it would be naive of the wife to expect a man not to have had some homoerotic process. Nowadays we would be suspicious of the man who did not acknowledge any homoerotic process at all; we would wonder when the Second Shoe would drop. Why is she so surprised?

Or there may be other factors, including issues (like connectivity) between her and him which have nothing to do with "homosexuality". The uniformed cloak of "homosexuality" is just the last, visible straw. But as the community is "joined" to the marriage, the narrative assumes he is homosexual and enforces limits; or a societal lesson must be "taught". There is no depth of understanding of the viscissitudinal energetics of the marriage, what she did or felt, what he did or felt: perhaps at this level of social response, gay is gay. And gay is not good. It is against God.

Now, his family will sit shiva, *i.e.,* they will treat him as dead, and he faces complete excommunication from the community which he has served, and which has served him, including heartfelt support during the death of his son. And who knows what the grieving for his son has to do with what he looks for on the Internet.

My wonder

My wonder is about this, and it is definitely not limited to Orthodox Jews, who only sing some of the earliest cultural notes of this song: when his

Orthodox community returns to their beds, and they have so-called heterosexual intercourse, what will that look like? Can I have it wrong to ask with whom and against what surrounding parameters will these orgasms occur? Must not the shadow of this homo-tabooing attitude toward lovemaking cast itself over and under the so-called straight intercourse, and subtly, if not profoundly, frame and influence it? There would be some insiders in this system who would say it will not because we are dealing with God's Will.

In this sense, those who argue for marriage only between heterosexuals acknowledge the reverberative impact of introducing such an astronomical shift in social and personal values, orientation, and, fundamentally, information, about Source. The Fundamentalists ask, "What will this homosexuality do to our heterosexuality?" Perhaps the better question is, "What has your (apparent homophobia) already done to your concept of your sexuality and by extension, your marriage, and by extension, your God?" What synapses are being supported, which ignored?

For me, who carries this system in my heritage, though somewhat hidden by filo layers of reforming insight, I think the resultant (Orthodox, orthodox, Catholic, Muslim, often parallel Christian) straightness must not be straight. Must it not be an enforced, bound, authoritarian, and circumscribed experience? Even though God includes forgiving, and the transmission of the male seed to its destination is central, the orthodox mind-set apparently may not account for or acknowledge the ricocheting, cyclotronic scanning our neurochemical system undergoes to get itself to its sequence of release.

Those who watch these processes clearly in slow-motion acknowledge that our journey to the orgasm release may resemble that of a wandering, wily Odysseus. And in the Odyssey, the gestalt instance of the coming together of Odysseus and Penelope has a tenfold, twenty-year (thirty-year?) circuit before it concludes. Paradoxically, God does not care how the seed is delivered, as long as it hits the target; hitting the target produces babies, if that's the only thing that counts. But that, at the very least, leaves us with the remaining hours of the days, with time, and incomprehension, on our hands and in our loins.

It may be wise to see that the core of our sexuality is energetic, and, to put it somewhat simplistically, spiritual. We don't understand some fuller meaning of this energetic until we understand that the objects or genders toward which our sexuality is directed are not essential, that what is eternal about the serious action of sexuality is its God-seeking, Ultimate-Reality-witnessing movement, outwards and inwards.

I ask the fellow how does he now view his Orthodoxy, and he is too confounded to respond. I proffer that he might see his exclusion as a shallowness in the tradition which would need understanding and compassion, but such shunning could not be tolerated now without his comprehension of its perhaps limited, superficial apperception of the Godhead. The fact that the Orthodox conviction has been held for (thousands of) years and is present throughout many faiths and societies does not make it true; more likely, it always contains within its tightened, tightening bindings – a revolution.

Like Job, he may be stripped of all his attachments, his wife, whom he loves, his daughters, whom he has well-raised, and his cantoring, wherein he sings God's praises.

And his wife and children will be caught rendering a soul-renting pattern of exclusion from what they have known, and need to know, a devout (and loving) husband and father, and, potentially, a whole man. Or, imperfectly, perhaps not; perhaps not at all. The issue is not at all as it seems, or even as I am seeing it. But the social narrative now wheeling into place is the one socially, sadly, explicated at the expense of reality. This is not an Orthodox problem alone; it is, I think, universal.

What I have come to envision is that the Orthodox injunction against homosexuality develops in the context of surrounding authoritarian societies (of gathered consciousness) who will stone to death the person who engages in homosexual activity. This deeper, undifferentiated response may be where we can see what the core issue is for human consciousness. The Orthodox solution is not the bottom line, even though in the Judeo-Christian nexus, we all listen to what it says, no matter how far from acting out that primal sequence we are. Even the extremes we have rejected effect the positions we currently hold and how we hold them.

And in some parts of the world, homosexual experience is met with violence and death. In a clear moment, we might lean over to our homophobic, murdering neighbors, and ask them, "What do you think the problem here is? What are you seeing?" In subtle ways, our current permissions arise out of swamps of fear and repression, and you may at times sense that you are carrying such traces of the past.

Here, the elders of the Jewish communities basically may not think the experience warrants death; and their lineage warns about killing people. But to survive in their social and political context – not to mention the context of primitive brain – they must ritually demise the violator, in a clever way which, like Abraham with Isaac, substitutes a symbolic death for the real thing.

Being exiled might lead to death at a number of levels, but there might be ways to escape, and who knows, in olden Biblical days, if lucky, if you did not die from excommunication, you might have found yourself ultimately in San Francisco or the Village, or some big, absorbing community like a city. Now, the possibility of finding a dwelling place for yourself and your inner experience may be in the hometown of your choice, with the inner freedom to choose and bring yourself to your whatever partner in wholeness. And do it straight and clear.

Another point which I think needs to be considered. Viewing a part of a religious and social system out of context is not what it is like to be inside the system. From the outside, we can raise rational questions about portions of a religion's mosaic and see potentials for toxicity, even destructiveness. But these systems develop over centuries, often examined and often unexamined, so raising questions from some outside as I may appear to have done may invite the response, "But you don't understand."

One response to this one is that systems are not just encapsulations, not influencing others. And we do not always take on the system patterns with the same energy that they are offered from within. The Orthodox position about homosexuality may not be the same as it appears to be the same in its fundamentalist Christian offsprings or with Muslims or with Buddhists And these carriers appear to be talking about the same phenomena, but the implementations of the insights may be carried in very different ways, in very different contexts.

And there is something about religious boundaries which very few get right. There seems to be a drive to universalize the insights, so that what I carry, you better had too. How many clerics would be able to say, "Our attitudes toward homosexuality come from our experience; yours may be different. And because we are neighbors, you can manifest your understanding, and I will manifest mine." The problem comes when your neighbor is abusing or killing a member of his family in the name of God. What, for God's sake, does that do to our current global, universal awareness?

Importance of historical perspective

A word of caution. The Jews, in the Bible and in their lineage, carry some of the oldest patterns in the West, good and toxic. And subsequent, *revisioniste* Christians have taken up these "values" in their own way, with similar, often un-Christian, uncharitable destructiveness, including about the significant so-called issue of homosexuality. This is why it is important to attempt some historical perspective about the patterns – no matter what your direct lineage – which you have grown up in and among; with your current vista of freedom, more power to you.

As you take the dive into your own inner experience, you may be surprised to find remnants of these past forms, patterns, rigidities, bigotries. You will find that you carry the very voices which in your freedom, you deny. The paradoxical nature of these holdings may have you shaking your head at yourself.

If you want to get more substantially free, which I recommend attempting, you will have to assemble these contradictions, these old battles, now set upon the table before you. You may apprehend the craziness of it all, or the rationales behind strange behaviors and attitudes toward behaviors.

You may see that your good time connects to the past of so-called civilization which comes to interfere with the clarity you now have, and that integrating the joy you face with men with the mix you have subtly absorbed may take some time – to revise the stitching. Perhaps much of the literature up to now has not dealt with the inner conflicts arising from the joy and how our inner sense of personal authority is thus severely challenged; so much of the overt conflict has been narratively stated as between the individual and a rejecting society.

What I have found, both heterosexually and homosexually – if it can be put that way – is that the variations you hold in the corners of your inner space are within your view, and that you are the custodian and shelver of these variations, many of which, early and late, you have "merely" taken on. While you may draw support from what others are sharing about their experience, from the outside, as it were, your inner vaults are where you will learn the most and where the greatest understanding and freedom eventually may be won, may be needed to be won.

You may get to see the direct line between outside and inside, how prohibitions, repressive tourniquets, calumnies, and terrors – even ecstasies – can come to reside within you, the unsuspecting child. And that in order to effect inner transformation, you may be very much on your so-called own, and not in any "ego" sense; the Self may have to go, in order for you to witness and watch your primitive brain synaptically revise.

Coming out has Second Shoes, held-energy systems which invite dissolution into radiance. And their resolutions, idiosyncratic to be sure, will be within each individual, including such as yourself. The "sexuality" you manifest may become felicitously invisible in the object sort of way; I think if you are lucky and wise, it may be a form of consciousness, a focal meditation, if you will.

No matter the superficial object, it can be straight because straight means connected, relational. You may have Zeus and Hera working for you, not in distracting (parental, tribal) conflict. You may be Innocent and Experienced, self-reliant in the Emersonian sense that you may have your own "homosexuality" (and "heterosexuality" – whatever), not those historical, trauma-based variants which the rest of us eagerly, terrifiedly, shove down your throat – or somewhere else.

Perhaps you will have to get a straight line on your "homosexuality" in order to live a full life, without ambivalence. Also with your heterosexuality, also with your sexuality. All need to be clear, source to delivery. You need to take out the judgment, the negativity, the repression. Sing a clear note. Then see what you have, simply and gratefully. Identify fears, accommodate to others. We all need compassion as well as companionate experience. You and your partners are merely here for a short time.

More

To agree to being gay means partially circumscribing, inwardly, what I sense and feel. No longer the acknowledged lure of feminine beauty, even lusted for. Thus named, the tyranny of heterosexuality is met in dutiful mirroring response by the tyranny of gay identity, not just socially held by the world outside me, but by myself, who has been taught that these trajectories must be quartered in a certain, sheltered way. In her demand for hearth-ful regularity, Hera may be cruel and stupid; the winds of Zeus pass over her skin and even away.

So the confession, "I am gay," has an absolute finality to it, destructive to the reality of the gods, and to God, who dumps His stuff in my lap and appears to abandon me. Rather, in this moment, perhaps speak, "I am moved, absolutely, in your (male) direction, and here is a single-minded, even desperation which urgently takes me past my ordinary self even, to take risks."

Also, for some, saying, "I am gay" is a site which one must achieve, in all its prideful and scruffy demeanor, in order to face down the demons, outer and inner. The riots at Stonewall show us that against these tyrannies, as starters, we must push back. But as has been discovered, that is only the beginning of a deeper process.

Circumscribed by ancient police harassments, vague lingering liberal disapprobria, and an inner sense that no one is supporting me to follow my passion, what remains is a boundary established by convenience and exploitation. Its implementers set the flaming sword in place and permanently go off somewhere for a beer. This sword of prohibition can radically predispose our entrance and exit from the sacred Garden, the inward chemistry where there is no shame, or let us hope so. At the site of Being, there are no categories. From this site, benign, essential Good has a chance of being witnessed.

Total exclusion

In Genesis we are instructed that our exclusion from the Garden is total, that there is a flaming sword, a spine rigid with sacred energy which prohibits access and easy, willful or inclined intention. "You cannot go in and out as you please," says Hera, "we have a home to keep, a dangerous voyage whose destiny depends upon the stability of the spars, the masts, and the – guy- wires."

And her directive comes to be identical with what it means to be true and, implied, centered. But the energy flows every which way, and I refuse to see that flow as unstable, difficult as that may be to negotiate through the day. The carpet floor spread out on the oasis sand is for the having, for our tender care.

When formally completing our passport application, in the box where it asks, Sexual Identity, we may come closer to our inner experience by writing in the space "Bisexual", but that is something quite different from both hetero- and homosexual identity. We all know about the sexual spectrum, the multifaceted, wandering grid upon which we walk, and fall, and soar. How much does crossing the dance floor to pick one partner or another determine a trajectory which, lines through the dots, proclaims a tendency, a viable statistic? I am this, I am that.

Rather say, "I am centered now. What a discovery that I can find myself in wholeness in your arms, and turning, then find another. What gift have the gods given me?" Is marriage possible in a traditional grid along a tradition scaled by infantile longings? Yet we remain faithful, amid this sometimes hurricane of desire. We are faithful within certain parameters, exclusive in moments and days of passion. We are faithful within loyal bonding to one individual, though like Scheherezhade, who tells 1000 different stories, yet she is all the characters in all the stories. Our intercourse with Scheherezhade at last wins over our prince, because of the longing for wholeness, for a unified sense of self which can coincide with convenience but is driven by seeing to the core of the onion, which spirally unfolds revealing at its center – apparent nothing, or better, nothing.

Sometimes we cannot see that core except by repetition, by finding the Gardens of Edens in a single and singular relationship. Like Penelope, we are waiting for our Odysseus to slay his plural-suitors-self, for him finally to enter the paradoxical world, the Garden(s) of unknowing and of honesty. Who else would we want to interact with, to intercourse with? In order to achieve singularity, we assume it must be with one Other.

Yet how hard to sustain. Some of us are not good lovers. We cannot sustain this unity, we are distracted inwardly by our dissociation, our lack of attentive unity, our brains rushing within the flood of high sensation, the promise of resolution of all our old, unhealed wounds.

The attempt to heal through labeling may be a start, but within minutes after, moments after, or during the orgasm elaboration, we lose our way and are bored. "So what?" our inner voice, taking its cue from God's silence on the matter, asks. Genetic heritage is all the tradition we can offer, a shallow response from within a shallow agency, or better yet, agent. There has to be a deeper rendering of our human response to the information of a desirable world.

Edens

So, there are Gardens of Edens, not one. Not until there is one. And we must perceive this plurality until it can be rendered in unity, acknowledging with honesty and truthfulness, the variations of desire. And their completion. Our intercourses, sexual and otherwise, take up what cannot be estimated into a single-Garden mind-set, within which all things can be seen and known; and it is perhaps dishonest to suggest that we don't begin with plurality which cannot be encompassed by a single word. That is what our soul is about.

Speaking about reporting our straightness, if held somehow without plurality, we are preoccupied in mere ritual, revealing to every portion in the bed with us how foolish such incomplete rationalizations can be. Likewise, if we are plural without singularity, similar, gigantic fissures appear on our earth's surface.

We can see how what we call "I am" is a record of the movement between plurality and singularity and back again. Our statement reverberates like a singing bowl, an achievement and a betrayal. The language centers of our brain at best reflect the movement between rational thought and its words, and energetic reality, an uneasy and compromised, traversing tack. Here we are as tightrope walkers high above the theological void.

Floating

This floating is what we have to teach when we teach reading, or better, when we teach words. Like head-dipping sacred scholars murmuring over texts, we can establish conventions which appear to bring consistency to this process, but "I am" is the hardest, most problematic affirmation we can speak, and all language and culture can be viewed as grounded upon this statement.

This floating is what we have to teach when we teach history. The illusion of the present is a platform from which all ventures into the past (and implied, future) are embarked. Our "I am" is as singular as Hera, as plural as Zeus, and their marriage in us is what brings us into a chemistry without the identifying markers of thought and ideation. Only conscientious awareness wherein having done its job, language disappears.

This floating is what we have to teach when we teach history, that we are always moving toward this enlightenment position from which to make right action, centered amid the point between inward and outward. And we make these actions when we are clear and not obstructed by traumatic process. We get to witness the apparent.

We may come to see there is only one flaming sword, but it resides in a million trillion moments, and yet it can transform into serenity and innocence in a thrice.

Looking at his portrait, I find my great-grandfather strong and beautiful. Would I want to hold him? A reverend minister, would he me? I want to witness his desire, his transmutation filled with pious attention, into satisfaction of individuality and identity.

Can we lie about this basic platform upon which we lie?

The unifying insight upon the gestalt of sexual identity, as well as of identity says that we are looking at the wrong this when we focus upon a single garden. We are returning to our first experience of unity, upon conception and the first, combinent moment of singularity after. Each subsequent division maintains that unity, but our experience is plural, multicellular, intelligent, as well.

Within the gestalt application of community, democracy includes voting as its ceremonial gathering, rough and indistinct as we now experience it. As inheritors of the Protestant revolution, we elect often because of our disbelief in authority, and our awareness of its singular tyrannies. Our understanding of unity and how we get there hopefully avoids authoritarianism. If we don't like democracy, within and without, where can we go? Possibly to the authority of radiance, not to the radiance of authority. How far does acknowledging "I am gay" – and more – free us from our historical, fear-based bondage, when we have not yet gotten over slavery?

With best wishes to you, Joshua, on your journey, Bill.

Addendum:

Though this letter is written years ago, as it were to an unknown soldier, I might have the same things to say, all trying to be helpful and honest. But what I would now prefer to do would be to ask for moments of dialogue with Joshua, wherein I could ask him about his experience, particularly his inner realms, and how he is shelving these experiences, their varietals. I want to see how he manages these transitions which have been superficially but significantly described. And by my questions and listening, I think I would give him the deepest support and respect and recognition as he enters a territory complex and potentially destructive and potentially ecstatic. If this letter means to give support, the dialogues would, I think, be more specific and deeper – more real.

CHAPTER FIFTEEN:

MARRIAGE AS GESTALT

Dover Beach

The sea is calm to-night.
The tide is full, the moon lies fair
Upon the straits; on the French coast the light
Gleams and is gone; the cliffs of England stand;
Glimmering and vast, out in the tranquil bay.
Come to the window, sweet is the night-air!
Only, from the long line of spray
Where the sea meets the moon-blanched land,
Listen! you hear the grating roar
Of pebbles which the waves draw back, and fling,
At their return, up the high strand,
Begin, and cease, and then again begin,
With tremulous cadence slow, and bring
The eternal note of sadness in.

Sophocles long ago
Heard it on the Aegean, and it brought
Into his mind the turbid ebb and flow
Of human misery; we
Find also in the sound a thought,
Hearing it by this distant northern sea.

The Sea of Faith
Was once, too, at the full, and round earth's shore
Lay like the folds of a bright girdle furled.
But now I only hear
Its melancholy, long, withdrawing roar,
Retreating, to the breath
Of the night-wind, down the vast edges drear
And naked shingles of the world.

Ah, love, let us be true
To one another! for the world, which seems
To lie before us like a land of dreams,
So various, so beautiful, so new,
Hath really neither joy, nor love, nor light,
Nor certitude, nor peace, nor help for pain;
And we are here as on a darkling plain
Swept with confused alarms of struggle and flight,
Where ignorant armies clash by night.

Matthew Arnold (1847-1851; 1867)

A love poem

After many years spent with Matthew Arnold's "Dover Beach", like others, I have come to see it primarily as a love poem, certainly a poem outlining the foundations of marriage, and more generally, relationship. Only relatively recently did I discover the poem was completed (1847-1851; 1867) while Arnold and his new bride were on their (delayed) honeymoon at Dover Beach; and then I thought, "Of course."

Matthew composes a somewhat loosely connected meditation for, in some way, his bride Frances, and it takes place in a cottage overlooking the pebbled strand of beach, under the white chalk cliffs of Dover. The poem falls into five stanzas, with the last articulating a three-part sequence which reveals significantly what is on Matthew's mind.

The first stanza describes the environmental setting, including the recurring beam from a (maybe French) lighthouse maybe twenty-odd miles across a calm, clear night English Channel. Its second part is more directly addressed to his wife, whom he invites to share the view, which he proceeds eloquently to describe. He invites her to listen to the rhythm of the grating roar of the beach pebbles as they are flung back and forth by the waves, adding specially, that such cadence brings "The eternal note of sadness in." Not asked what she hears or thinks about her husband's perception, already Frances is being set aside as Matthew's meditational momentum is absorbed in his own process of thought experience, including his capacity to project upon the sea and landscape feelings, including "eternal sadness", a poetic phrase which might be evocative for, say, a mid-19th Century congregation.

The second stanza elevates the next thought moment (I find the transition awkward, or expositionally, didactically formal) into a wider historical long-shot association to include Sophocles, Greek tragedian and chronicler of "human misery", with whom, in a preacherly sort of way, Matthew feels a misery-sensing kinship, though they are miles and centuries apart. Unlike one Shavian character who proposes that there is a constant level of tears for all the world, Arnold sees misery as an ebb and flow sort of thing, in and out.

Sea of Faith

Patently, he adds another idea to his list, namely that in the past, the Sea of Faith surrounded the world, but like the sea before him, that is now retreating down the sloping beach pebbles of cultural and personal consciousness. A few observations might be called for here.

1. There is literally no (watery) named Sea of Faith (yet), including on the moon or on Arcturus.

2. The Sea of Faith can refer historically to a time (we could place it at any time) when everyone subscribed to the same orders of apparently doubtless faith and belief, such as before the Renaissance, or before the Reformation, or before the Industrial Revolution. Or before the recent challenges expressed in the debates between Wilberforce and Huxley, precursors to Darwin's so-called faith-busting presence.

   There is a possible Eurocentrism within this idea as Arnold carries it, namely that ultimately as England and its cultural Faith process goes, so goes the world; if faith is compromised in Europe, that effects and declares the world's Faith condition. There is no significant mention of retreating Faith amid eastern religions in Ceylon. As an emerging cultural critic, Arnold senses and elaborates upon this vision in his other works; as he records the mind of his (global) culture, so his culture is reflected in his own process and thought, as it is for all of us. We can be witnessed as expressions of our cultures.

3. The Sea of Faith is personal, even adolescent in context. There is a pubertal edge which adolescents can hit (some of us hit it earlier, some later), when the systemic encapsulation of religious belief systems becomes constraining to our deeper, deepest spiritual longings. Some "individuating" people turn to atheism, or agnosticism, or universalism, or to alternative forms of focus; some retreat from the endeavor altogether to master reality by social, even personal means, with no direct concern for issues of Faith.

The social organs of explications of this focus traditionally have been religions, the personal foci have been through personality and identity. The problem of a retreating Sea of Faith might come down to confronting, experiencing within and without, the God, or pivot point of Ultimate Reality, which can, or more likely cannot, be known.

4. The Sea of Faith is developmental, appropriate to the learning of a young (marrying) Victorian man, who is encountering a shift of sensibility and sensuality which might be formidable and formative. The Sea of Faith can refer to early childhood moments when in Eriksonian terms, the issue of Trust vs. Mistrust comes to bear. As infants, we feel enwrapped by our maternal and paternal surround; as adolescents, we extend our individuating process beyond those of ordinary family and Church. Our level of basic trust is challenged, particularly by the incursions on our own process by that of a significant and signifying Other, as well as by shared intimacies, including that of orgasm, itself a building block of connection but significantly also of individuation.

What Arnold reveals here, both directly and indirectly, is that there is an underlying Cultural – read personal – depressive, some call it melancholic undertow, like the retreating, dreary winds and tide, which follows hard upon the elegance of a swaddling, supporting girdle. Pillow talk here might confess to a post-coital *tristesse*. The now rapidly growing-up adolescent or young adult begins or consolidates both within and without a transition of individuation.

In the coupling with his spouse (or the – Victorian – confrontation with coupling), Matthew discovers a platform for sensate elaboration not only of himself as body-merger, but as of separate penetrator/withdrawer – advancer and retreater. His is an historical presence or identity/locus which moves with him (to the window), while she remains by the fire, or in the bed. Perhaps a new axis of trust and focus is emerging in the early experience of marriage, a new energetic sense of balance and High. From this High, we can expect Matthew's trauma sites to become visible, and there are two stages to the revelation of these sites.

The most famous final stanza has a starkness about it which follows the High-low sequences of tragic insight and parallels the early learning of relationship. In the face of loss of external Cultural supports, both outside and within, we arm ourselves into a cultural dichotomy – there is Me, and there is the World. I don't think Arnold here means the earth when he acknowledges the phenomenon of projection, but he does mean the cognitively apprehended World as separate from Self.

And when we pass into the vision of the corruption of the world and of how we project onto its imago our own longings, we are left with a potentially profound and organizing insight, namely that the world does not have the ideals upon which we project these longings, for certainty, for beauty, for help for pain.

The world, specifically the global earth, does hold herbs and water, and food and things that can very much, actually crucially, help us out, but they require our human agency to, say, make marijuana into medical marijuana, or to drink well water. The World also provides certainty that there will be sun and weather, not saying what kind. Here is an important developmental cusp which starts early in our lives but which accelerates exponentially within marriage, including the honeymoon accommodations of our Self and Other constructions.

Intercourse here means at least the delineation of the boundaries and of derived expectations upon which our adult assumptions of responsibility are grounded. Though dependent upon the Outside for sustenance, we formulate a world-view which acknowledges that as part of that world, we must interact with it and with some level of agency. If only that we ask for what we want and understand what we need. At the most elemental and soul levels, this is marriage stuff.

The three aspects of the final stanza rest on the starkness of the vision of the World and of the recognition of projection as a perhaps morbid function in our psychology. Firstly, Matthew proffers the solution, or a solution, to the dilemma which every person faces, namely, is there a summary position about our relationship to the World, when we acknowledge that it does not have an actively welcoming human-friendly meaning? When I ask people about this – friends, students, clients, professionals – we all fall back into our relationships with our families and our friends: when the world is going to hell in a random basket, our effort will be to keep the line of clarity and truth with those we love, who also are meaning-systems seeking connection beyond the solipsism which is handmaiden to the phenomena of projection. This is a readily accessed movement of the brain, old as its hills.

I suggest that this formulation/discovery can involve tragic, trauma process, for it leaves us on a darkling plain. The only truth we can begin to approximate is that which is standing, loving, before us; and those who are struggling in armed, actively warring combat are ignorant of this insight about projection. Their clashing reflects their lack of enlightenment, and they do not have the first and crucial tool, the insight about projection, with which to lighten their path out of their often mortal struggle. Glad they have at least an enemy, they do not ask, "What in myself am I projecting upon my 'enemy' such that I seek to destroy it?"

Encapsulations are the rule

Here is a broad social message, but it is also a personal message at two levels. Most of our interactions are occurring on the darkening plain with fellow actors projecting their trauma agenda at a mile a minute, willy-nilly outward, sometimes heard, sometimes responded to, sometimes challenged, sometimes merely mirrored. See works of Strindberg, Albee, even Updike, for particularly contemporary haunting descriptions of these phenomena within couples.

Social encapsulations are the rule, and the armies within a single marriage continue to clash ignorantly because these are the brain-disturbing, trauma-based patterns demanding resolution. To find a vision wherein projection-limited systems truly encounter each other and establish a different possibility beyond encapsulation, one might examine the Christmas sporting conducted by World War I enemies upon No Man's Land, or the writings of some visionaries such as D.H. Lawrence or William Blake, who hang out with frequency on the battlefield edge of human limitation.

And as Arnold reflects in another poem, "The Buried Life" (1862), to be true to one another is not that easy, given the ways we hide from ourselves, not to mention others. I do not think being true to one another means being merely monogamically exclusively faithful to our spouse; that interpretation strikes me as shallow. Rather, it is this difficulty of assessing our own truth which prefigures the Freudian reformation – toward internality – and continues to vitiate our desire to embody the truth, of our words of connection to others, and of Being itself.

The darkest part of Matthew's vision can be encompassed by the ways in which the cultural texts we have ingested, which he unconsciously satirizes in the academic tone of the third and fourth stanzas, often abandon us to an apparent lifelessness which also has been transmitted from generation to generation, a sustained shock pattern which makes it impossible to see inwardly. Our ego sense of consciousness consolidated by our so-called Self floats on a neurochemical sea which we can barely assess or appropriate, its underlying, unattended conflicts darkly perceived as "ignorant armies". Former lives, prenatal transmission of personality and cultural absurdities barely begin to describe or account for the conflicts.

This vision, perhaps coming rightfully hard upon the honeymoon's ecstasies, reveal the power of those ecstasies to evoke (trigger) the underlying traumata emerging for resolution. In "Dover Beach," Matthew gives up the elegiac, historical tonalities which frame his initial inherited perspectives for a hard-core venture into an active grasp of individuals facing reality without Cultural supports or even the clever device of projection to help put the problem into words.

The key phrases "naked shingles of the world" and "bright girdle" may remind us of honeymoon realities which sponsor the withdrawal from verbal, verbalizable experience. Even his final images have a youthful starkness which reveal how only partially efficacious the language and cognitive centers of the brain are in this confrontation.

For the function of marriage, our beneficent option is for each partner to be energetically held as their held-energy patterns emerge and dissolve. Both spouses learn to surrender into a somehow preverbal equality. Matthew is laying down the tracks upon which the marriage (all marriages?) may roll; the honeymoon might appear to conclude, or to be obliterated by the triggered emergent, resolution-seeking patterns – the nightly clashings; yet the marriage begins here.

Addendum:

This spring, I asked my students, "How many people (characters) are there in 'Dover Beach'?" One seventeen year-old woman replied, "One. There should be two, Matthew and Frances, but it's all Matthew, and he's posturing and encapsulated. I wouldn't date him." Well, there we are.

How to focus

Susan, a frequently and so-far fortunately unsuccessfully suicidal young student, notes that her favorite love story is Romeo and Juliet, and she tells me that now someone has recast this story of forbidden love as between a star-crossed young maiden and a zombie. She notes it is a duplication of an older pattern; and she looks back and finds Shakespeare is not the first to tell the narrative.

Here is one of the important reasons for teaching literature, so that our students can recognize familiar plots, characterizations, solutions, and can know what is repeated, and perhaps basic, from that which is impulsively produced, not thought out, not understood, and not the best way to spend our remaining time here on earth (always the artistic, moral question, particularly even for Susan). The repetitions of literature are valuable because they serve didactically to warn and encourage, and they provide access to realms beyond narrative.

Our literature gives us a vessel on the sea of preverbal experience we are trying to master, through category, insight, narrative, emotion, and the like. We can move toward economy of experience, cultural soundbites, if you will, if the achieved synthesis or sauce reduction returns us not to just knowledge of recognition but to knowledge of how to accurately focus upon the mystery at the core of the comparison or of equivalency between narrative versions. Wherein our freedom and our responsibility lie. And where we can begin to train ourselves to relate to so-called other people.

Petruchio helps Katarina

In "The Taming of the Shrew", Petruchio helps Katarina to reduce the tyranny of her habitual, addictive anger by providing a disciplined focus on her pattern, which from his own despotic and choleric temperament, he knows all too well. He does not say how or if he has any ability to modify such predisposition within himself, but he can spot it when he sees it in another. He knows at least the first steps toward transformation; initially he is still in AA (Angers Anonymous?), though perhaps further along than his to-be wife.

Traditionally, this transformation, Katarina's and, surprise, Petruchio's, is a crucial Christian insight and intervention, wherein some fixed pattern, death-certain and hardwired, transmogrifies into balance and living radiance. And, though in the struggles between some Christians and Jews who try to establish differences where there are perhaps none, the insight is well-prefigured in the story of the Exodus and in the Sacrifice of Isaac by Abraham, among other Torah tales.

What is revealed in the kiss in the street scene is the possibility of acknowledging shame within public space.

> *Katarina:* Husband, let's follow, to see the end of this ado.
> *Petruchio*: First kiss me, Kate, and we will.
> *Katarina*: What, in the midst of the street?
> *Petruchio*: What, art thou ashamed of me?
> *Katarina*: No, sir, God forbid; but ashamed to kiss.
> *Petruchio*: Why, then let's home again. Come, sirrah, let's away.
> *Katarina*: Nay, I will give thee a kiss: now pray thee, love, stay.
> *Petruchio*: Is not this well? Come, my sweet Kate:
>   Better once than never, for never too late.

[*Taming of the Shrew,* V.i.129-135]

By saying in effect, "I am not ashamed of you but ashamed to kiss (in a public way)", Katarina takes the pattern to a deeper level and dissolves it; she thus becomes equal to and thus master of the previously frightening and dominating, repressive pattern, including that of the institutional function of repression itself.

The public space which frames the kiss can be read here as a recognition not just of social mores, but of the ability to tolerate the rightness of kissing, no matter where they are, including in front of everybody; this is a matter of the deepest privacy being reworked and expanded. And having set this point within the gestalt personality of the play, it becomes absorbed and invisible, nothing to be afraid (or – its psychological narrative – angry) about.

Petruchio can now acknowledge her teaching and learning position: "Is this not wonderful?" he proffers, here on the receiving end of a witnessing self-acceptance which, in spite of his expertise, heretofore he has never witnessed. He can never experience his potentially crude, isolating bullying – a ruse awaiting finally welcome challenge from his heretofore undiscovered equal – the same again. Jonathan Miller's television production of the play [*Taming of the Shrew. The Shakespeare Collection. British Broadcasting Corporation, 1980.*] insightfully, intelligently characterizes this crucial scene better than most productions, as does his surrounding commentary, though I don't think he acknowledges its importance quite as much as I am doing here. I suspect here we may be seeing something about Shakespeare's own private understanding and experience of marriage and relationship.

Petruchio is the individual who by hook and crook, is escorted into his area of incompetence by his competency. Here is the companionate lesson he can experience, and the more Kate takes on the ostensible primitive goal of obedience, which Hortensio's widow rightly objects to, the more he is exposed to his own limits as a Puritan God-obedient.

Once again, the Shakespearean heroine holds the advanced cards of spiritual and emotional development; the feminine (overtly declared by so-called female dramatis personae – not played by real women on Shakespeare's stage) has the flexibility to transform and to learn, whereas the male-identified carriers of the pattern are too rigidly bound to them by their need to establish a self which is primitively, immaturely over-determined. One can see this relationship as gestalt-illuminated, with all the promise and visibility of gestalt insight; the marriage is a marriage of parts within a self, and the transformation, as far as we can see, is satisfyingly deep.

As we face a happy marriage, Harold Bloom's view of *Taming*, we witness the ability to move into the trauma-determined rigidities and watch them melt in the holding embrace of our spouse, who knows their costly burdens and the moment of their release. As Katarina's equality *vis-a-vis* her anger-anguished pattern emerges, so does her capacity to claim her equality before her marriage space between and with Petruchio. Here is the perhaps only place of interest in marriage, where we can see reality as equals and equal to the task.

CHAPTER SIXTEEN:

FURTHER APPLICATIONS: NOAH

Graduation address

Here is an application of gestalt, energetic, and developmental theory, a commencement speech I delivered at a special education high school for severely disturbed adolescents where I have taught for over 50 years. I have now added some portions of the original meditation which I initially had cut because of speech time limits.

It is wonderful to see you, your significant self with your significant others – family and friends, staff and others, here today. What this ceremony represents is awesome. I have a lot to share and a short time to say it, so the following will be a bit compressed. As you have in the past, bear with me.

I am going to cut to the chase and present the essence of a series of meditations upon a story, some of which most of you and I have experienced together over the past months and years.

Almost everyone in this room has had a brain, or body scan, a CAT or MRI, or knows someone who has. The remarkable technology developed over recent decades reminds us that we are self-scanning creatures; our neurology reviews itself, at least ten times a second, or if you are 18, over 5 trillion, 676 million, 480 thousand times, plus nine months (or an additional 236,520,000 scans). That's a lot of information gathering; no wonder we can get fatigued.

While there are billions of individual brains scanning, we also have cultural scans, recorded in history, scientific research, sports, the arts, and myth, ones that go on for thousands of years, recorded in bibles and art, literature, history, politics, music, economics, religion, psychology, sports, and jokes and cartoons, including topics we are advised not to talk about if we want to avoid controversy.

Each new perhaps windshield-wiper scan of our systems alerts us to problematic areas of human experience, ones which, after millennia, we repeatedly discover we have only begun to address. These scans are held in easy-to-tell story sequences which convey knowledge about how we develop, how we work. They are often recorded in tales we tell children like Hansel and Gretel, Beowulf, and Snow White. Important issues keep returning for reconsideration; each time we listen to them, we are hoping for a deeper, more accurate view of ourselves and of reality.

Our civilization, if we can call it that, is in revolution, and some people are saying the cultural tracking is too old, too repetitive, too expensive to duplicate through each generation if there is no significant change. Better strike out parts of the past with the new synaptic connections, culturally and personally – if we can. Yet there remain some important parts of our scanning which are conveyed in these easy-to-tell-and-remember sequences which relate in a kind of code – knowledge about how we develop and how we work, and some things we know very little about. Sequences of scientific research exploration as well as favorite ancient stories like the Odyssey and Creation and the Garden of Eden.

While sometimes functional, our understanding has been shallow, so that there are whole sections of our now world culture which have, to put it mildly, an unbalanced quality about them, and, armed with Facebook, Twitter, the Internet cloud, and the other media monster-dwarfs, we can find no excuse for not knowing about so much more of the world and our inner experience than we thought acceptable, or even possible.

Since we looked back at our earth and saw its photographic image from space, since we established an Internet of unavoidable informational connections, world cultures have been in a deeper revolution than was hinted at in the awarenesses of the last century with its so-called World Wars, and desires for World Peace. The scanning has been augmented, the nature of our vigilance more strategic. And we are being flooded with new information and ways of conveying it. And it looks like nobody is going to escape.

Like the young intern doctor who is overstimulated by all the data in the emergency room, we have to learn what is essential and act decisively in that direction. In history, we take up so-called facts and render them into myth, which helps us to understand how our cultural scan is going. Each scan may take us beyond subsistence levels of awareness. Paradoxically, if we are too much in the narrative details of the story, too fundamentalist in the wrong way, we will not be prepared. And we know the elephant of fundamentalism is somewhere in the room: it's probably best to deal with it.

The scans, whether legends, stories, or myths, all convey something important about human experience and in that sense, all are true in a shared sense that we can say when they are not true. Developing something as a fact does not tell us quite how we carry that information, or how we come to understand it as such. And living with a myth makes the narratives of that myth essentially true at some levels, even if the story is filled with improbabilities, even impossibilities. We state and carry the truth in complex, sometimes paradoxical ways.

In regard to an unprecedented flooding of global and personal information, one traditional scan sequence which bears looking at is the – shall we call it myth – of Noah and the Ark. Like all children's stories, it instructs in developmental and spiritual lessons which we may more fully understand during the harvest time of adulthood. There are problems with this story, but its outline, as brain, cultural scan, narrates a universal developmental, even existential process we all go through, particularly starting when we are very young. At a number of levels, it is deeply true, as true as we are gathered here now. I think the story – sort of like a meditation – falls into four important parts or phases which I shall say something about.

Then I will tell you a joke.

Flooding

Phase 1: The flood:
You will remember that God gets fed up with the mess of humanity – too many economic bubbles, futile wars, holocausts, terrorizing abductions, predictable yet unavoided atrocities, and aimless addictions, exploitations, and bad behaviors. So God plans to wipe out the wicked and corrupt human race with a gigantic flood and to start all over again. But first he connects with the straight and narrow Noah, whom he instructs in the building of an Ark. Noah, you will remember, lives in his usual uprighteousness, while his neighbors continue to live the degraded consciousness of apparently easy, impulsive, unmindful lives. As grasshoppers, they mock the ant-like Noah.

When the rains come, as they surely do, the entire world is flooded, and everything is drowned and lost, except what Noah has brought onto the Ark, including his family and one male and female pair of each of the animals and samples of everything in which there is breath of life.

There are at least two kinds of flooding – external and internal. Setting global warming aside, I am going to focus primarily upon internal flooding, often in response to too much external information, data coming at us from the outside.

Many times the world is too much with us, and we are overcome with sensation, and frustrated with reality – how are we going to respond with clarity to all these new and old stimuli? One sign that we are overstimulated is that we think globally, in the bad way, and wonder whether we can get rid of everything and start all over again. Our brains seek and make summary judgments. Let's push the whole meal off the table, or even push the whole table over, or maybe even the whole house, or the nation? Sound familiar?

When we start to experience flooding, we need to find a way to reduce the stimuli socially, physically, emotionally – outside and inside. This may involve saying "Hold", even when everyone else is saying "Go." By acknowledging that we somehow experience the flood, the overstimulation, we see that we need to reorganize how we take things in emotionally, cognitively – neurochemically. When our Ark is in place, we can then sail upon the flood, not disastrously within it. Here is a model of consciousness and of personality, floating above an often precarious neurochemical sea. It is a real strategy, but curiously, it is temporary.

As infants, we are God, that Everything which is, that which is Chosen, that which is Only Begotten. There is a recognizable overwhelm process when we tantrum, particularly after about age one and one-half, when our developing brain significantly readdresses its priorities.

So, the Noah myth informs us that experiencing sensate and emotional flooding, as infants, somehow we construct a kind of Ark to mentally and emotionally hold that which is nearest and most important to us, our families, and all the living creatures, which we somehow also recognize as being male and female.

And with this power of circumscribing discrimination, we float, until, like Noah, we land, reentering, renegotiating with the exterior world. And we repeat the same globalizing vision of all creation but within a reduced parameter; some would call this a shrinking.

The Ark

Phase 2: Building the Ark:
The Ark we build is specific to our immediate surroundings, including our thoughts, internal states, a cognitive and emotional process having to do with flooding information and boundaries, old and new. And at some point, this energetic, neurochemical process has to recognize itself as scanningly real, hence the legitimate attempt made in the curious literalness of traditional fundamentalist thinking.

In the Biblical version, the Ark's dimensions are quite specific – 300 cubits long, 50 cubits wide and 30 high, with three decks. Quite the cruise ship. I think such specificity is a part of the mythic code instructing us to pay attention to detail about the qualities of our life prior to the flood. What are the specific experiences of the flood, and where can we put our attention? In Robert Frost's terms, when we draw a line around ourSelf, we want to know what we are walling in and what we are walling out. How playful can we be? How can we determine what is necessary? The solution lies in the concrete recognition that we are real people, traditionally seen as a combination of spirit and matter.

What are the specific measurements of our Ark? As very young children, they are built in familiar parameters of those closest to us – our family, our friends, our room, our bed, our prayers. We set an emotional priority with our pet dog Rusty, not all the Rustys which we may be beginning to realize there are in the universe: "I don't love all the dogs in the world as I do my own Rusty." We can hear the cognitive perception tracks being laid down in that realization. Or its more adolescent reformulation, "I love every dog in the world."

In school, we learn to be playful with ideas, refining our understanding of what is true in our study of history, literature, language structure, science, and philosophy, and becoming adept at slaloming around and through these illuminating, sometimes dangerous gates.

As young adults, measurements are taken in therapeutic attention, in negotiating dreams, in recognizing stress triggers, target behaviors, in interactions with friends, in accurate descriptions of our neurochemistries as we experience them from within, to people who listen with "medication" ears. The measurements are garnered in the intelligence of the cell, each cell.

Sustain our fundamental integrity

When we are conceived, we begin as diploid, male and female, sperm and egg, and then, catastrophically and developmentally, we transform into first cell. Now we are both two and uniquely one. We never forget this unified, combinant moment, no matter how many trillions of times we subdivide. We refer to this sense of unity throughout our lives, on many different levels. We are never really that far from it, no matter what we do. One definition of success in life will be to sustain our fundamental integrity, to bring this integrity to our lives, as well as to the human systems which mirror this earliest uniting, unified moment, the Others.

So when the flood comes, we pull the wagons into a circle and place an edge around what we know, creating a unity, a unit. This could be the unity of our individuality, or of our family, or our tribe, or our nation, or our alliances, or the world. Our Arks are constructed toward such safety against the plural flood, which means like intelligent little cells, we take in the nutrients, and we recognize and expel the toxins and waste. And we relate cooperatively to neighboring cells.

This integrational process will mean that our fixed patterns may dissolve into what the mystics call radiance, so that we may have moments of freedom in each day, maybe whole days and weeks and months and years of it – real freedom, not just political and social freedoms which imitate and support but do not substitute for the perhaps more real personal, inward spaciousness.

Myths can distort life

Phase 3. Ark work:
Unfortunately, the Noah myth has a deceptively simple linear sequence to it. God warns Noah of the flood, Noah builds the Ark, then the Flood happens, then Noah survives. In real life, the flood sometimes comes first, and we have to build the Ark in the middle of advancing waters. Myths can distort real life like that, hopefully toward making the patterns they describe easier to learn. Often the flood includes lack of preparation, registered in shock, and a watertight Ark has to be constructed both in dry dock and modified in a flooding world. And as with any new vessel, there are leaks.

So, floating above the Flood includes fashioning the Ark, fine tuning it, so that a conviction of real safety is pervasive. And thorough. As we go into

Ark retreat – or better, suspension – a survival mode, the construction and adjustment of the Ark continues.

Here, our success may include our ability to witness the Ark walls, repair and redefine them so that they work more smoothly, with greater speed, grace, and even, in the image of the cells, with appropriate porosity.

In olden days, if we saw someone walking down the street alone, talking out loud, we would be concerned for them; we might suggest a shift in medication. Now we assume they are talking on the phone to someone real in real time. The privacy of public places and our cues about them have changed. And we, you even more, are redefining the lines between public and private. All the more reason as individuals and as a society, we have to find places where we can be private and alone. The Ark includes separate time, safe time. Time to be alone and ok with that. We need to celebrate this ruminative time.

Furthermore, if Dr. Phil and 60 Minutes, and Facebook strip away all our secrets, the places where we thought we could be alone with ourselves – now we will have to find new, deeper centers where we can be alone, if only so that later, with Others, we can be together better.

For centuries we have been increasingly exposed, our private process revealed in politics, religion, and literature, and our desires have been exploited. We have become addicted to adrenaline of the newscasts, of the music, the public media and its games, of sudden food, of the radical flooding stimuli which promise distracting activity but which are driving us crazy.

So I think one important measure of a successful life will be our power to Ark above and amid the Flood and to land in a satisfying way upon the often increasingly toxic earth. Each occasion, each relationship, is an opportunity to start anew, to clear our decks, to resolve the traumata which currently tilt our vessel, and to find a good place to land. In the most basic way, our Noah process epitomizes the American Dream, the pursuit of individual happiness within liberty, and we can measure our success by this very personal standard. It is a problem of infantile developmental experience, of the developing brain, of adulthood, as well as of civilization and how each of us holds it.

What we learn in the withdrawal aspect of Ark experience is that at the center of what we might call Arkwork is a quiet stillness, with no movement, no need for movement, no restriction from movement. It is a floating point of generation of all significant and lasting action and is separate from mere activity. Is it curious that quiet should parent sound, stillness parent action?

Knowing and not knowing

At the center of our Ark is knowing and not knowing at the same time. We all reflect differing stages of resolution, differing times of day when we are more centered. Being centered is being on our line – Olympic skaters can be on their line up to five minutes at a time, but many, even the most experienced cannot. Look at the trouble we can get into even when we are dancing with the stars.

Word quickly spreads when someone maintains a line with some consistency. Tom Brady, Gandhi, the Buddha, our baby sister, ourself. But our falling off is regular, and when it happens, we are encouraged to pick our self up, dust our self off and to start all over again. That takes us back to God's problem at the beginning of the story.

At the center of what we may discover in the Ark is freedom, and silence, and a positioning for action, but not out of necessity – it is the moment wherein we are at play. Everyone in this room has glimpses of this state of mind, and if the question were properly phrased, everyone would say that serious playfulness is what we want to manifest: the playfulness of considered experiments, of rewarding negotiations, of significant education, when learning is unencumbered, focused, and spontaneously brilliant. The playful genius of the infant or child, prior to tantrum, or of an haggard student suddenly taking on a new, liberating understanding. A sufficient and soul-sustaining happiness.

We are creatures of radiance, of light, and we enter the room which includes people who cannot participate directly or cleanly with that radiance, and they give us messages about its impossibility, about our impossibility. For our own protection, we have to listen to them and monitor our behavior, and even our radiance, if we could.

But we must realize that this radiance is what we are guarding when we become flooded. Whole icebergs of misunderstanding can be delineated by our cognitive thinking, and they drop into the sea as inconsequential. Whole mountain ranges of synaptic alignments can be transformed in a single moment of conversion, to a new way of thinking about others, about ourselves. How we integrate the newness into regularity, connect to our memory, is a continuing process and a sign of integrity, which we can relax into.

What we are currently challenged by are the external floods – the stimuli which are not central to our core, distracting – in the old Biblical mythic term, tempting – us away from our core. At the center of which is our radiance, our stillness, our silences. Our freedom, and, though they appear there as something like nothing, our selves.

Landing on Mt. Ararat

Phase 4. This brings us to the landing:
Ararat, where Noah's Ark lands, is a real mountain range at the interface of Turkey, Iran, and Armenia, and there is an old volcano specifically called Mount Ararat; but I don't suggest, as literalists have done, taking a trip there to find the remnants of the Ark. Just as the Ark is neurochemical, so Ararat is a mental site, set within a neurology which scans itself as three-dimensionally physical. And, being mythic, the place of Mount Ararat is fundamentally true in the physical, electrical neurochemical way we are true.

The reentry process, the landing of Noah's Ark upon the mythic Mount Ararat is crucial to taking responsibility with a corrupt, and vivid world. The old view has been washed away, but we repopulate the world with flawed beings. Somehow we have accommodated to the corruption in a functional way; we have maybe a sense of what we can do from that place of new and old understanding.

Interestingly, we discover that we need to be able to flood. And to suspend, and to float, and to land. We have to restore the cellular integrity at all levels, including by getting a good night's sleep. And we give ourselves some separate time, a quiet room, an inner sense of space, even void, and deep silence which, funny enough, is at our center.

And when the Facebooks come to invade our privacy and bring in Orwellian supervision in the name of friendship, and we are made to confess all our secrets on talkshows, to be publically forgiven, what will the form of self, or non-self look like?

Here's an answer: It will be a calm center, voidy, and creative. We shall have to lose the defenses of our closeted selves and see that even when we give up the secrets, we are more than what we say we are; and we do not have to believe everything we say about that. Paradoxically, we are also more visible and invisible.

We can begin, and our scientists will confess we are only beginning, to reestablish the vision of the cellular intake of nutrients, the expulsion of wastes, and the identification of toxins. A smart cell performs all of these basic truths in a self-evident way.

The child begins

How does Noah do it? The child begins again, seeing the changes which it has manifest, and the sameness. But in the flooding sequence, including the tears, we can reenter the world with a greater sense of the core which has been threatened and the core which needs to be protected.

Maybe this School has been a Noah's Ark, a place of floating after the judgment and the flooding. Maybe the core has been more clearly revealed, and the cells have learned better how to take in the nutrients and shed the effluvia. Maybe our time together has been an experience where you could begin to build your own Ark which can float above and amid the turbulent flooding. Maybe this is the place where you have begun to land. I hope so.

Maybe some enlightenment about what as children we can do to make the parental world better has been modified and made more real, the burdens and the joys clarified. Maybe we all can have a more reasonable approach to the problematic world we face, knowing and returning to our core. That may be the ultimate lesson we learn through learning. I hope so.

When faced with a world which is not humanely, fairly organized, one where the corruption and irritation dominates beyond our point of tolerance, like the infant who is overstimulated at the party, we take, or are taken, to some quieter room. When a child indicates its fatigue level, we give it a "Time Out", a place to "center down", as the Quakers put it. But in that Time Out, that function/aspect of the Ark, has to be learned so reality can be faced.

It takes six spiritual days for God to establish a Sabbath, and maybe 210 thousand years for us to realize that there is Sabbath, not only once a human week, but in every day, and in every moment. There is a still resting point at every point and subpoint in the atoms, and in the center of atomic and sub-atomic structure. And often we forget that we are encompassing that stillpoint quite literally in our bodies.

I want you to remember Noah's transition sequence: prepare, float, land. There is a point to watch out for, as you are negotiating this sequence in a small and big way today, and that is the reentry. Now aged 600 (Biblical) years, floating Noah waits for a sign of the abatement of the floodwaters, and he sends out birds to see if the Flood is over. After some unproductive experiment with a raven, one investigative dove finally comes back with an olive branch in its mouth, a traditional sign of peace. He keeps sending out the dove until it does not return, meaning it has found a way to sustain its own life, independent of Noah and his Ark. The floodwaters recede, and the Ark lands safely on Mt Ararat, and Noah and his family and the animals and plants repopulate the world.

World of creation

Noah prepares for and lands in a world of creation, including heterosexual coupling. Let me say a couple of words about Noah's discovery about the heterosexual world, the world of creation generated by male and female. For any child, this is a central piece of information, one some regression therapists think it already knows and can recall; but how that information is held and stored, in short, understood, can be a problem. Being created and even creating children does not say very much about our sexuality, so how we hold this heterosexual insight is significant. The current external flooding of information about gender demonstrates that we have been shallow in our cultural and personal understanding of our sexuality.

I see a difference between sexuality and the gender through which it is expressed. You have discovered how your sexuality can be misapprehended, by you and others; please remember, there are mysteries, sacred mysteries within your intimacies which include aspects and depths which will take you even further than some of the places which you have courageously already established.

There is a deeper reality which can be appropriated – you, we, are both more and less than we thought, and there is more in that less than we thought. The world pulls for male and female, sperm and egg, but life takes place amid a very broad spectrum of creative energy, and if we want to go to the root of our gender capacities, they transcend the ordinary median rules which society has given and which still enthrall and sometimes destroy its essence, our essence.

There is an historical trajectory wherein homosexuality was repressed, to the point of killing. People were stoned to death. Some parents have said, "Better my son dead than gay," and some youths, hitting the interface between society and their own suppressive dynamics, have suicided.

An entire section of our sexuality and knowledge was cut off from ourselves. And though they say that same-sex marriage will not effect the heterosexual world, or marriages, I believe it will, and positively, because at the root of this recovering world are deeper truths which effect how we move and interact in the world not just as gendered males and females, but also as spiritual creatures. Just because we can combine sperm and egg, engender children, does not tell us quite how God does it in us, Its crazy creations. There is a lot between initiation and conception. And merely creating, or being created, doesn't make us straight.

We quickly move beyond our commonplace homosexualties and heterosexualities into what might be termed an energetic directness, beyond custom or legislation which goes past the shape of objects; at such a core, we may be able to witness some ultimate, perhaps for lack of a better term, sacred straightness, beyond our sometimes quirky affirmations about who or what is appropriate for our loving.

But if we survive our current dark – whatever – transition, face the universe which is engendered when we discover that our sexuality is more than we thought, and is still more than we thought no matter how we align our bodies, we shall discover that our heterosexualities are more complex than we thought, just as our homosexualities, or other proposed identities are. The gender and identity wars try to pin down our "Force" – Obi-Wan Knobe's term – but they cannot.

Thus worked, our shallow identity can only resolve realistically with a sense of humility and awe. And no matter what its shape, I think this wonder is the way to hold it: here is our ultimate straightness. No matter what our twists and turns, I urge you to be centered, to seek centeredness, even your original integrity, in your search. The deeper we go, the farther we may see. Forster characterizes this ancient longing for righteousness when he writes, "Only connect." And you will be wonderful partners.

Where's the gestalt?

You may say, OK, Redpath, where's the gestalt, the unifying vision? Well, it is just this. Firstly, all of these Noah sequences, the flooding, the Ark building, the float, the landing, apply to us as single individuals; if it is a dream, we are all of its parts.

I recall the irony with which I viewed the National Geographic Society's report of a tour to the Ararat volcano husk to find the place where Noah's Ark landed. They could not find it there, though they might find it in the fundamentalist way of thinking which it describes. If Ararat is within us and interior, then also its exterior reality can be apprehended.

What happens after the Ark's landing is of immense interest, because it records a High vibratory state or neurochemistry out of which a civilization, including compromise and abandonment, apparently unavoidable, follows. Noah comes out of an initiating environment in which there is judgment into the world wherein there is the possibility of peace, internal and external. He begins a successful life, populating it with what he knows; and he has faced what he does not know. And in our site-specific connection with our bodies and spirit, we connect to the real world in front of us, full of success and, dangerously, of catastrophic Second Shoes.

There is a sequence when we discover the Stillpoint in the center of things when all the old debts come flooding forward for resolution, and it seems we are being punished for our success. Again, we have to deal with this second internal flooding, renew the specific vision upon which we can then build our Ark to float, until we can land again.

The trick is to read the unavoidability of that second-stage crash in the pattern not as a problem in mastery but as an opportunity. Again, you may see that your radiance will set off, as it already has, very difficult patterns in your environment, and though you may set them off, they have little or nothing to do with you. That fact may reduce some of our ego, challenge some of our unresolved narcissism, but it will also give us a direction.

Here, Noah's hidden lesson is about causality, as opposed to magic: if I do this, then something – else – happens. The causality of the Ark rescues us from the Flood, which threatens to take away our oxygen in a subsuming blurring of subject and object. The story, like the Ark itself, reassures us of this floating awareness, the capacity of the mind to focus, on itself and on others. The line between becomes enchanting, bridged by a kiss.

Chorionic at its earliest position, the division between the Ark and the water allows us to peel off from the uterine wall and breathe in separation from a flooding blur, conviction turned into First Error: we have always been alone; we have never been alone. The Ark is also cognitive and allows us to process, see and experience this division.

Children of radiance

As children of radiance, we know that most of what appears to happen to us has an imbalanced quality about it. The patterns we are called upon to solve mostly don't have anything to do with us – we have merely, in our radiance, set them off in ourselves and in others. If we master how we project onto the outside world what is true and difficult in our inside, we have more than half the game won.

As we stay in the stuckness which surrounds us internally as well as externally, and observe, we will find the universal spiritual truth that out of nothing, something comes, and with that movement, we will experience hope. I don't think hope can be delivered as a commodity, but it can be discovered – in our profoundest sense of oxygenation, inspired. When hope appears, we will know that there is movement at the deepest levels, not the feigned and shallow efforts with which we are so often faddishly distracted.

Let's not be distracted; the mechanism is twin-stroked, easy to learn, harder to implement, and at its base, the radiance carries us past hope itself into a place of centeredness. The Ark is silent, radical; it sustains void, it is stillpointed, and the Ararat in ourselves and in the world is the same, for ourselves and for the Others we meet. I think meeting ourselves and others at this level, in varying degrees of tolerance and intimacy, declaring what our limits are, what our desires to share these sacred places within and without – is the only game in town. Every material achievement can support this goal, and if these achievements are not leading to this apprehension of our ultimate reality, I wonder what good are they?

At the same moment

Secondly, the parts of the Noah story, its sites, its characters, are happening at the same time, even the same moment. We are all in various phases of something which the myth has spread out for us in a causal, linear narrative. And so as we reenter the world, we know that there are other Noahs, facing other floods, other Arks, other people trying to land. Most of our misunderstandings between people can be characterized within this famous story.

As creatures of radiance – embodied, electrified stardust – we must return to the literalness of our being. We spirits are flesh and blood, which stubs its toe. If we see brains scanning for the literal truth of their being in fundamentalist thought, let's see that process for what it is, not for what it is not. We can hold fantastical statements as true, but not true in the way we thought. At some point, our brains must return to the knowledge of the mystery of our creation. Upon this Ararat which we have forgotten or, in our dissociation, we forget, you members of the graduating class are now landing. And will continue to land.

In summary:

Phase One: Flooding

Say "Hold" when things start to flood. Listen to your own place in the myth, just as landing on Ararat also takes observance. Say "Go" to the flood when your Ark is in place.

Phase Two: Building the Ark.

Carefully build the Ark to suit your specific needs. The more carefully you measure what is required, the more watertight for the rising waters your vessel will become. Build a Time Out or Quiet Room, a therapeutic relationship, a friendship, a meditational practice wherein you can declare your solitude, and nurture yourself in the silence, both literal and internal. Find Stillpoint, where there is no movement, no need for movement, and no restriction from movement. This can be the basis of friendship, or marriage, or even international peace.

Phase Three: Arkwork.

Encapsulate. Establish balance. Float.

Phase Four: Mt Ararat.

When you, and the people around you are ready, re-engage from that place of individuation, at whatever scale you can, carefully. The world may seem new, but it frequently is as corrupt as before the Flood, your flood. Develop strategies which will help you to be the matador when the cultural bull starts to charge. These will include knowing that though you may appear to trigger people's patterns, their actions, their abuses, their tragic sadnesses – radical as they seem, and culturally embedded as they are transmitted – rarely have much to do with you. Like Noah, these Other, human systems, are also trying to land, and with that in mind, you can meet them.

Know that we are all Noahs, including you, in various levels of flood repair and healing, and that the phases of the Noah story are going on simultaneously. Our systems which appear to have action and individuality also hold significantly silence, Sabbath, void, in the same moment. And we can play, as loners or as lovers, along this entire sequence.

Know the story so you can be straight about it, not confused. No matter in what body form or with what body parts we engage, we can be direct and righteous; we can produce right action when we move from our center.

I shall close with a story I have told before. It is a story of hope and of landing.

Dr. John Watson is sometimes irritated by the all-knowing clarity of his friend and experienced intuitive, Sherlock Holmes. Holmes always knows more than everything. Still, they are very close friends. And they go camping, and they get ready for sleep, each getting into his own sleeping bag, and they fall asleep.

Watson awakes in the middle of the night and looks up at the sky, and he senses Sherlock Holmes is also awake. And he asks his friend, "Sherlock, what do you make of the stars above us?"

Sherlock replies, "Well, we are in the fourth house of Aquarius, and there would be astrologers, particularly north of Belsize Park in London NW3, who meet during times like these at 4pm on Saturdays, and I can see the North Star which has guided millions of people on their journeys through life, and I know that the light from the stars takes a long time to get to earth, and I know that some of the light is from stars that have already died. And other things. So, John, what do you make of the stars?"

John answers, "I think somebody has stolen our tent."

I hope the best for all of us Noahs, learning what to pay attention to and for what. There are surprises, good surprises waiting for us ahead. We are only beginning.

CHAPTER SEVENTEEN:

SUCCESSFUL LIFE – ADDENDUM TO NOAH SPEECH

Era of barbarity

According to the Urantia Papers, we are in an era of barbarity – of war, inequality, and imbalance – and, though there are some contraindications, I think this is a good strategy. It means we have to go to another level of awareness and embodiment, and that we have just begun to take that journey's first steps. So we can ask, "What constitutes a successful life?"

In the past, success has been estimated at a number of levels, including financial success, family success, professional success, scientific, literary accomplishment, social and political success. Within the past two centuries, in an era of some plentitude, access to some of these realms has been sustained. Now, because of what we know, we have to sort of add two more realms, psychological and spiritual success. These additions especially mean for gifted young people, that you have had to include and focus on these latter goals, even to bring yourself to the more public recognitions of achievement. Not because psychological and spiritual success have not been there all the time, but because we misuse the term success if we do not include these aspects in some reversed priority way.

For you, each day carries its turns, its moments. Nothing is guaranteed. You are pioneers within your own neurochemistries, and it is awesome watching you maneuver and gain your center, often with skill and grace.

Neurological pathways alter the increasing skill at these traverses which will be part of your psychological, personal success, part of what you offer the world. As we walk down the street, we broadcast the state of the art, the information of challenges met, ravines delved into, all leading toward a life of depth and hopefully of meaning.

Yours is a special map, and part of your success is in making it available and accessible to the world. Increasingly, we live in a world of global, cloud proportions; your ability to find your core radiance and continue to identify it, often amid a destructing and fragmented world, will matter. You can be a beacon for the world within and around you.

Your expertises include negotiating mood swings, fractionation, dissociative states, as well as emotional brilliance and clarity amid these turbulences. The world is sorely sore and needs to hear the notes you sing. It needs your integrity, your ability to bring into some semblance of unity the widest and often the most difficult areas of human experience. You have begun to develop vocabularies and strategies for the ascent. We will observe each other, give each other support in these endeavors – "How goes it with you?" – we will look at our partner, riding their horse next to ours.

We may be able to achieve many invisible things, invisible to the regular worlds, and be honored for those achievements. We may succeed famously in the real world, but like Steve Jobs, whom we sometimes admire, we end up looking at his private reconciliations, his personal sacrifices and attempts to bring himself into some kind of spiritual balance. And we shall bring this perspective to each table we sit at, respecting others for their reconciliations and their difficulties achieving others. We can be watchdogs for ourselves and for others.

Our ultimate success

Our ultimate success will strategically include our within, watching how what is permanent and radiant within ourselves gets expressed with increasing skill and accuracy to the wounded world through which we wander. Having learned how to restore ourselves, we can then understand the dilemmas which others, including whole societies, face, and maybe we can place a stable hand under their wobble and help them to find stability as well.

Success will mean learning how to filter out irrelevant stimulus. Society has garnered how to get our attention, usually to cater to our for lack of a better term, adrenaline, to which we become addicted. Advertisements excite us with threats of abandonment, then promise relief with the purchase of an idea, or an object.

Your success will be in setting upon a meaning system for yourself. My mother used to say, "We have to create our own meaning system." But usually communities are based upon shared meaning systems, then the plurality becomes too much, we are flooded with too many meaning systems, each competing for our attention.

One strategy is to float above all of this flood, and become, perhaps momentarily, enlightened. We know all the arguments and their opposite ideas. One week butter is ok, another it is not. Smoking generally is not ok, nor driving under the influence, but being careful with whom we love and how is.

One sign of success will be to recognize our patterns, and watch them complete; all patterns are seeking completion, and they end in stability, not fractionation. This includes violence, which appears to seek some completion but rarely achieves it. Our success will be how we handle the violence which comes our ways, psychological and physical. You already have found these challenges daunting.

Success may involve gaining forgiveness – a complex and abused word to be sure – for yourself, some kind of accommodation to how you have taken in, or have not taken in the world. Your success may be in helping others with the same problem.

We have been manipulated into believing things we cannot believe in. For reasons we ultimately do not understand. We want to be free, but our freedom is negatively gained. We know what is not true, and it is mostly what other people say *is* true. So the question for ideas is how will we hold them.

Dance with

In a successful life, we have things which feel good and appropriate, learning how to dance with someone we love, and learning there are things which we are educated to feel good about.

There are moments when we are clear, and there are threads of clarity which we have, when we are inwardly straight, no matter what our sexuality or emotional predilections. Now, we are what biblical people might call righteous.

We can be cool, which means enlightened, not attached to the winds of personality and politics. We can see broader patterns and maybe support them. We can attach, and feel the ecstacy of attachment, of being clear, with our bodies, our minds and our hearts. That means that our actions come from our sense of Being, our neurological core, not of doing or becoming.

When we act from our neurological core, we express a knowledge which is profound and not shallow. Delicate and strong, suspended in the air, like the island-clots in "Pan's Labyrinth", floating above universal meaning, and centered within and above gravity.

When we are in truly centered mind-sets, we can bridge the paradox of mind and body and voice, as religious mystics do, and make extravagant statements. The things we say may not be rationally true but they speak to perhaps some centered, exalted state of Being, and that state is literally, neurochemically true.

How playful can we be? How can we determine what is necessary? In history, we take up so-called facts and render them into myth, which helps us to understand how our cultural scan is going. Each scan may take us beyond subsistence levels of awareness. We live in a new world, with new ambitious values, and new boundaries. New space-surmounting cell phones and the Internet allow us to move closer to each other, more dependent upon the sense of the others in our lonely world. The rest is silence.

CHAPTER EIGHTEEN:

EDUCATIONAL EXTRAPOLATION

The following is a letter I wrote in 2011 to a friend of mine, who was teaching art history to undergraduates at a major university. It reveals some of my perspective on how the energetic gets acknowledged in traditional humanities studies.

Reason for a liberal education

In college, we take many courses which expose us to different disciplines and within those disciplines, different theories and investigations about each area of experience. A liberal education thus can lead us into awareness of plural groupings of thought and perspective. We discover that we can focus in particulate ways, we can slow down perceptive, cognitive time, as it were, enabling ourselves to see with greater specificity and efficacy: ultimately, we can observe and influence genes and subatomic particles. This specialization is charming and seductive, leading us into realms of greater and lesser knowledge. And God loads his Table with many specific foods, ultimately delicacies, which we are thus enabled to absorb and appreciate.

Also, a liberal education gives another kind of knowledge. By exposing ourselves to differing disciplines, we inhabit systems of ideas and experience and discover that we can move from one to another, that we can be absorbed by one and another, and that somehow, in our flexibility, we are separate from these systems. We are free to move in and out of them, to focus here and there. We carry our focus through many separate frames.

This liberating, differentiating experience garners what we can come to call intelligence. Insofar as native intelligence can be trained, or enhanced, or developed wherein it formerly was not apparent, or dormant, this tradition of focus establishes an hopeful median, at least, for social education. Such intelligence, prefigured in freeform sandbox play, amounts to and is intimately linked to liberty, not being ultimately constricted by any one system, including those which we may be dedicated to preserve. Often individuals with a liberal education will reside in clusters of belief and sorts of cognition which do not float too far from society's established docks of agreed-upon insight clusters; and many docks are attractive. Such training, if it takes, may be significantly desirable, even practical, for the flexible sensibility can move presumably with greater ease than most inexperienced ones.

Yet for the individual who in this way has been educated, there is a hidden awareness of the suspended quality of all belief, even of all so-called information. Thus the psychological effects of the liberal education on personality, both problematic and salutary, can be profound. For one, we can enter an universal abyss wherein there is no meaning, a traditionally Godless place which may cause our belief and conviction systems to be held all the more closely for the warmth and support they appear to provide, often at the expense of our capacity to witness Reality.

Another effect is that of rarified awareness of the transient nature of our variegated intelligences, overriding which is our intelligence, or focused consciousness, itself, capable of entering and leaving all systems in – ideally – egoless freedom. Each idea system may appear to serve our proposed self, but for the enlightened sensibility, selfless awareness rather than allegiance can be the only satisfying goal, if it can be so called.

It is this subtext of the liberal education which finds its most current explications in the culture of scientific exploration, where experiment grounds ideas in scientific, *i.e.*, revisable, self-revising, expandable fact platforms. As currently taught, traditional humanities studies frequently suffer from what might be called research exhaustion, wherein the deeper purpose of the studies is obscure, abandoning us at its solipsistic boundary encapsulation. Efficacy and site-specific integration of its discoveries for the student is remaindered to post-graduate growth and therapy modalities.

Significantly, what emerges as a liberal value is the ability of a person to enter each system fully, empathically, so that the secret places of the system's origin and strength can be observed, even possessed – understood. Here empathy is a psychological aptitude of high order and essential for self-knowledge and leadership, personal and social. It is so interesting that this ability is usually not named – we sort of back into it as a goal, as we move from one classroom to another.

One further aspect of liberal education – the term contains the oxymoronic – is that it seems to require some, though not always the deepest, involvement for student and teacher at the experiential level. Our teachers show us how the ideas or judgments, or awareness are carried by themselves and by other people. The best teachers reveal this process empathically, with integrity being the most interesting benchmark for sustaining the basic freedom which thus has been discovered.

Integrity here can mean an over-riding unification of consciousness, separate from any individual part; and it rests in the clarifying experience of what has been called Being, separate from emotional and cognitive attachments. This Being state is garnered as increasingly important, in the crossover moment as we move between classrooms, from one idea system or cluster to another, from one brain agency to its neighbor. With speed and grace, we finger-track roads in the sandbox sand only to wipe them out and set in others.

The old conflict

In the development of individual consciousness, particularly with young leaders-in-training, the old conflict between the freedom – Zeus' polymorphous, initiating creativity – to inhabit any idea or system is matched by the social, Hera-based need for order and social cohesion, so that society's constituents not be prone to perpetrating reckless – and costly – randomness. If we encourage individuals to be more Zeus in their applications of individual liberty, they may become unrecognizable, or appear to be rebellious toward the Heran realities. We often defy Heran values for order – ordinariness – *per se,* as much as we oppose anything in the specific ways those values are manifest.

For leadership, we need individuals able to move past the ordinary envelop's edge in order to help steer our social boat toward safe and productive outcomes. If they hang too far out, they become undecodable and cannot function as current leaders; though they may be recognized later by social critic-delineators and historians as pioneers.

Yet in the Protestant form of democracy to which we now aspire, leadership includes the leader who votes, and that means every adult. We all have a direct connection to and participation with Ultimate Reality, and that includes social and political forms through which that Reality is encountered. The liberal education instructs in the temporariness of political and social faiths, in their toxicities as well as their virtues. And how we all need to be as vigilant about those toxicities as we are of the virtues, right down to the common citizen; hence the vote.

For the most part, society's formulations about Reality can include huge assemblies of rigidity, impaction, and corruption, waiting to heal; and so the liberally-educated person approaches these systems knowing their transient nature and the ways they can be desperately held. We experience, personally and with texts, why versions of the truth are merely versions. Our independence, our liberty, rooted in a clear, still sense of Being, is our only real, dependable truth, and in this knowledge we are both transcendent and system-subversive. No singular social or political system can bring us to total belief, and thus to total submission or totalitarian agency. Belief may be valued, but the crucial viable point is knowledge, knowledge centered amid the experience of Being. From any position in society, each so-called individual is leader, able to see beyond current bouncing horizons, and our directives voiced from our crow's nest may carry particular weight for the helmsmen, our political representatives, below. With knowledge may come understanding.

Alternatively, belief and cognitive systems can be approached and engaged in as yet another means: with total devotion total surrender can be experienced, with its concomitant cognitive dissolve, returning us to what for lack of a better term might be called theological awe. I suggest it is this awe from which all knowledge and desire for knowledge of Reality springs. As Job discovers on his enforced march of suffering, Being is ultimately beyond attachment, beyond narrative: silent, preverbal, and nameless.

To train individuals in this discipline of flexibility is to invite misunderstanding, partial embodiment, and casual and disastrous manipulations. People can live and die at secondary, not primary levels of awareness. Not to train individuals in this polymorphism experience is to engender slow, corroding despair, often amid evoked and catastrophic trench-warfare anarchy. Within democratic pluralism, we voters regularly upend the glass globe to evoke a somewhat circumscribed storm and watch the flakes descend into a somewhat new order. We gently, hopefully creatively, skirt flossing chaos – but on our terms.

The texts of culture become the agenda for study

Liberal education takes raw social data and institutionalizes its transmission. Culture exists separate from the school, yet because experience and knowledge are the touchstone for what is important, and culture incarnates these attributes, the texts of culture regularly become the agenda for study. Yet one significant, perhaps the major subtext of all critical approaches to these agenda is that they can lead the student participants to states not of doing or becoming, but of sustained Being.

Even at the most prestigious universities – often biased toward creative doing – the conflict persists between educating the young leaders in their own capacities for differentiated experience, including, increasingly, their own traumatic past, and finding a collective vocabulary and set of concerns which they can readily join. Success is measured externally in accomplishments in the manifest world, and internally in creative, artistic, even so-called theological understanding.

Increasingly for observing older generations in the liberal lineages, these academic achievements slough off as perhaps easily grasped; and what emerges are the more individual mature triumphs of awareness, the mastering of addictions, of absurd and devastating loss, the separations and attachments, of immense, capricious good luck, the conversions of consciousness, all of which the liberal education hints at, even promises to help inspire, but in a nitty-gritty turning-point way, it seldom engages at the Being/Reality level.

Enthralled by ideas and experiments and garnering statistics, we delay confronting the initiating moment when out of nothing, something comes; or better, we come. Perhaps as much by a process of elimination as anything else, the liberal education often can only remind us of how important this initiating movement is; it identifies the incompletions and prepares us for our own continuing returns to the drawing board. Our cultural endeavors are all homestretch, bringing us to a goalless finish-line.

Only with more experienced graduates can the full scope of the liberal education be garnered, and the reportage from many of these graduates is often laudatory and happy. The impact of the liberal education has been strong, and it has been held with enthusiasm. But rarely does the reportage amount to: "The work I initiated at my college directly led me to a state of enlightenment about reality, or to a deeper apprehension of God, in myself and in the Other, transcending everything I learned as an undergraduate."

Somehow there is a final step, important to be sure, where the tradition shelves off and is not expected to go or to be part of the link to the personal issues which come to mean the most to graduates: not the money, nor the status, the demonstrated competencies, but the mastery of patterns, of family, of relationship to Ultimate Reality, established within but more importantly beyond construct or, for that matter, often, academic witness.

Somehow, perhaps because of the pluralistic, secular framing of current education, this mastery of individual experience is not expected. Here the achievements which are important seem more personal, more a function of mature vision and balance, than of exterior accomplishments. The problems which need resolving are solved at more therapeutic and spiritual levels in ways which the liberal education of youth does not directly acknowledge. One law school graduate seven years out said to a younger law school graduate primed with grandiosity for New York and thinking he knew what he was heading for, "Come back after five years and tell me what you see and what you think is important."

The return to basic experience for people of already immense talent and experience is time-consuming, and it brings their systems to their deepest rigidities and impactions, from which it is hard to self-extract, to self-liberate, particularly by standard classical forms of instruction. Ironic, then, if the way out of these ineducable intractabilities is to entrain our souls not to do, nor even to observe, but to find in the present a yielding into states of Being. This is not an objective we would share with our supervisor on some political or organizational ladder, where the leader is inspiring us toward the intensity of productivity which belief in a particular system brings, at the expense of a deeper, goalless knowledge, and with it, hopefully, understanding.

But when we hear someone describe their career, their success, this quiet note is what we often are listening for. Training ourselves to tolerate a deeper freedom which liberal education may be identifying, even promising, often means we have to limit our allegiance to specific systems, including language-based cognition, if we are to keep our eye on Truth, which always includes the transcendent. Classically, this conundrum can lead to system-myopia – bubbles, political grandiosity, collectively-held illusions, etc. – and related issues of loyalty. Cognitively protestant, the liberally educated individual is always potentially a double agent and then some. And, appropriately focused, this functionality is what makes him/her useful, even creative for society, which now must include its membership in a global plurality. Perhaps this capacity for flexible ego-dissolve is at the heart of learning as we negotiate the international, webbed world.

Self-liberation can occur through exterior process, good works, etc., but it also means heading into abysmal swamps, where there are few guides, and disorientation is a rule rather than an exception. After disciplining our intellect and sensibilities, we are left with impactions which do not move, the places where we are stuck. Time and changes move quickly enough, but the patterns where there is no movement, these sites bring us to our knees and ultimately do us in, intellectually, physically, emotionally, and spiritually.

From very beginnings

When we discover that these stress points have been set in from our very beginnings, how they are set in and maintained becomes a daily question of some import. We find new interest in the assembly of history, personal as well as cultural, and the list of visible transcendent, consistently transcending beings becomes very short. Yet we look for these to model ourselves with. Like instruments in the surrounding orchestra, we tune to their oboe concert A, and we move toward increasing whatever moments of such righteousness and clarity we already have carved out in each day.

And we face the reality that these held-energy patterns are what we are, until we discover the spiritual freedoms which demonstrate that we are not our repetitions, or don't have to be: we are our traumata until we are not.

Wisely, a prophet instructs, "Build your house not on sand, but on a rock." But if the rock upon which we build our personality domain is the rock of our impactions, then our firmest place upon which to build our sense of self must be upon something like a non-self, a place imitated by the liberally-educated intellect – flexible, differentiated, non-attached, and empathic. In short, we may be able to build our dwelling place upon its most secure foundation, not the rock, which in dissociation we imperfectly, yet daily, encounter, but upon the most stabile aspect of ourselves we know, namely light itself.

Intellectual enlightenment does not always lead to spiritual enlightenment, though after all our getting and spending, that is what we respect and desire. Our liberal education provokes and imitates and brings forward as sure as shooting the impactions, floating to the top of our awareness, the incompetencies to which we rise; but it does not tell us that these sites are where we must focus, and that its arsenal of arts, letters, and histories of all sorts are often woefully inadequate to this later, individuating task. In spite of history, in spite of poetry, in spite of science – all of which ironically may accurately describe even this problem – yet now we are very much on our own.

It is this very-much-on-our-own position which, when push comes to shove, our liberal education may not be able to help us with, and which the liberal education as a quest lineage leads us up to, only to turn away from. The self we possess in so many other ways is beyond ordinary assessment. This positioning is potentially too hard to acculturate, too difficult to evaluate, too multifaceted and sudden to be studied. Or it may be that for our growth, we shall have to remove all traditional handholds in order to succeed. In the neurochemical transforming moments, we have to go off the cultural instruments. Can this gleaning capacity be the essence of the success game, its definition? In whatever air, for how much of my day do I fly free?

Knowing this universal challenge, we can prepare students through biography, through narratives, through traditional landmarks such as the Stations of the Cross; but taking a student to the edge of its differentiated awareness to a new competency may require validating the stuck places they will inevitably encounter, perhaps more than utilizing the clever, brilliant successful synaptic sequences which bring them to the hallowed halls of College in the first place. Here they can be told that even as alpha males and females, they are in the right place, and paradoxically, their expertise in dealing with these impactions is what will deepen their focus and impact as educator-leaders, not just in local jurisdictions, but in more Zeus-supporting global, filled-cloud realms.

Allegory of the Cave

Plato (are we surprised to find him here, again?) describes this process in the Allegory of the Cave, where the liberated soul must go back and escort his former prisoner peers in how to move into the liberal, non-attached consciousness of enlightenment and of non-goal-oriented states of light, pure (B)eing, the Good. Of course, the Allegory illustrates a gestalt: the liberated parts of each one of us must continuously return to our imprisoned parts if any integrity is to be manifest; so we can have a true measure of our growth.

But I find Plato does not quite say how this encounter is to be done; he knows the process is slow, painful, and full of resistence. His story implies a prisoner unshackling, perhaps like Hercules for bound Prometheus. Here, the nature of the shackles, their shocky formulation and non-intentional dissolve, should be the place of focus, as well as the moment just before Prometheus again stands up.

When instructing undergraduates in looking at a painting, both the clarity and opacity of vision, exterior and interior, is the grid for learning which is being set out by teacher and student. The instruction is about light, inner and outer. That some established teachers avoid such concentration, or even not approve of it should not be a surprise, even, particularly, at the most adventitious academic settings. The precarious marriage adjustment of Zeus and Hera reengages repeatedly each time a student or a teacher opens their eyes or their mouth. We can descriptively lead the horse to water, but the horse itself must drink. And to add to the complexity, we are the leader, the horse, and the water.

Challenging the privileged status quo in a young gifted individual may not garner praise, even support for the challenger. Even though their experience already includes over 5.6 billion self-scans of their brain, the cutting edge of learning returns these adolescents always to the paradox of experience and innocence and the difficulty in an achieving, goal-focused society to value the liberating truth of Being. Once mastering the tasks of food and shelter and necessities, are we to be left to play with goalless time? The great meditation lineages, including breath and stillpoint and juxtaposition, may snap an orienting line; yet often they also do not.

Educating these students to witness light is as delicate a task as any; instructing includes seeing and not-seeing, proportion and perspective, not to mention observing the hard-upon rush of Hera to restore the hearth Zeus causes to be initiated and immanently disrupts. Given their current trajectories, these young people may not think Being is a serious task to engage with because herein they find themselves initially so very much alone. Yet supported by insight and self-soothing neurochemistries of irony and humor, we seek to individuate through our afflictions, where we have to Be on our own in new ways which may bring enlightenment and surprise.

In short, we often learn cleverly, only to discover we are, in segments, ignorant and not wise. Our education has not demanded early depth from us; for some trained in liberal education, it never is experienced. Our core becomes visible only after time and the usual suspect, suffering. Yet this liberating insight may be the best we can offer the self-satisfied, self-assured world, our neighbor.

We are entering a catholic, global consciousness, wherein partisanship precludes participation, and maybe associating young people with this challenge earlier than we have done may be a wise thing to do.

SELECTIVE INDEX

A

Abel 66, 100, 246 - 251, 263, 266
Abraham 182, 204, 248, 270, 299, 315
A Child is Being Beaten 270, 276
Adam 17, 18, 60, 64, 66, 100, 178 - 179, 185, 188, 206, 247, 250
Aeschylus 183
Allegory 55, 102, 164, 166, 168 - 169, 171 - 172, 344
a man who had fallen among thieves 4, 151, 153 - 154
Angels in America 292
anima 110 - 111, 118, 122
animus 110 - 111, 118
Ariadne 101
Aristotle 9, 67, 107 - 108, 131, 182, 184, 201, 225
Ark 13, 319 - 331
Arnold, Frances 308 - 309, 314
Arnold, Matthew 109, 308
Astaire and Rogers 162
Athena 15
atman 60
atom 68, 225
aura 27, 110, 246, 251 - 252

autarchic fantasy 178

B

Beowulf 318
Bergler, Edmund 155, 159, 178, 273, 279
Bible 102, 120, 214, 220, 246 - 247, 300
Biblical Time 108, 117, 227
Blake, William 28, 284, 313
blastocyst 102, 184, 197, 253, 262
Bloom, Harold 280, 316
Boy 265 - 266, 269 - 280
Brooks/Scofield 234
Buddha 2, 23, 69, 181, 194, 324
Buddhist 8, 12, 56, 68, 176 - 177, 193 - 194, 209 - 210, 215, 217
Burning Bush 69, 112, 195

C

Cain 66, 100, 246 - 251, 257, 263, 266
Captain Archbold 259
Cave 55, 102, 164 - 166, 169, 171, 344
Chosen 176 - 177, 203, 244, 320
Christ 41, 69, 71 - 72, 194 - 195, 196, 207, 215 - 216, 237 - 238, 258, 260, 268 - 270, 277

Christian myth 41, 97, 183, 236 - 237, 239, 254, 266
Civil War 36, 206, 219, 240
Clark, Kenneth 133
Cohn, Roy 292
Conrad, Joseph 243 - 263
Cordelia 232 - 233
Corinthians 126
Crane, Stephen 219
crucifixion 209, 254
Cummings, E.E. 152, 199
Cyrano de Bergerac 269

D

Dali, Salvatore 199
Darwin, Darwinian 227
Dante 120, 197, 309
David 16
default mode network 5 - 6, 31, 136, 167, 180, 214
DeGuiche 269
deoxygenation 46, 51, 56, 100, 137, 218, 222, 223, 273
Developmental Bible 220
Dickenson, Emily 63
Didi 265, 266, 269 - 275, 278 - 279
dies for our sins 201, 203
diploid 12, 111, 131, 322
Disney 190
Donne, John 55
Dover Beach 307 - 308, 313 - 314
Dr. Phil 323

E

eagle 193
Eden 17 - 20, 37, 64, 66, 97, 99, 138, 160, 171, 183 - 189, 236, 248, 267, 318
Edgar 230, 232, 234
Edmund 159, 178, 230, 232, 234, 279
Eliot, T.S. 13

EMDR 55
Emerson, Ralph Waldo 278 - 279
Emerson, William 168, 202, 253
Enlightenment 29, 38, 40, 136, 184, 192, 194, 211 - 212, 268
e pluribus unum 103, 288
Erikson, Erik 310
Eve 10, 17 - 18, 61, 64, 66, 100, 179, 185 - 188, 191, 211
Expulsion 18, 38, 185, 189, 236, 267

F

Facebook 318, 323
Fagles, Robert 163
faith 14, 24 - 25, 40, 154, 174, 202, 213, 254, 309
fallopian 127
Faust 222, 224
Flood 322 - 323, 326, 329, 331
force 291
Forster, E.M. 328
Fortinbras 269
Frankenstein 102, 182
Freud, Sigmund 279, Freudian 150, 270, 276
Frost, Robert 134 - 143, 148, 321

G

Genesis 17, 38, 61, 175, 178 - 179, 186, 188, 190, 209, 267, 276, 303
Gloucester 231, 234
Gnostic 68, 70 - 71
Gogo 265 - 266, 269 - 275, 278, 279
gold 67, 69 - 71, 114, 118, 124 - 125, 143, 145
Golden Rule 158
Goneril 233 - 234
Good Samaritan 152, 154, 159
Gospel of John 214, 220
Guns of August 33

H

hamartia 182, 254, 259
Hamlet 11, 39 - 40, 56, 160 - 161, 269, 277
Hansel and Gretel 102, 318
haploid 12, 111
Heart of Darkness 243, 249
he dies for our sins 203
Hegel 103, 111
Heisenberg 51
Hell 120, 124, 193, 197, 221 - 223
Hera 139, 150, 284 - 286, 292, 302 - 303, 305, 339, 345
High 9 - 10, 20, 36, 40, 49, 63, 97, 110 - 111, 118 - 120, 136 - 138, 140, 146 - 149, 171 - 172, 183 - 184, 193, 211, 239, 250, 251, 288, 295, 311, 329
Holmes, Sherlock 331 - 332
Holy Eucharist 237
Holy Spirit 178, 180
Horatio 269
How to Change Your Mind 5
Hubris 20, 182
Humbert, Humbert 103 - 105

I

Ibsen, Henrik 10, 198
Incarnation 175
Innocence 5, 18 - 19, 28, 136, 163, 251 - 252, 284, 287, 294
Insusceptibles, The 143, 148, 172
Internalist Movement 102
Internet 73, 297, 318, 336
Isaac 182, 204, 248, 270, 299, 315

J

Jacob's Ladder 125, 129
Job 340
Jobs, Steve 334
Joshua 281, 306

Judeo-Christian 38, 97, 299
Judgment Day 212
Jung, C.G. 69, 102 - 103, 225, 276

K

Katarina 315 - 316
Keats, John 55
Kent 233 - 234
King Lear 56, 183, 230, 235, 238 - 239
King of Kings 177, 195
Knievel, Evel 100
Krishnamurti 44
Kurosawa 230, 235
Kurtz 243, 249, 250, 254

L

Labyrinth 22, 99, 101 - 102, 133, 183, 336
Lawrence, D.H. 313
Lear 56, 183, 230 - 235, 238 - 239
Leggatt 245 - 259, 261 - 263
Levine, Peter ix, 189, 280
life force 175, 291
linear time 3, 4, 7, 9, 11, 18, 32, 184, 186, 190
Locke, John 13
Lin, Maya 36
Lolita 103 - 104, 106 - 107
Lord Jim 254
Lucky 265, 270 - 271, 275, 277, 279
Luke 152, 153, 155
Luther, Martin 10, 72

M

Magnificent Ambersons 161
Marlow 249
Melville, Herman 219
Mercier, Vivian 266
Merope 182
Merton, Thomas 13
Metman, Philip 103
Michael 5, 46

Michaelangelo 258
Miller, Arthur 10, 316
mind-body 4, 45, 48, 88, 147, 214, 281, 283
minotaur 98
miracles 213, 215, 217, 218
Melville, Herman 219
Moby Dick 219

N

Nabakov, Vladimir 103 - 104, 122
National Geographic 328
negrido 46, 69, 70
Noah vii, 13, 319 - 320, 322 - 323, 325 - 333

O

Obi-Wan Knobe 328
Oedipus 23, 41, 107 - 108, 163, 183, 234, 274
Olivier, Laurence 248
Olympic 27, 324
only begotten 203
Oresteia 183
Orestes 15
Orwellian 325
oxygen 32, 45 - 47, 50 - 51, 54, 56 - 58, 74, 78, 82 - 83, 89, 121, 169, 190, 213, 218, 223, 237, 238, 255, 261, 267, 278, 329

P

Pan's Labyrinth 336
Penelope 162, 298, 304
perfect sacrifice 207, 210, 237
Perls, Fritz 103
Peter Principle 38 - 39, 40, 255
Petruchio 315 - 316
Pieta 258
placenta 102, 198, 208
Plato 4, 11, 55, 59, 102 - 103, 164 - 171, 193 - 195, 344

Platoon 219
Playboy of the Western World 287
Pollan, Michael 5
Pozzo 265, 270 - 271, 275, 277, 279
praxis 162, 250, 260, 274
pre-Edenic 20, 164
Prisoner 164, 166 - 171
Projection 36, 205
Prometheus Bound 183
protestant 41, 206, 240, 278, 306, 339, 342
Purgatory 120

Q

Quakers 326
Quilty, Clare 103

R

radiance 17, 42, 51 - 52, 54, 69, 70, 99, 108, 142, 149 - 151, 158, 165, 177, 184, 209, 222, 238, 268, 279, 301, 306, 315, 322, 324, 329, 330, 334
Ran 230, 233 - 235
Rashomon 233
Reich, Wilhelm 51
Regan 233 - 234
Republic, The 164, 166, 171
Rich, Adrienne 144, 148
Road film 104
Roosevelt, Teddy 84
Roxanne 269

S

Sabbath 326, 331
Salvation 188 - 189, 192 - 194, 196, 202, 270
Santa Claus 124
Sartre 188
Satan 18, 66, 221 - 222
scan 43 - 47, 62, 80, 82, 87, 108, 109,

137, 142, 172, 183, 225, 226, 227, 228, 284, 317 - 319, 336
Scheherezhade 303 - 304
Sea of Faith 308 - 310
Second Coming 195
Second Moment 63, 65
Second Shoe 9 - 10, 20, 39 - 40, 42, 63 - 64, 89 - 90, 112, 123, 136, 138, 288, 295, 297, 301, 329
Sephora 245 - 249, 256, 257, 259, 262
sequelae 290
serious action 59 - 60, 107 - 108, 156, 170 - 171, 184, 201, 260, 298
Serpent 186, 187
Shakespeare 11, 39 - 40, 56, 150, 161, 183, 230, 235, 239, 314, 316
shiva 296, 297
sins 36, 197 - 199, 201 - 208, 237, 240, 267, 277
sins of the world 36, 197 - 198, 203, 207, 237, 240
60 Minutes 323
Socrates 166, 168 - 171
Solness 10
Son of God 180 - 181, 195 - 196, 203, 213
Sophocles 4, 107, 163, 183, 307, 309
Soul 12, 13, 176
Source 13, 17, 51, 54, 61, 70, 164 - 165, 169, 171, 173, 175, 177, 298
Sphinx 100, 238
SSRI 41
stasis 79, 156, 162, 269
Stations of the Cross 211, 344
Stillpoint 13, 16 - 17, 27, 38, 44, 94, 127, 135 - 137, 139, 140 - 142, 143, 170, 188, 226, 227, 283, 285, 289, 329, 331
Stopping By Woods on a Snowy Evening 134 - 135, 139
St. Paul 125, 215
Sufi 55, 195

Synge, John Millington 287

T

tabula rasa 13, 252
Taming of the Shrew 315 - 316
TE 44 - 45, 50, 73 - 75, 83 - 84, 89, 91, 93, 169, 183, 207, 227
temptation 187
Ten Commandments 34, 112, 125
Thakar, Vimala 44, 214
The Christ 194, 195
The Demon Lover 112, 116, 122 - 123, 126, 129
The Father 220
The Good 11, 165, 195
The Red Badge of Courage 219
The Secret Sharer 4, 243 - 245, 249 - 250, 252, 257 - 258, 261 - 262
Time Out 326, 331
Torah, Torahic 108, 247 - 250, 315
tragedy ix, 19, 107, 108, 131, 161, 181 - 184, 201, 235
tragictatus 182 - 183, 212
Trauma Energetics 1, 4, 19, 44 - 45, 49, 141, 280
Tuchman, Barbara 33
23rd Psalm 184, 244
Twitter 318

U

Ultimate Reality 15, 17, 24, 63, 64, 65, 66, 108, 174 - 177, 179, 193, 194, 204, 210, 213, 219 - 220, 222, 226, 238, 251 - 252, 266, 268, 310, 339, 342
Un Chien Andalou 199
unconscious conscience 159
Updike, John 122, 312
Urantia Papers 333
uterine 102, 111, 184 - 185, 197 - 199, 201, 232, 238, 253, 256, 262, 329

V

Valhalla 32
Via Dolorosa 108
Vietnam 36, 219
Virgin Birth 177 - 180, 204
Vladimir 265 - 266, 274 - 275, 277 - 278
void 5 - 6, 11 - 12, 16, 29, 33, 35, 61 - 62, 94, 173, 186, 226, 251, 297, 305, 325, 330 - 331

W

Waiting For Godot 265 - 266, 269, 271, 274 - 276, 278 - 280
War and trauma 218
Waterloo 219
Watson, Dr. John 331
Welles, Orson 161
Whitman, Walt 109
Who's Afraid of Virginia Woolf 233
Willy Loman 10
Winter's Tale 183
Wizard of Oz 160
Wollstonecraft-Godwin, Mary, Shelley 102
World War 4, 33, 37, 132, 219, 313

Z

Zen 49, 55, 195, 274
Zeus 139, 148, 150, 284 - 286, 292, 302, 305, 339, 344 - 345

www.ingramcontent.com/pod-product-compliance
Lightning Source LLC
Chambersburg PA
CBHW020638300426
44112CB00007B/155